A Street Survival Guide for
Public Safety Officers

*The Cop Doc's Strategies for Surviving
Trauma, Loss, and Terrorism*

A Street Survival Guide for
Public Safety Officers

The Cop Doc's Strategies for Surviving Trauma, Loss, and Terrorism

Dr. Daniel Rudofossi
Sgt. NYPD (Ret.)

CRC Press
Taylor & Francis Group
Boca Raton London New York

CRC Press is an imprint of the
Taylor & Francis Group, an **informa** business

CRC Press
Taylor & Francis Group
6000 Broken Sound Parkway NW, Suite 300
Boca Raton, FL 33487-2742

© 2012 by Taylor & Francis Group, LLC
CRC Press is an imprint of Taylor & Francis Group, an Informa business

No claim to original U.S. Government works

Printed in the United States of America on acid-free paper
Version Date: 20111110

International Standard Book Number: 978-1-4398-4577-6 (Paperback)

Library of Congress Cataloging-in-Publication Data

Rudofossi, Daniel Carmine, 1961-
    A street survival guide for public safety officers : the cop doc's strategies for survivng trauma, loss, and terrorism / Daniel Rudofossi.
        p. cm.
    Includes bibliographical references and index.
    ISBN 978-1-4398-4577-6 (pbk. : alk. paper)
    1. Police--Job stress. 2. Police--Mental health. 3. Post-traumatic stress disorder. 4. Loss (Psychology) 5. Police psychology. I. Title.

HV7936.J63R83 2012
363.201'9--dc23   2011045941

Visit the Taylor & Francis Web site at
http://www.taylorandfrancis.com

and the CRC Press Web site at
http://www.crcpress.com

Contents

Foreword

Dr. Dan Rudofossi has hit a home run with this one. He has not gotten lost in the vagaries of political correctness, but touches the hearts of every man or woman who has worn a badge, whether as a firefighter, EMT, paramedic, ER nurse, MD, or police officer. He reaches inside and talks about those things, the "it" that none of us ever talk about. This book goes beyond superficial descriptions and gets at the real meaning within each of us using his *eco-ethological existential analysis*.

Dr. Rudofossi writes about the pain, the guilt, the shame, and the conflict we have all felt at one time or another. This is the "it." Dr. Dan talks about it in ways that only someone who has felt or experienced "it" could do. This is language and understanding from the trenches.

Dr. Rudofossi follows up his own words with very detailed case examples. These men and women are real and this book paints them with a very human brush, highlighting trauma, pain, and the path to healing. He describes the disenfranchised nature of these experiences—public safety professionals are not supposed to "feel," but we do. Dr. Rudofossi describes personality changes necessary to survive in this eco-ethological system "as each wound reshapes and interacts with each new one, leaving a deeper scarring."

Dr. Dan Rudofossi has gone beyond normal self-help books and written one that can work for police officers, firefighters, paramedics, EMTs, ER nurses, and MDs. This book will help to normalize their daily experiences, which go well beyond what most would consider normal. He helps us to understand the impact of those experiences for that unique population that will go into trauma again and again, day after day subjecting themselves to experiences that would overwhelm a normal population. As he describes the impact of trauma on public safety personnel, he helps us to identify those darkest places where we keep the secrets and shame resulting from our own exposure to trauma and our own unique eco-ethological perspective.

Dr. Rudofossi describes the often superhuman conflicting demands in response to trauma—police, firefighters, ER nurses, EMTs, and paramedics are often told it's "just an incident." But this book describes how it is not just an incident but instead is complex and hits hard on many levels of experience and existence.

Albert Einstein said, "There is no greater tragedy in life than when that which lives inside a man dies while the rest of him lives on." This book is about survival! It is about survival on the most basic level. Dr. Rudofossi talks about ways to survive the emotional onslaught and to keep that unique individual within each of us alive. We have all felt this pain and seen some of our coworkers who did not survive on the emotional level. They retired on a PTSD disability or went through five, six, or even seven marriages. They died inside while the rest of them lived on. This is the eco-ethological material Dr. Rudofossi is talking about. As I read the material, it seemed as though he was writing about some of my best friends in public safety.

Again, Dr. Rudofossi avoids the bland wasteland of political correctness and tells it like it is. When he writes about the importance of sharing the trauma with a cop doc or another therapist who understands public safety work, he provides a step-by-step approach to finding the right person to talk with.

Dr. Rudofossi states that it is impossible to successfully treat a public safety officer independent of the world he or she lives and works in. He specifically lists important attributes in anyone you are going to trust with your emotional well-being, *including the importance of understanding the nature of true evil in the world.*

This book is a step-by-step manual for public safety officers in surviving complex trauma and should be mandatory reading for all recruits, veteran officers, and those clinicians working with this population. It's not just for new personnel.

This book describes the impact of trauma in a three-dimensional way— ecological "impact on denial, avoidance, and delaying ... how you experience losses," tackled with Dr. Dan's eco-ethological existential analytic approach.

Every cop, firefighter, paramedic, EMT, ER nurse, and MD will find themselves in more than one of these pages with hope and means for minimizing the impact of complex trauma. We are losing far too many public safety officers to the emotional hazards of this work. It's time we all took care of ourselves, and this book is a great step in that direction.

Cop Doc Dennis Conroy
Author of Cops at Risk
St. Paul Minnesota Retired Sgt. and Licensed Clinical Psychologist
USMC Vietnam Veteran and IACP Psychological Services Section

Acknowledgments

First, and in profound appreciation for my ability to have survived and grown in my faith in the highest being—the highest spiritual force, God! I often reflect, as many greater folk than I have said, "There go I but for the grace of God." It has been my good fortune to have so many blessings that follow:

Thank you Taylor and Francis, Ms. Carolyn Spence, sr. acquisition editor, for seeing in my book a valuable addition to the literature on terrorism, trauma, and loss—that is a privilege and honor: I thank the excellent editor's staff at CRC Press, especially Ms. Samantha White, sr. science editor, and the copy editors for their high level of commitment, professionalism, and amiable approach to a complex process with equanimity.

Cop Doc Dennis Conroy, who gave much of his time in reading through my guide and honoring me with his foreword to my guide, is in his own right a legend among cop docs with a U.S. Marine service record, scores of years as a St. Paul Minnesota police sergeant, and the director of their psychological services/EAP. The 1993 classic *Cops at Risk* is destined for being a classic, as it is now, also in the future. He is a true friend and peer with a lot of wisdom— rare and incisive—always willing to offer a helping hand to a fellow cop doc.

Cop Doc Antoon Leenaars, outside of his Canadian wit, is an on-target premiere expert on suicide in the world. He knows more about this tragic moment and epidemic than anyone alive today. His erudition presages not only knowledge but also healing from and preventing such tragedies. He is simply the leader, and it is with his generosity and genius I have been blessed to have my preface written.

My close friend and mentor of the highest caliber, Cop Dr. Al Benner, who died this past year, inspired me by his political honesty, integrity, and fellowship during rough times. Indisputably, Doc Benner lives on as the cop doc's cop doc. His service is legendary. His courage was indefatigable! A true pioneer who broke through unexplored paths in police psychology by his incredible ingenuity, humility, fraternity, and professionalism. Dr. Professor R.R. Ellis, a superb clinical psychologist, did this best by his humanity, being the superb educator, clinical supervisor, and gentleman he was. A decade and a half of our lives evolved together into a personal friendship and collegiate relationship. Dr. Ellis gave countless hours in editing with a wonderful openness, sense of humor, and love; his sagacious and acute critiques are magnificent. What he planted in his students are harvests in the here and now; although his death also has left a gap in many ways, his work is alive and so is his soulfulness. I can never leave out the enlightened genius and erudite supervision of Dr. Charles Brenner, the father of the science of conflict as a psychodynamic psychotherapist. It is not only his cognitive genius but also his emotional "genius" as well that surfeits over his fecund mind: if one grabs Diogenes' torch in darkness—in search of an honest man with humanity and humility—he or she would find him in Dr. Brenner. His mindful creativity lives on in all his fellows and postdocs. I am grateful for the privilege afforded by his generous sharing of perspective extending way beyond "the hours" of clinical supervision—my eco-ethological approach toward Police and Public Safety Complex (PPS-CPTSD) has benefited from his fecund perspicuity. Dr. Al Ellis's inimitable style and clinical supervision also remain invaluable. Dr. Stuart Young, physician, novelist, coauthor, extraordinary scholar, colleague, and friend for life—a true breakfast club pal. Always present and wise—a treasure in my life. Dr. K. Doyle, colleague and friend, of extraordinary integrity who gave of her energy, support of my ideas, and editorial suggestions and my 3-year journey at the Institute for Rational Emotive Behavior Therapy. Dr. N. Pelusi, an excellent leader in Rational Emotive Behavior Therapy (REBT/CBT) and, for a good dose of humor, PRN. Dr. R. Balter, PhD, JD, a rare friend, as judicious as she is keen in her wisdom as an attorney and psychologist. Dr. Terry Jordan, whose research brilliance helped me in my passage from doctoral candidate through my dissertation to my own scientific stanchion and ingenuity as a researcher and a clinician in counseling psychology, and a decade and a half as a colleague working in tandem through different clinical and research populations—our ongoing friendship for many years is a rich treasure I cherish. Thank you, Dr. Bill Schiff, for your brilliant teaching as an ecological physicist and support toward my own ecological-ethological approach in understanding complex trauma with police at NYU in 1993–1994. Dr. Bill Worden's superb advice and poignant insights into trauma and grief are so appreciated.

I have been greatly enriched by Dr. Bob Scharf's and Dr. R. Weiss's inimitable psychoanalytic ability, skill, ingenuity, and humanity: with cherished gratitude to the New York Psychoanalytic Institute and Society. Thank you, Dr. Bob Barnes, president of the Viktor Frankl Institute and Hardings Simmons University, for your incredible courage, fraternity, wisdom, kindness, and finest of humane excellence and education. Without doubt, the achievement of the diplomate clinician as an existential analyst was sown in the long hours of supervision through the generosity and clinical skill of Dr. Ann Graber. Professor Jo Anne Thorp, a most astute of forensic observers: a great friend with genuine brilliance and generosity I have learned from first hand. A true classic artist, Emmanuel Defiliciantonio Martin, MFA film director and producer and another great buddy, who has a touch of genius in every film coupled with an angelic light to pull the humanity out of the worst spots decent persons can find themselves caught in.

Dear friends, thank you for your support and intellectual stimulation: Assistant Chief Chaplin Shiomo Tizel, MTA Police Department for humanitarian work above and beyond the call of duty 24/7 with compassion of an angel! C. O. Captain Sosnowik of Leadership Training, NYPD, a brilliant friend and leader with integrity and creativity that leaves room for pause in all ranks that enter with cynicism and leave with passion and commitment. TLC Commissioner, Bob Lintell, who makes a cab ride safe and DEA Ret. President Ed Lintell, a sleuth's sleuth. S. Southwick, MD, R. Montgomery, DDS MPH, S. Luke, MA, Steve Southwick, MD, Jo Ann Thorpe, MA, Catrine Giery, MA, Det. M. Hennessy, Mary Hennessey, MSW, J. Krieger, MA, Bert Breiner, PhD, Michael Perlin, JD, Bill Worden, PhD, N. Pelusi, PhD, B. Schayes, MD, S. Young, MD, M. O' Keefe, PhD, E. Alpert, JD, M. Bellsheren, P. Stevens, PhD, H. Schwartz, L. Ellis, PhD, E. Albert, MPH, JD, D. Valentine, MD, K. Doka, PhD, M. Yusaf, PhD, R. Balter, JD, PhD, W. Schiff, PhD, E. Nalplant, PhD, R. Hirsch, EdD, R. Katz, PhD, D. Cohen, PhD, B. Hutzell, PhD, V. Hutzell, PhD, O. Cruz, MA, D. Panitz, MA, and Luigi Valenti! The best photographer I know, Det. Sal Vitale, thanks ... as well as my friend and photographer Paul David and CCC. Being a cop doc was strongly supported by the vision of the finest of the finest bosses on the job and off: Retired Chief Mansfield, MA, and Inspector V. Werbkay, MA, selfless leaders who gave much of their time, support, and commitment to ensuring I could deliver police members the best of care. Thanks to Mr. Genet, MBA, and of course the SBA president Sgt. Ed Mullin, PBA, and Pat Lynch, LBA and CBA, and of course thanks to each peer support officer, a person who always exemplified what I considered to be outstanding commitment and skills: the heart and soul of NYPD.

Det. Jimmie Giery, a cop's cop, fourth-generation crime scene investigator, the best of the best, a true buddy! Lt. J. LaTorre, another true buddy who covered my back and sprung for Macanudo cigars on the PA deck, and to boot Cappuccino, one of my best buddies! Sgt. Louis Vilenti, MA, dapper— true blue pal to director in New York State Counterterrorism Unit. To my other crime-stopping street colleagues: the midnight crew PSA 1, 3, 3A, and 4; my partner Capt. D. Sosnowik, MA, now the commanding officer (CO) of Police Academy Executive Development; Chief G. Anderson, J. Dillon; G. Suarez, JD; V. Sheehan; B. Sans Castett; Lt. J. LaTorre, BA; Lt. B. Chlan; Lt. P. Kelly, MA, JD; Lt. S. Jones, MA; Sgt. B. McNally; Sgt. A. Medina; Sgt. M. Miselewisch; Sgt. Jerry Wong; Sgt. Louis Vilenti, MA; Det. M. Hennessy; Det. R. Otting, MA; Det. S. Mohammed; Det. James Geary; PBA Delegate

M. Gilligan, Phil Gibutosi, special agent M. Chiu—you all remain the finest! I salute you all, now and always!

Inside the beat of the NYPD cop docs I have the following salutation to offer: Chief surgeons Thomas and Dr. M. Symond, who served as my personal supervisors in the NYPD (both deceased and served till their deaths), I salute you! Chief surgeon for the IEMRA, Interpol, and International Police Association, Dr. Doug King, a stellar cop doc; FBI special agent J. Reese; Dr. H. Schlossberg, Det. NYPD (a psychologist with a gun); Det. Dr. G. Mack, NYPD; and fellow Sgt. Dr. Henry: an honor to be in your company! My gratitude for PC, NYPD, Dr. R. Kelly, JD, LLM, who appointed me as the first uniform psychologist with Chief Mansfield and Inspector Werbkay, the ingenuity and courage of Commissioner John Walsh, HRA PD, appointing me the honor of being the police surgeon on call. Thanks to Mr. Genet, MBA, a leader/founder of MAP, now known as POPPA, who gave so much of his time, support, and commitment to all of us, including myself as the cop doc and cop PSOs, ensuring the best of care to each member. Other gratitude to SBA President Sgt. Ed Mullin, PBA, Pat Lynch, LBA and CBA, and of course thanks to each peer support officer, to a person who always exemplified what I considered was outstanding in commitment and skills: the heart and soul of NYPD. Chief Bobby Basso, Major Inspector General New York Guard, a true friend and brilliant police executive with heart and soul. EMT/firefighter Kat Rosemond of Virginia, who has taken my work and run with it in aiding her deputy sheriffs, firefighters, and EMTs! John Carr of Rhode Island PD and DEA/FBI, who is a staunch friend and colleague. Friend and mentor Lt. Col David Grossman, who incredibly has taken on the world of terror and extremists with a new theory that ingeniously tackles the terrorists, his inimitable killology. My non-PC friend Col. Danny McKnight of *Black Hawk Down* and Rains of Mogadishu, who like the modern Audie Murphy makes the fighting Irish proud, even if you are not Irish, with his style of training and leadership in the war on terror.

I thank my family: Mom, an inspiration to me in her abundance of lifelong love—through thick and thin—whose compassion lightened my darkest moments of trauma. In beloved memory of two of the most courageous men: my father, Harry, a combat veteran with four ribbons in WWII, USN, and my grandfather Morris, an infantryman in WWI, U.S. Army. To WWII decorated veteran pop, Mr. I. Friedman, I salute your courage, humanity, and friendship! To my son Jonathan, USMC, my hero, who keeps me laughing with his humor and love and text messages that keep me on my toes—he is so much better at it than his dad, he is the mechanical genius that can get anything back up and running. Their war stories will never be forgotten, nor will their courage. My grandmothers, who loved wholeheartedly. To my sisters, who are lifelong friends: Vicky and Mara. Spiritually—Rabbis Kalman Packouz, J. Kolakowski, and Z. Marcus: thank you for your timeless noetic wisdom and for combating complacency with anti-Semitism/racism hidden and disenfranchised. In partnership with the finest officer-patients I owe my education and wisdom still learning from you all. Each journey hopefully enlightened your path as it did mine! To cop doc peers paving new roads without forgetting our own beaten paths! To my students at New York University, the brightest and finest—the best with love!

Preface

Not at all surprisingly, I was extremely honored to be asked to write a preface to an extraordinarily fine book written by an equally extraordinary cop doc: Dr. Daniel Rudofossi. Doc Dan—as his officer-patients call him—was a street cop and is a licensed psychologist. Part of my qualifications in this present instance is that I also have a long history of working with police officers and treating traumatized officer-patients. Doc Dan called on me as a peer "doc cop." I answered his call with affinity. Over the past 30 years, I have treated police officers and worked with them in cases of wrongful death, suicide, homicide, and homicide-suicide, including that of officers.

Dr. Daniel Rudofossi has done the kind of work with fellow officer-patients that I highly endorse. He has embedded his intensive policing within the larger context of psychological treatment. His previous published work of this genre includes *Working with Traumatized Police Officer-Patients* and *A Cop Doc's Guide to Public Safety Complex Trauma Syndrome*. This book is the third, so to speak, of his intended trilogy, *A Street Survival Guide for Public Safety Officers: The Cop Doc's Strategies for Surviving Trauma, Loss, and Terrorism*.

Policing is stress. The nature of police work is stressful. This has been known for millennia. It is known that trauma and loss carry on throughout life. It does not simply go away. Trauma has a shadowy presence. Trauma is a wound or injury. Police officers, and public safety and security personnel experience, witness, and are confronted with events that are outside the range of normal human experience. September 11, 2001, is a good example. Officers are more frequently traumatized than people in the general public, not only by one event but continuously. Many events involve actual and threatened death and serious injury. There are threats to the physical and psychological integrity of self and others. It would be normal (not crazy or abnormal) to respond with intense fear, helplessness, and horror.

Traumatic events, Doc Dan says, would "horrify, repulse, disgust, and infuriate any sane person." Doc Dan, being well aware of this, asks the now obvious question, "Why shouldn't that be true for police officers?" Regrettably, after traumatic experiences, a common response is: "Tragedy happens, learn to deal with it" or "Snap out of it" or "Just get over it." Silence, of course, is a core part of a cop's existence. Silence is powerful, but it may also become dysfunctional, even lethal. Not only alcohol, sex, and violence are aftershocks, but also suicide—and all too often, homicide-suicide. Indeed, avoidance only exacerbates the problem. Forgetting, avoidance, phobias, and inhibition, as was first well documented in survivors of posttraumatic stress disorder (PTSD) among Vietnam veterans, only traumatize the officer more. The officer is "numbed out" or "zoned out." Doc Dan, in this book, breaks down the blue wall of silence ("Don't talk about it"). Loss or trauma all too often result in the officer becoming "disenfranchised," a core loss in the blue culture that many officers experience. He or she is then caught in a catch-22 of persistently reexperiencing the event (such as recurrent and intrusive distressing recollections, recurrent disturbing dreams, and acting as if the event was reoccurring) and persistent avoidance (such as efforts to avoid activities and duties, having an affair, leaving the force, and restricting affect), with increased symptoms of difficulty falling or staying asleep, irritability, difficulty concentrating, hypervigilance, and exaggerated startle response. Doc Dan does not call it a disorder, but a "complex"—"a complex experience that is disturbing, compelling, and adding that makes the experience traumatic." Yet, Doc Dan offers hope; despite taboos ("You have to be the tough guy"), he suggests that officers can heal and he offers here a practical guide to do so. Doc Dan shows us a unique path to healing, and thus better policing.

This is not a feel good book; it is an arduous challenge. This book, in fact, asks some tough questions: What are the painful short- and long-term consequences of a trauma for the officer? What are preexisting personality styles of coping? What are the existential factors that affect the consequences—what, as I noted, he calls complexes? What are the guides to treatment and intervention that might allow an officer to courageously overcome not only the shocks but also the aftershocks? What are the barriers, called blue walls, to wellness in policing? (Doc Dan amply calls it the "officer's wall of China.") What can be done to more effectively educate and help our fellow officers? And, of course, there is the dire service/system question: Will we continue to allow our officers to suffer the traumatization? (Like me, he expects the platitudes and bureaucratic inefficiencies.) Doc Dan asks key questions; he uses the Socratic method—Socrates knew that it empowered the person, not the teacher. Doc Dan does so. There are many of what he calls existential questions throughout the guide—about the heart and soul of officers.

What were the shock and aftershock of the gruesome murder, rape of a child, partner's suicide, domestic violence, assaults, and 9/11? Doc Dan asks: "Why have certain events impacted you the way they uniquely do?" Doc Dan takes an enlightening step: he searches out, for perhaps the first time, the commonalities in police personality styles. His dictum: By understanding your unique personality style, you can heal better.

Knowing is key. This is as true in police investigations as it is of oneself. Doc Dan offers what he calls tragic optimism. What he means is police courage and hope. Doc Dan says to the officer, "You are an intelligent, competent learner." In this book, he speaks to and shares meaning with the officer. He calls on officers to accept what they cannot change and to have the courage to change what they can—in their own distinctive way. He argues that each officer's unique adaptation makes superb sense. Dr. Rudofossi is police officer-centered. He does not eschew complexities, but—and this is important—he also believes in the officer's ability to stop, pause, and reflect. Healing is possible. Here he follows the wisdom of Jacob Bronowski in the famed book *The Ascent of Man*. Both believe what makes a person a person—and an officer an officer—is the ability to wait, to think, to talk, to pause, to reflect, and so on, before the act.

This book is not a dummy's guide. Ironically, one can buy cookbooks and manuals today. Yet, they offer false hope. Doc Dan offers wisdom, a rarity today. There are no platitudes or Pollyannaish optimism. Rather, the book is answers. He states, "Being healthy is achieved by gaining insight." He shows the officer his trauma, her loss, and his unique personality style—and her strengths and so on. He states, and I know this to be true of police officers, that you will not break. He says, "You will survive." You, the officer, have worked hard as a cop; now you can trust that strength to work hard on wellness. He offers what he calls CPR: an acronym for compassion, passion, and resolution. Doc Dan offers "a guide, a path, a bridge." "To serve," he writes, "is a profile of courage." He puts forward some scripts: Don't give up. Don't buy into the blue walls. Truth is healing. Choose life.

The officer needs to trust her or his courage—you have survived stress, beyond what you imagined the day you first wore the badge. I strongly believe that your life—and mine—is like the Greek Sisyphus's. Each day we must ceaselessly roll our unique rock to the top of the mountain, and the next day you must persevere and do the same. This is not to be condemned; this is life. Indeed, if you believe Homer, Sisyphus was the wisest and most prudent of humans. Doc Dan does not inoculate the officer against trauma; he does something better. He helps the officer get in touch with his Sisyphusean strength (what are called protective factors) that builds the natural surviving of the aftershock of everyday policing, deep within the heart and soul. This book is truly a gift.

There is one further point that Doc Dan makes that I wish to echo, namely, because it has caused needless deaths among police. Dr. Rudofossi states that the therapist you chose, if you do, to work with, should not be a random choice out of the blue. I have investigated the tragic suicides of officers and have learned that some therapists do not know or understand cops. These therapists do not cope well and want to keep things hidden. They minimize, underestimate, and avoid anxiety too. They have "white walls"—and are often unaware of the barriers. (Cops call them "doc crazy.") These people are naïve and have no background working with police or public safety officers. I have investigated therapists who have seen an officer who killed, just prior to the tragedy, and these professionals do not discuss risk—of homicide or suicide. One could see this as the officer being noncompliant with treatment. But more accurately, it was the therapist's naïvety, if not suicidogenic nature.

Under the heading of therapist variables for effective therapy, there could be an endless list of factors. The research, in fact, has long shown that there is considerable consensus among officers about what was most helpful. The officer-patients will state the therapist. Some therapists are more effective. There are, of course, counselor factors that are harmful, some that deteriorate the healing process, and some that are suicidogenic. Like mine, Doc Dan's advice is choose carefully and wisely.

To conclude, Dr. Rudofossi is "one of us": he is a "cop doc." He was a police officer with the New York Police Department (NYPD), having spent more than a decade as a street cop, and was the first uniformed psychologist in the NYPD. Not only has this given him an insider perspective, "a cop doc on the job," but also he has interviewed, assessed, and treated hundreds of officers, many suffering from PTSD, including after 9/11. This alone is reason for all police and public safety personnel, and those mental health professionals seeking competency to work with them, and their families to read this book. Surviving policing will be easier using Doc Dan's guide.

I support and applaud Dr. Rudofossi's efforts and give him every encouragement in his exciting and healing endeavor. I recommend the book to every serving and aspiring police officer for both its brilliantly written expression (he knows how to tell a story) and insightful clinical implications.

Antoon A. Leenaars, PhD, CPsych, CPQ
Author, Suicide and Homicide-Suicide among Police

Introduction

This book may be considered a sequel to my first two books: *Working with Traumatized Police Officer Patients: A Clinician's Guide to Complex PTSD Syndromes in Public-Safety Professionals* and *A Cop Doc's Guide to Public Safety Trauma Syndromes: Using Five Police Personality Styles* (Rudofossi, 2007, 2009). I continue being a cop doc as chief psychologist of the Detective Crime Clinic, New York and New Jersey Metropolitan Police and Captain in NY Guard and police surgeon/psychologist in FOP/NY Amtrack Railroad Police. In my four decades of life I have had the privilege of some priceless experiences: retired police sergeant of the NYPD and licensed psychologist, and retired administrative clinician (cop doc) for the Drug Enforcement Administration Employee Assistance Program, to clinician's and police supervisors, and support staff. I have supervised over 500 plus clinicians for clinical quality emergency intervention while honing my own skills and empathic ear. The NYPD comprises around 40,000 to 50,000 police officers excluding support staff of the highest caliber. The DEA consists of approximately 10,000 agents and support staff in the same line of fire as street cops. This is my second decade in the saddle as a cop doc where my theory of police complex trauma and my treatment titled eco-ethological existential analysis has been refined. What I have taken from the other two books is the case examples that have been so well received and, without oversimplification, sifted them into a down-to-earth conversation. That conversation is what you have in your hand.

I am reaching out to the cop audience as much as the firefighter, EMT, ER RN, and other first responders, including peer support officers and other cop docs, police managers, and clinicians who desire to work with this worthy population. You have in your hands an insider's perspective about what public safety officers experience on the job and a step beyond my other two books. Here I am applying my experience and chiseling out interventions that distill the down-to-earth work between a cop doc and public safety officer. This book is meant most for the public safety officer and for those who love and work with this worthiest of populations.

Hence, this book takes off with conversations with a cop doc in the heat of the war zones of loss—launching an effective approach while distilling meaning stuck in the bog of cynicism. That cynic attitude is still plaguing officers in their fields of despair. It is these conversations between cop doc and public safety officer that illustrate via the use of case examples in my first two books the "why" and "how" an officer is brought from the chiseled streets of despair, cynicism, hopelessness, rage, and depression to "how" and "why" sowing his or her own garden of tragic optimism as motivation in life, living, and redemption is what makes him or her unique and humane and his or her work worthwhile. Further, these conversations highlight my theory and therapy in this book as the heart and soul at the gut level of the officer on the street of experience for his or her own use in his or her day-to-day life and living. The emphasis is like the memo book officers use on the streets when responding to challenging events—except my guide is not technical— it offers healing, hope, and help in reclaiming their courage, strength, and humane limitations in their personal calling day to day. This book opens the interventions to officers, their spouses and families, and the communities they live in from a perspective that returns to the officer what is meaningful in his or her life and the lives he or she touches day to day through internal witnessing. Internal witnessing, as I call it, is no easy task, and I will show how to do it in a language and depth that a street cop, firefighter, and EMT sipping some hot Joe could understand and use while slopping down a donut without getting scalded by the heat of hell's kitchen!

Offering insights that glean a viewpoint of public safety trauma and loss for officers to understand in the form of a conversation between the gray line healing the rift between an officer as an enforcer and as a healer of wounded lives and situations called complex traumas. These collisions of what I call identity modes occur in the web of existential crisis moments. Moments existentially all too systemic in the front lines of public safety work. It is in my experience as a cop doc that I pull together those existential crisis moments and work through the conflicted identity modes that cause so much strain and stress—reinfranchising hidden meaning for motivation in the hard work of healing that confronts us. It is from this perspective that I have been able to define a problem with what may be viewed as an easy solution to public safety stress. That easy solution identifies the endemic problem as administrative stress and the solution as generic clinical debriefings. The problem with the few guides or books published on public safety stress is they give global pictures and contend that the real stress is administrative.

The problem itself lies in the types of questions and assumptions underlying most researcher bias in this field; this has now extended to the much enlarged domain of the paraprofessional peer support programs. Administrative stress, common to every profession, has been overemphasized rather than events associated with trauma and grief responses that police experience. This misplaced emphasis on administrative stress is due, in part, to the understandable denial of officers (conscious and unconscious) to identify their own trauma and grief. This, in turn, is also denied by many police administrators and the communities officers serve. It may be, in part, easier to sweep loss under the umbrella of trauma and close that broad cover away and tuck the tears that rain on the officer into a nice neat generic box that is compartmentalized deep within. Instead, I offer a viewpoint that opens up a healing in a conversation with you as an officer or a family member of an officer. That is even after experiencing a trauma in its full color and complexity, which likely has forced a response from you as an enforcer of public safety and a street corner—healer of wounded souls. The collision of public safety demands hurls conflict at quantum speed that can tear open your soul. It has become endemic in either an overtly skeptical view of the job of public safety and its culture, or a view that is overly optimistic. Extreme optimism in my own biased view is that a few peer support sessions will rescue a fellow officer from the swells of grief that multiple experiences of trauma and loss drown one in.

If you are the officer who picks up this book, you are invited to a conversation throughout the guide. A guide that reaches officers at their level and in their words. That is because I was one, as well as street cop and boss. I have never lost touch with being in public service, which continues to this moment in my service to public safety officers and their families.

The term *police* is used synonymously with public safety professionals that are both public and private, as well as their spouses and families. Each chapter has a specific domain, mapping out the spires of loss into a hub that coheres a perspective of complex trauma with individual differences in clear focus. Theory is wed to practice and practice to effective interventions to and for officers in their own language. This book is a self-help guide as much as an initiation into the reality of public safety work that is validating, and taking that reality and moving it from doom and gloom into a glimmer of what is meaningful and motivational in the face of that very loss in the complex configurations that envelope each existential moment in the depicted officer's life. The key here is my theory and technique of doing an eco-ethological existential analysis delivered in a way that officers and their families can understand and use in their day-to-day lives when trauma, loss, terrorism, and swift changes captivate their focus, and the meaning in life and living is left on the fringes as borders receding into the dim past that reifies the present—the doom and gloom police cynicism so many officers speak about in locker rooms. Real police authors romanticize but are distilled for consumption by an approach created by a cop doc who has been there, done that, experienced some heavy losses and traumas, and knows how to crack the egg of petrified trauma into the sowing of tragic optimism. This distilling so hidden in the therapy hours and the resilience he evokes in each case anew is delivered into your hand for immediate consumption.

It is not a dummies guide but a respectful journey for each of the five personality styles officers bring to the table of therapy. The coordinates of intervention are laid out for each officer-patient's style via their own words and stories. Yet it is not just their stories, but one that is etched in the frames of the hours of therapy for use on the streets in which they will return to drum out their beats for the most productive years of their lives. The costs of burnout, cynicism, and withdrawal from the existential vacuum and chaos exact a living death for many. This work holds out the existential psychological imagination to the officers—it highlights lessons learned and forgotten in the harsh repetition of loss in trauma.

It ought to be of more than a passing note for you as a reader that many officers in local, state, and federal public safety have an equivalent of an associate's degree in education. I write to you on par with respect for your intelligence and ability as a smart officer. The guide in your hand identifies problems encountered, solutions sought, and wisdom culled from experiences with hundreds of officers where faith, strength, and courage are stoked into workable motivation for inspiration in dealing with the invariable losses and trauma encountered in your field of police, medic, firefighting, and correctional work. The examples highlight each of the five personality styles from different dimensions of loss that is reinfranchised through an eco-ethological existential analysis. In addressing the cases presented, you as an officer or your family members are educated in clear and fundamental lessons learned. This is done in a way that does not overburden you as a reader with jargon or insult the expectation of a respectful valuing of your maturity and ability to learn how to value and internally witness your own courage, responsibleness, and calling as strength in choosing how and why to turn losses into healthful motivation for life and living.

Final Note: This book is not in place of therapy. It is a self-initiated guide for you, your wife or husband, and SOs that can be expanded with peer support. In many instances mental health professionals with expertise in grief and trauma therapy, and ideally with public safety experience, are indispensible allies and trained healers.

Police and Public Safety Complex PTSD (PPS-CPTSD)

1

Understanding My Own Police and Public Safety Complex Trauma

What's the Real Deal, Doc Dan?

The real deal begins with what you have become accustomed to as fact in our police and public safety culture:

"Tragedy happens, learn to deal with it!"
"Toughen up buddy, cops don't whine."
"When you are in, you are the best—when you retire, you are a pest!"
"Once a cop, always a cop, 24 hours by 7 days a week!"

You in public safety have been through the drill and can hear the barking out of mobilization orders with six different plans and alternatives for each reactive wave in any emergency. You know full well the value of discipline: in fact, you have likely heard the terms *trauma*, *grief*, and *terrorism*.

But what do these words *trauma*, *grief*, and *terrorism* mean to you as an individual public safety officer or you as a family member of an officer?

From the start, it is you I am addressing as an individual officer and a peer. Yes, a peer. I have been a street cop: I have been there when the chaos has hit the fan and know how hard it is to deal with piles of bureaucratic shuffles. Pinheads are in place in countless lines to tell you who you are and how to do your job. The layers of paperwork can flood your sensibilities. At times, paperwork can cloud your ability to think as clearly as you would like to believe you are thinking. Yet, the layers of the bureaucratic tangles are stapled into your daily package with the commanding officer barking out, "Hey, I did it! Now it's your turn—you can do it! Guess what? You do it, or leave!" Most of us can't just get up and leave. We can't afford it. Further, you did not endure all the work, commitment, and love of your job that you are likely to hate as well.

Well, it is the pinhead bureaucracy in part that is at times so overwhelming. But, even the pinheads need to be there and have their place in a bureaucracy. Yes, the sad truth is the layers of any agency, department, bureau, or administration can make you cry no different than peeling away the layers of an onion that spoiled. I can stop right now and tell you how many degrees I have, how many therapies I have trained in and learned, and why you ought to listen to me. I will not do that. Why? Because I am talking to you as I genuinely consider you: I consider you a brother or sister officer—this survival guide is one I want you to use, and not put down.

I am being real with you and want you to be real with not only me, but also with you, yes you! I did not want to, and will not write a guide that you cannot connect to and use for yourself. I will discuss some technical and important information to navigate your way around losses. Losses that surround your experiences of trauma, especially as inflicted by terrorists. Domestic and foreign terrorists may not terrorize you as they do civilians: But, the quick trap of burning out and spacing out can do the equivalent damage. Terrorists try to tack your sacred center. That is, tack you down from the most important place, which is your own special place of courage, tragic optimism, and resilience.

In my own work both the tragic and redeeming moment was realizing how much of these dimensions are hidden from conscious awareness. Redeeming is crucial in your connecting to the inner source within you. In helping you connect to that eternal source within, I will give you my own theory and therapy approach to trauma, loss, and terrorism as a doc who is also a cop. This is not a pretty book. It is not a feel good book. It is not an image book. It is not a reality guidebook. It is also not the next American idol book or reality guide.

It is a guide for you—from me—and I mean you. I will draw from my years of experience with working with the finest, bravest, and brightest public safety folks. Public safety officers are the salt of the earth: I pray God I may be considered along with you as an earthy, pithy, and genuine peer for all prosperity. With this roll call address I now call you to the most important duty of all: the duty you owe yourself, your families, and friends. It begins with you first. Beginning with you enables you to help a group of folks as large as the community, department, bureau, administration, or agency you work for.

This is true whether you work for a public or even a private agency where you put your life in danger: mental, physical, or emotional for the public trust. You are indeed a public servant, and you are the exact reader I seek to support, challenge, confirm, affirm, and travel within your day-to-day journey. I will do that journey with you as one of the few real cop docs out there in the field of service. Meaning, frankly I have walked in your shoes in fires, emergency medical situations, police situations, and a crisis of peers. I have done that walk many times literally, and even more times vicariously. This guide then is our guide, and it is time we open the new book and start with our first chapter. Let's begin together, and please continue with me. Even if you are alone, feel isolated due to job-related stressors, or you're an executive or rookie, and even if all seems well and fine or you are in the dumps, please, stop and pause. It is time to take on my invitation as a partner with me—let's do it! No time like the present. Consider yourself the operator and me the recorder. For those of us who have worked with a partner in the field of real policing, emergency medical technician, firefighter, National Guard, emergency nursing, and medical work—no further explanation is needed—let's begin.

Dismounting from the Saddle: When Complex Trauma Hits Home—Existential Questions!

It is common for a street cop, emergency medical technician, paramedic, firefighter, emergency room nurse, or emergency room physician/psychologist to sometimes ask compelling questions from his or her hip of experience. Questions asked well after dismounting from your saddle—that is, after one of those events you would rather not remember, has passed, and you cannot forget "it"! Sometimes you may even ask yourself the following questions or make the following statements in the heat of the chaos of "it," or as we may call it, a complex traumatic event:

"How did I get here?"
"I can't believe this event is happening."
"I must be dreaming."
"Am I going to make it through this?"
"Am I going to be put up on trial and shaken down and lose all I have worked so hard for?"
"I need to be professional, God can get me through 'it,' but I must really be going crazy."
"No one has ever been this badly off before—and in a panic to boot— why me, dear God?"
"How could the job let me down when I have been such a good soldier?"
"I do my job so well, how could I have let down my guard, and not seen 'it' coming?"

These we can call existential questions. Why? Because these questions remind you of your existence, not just physical and logistic expertise. They tap your heart rhythms and beg questions that ask of you: What is your existence all about? In other words, these potentially complex and traumatic events provoke thoughtful and deep questions in all of us, right down to the real meat and potatoes of life and living: right to the heart of the matter of what counts is the questions you ask yourself when sirens are turned off. When you dim the turret lights and the flashes seared in your eyes from the events you wish you never witnessed and participated in—that pop out at you!

That heart of the matter is where you hide inside: that place hidden in quiet moments comes out and haunts you in full color. That moment of loss and trauma may have passed in physical time that you can count in minutes, hours, days, weeks, months, and even years in the space of your minds. Yet "it" is still a shadowy presence. It is that human space that is so uniquely yours that may plague you deep inside your core. That is speaking from your gut—in your own private space, which with the right therapist, together the pain and loss you endure is made less toxic.

But, let's hold off on therapy for a while and take a look at some questions that act as signals that tell you that some events are traumatic and existentially gut wrenching:

"Where am I at this point in life?"

"I almost lost my life in the fire. What did I do for this to happen?"

"Why do I have a cut in my face from a perp, a scar for life on my cheek?"

"Am I really a good emergency medical technician or a fraud—not yet figured out?"

"How did I get here? An official misconduct charge by inspections and IAB is pending."

"I told that pompous civilian to shove his complaint. Now I'm screwed with CCRB?"

"Where else can I police? I only know how to patrol 'iron horses' [trains] and transit stations."

"How can I forget about 'it'? Did I really do the best to save that kid from choking?"

"I am sick and keep seeing the DOA, and dreamt I was kissing her. Am I a freak?"

"Can I ever be a normal person again, and go back to being innocent and naïve?"

"Did I really do the right thing—or am I really out in la la land?"

"I was a choir boy and now I am at choir practice and wild sex. What happened?"

"Civilians understand squat. We all know it, so what can I do but humor them?"

Public Safety Officers and Existential Questions: Eco-Ethological Existential Analysis

Existential questions as those above in reality ask us questions where we breathe. In other words, these questions are markers in our lives and where and how we move in the orbits of our daily beats: those beats can be the patrol sector, whether vertical or horizontal. Those orbits can be in the ER room as an EMT/medic bringing in the kid that got ran over by the bus and is alive. It can be as a patrol officer active in the Armed Forces who witnessed an elderly man get tapped by a van and heard the driver say, "Hey, the old creep should have looked out. Gotta go and the elderly man is now brain damaged." Maybe you are the ER RN or ER MD doing the traumatic brain injury (TBI) assessment on that elderly man. Perhaps you are the firefighter going in the tunnel with a Scott pack and feel your own life closing in on you and aware you may get stuck: panic sets in and you can't talk.

Existential questions and problems are real, and they strike at the core of meaning in your life or the eclipsing of that meaning. These questions ask you in your own voice:

"Did you really act as you believe you know you should have and must have acted?"

"Was your heart in the right place, or did you not give care as you should have?"

"Are you responsible for the mess you just experienced, or were you hurled into the chaos?"

These key questions shake your view of the world. They shake not just the way you think, and why you think that way, but what you really care about that is meaningful in your own life. I do not mean some sweeping brush applied to the whole department, but for you! Yes, you!

When you say *me*, it is not really a dirty word. In fact, in moderation it is one of the healthiest words. For you as a public safety officer or family member of an officer, you are living in a world where you can honestly tell yourself, "You serve others constantly and have forgotten about the 'me' within the 'we'!"

It is important to pause right here and now. Please reflect for a moment as a public safety officer and humane being—how important is that word *me* to you?" Some of the folks reading this book, including you, may say, "Hey Doc, wait a minute. I enjoy life. I have a sweet drink, know how to eat well, live well, and can shake off all the bad stuff dealt with as a public safety officer. I am truly okay! I have even learned to move with changes and dance with changes."

That is a compelling argument you are taught to tell yourself. It does not really cut it. Let's be real—right here and now. While you can have fun at times, you do know where to go for immediate satisfaction on any material or even fantasy level. Yet, deep in your personal sense and core, being a public safety officer is a lot more than that. You know that as well!

You did not join to just wear a shield. It is what that shield really means to you and how much you are now ready to renew your hope, courage, and optimism. Not just any mainstream pitch feels good for you. But, when you think back to the way you used to put on your uniform and the pride you felt in wearing the shield—that feels real good. Yes, the job changes with time, but so do you! I am not going to tell you to buck up. I am not going to tell you to shore up your feelings and march on with blind optimism, all-encompassing hope, and blind courage. Why? Because that is shoving jargon down your throat and it is you whom I respect too much—as you are, in essence, at a core level a brother and sister officer. The "I" in you is critically important because that is exactly what urges you to be the best you can be. The "I" also may push you to be the worse you can be.

To be the best you can be, you will need to deeply drink from the strength within your own well. A well that is hidden in the dim spark that needs to be awakened in the daily work you did and will do in the future. That begs you to have optimism while facing the reality of tragic reality.

Tragic Optimism as Courage to Command Presence and Respect (Self and Others)

I am going to be real and explore what these terms mean to you personally. I will do that job with you by adding the real dose that you need to make sense with and be real with you—by adding in the missing word *tragic*, that is, *tragic* optimism: your courage and hope in the tragic you experience in the space of your work as a public safety officer!

Tragic optimism are the words a public safety officer on the front line, Dr. Viktor Frankl, coined when he survived the living hell of terrorism under the Third Reich. Public service doc in a regime that killed his wife and children, and bent on killing him, Dr. Frankl held on to his optimism and faith. Faith in the face of tragedy till Viktor tasted victory.

Frankl suffered hell, where he lost his wife to murder, his parents and siblings, his profession, and all of his work, while he held on to his faith in ultimate meaning in life, his refusal to let despair set in. If that is not victory, and a fellow public service officer to learn from, I do not know whom to look for inspiration. For you, as an officer always in the front line of ultimate risk—tragic optimism—faith in ultimate meaning is well worth keeping alive. In order to do this, I need to have you revisit the tragic experiences in your own life without giving up your own existential meaning of what type of questions within you cry out for answers. Answers to questions you have. Even if you have never actually asked any out loud. Perhaps questions you never even dared to ask—not only another person, but even yourself.

Silence in Traumatic Loss—Deadly Rounds— One More Round Please! Which One?

You have learned larger than life public safety rules you live night in, day out. You have learned to suffer in silence by being a good soldier cop, good soldier firefighter, good soldier emergency medical technician/medic/ER nurse, and physician. Silence is powerful, silence is a core part of your existence, but existence asks questions of you. The existential questions you confront are how to live with experiences most folks do not go through in a lifetime. Questions you may ask are not only gut wrenching, but heart breaking, such as:

"How do you keep a professional attitude at all times, at least before 'them'—the public?"

"How and what does your professional attitude mean to you as an individual?"

"How do you keep to standard operating procedures [SOP] when you have been hit in your gut as a deep cover, with no justice except what the law of the war zone 'might make right'?"

"What does armor that is supposed to protect you do to you over time in the space you exist in?"

"How does the blue, red, orange, and white wall help with the real stuff you're dealing with?"

"Can you maintain functioning as losses etch memory tracks echoing in your brains chambers?"

"How do you regroup after you just failed in reviving a kid choking on a piece of candy?"

"Can you redirect and regroup after you lost your partner on the job?"

"Will you ever recover losing your partner on the job, and now in your personal life?"

"How can you lose your job, face losing your partner, and dealing with job-related trials?"

"Did you really get wasted and go out to a bar and do what you did with
    a stranger?"
"Did you wake up alone and depressed once again, feeling spent and
    ragged inside?"

If these questions have come across the roll call of your mind, take out
the flip side of your memo book and open the scratch sheet column for personal notes at the back of this guide (see Appendix A).

Cop-In: No Cop-Outs!

Questions track our guide as I intend to answer how and why these questions
and events can open you to cop-in, not cop-out! You will be able to work on
how to figure out why these questions become building blocks that can guide
you and affect you. I will share with you what you can do to help yourself.
You are left with choices and responsibility. I offer you new knowledge. I
will provoke you to develop even deeper wells of wisdom as a unique and
individual public safety officer! It begins with realizing the power to affect
change in your life and your loved ones by appreciating the complex impact
losses have on you.
    Losses are hard to color in and realize when unnoticed and unresolved.
It is as if you have swallowed a toxic pill: as we know, a toxic pill swallowed,
whether by accident or intentionally, can ultimately destroy you. That is, a
toxic pill that you are not aware of. Such colorless toxic pills are an accumulation of losses and trauma unacknowledged by you and your loved ones.
My antidote is based on the field of what you, as an officer, let yourself disclose. Your disclosure begins with first understanding my approach, which
includes learning how the ecology of your beat impacts on why certain
behaviors, ideas, and emotions are meaningful, or not meaningful, to you
from a survival point of view. Survival is half of the reality, including the culture of trauma and loss as part of your own survival equation. Other actors
and influences come into play.

Public Safety Officer Reality Equation:
Your Own Existential Self Analysis

Hold on to your saddle because the most important experience of the reality equation is the part with no material hold on you, your life, and living: it
is what makes you uniquely different by being an officer living in your own

eco-ethological niche. How and why you select certain traumas and defenses against feeling "it," and the way you adapt within your niche, is imprinted with your own mark and style. It is also your humane being that is different from any other: your own distinctly humane style of public safety. Learning from the case examples to follow will highlight how to get ready for using an eco-ethological existential analysis.

What Does the Eco-Ethological Existential Analysis Ask of Me?

Eco-ethological existential analysis asks of you questions that sink into your own heart of hearts. That is, the soulfulness that makes you, well in truth, you! That "you" is what is so hidden under layers of that rotting onion of losses and trauma. My job here is bringing a glimpse of your own hidden wisdom to the light of your day-to-day experiences. Hidden wisdom will not change much in terms of eco-ethological dimensions of events you experience. What you will change are your thoughts and, in turn, your feelings, as well as your inner sight and will to meaning lighting up the caves of your own eco-ethological niche. Your views, ideas, and behaviors within your ecology and the ethological niche you live in for at least a third of your days will never look the same. That is provided you work on understanding and applying your own self eco-ethological existential analysis. This will optimally be done with a clinician you can trust to work on "it" with you.

Eco-ethological existential analysis will make all the difference to you and your ability to understand and appreciate you, your peers, and the community you work in day in and day out. In other words, the difference is the existential questions and the guide that I insist must be done one officer at a time. One officer at a time hopefully making more sense to you as to why your participation and investment is both unique and needed. You are worth it, and that is why I insist to peers on the job the fact that time and energy are hardly wasted on the real deal. The real deal begins with understanding you first and caring for yourself. You cannot truly help others before you help yourself.

My view from assessing, diagnosing, and treating hundreds of brothers and sisters in public safety has led me to write this book. Too many need a compass and direction. It is hard to understand that fact of being lost when you are lost. Once you realize you are lost, it is easier to let another peer in and help you move toward being found. Further, it begins with an admission that "I am not so okay, Doc, and I know you've been there in the saddle."

"I know you can hop in and be my navigator—or if you prefer, you are the operator in the radio motor patrol car and I am the recorder." A point to be made right here is that like you, I am no dummy: I do not think of you as a dummy! This is not another dummies guide. In fact, the evidence is you have my book in your hand. You are reading and seeking to understand your own experience of trauma, loss, and terrorism. Your own evidence is you care enough about you and your loved ones to make this effort! Your desire to learn how to get a grip on what trauma is for yourself will be shared with you in down-to-earth terms. I will do that as a cop doc to cops in narratives that guide your passage to understanding that is practical and real.

When *cop* is mentioned what I mean is you as a public safety officer: EMT, firefighter, ER RN, ER MD, parole and probation officer, S/A or DI or intel analyst, public or private security officer on duty or off duty, active or retired. I am not lumping you together with everyone else, or anyone else, but rather showing you how big your family is. Like all families, conflict exists and different jobs are performed. But like a family, care to cover each other's back starts with your own. So with that said, let's move on together. What is trauma? Trauma is a wide hole that rips your expectations open. Your expectations in your mind's map are torn in a different direction not to your own liking. That map in your mind is shaped by the ecology in your day-to-day experiences. It is then, one may say, always in part, a loss or losses that lead to an effort for you to fill that loss in your own ecological niche. Trauma hits when what you expect in your map as a guide to help orient you is shattered by an experience that is unexpected. That experience hits you by surprise. As a rescuer first responder you are hardly guilty of whining about your losses. In fact, the problem is, if you are like the majority of officers, you are likely to deny your losses. What is borne out by reality is your expectations are ripped apart with the timing of "it"—the traumatic event. An event that you have more than likely become stuck in. That is the moment "it" hits you in your guts, you are deeply struck by profound loss. The timing of "it" is almost always unexpected. So it follows with that unexpected edge of surprise and shock that may provoke you to ask a good question of me such as, "Doc Dan, hey, when does trauma really occur? Is it when you are on the scene, or later, or what?"

It generally occurs after the street has been cleared. The makeshift emergency triage is done on some dirty, impersonal, and cold street corner. The spraying of rounds may leave the combat zone littered with civilians down. Perhaps some shells were sprayed in a dry run by bad guys; left unaccounted, no one has been hit and it gets deep sixed as unfounded. Unfounded shells fired in target practice by the guys may go as unfounded, but not forgotten as you may be the target of their practice. You are misinformed that the trauma is for the weak or the newbies, not you! In spite of education attempts about trauma, old fears survive well. Well, what can you do in an acceptable way when the ecology of your own space is ripped open with intense repeated losses accumulated over time on the job?

Good question again. Well, it is sometimes drowned when you are at a watering hole, or what Joseph Wambaugh, a fellow police sergeant who patrolled LA, called off-duty "choir practice" (Wambaugh, 1987). Choir practice in the "concrete jungle" of war zones may be politically incorrect, but it is the bull's-eye truth about after hours bar hopping. War zones can occur at any time in the world of public safety. For example, in the Wall Street or South Street Seaport neighboring the Twin Towers' site.

Let's return to the watering hole that is drunk from in your attempt to fill that emptiness the hole has left. That empty hole rips open with shock and terror when citizens you are sworn to protect are taken out with terror tactics. In your attempt to cope, you may choose to fill your holes with chemicals, sex, and violence just as you witness sudden and shocking attacks in the war zones in the city or rural areas you serve. Questions seasoned public safety officers working in rough areas of the cities and rural areas struggle with are:

Isn't it worse to be attacked at home than a place foreign to one's own
     soil, for who is the enemy on the home front?
Who is your real friend in your precinct, firehouse, or medic station?
How do you orient yourself when the very map you used as coordinates
     is taken from you one layer at a time?

Reality sets in hard and fast. Nowadays the bravest soldiers at home or abroad have the same fights and struggles with guerilla warfare by terrorists—urban, domestic, or foreign! In a moment after the shots are fired, or a building fire has gotten out of your control, or a man or woman is down, has gone south. Perhaps a kid who was molested and beaten and is dying on the street corner in a huge garbage disposal, moaning and crying, exhales his last breath close to your face as you try to comfort him. Perhaps you can smell the blood, urine, and vomit that will wretch in your lungs as long as you live, as you are telling yourself:

"Get a grasp—calm down: I need to forget this nightmare and no one
     can understand it!"
"How could God allow this to happen? It is way beyond to talk about
     anyhow."
"What did I do to deserve this and how could I ever be normal again?"
"It is what 'it' is all about—forget about it—life is a nightmare!"

That nightmare that turns into a daydream of trauma and losses in your daily beats and sectors: What can you call a day-mare?

Public Safety Complex Trauma Syndromes: Keep It Simple, Complex Is Complex!

Why this term? I do not feel *disorder*, nor negative labels and how they are perceived, really matches the experience a public safety officer such as you develops. I intend to go over some basics that you could use in identifying and understanding how complex police trauma syndromes develop. It is not an incident but a complex experience that is disturbing, compelling, and addicting that makes that experience traumatic. What makes it traumatic for you also is an experience you feel as a tragedy. In fact, around 97% of officers likely call "it" just that—tragic. In fact, public safety officers, regardless of differences, tend to minimize their own pain and suffering. You especially learn to numb your own existential pain in your gut when you feel this pain in your heart and soul. You may numb this existential pain by becoming increasingly aggressive. Perhaps you are amusing yourself by increasing your risk-taking behaviors. Among risky behaviors are drinking, gambling, and sexing out your losses.

Stop, Pause, and Reflect: When and Why Did I Lose My Sense of Loss, or Did I?

Go back and remember the academy days, where you were likely taught informally that it is part of the job and routine to unload at the bar. Perhaps have a fling now and then, or take a little risk to stay and feel alive. I ask you to challenge that way of thinking even if it is your own thinking at present. It may feel like a worn-in shoe for convenience to escape the angst of the job by choir practice. Truth be told, it leaves a hole in the sole of your heel: a rough spot in your Achilles' arch. That arching denial, suppression, and holding back your feelings is deadly over time to your well-being, mentally, physically, and existentially.

When you are feeling compelled to rush to a scene and then get deep into a homicide, a train wreck, an emotionally disturbed person, it is not easy to brush off the losses and get back on track. It is very hard and difficult to even process as an individual. When you are forced to go on one, two, and three jobs, it is "your job," "your duty," even "your calling." But stop and pause for a moment. Is it not truly a gruesome scene to see human beings dying after being stabbed, shot, and attacked by terrorism? Pause for a moment with your own slowed-down reflection.

What may not have occurred to you will become self-evident when you realize something has forcibly changed in your own way of thinking about such events as murder, terror, and mayhem. But what change takes place in the way you are thinking and processing the events of trauma in your own mind now? What makes "it" for the moment comfortable or even standard operating procedure? How did you get from shock and slowed vision to processing gruesome murders, rape, violence, and assaults so passively as to think about "it" as routine. Something inside of you is likely to question these events in a whisper as to what you really are feeling, thinking, or experiencing in different public safety situations. Some of those public safety situations are when you do emergency operations and rescue; recovery of dead/body parts; pursuit, apprehension, and arrest; and notification of victims' family and friends.

This process most of you have heard of, called numbing out, zoning out, even zombie out, is really at the heart of the matter when you deny your human response to a tragic situation. How you interpret and cope with "it" as an emotional memory is separate from how you act at and on the scene by emotionally distancing yourself from it by SOP. It is as if a distance exists from how "it" affects you over time, let's say a surrealistic distance.

Complex trauma events you experience accumulate toxic effects over time. Sudden memories, to or away from the reminders or clues you remember, emerge from the shadows of what SOP ensures. SOP serves and shapes survival in the physical reality of the moment of trauma. SOP also reinforces and shapes the most intense denial of the losses.

Think about it this way: if you watched the white shark in *Jaws* torpedo swimmers and chomp on surf boarders, you likely felt a moment of fear, excitement, and relief as you watched in relative safety and reflected quietly, "Wow! I am safe."

That relief at the time you crunched or held that popcorn kernel in your jaws clenched tight stayed in a memory bit as a flash in your mind. That flash recorded an information bite to be recovered when a similar associated event emerged. You may even have remembered when you talked it over with your popcorn-wielding buddies that it was a fun movie. You all got a laugh out of it. Notice you enjoyed and satisfied your animal side of devouring your popcorn while watching the shark eat the victim, and then laughed at the fact you were far from being in danger. Vicarious experiences like that tell us a lot about one side of human nature. Keep that in mind. Yet years later, let's move to a different place in your life when you are really swimming in the Bahamas and you see a flash in the water, and the next thing you know, you are hyperventilating and imagine you just saw a shark. Not just any shark, but a huge 20-foot white shark encircling you. You felt scared "almost to death."

SOP: Placing Fear of Death and Harm in Your Scope of Practice

You may in some circumstances get a tingle, a thrill, and even dare that fear. Why? Daring a fear makes very good sense as much as SOP does for officers. It reduces anxiety and makes it more likely it will trigger a need to dare to do it again. You may even swim deeper to redirect that fear away. But why is this so entrenched on our animal side from an ethological and ecological niche perspective?

This is so because it allows you to be in control rather than the event being in control of you. This is so natural the great ethologist Dr. Desmond Morris calls it mobbing, such as a group of seals mobbing a great white shark and driving it away (Morris, 1994). Looking at mobbing and applying it to policing makes great sense. In fact, your need to conquer fear by jumping in and seeking more trauma events is called countertraumatic. In many situations it may even be part of an unknown addiction you have learned, and in some way reinforces a biological tendency in yourself. That tendency may be a seeking out of ethological stimulation and defense against trauma and loss. Almost as if your conquest is a way to prove your mastery of "it."

Addiction may include your need to act out and conquer your fear. This happens by immersing yourself in what you fear most compulsively and thereby mastering your worst fear. Noticing and attending to an experience leaves you with the illusion of control and mastery: you're in the driver's seat. I would like you to think about what you may be doing now, as addiction is strongly shaped and makes superb sense from an ethological point of view. How? Your own survival in unpredictable and chaotic eco-ethological niches repeatedly leaves you with the idea, "Hey I have survived once again." It also gives you an existential sense of being an indestructible soldier, or as you may think, an immortal soldier.

However, you may even avoid dipping your heel in the sea at the slightest hint a shark may be lurking in the gray fog that glistens dimly in the shadow of the looming sunset. One such person who is mortified about the idea of being a human lunch for a white shark is me. My own response to *Jaws*, for example, embraced the denial mechanism of fear and avoided being eaten by a San Diego as well as formally a New Jersey Shore white shark! That may be your response. Well, while similar to watching *Jaws*, you may experience an as if sensation without really being eaten by a white shark. Cues that act as warning signals reinforce whether you will avoid, jump in, deny any response, or act indifferent to swimming in a beach. Now let's take the example of *Jaws* and move to experiencing real life and death trauma events.

Events that you witness, participate in, and experience with the intensity and frequency you do.

Stop and think about the reality of having been taught a lot of jobs that are routine and likely having been told, "Well firm up, and stop whining about it!" Maybe you heard, "Hey, toughen up or bail out, and if you are not happy, then toss burgers at McD's once again, kid!" The result of being shaped by trauma events with the weight of life and death conspires to create your own unique adaptation. From an eco-ethological perspective, your own unique adaptation makes superb sense. Keep in mind as you move on in this guide that fact is pivotal as to how and why you will at least, in part, heal the wounds in your own trauma experiences—if you are willing to stay with me. Leaving no public safety officer behind, which means you. Let's look at another example in ecological niches of policing. A homicide DOA is a real human lying with urine that seeps out when the body pops in sweltering heat. Stench that burns emotional memories for decades of smelling wretched rotten eggs. A trigger that may reinforce smelling that DOA again is when you smell eggs overcooked on a stove.

A case is Officer Irving, a WWII veteran who liberated Dachau death camp. When he smelled certain fumes or food items, he immediately had the experience of repulsion and gagged. When we uncovered his losses, he remembered seeing the victims left as piles of bones and flesh and reexperienced his rage at the terrorists' mass murder. The associated sense of smell was ever present as a door to trauma ready to emerge at any time. Visual memories of a crime scene may reemerge when drinking strong coffee. In other words, the sense of taste may trigger a visual and then dominant sense of smell associated with the trauma. For example, a crime scene may be remembered in a triggered memory visually imprinted, but where smells of dry coffee as burnt offerings on an old GE stove were used to overwhelm the DOA stench. No Hollywood pretty scenes.

Perhaps you are an ER nurse, medic, or physician doing defibrillation on the dying handsome corporate attorney who took a hit snorting cocaine and is hemorrhaging with fatal convulsions. You remember on certain warm days smells that permeate the air and trigger these visual and then auditory senses of the crime scene.

You may be a city EMT who can remember responding to a job 3 years ago of a "female child down" who on scene was molested and left for dead. You remember the groaning near a garbage disposal. A cat meows and now you get a jolt and see it all over again, although it was 13 years ago when you experienced the complex trauma. It may have been your rookie run responding to a "junkie" dying of an overdose and begging you to end the pain. As you arrived on the scene as a firefighter and realized that is the teen son of a parish minister you know. Like these events that are so hard to cope with, you may want to wash away the memories with addictive behavior. Strong booze, sex, or gambling can win back some of the losses you have to swallow day by day—so it seems in the moment. However, these memories remain toxic in your brain and do not vanish, as much as you may try to have "it" go away and hope to control "it." You may succeed in suppressing some memories from your own conscious awareness. When you realize you can survive and function like many trained mental health professionals and bosses on the job, you may mistake functioning for healthy adaptation. You're functioning well does not stop the reality that your trauma experiences may remain frozen in your mind. That frozen time is set in the space of your own emotional, mental, and visual memory imprinted in your brain.

Ethological Memory Imprints of PPS-Complex Trauma Experiences

That imprint is like a dark inkwell stain in your brain. That stain colors your experience in a way that affects your ethological survival strategy. That survival strategy is imprinted in a dimension of human experience we can firmly place as the ethological. Ethological dimensions are not only exclusive to humans but represent biopsychological patterns of behaviors in all animals. Ethological is used in my theory and therapy of complex trauma and grief. In part, motivation at a basic level of survival is at the center of the why and how public safety officers act, think, and react to events that can be characterized as traumatic on a daily basis. In part, your reacting on a survival dimension as an animal is undeniable.

Stop, pause, and think, and you will likely recall many peers who say almost without thought when asked about their adrenalin rush and excitement at a disorder control situation, a plane crash, or a tornado, that they went into survival mode.

That survival mode runs a lot deeper than you may consciously be aware of, and certainly educated about. In my type of therapy for grief and trauma, you are helped with a method that includes taking a tough look at terrorism (domestic or foreign) in its center of ethological and ecological niches, where it develops. The real human and spiritual side of your experiences is something that is not alien from your ethological experience of fear, anger/rage, and excitement.

All animals experience these emotions with different ways of expression as well. Ethological includes territorial, ecological influences, the niche in which you operate and think, and patterns that overlap survival needs and existential meaning. Ignoring the tragic as a human experience and within the unique aspects of language is not only dangerous, but misses the target of your experience. Stop, pause, and reflect on any of the events presented in this guide for a moment.

Whether you are the toughest firefighter, police officer, EMT, ER MD, ER nurse, or field medic, is there not some aspect of any of those events that you do not connect with as truly tragic? I doubt you did not feel, think, or experience a twinge in your gut and an ache in your soul when you read some of the trauma events our peers endured thus far. Let's not avoid the reality and take it further down the line of your experiences. What you do is not just "a job" as civilians think: it is "the job"—that is, the sector, the precinct, the firehouse, the police service house, the medic station you mean by "being on the job."

The survival of your partner or your squad is what counts not only first, but last. That survival is ethological and imprinted in your ecological map and eco-ethological niches. Not only for survival imprints, but the meaning you get in achieving your goals, including surviving your tour, is intertwined. It is the area of your beat, the detail or unit you are working in, that is all important over time. The ecology is the setting for the trauma you are experiencing and the way you must survive on a daily basis. This is unusually sensible ethologically, as some bad guy is deterred from ever thinking you are weak, and can take advantage of weakness as an edge to ambush you. Eco-ethological niches include knowing the geography and the cover buildings, and even the johnny pumps that afford your survival if you are ambushed, that is, ethologically driven tactics. Your own physical and psychological survival responses and where and to whom you are responding to are as different as the color of the day. In sum, the most crucial factors are framed in an ecology niche with ethological importance shaped for your very individual and unit survival. In the survival mode all the hoorahs are valuable in shaping your responses. But the one hoorah you are looking out for in reality comes down to your partner and unit while doing your job. That is when it really reaches your gut. In that way the job appears routine. As a habit it becomes familiar—as you have heard countless times on the job— "it's simple as that," right?

Is it as simple as all that? Well yes, that is right, in part, but not exactly. It becomes routine until the unexpected happens. You do not have the map to guide you when a novel moment occurs. It is never as simple as that, even though you may say that automatically—specific responses to novel encounters are always unique. Those specific responses depend on your personality and on your own experiences of losses and successes in your eco-ethological niches. The style you may have processed in your own experiences and expectations is learned and helps you predict in your own map, to act or not to act in a crisis you encounter. But that does capture the existential tragic moment you experience within the complexity of your learned eco-ethological niches as an officer.

For example, it is not as simple as all that when you attempt a rescue of your partner, who may be fatally shot and dying in your arms calling for his wife, perhaps his mother? Well, was your experience of seeing the gal shot in the head and not knowing what to do at that point except get a bus (ambulance) on scene immediately as simple as all that? You may be the EMT on the scene, and you may be trying to locate the entry wound and stop bleeding as the FD medic gets on the scene and joins in the rush to the hospital—not so simple. The triage ER nurse is prepping the patient for the ER doc and surgery. Which one of these public safety officers are you? Stop! Think about how real that scene is—routine and simple as all that, right? Wrong!

It is not routine even if you got used to "it," and it may not bother you at first: these events are traumatic and they accumulate like toxins each time your blood pressure rises. Your internal alert goes into operational mode and functions as the professional you are. But remember, operational mode and functioning do not mean healthy—they mean you can do the job. Please once again, stop, pause, and reflect for a moment. Now think of each of your brother and sister public safety officers in the chain of rescue and recovery operations who suffer tragic losses. Losses such as a real human being dying, sometimes by murder, sometimes by accident, sometimes in an emergency medical situation. Do you really believe you have the ability to turn off and tune out your real emotions to the tragic losses you face?

If you only operated on an eco-ethological dimension and not as an animal, but as a robot, maybe the answer would be yes. But even then, likely the answer would be no. Animals arguably experience grief and, for that matter, trauma. Perhaps rethinking is called for here. Please ask yourself if it is really possible to have a type of optimism even in the face of the accumulation of tragic moments in your life history. It may be possible that optimism in the face of the truly tragic is just, after all, an illusion that only the uninitiated civilian mentality can hold on to. Well, the tragic is actually secondary when you cannot even call tragic tragic in the first place. The answer is yes, in part, it may just be an illusion. After all, you can function well under fire, and in fact, for many times under fire, even for a 20- or 30-year career. That functional part is automatic, and on the surface, the emotional, physical, and mental dimension that defines your psychology as a human being from a uniquely human bio-psychosocial perspective.

Existential Analysis of the Eco-Ethological Impact of Complex Trauma: Soulful Rhythms

This is the human biopsychosocial picture. It's a good frame, but not the full picture by a long shot: the larger picture is the overarching motivation that makes you a uniquely humane being with a heart and soul. It is what you do in terms of coming to grips with your own existential moment as a humane being in a humane way. In other words how you deal with what you experienced in a heartfelt way, even if denied, does not cover over what you really feel and experience to keep you healthy. For example, as many public safety officers who are humane beings in their heart of hearts may sit with and swallow what happened on the street today, yesterday, and tomorrow. Outside of the upset and pain, you still care enough to help the homeless person with a coffee bought from your own funds off duty, or walk the elderly lady to her community center, or share a moment with a mentally ill person and inquire how she is doing. Any of these existential meaningful moments are not searched for but are actually a core of your self-expression and strength. These meaningful moments exist and transcend the influences that are shaped by you and your relationship within your own eco-ethological niche. It is essentially what defines a dimension of your essence: responding in your own unique style of who you are and how you act in deed as well as heart. The great jazz player Louis Armstrong Jr. called it soul! In the eco-ethological existential analysis your own healing includes sowing extraordinary moments. Timeless moments where you give silently a part of who you really are to another human being in need: in deed. No terrorist, complex loss, or trauma can turn off what is your own motivation and expression. It is your choice to not give in to the closure of conscious awareness and openness toward the existential dimension in you.

This is nowhere near the depth of existential potential that lies in your heart and soul. Like trauma, the antidote lies within the toxic frames that gnaw away as questions you hardly ever ask aloud. Not asked aloud does not mean they are not asked in your soprano conscience. Although you may have never asked yourself certain questions within hearing of another person, it may be a relief—a relief, believe you and me, to know a reality I will share with you: cop doc to public safety officer. The questions that gnaw in your silent echoes within your soul are asked in the therapy room. Sometimes I pull them and sometimes they are offered as gifts in the therapeutic hour as follows:

"How can a human being stoop so low to do what she did?"
"How is it possible for him to leave his humanity card behind in the dust of such reckless evil?"

infiltrate your entire way of being and existing on a spiritual level. That alert survival mode submerges you into the sea of chaos. That chaos and splitting into different identity modes is what helps you function night in and day out.

Adaptive Functional Dissociation Pounding Your Public Safety Beat Experiences

It is possible to be okay in your day-to-day surfing in the sea of chaos of losses because of what I call adaptive functional dissociation. That is, the ability to alter your state of consciousness by being fully alert to your ecological niche, where you master the unique map that works very well in your own survival strategy. You adapt so well to this survival strategy map and so expert in your mapping survival strategy that you can lose the reality of who you really are and your own unique meaning and hope in your own life and living. This is in part within your will and in larger part not within your awareness, except in a vague and hazy way, like foam in the surf. Many officers have told me and I could relate to the idea, "Hey Doc, I would rather take a hit or even a beating than deal with the BS from the job!" Well maybe you do not say it out loud, but most officers I know say, "How could you just forget what you just experienced without going crazy?" How do you manage to keep hope and keep doing your job like a sanitation man—the more you clean up [again, fill in the blanks] _____, the more _____ accumulates.

Many officers tell me, "Hey Doc, in my case I am different and I am healthier—I get close to my work partners and laugh about something in 'it.'" That "it" again:

"I may drink 'it' off, and then for me it works. I am able to handle my drinks."
"I may work out and feel better. That is my way of dealing with 'it.'"
"At times it gets so overwhelming I may isolate and stay alone. It helps me, okay!"
"I try to have sex even with a stranger to help work it off, and it hurts no one. She's willing, so why not?"
"I may even hurt myself to end the pain and feel alive—anything but sitting with the memories of 'it'. But you know what? I am in charge of me. Simple as that!"

Redirect your attention to loss and "its" impact. That is reality. Denial is illusion at best.

After hearing how your peers attempt to process loss, let me redirect your attention for a moment and ask you to look at the different attempts many officers use to help themselves. Please pay heavy attention to the following question: Do you still think your work is simple, routine, and you should let it roll off like a duck?

I know I like Peking duck as much as the next fellow, especially in China in 2003, where I loved eating Peking and Beijing duck. Duck authentically basted and made to perfection—but tasty as duck is, I do not want to be one. I doubt you want to act like a duck. All this "duck stuff" is telling of the culture we work in, and the rules we learn to live by. I am not trying to be funny. I am being very serious when I say ducking is just not going to cut it, but cut you. Ducking and letting the trauma roll off will not stop the target from getting hit—it may delay it—but it will hit you head on. The more you try to avoid "it" like the white shark in the sea of losses "it" will reemerge and strike hard and torpedo you when you least expect it: expect it!

So what can you do if you cannot deny or duck from the trauma you experience? Well, first you can call the impact of most tragic experiences that are really hard to deal with psychologically complex trauma events. You can follow up by realizing the effect it has on you as a syndrome. It is important to realize why. It is not abnormal to experience what may become symptomatic after you experience a complex trauma event. If someone has been through a marathon, you do not expect him or her to be able to be able to roll out of bed, but rather roll into bed and put up the pillow and sleep.

You have learned in the academy that the adrenalin rushes are like a locomotive. The rush impacts your breathing and heart rate. I am going to go over that and talk to you in realistic terms. That rush is not temporary. Imprints of trauma are unique as fingerprints in the detection of officer's responses and memories of each trauma event.

Every time you experience a complex trauma event a buildup of your ability to tolerate a level of stress occurs in your body. Along with your higher thresholds of stress, a memory becomes more colorful and more intense. This is one aspect of what has been called inoculation to complex traumatic events. The belief is it becomes easier to handle more tragedies we encounter by accumulating experiences of tragic importance: from an ethological and ecological view, that is partially true. Think about it, you develop a tougher skin with more wear and tear. Folk wisdom has it you can let "it" roll off your back as you experience more situations and events—your sophistication increases; again this is in part, true. The blue police, red firefighter, and white medic culture all tell you comforting words of tough love of a sweet grandpa and grandma. They may say, if you were raised in Brooklyn, New York, like me: "If you feel the kitchen is too hot, get out: if you can't let it roll off your back, then you aren't made of the real fiber necessary to be a firefighter, cop, or EMT. Toughen up."

Well that is folktales, and like some tales, it is best to let go of what is not so good and does not work in the long run, and even shorter run for you.

You are asked to be your own captain and leader of your own ship. But you may ask me now, "Hey Doc, what do you mean when you say, in part, it is true that we gain immunity and inoculation to complex trauma events?" As with pregnancy, you cannot be partly pregnant, but either pregnant or not pregnant. In your case, immunity and inoculation mean delay, not cure and not healing. In other words, you adapt to living with terrorism and criminal violence, which you need to do to function. That adaptation is functional and important on the job. On the job, "it" does not get in your face, heart, and soul, but reality sets in and it does get in your face, heart, and soul.

That pain accumulates as you learn to adapt to your ecological niche and in your survival mode ethologically with expertise. Inoculation and immunity are a healthy experience for physical and emotional survival. However, truth be told, adaptive functional dissociation is not healthy in the dimensions of your own life, and living meaningfully after the "job" or "when you leave your assignment."

Let's look at an example to illustrate this point, being immune to feeling the heat that lets you know there is a fire, and being blind to smoke is not only hazardous to your breathing in the short run, but fatal in the long run. Inoculation and immunity help your body survive and your emotional ability to adapt as a public safety officer "on the job." It works against you unless you understand that this learned and biological survival drive needs counterbalance. Your inner sight to your existential wisdom will help in balancing the driving force behind your adaptive functional dissociation. Inoculation, as is true of immunity, is not an all good thing, nor is it all bad. The impact of inoculation in part is out of your own control, but with your own understanding and hard work it can work for you.

Dan the Cop: A Case Example

Let's get specific here with a case example again. Let's take Dan the cop on the beat, who is a good street cop. Well, when we go back far enough to his first homicide, it turns out it was both shocking and fascinating. It was shocking to see a fellow human being punctured in his chest with a little bullet entry wound and with little bleeding. The person Officer Dan observed lay "frozen stiff" in a two-door sedan. Neither Officer Dan nor his field training officer knew it was a homicide at first. They speculated it was a homeless man who tragically wanted to warm up and he tried to get in the car to get some

warmth. Another speculation was he possibly owned the car and got disoriented when the cold air overwhelmed him after one too many beers. In fact,
not looking like a suspicious death or homicide, he appeared to be "a freezer"
who sadly died homeless in a car in his effort to heat up from the elements of
a brutal New York winter.

The medical examiner (ME) came on the scene and she felt around the
DOA fellow. Officers Dan and Marty placed gloves on their hands while turning the stiff and cold body around for her to check. "Bingo," she exclaimed
as the field training officer wisely grinned and said, "See kid, that is a clean
hit—the old guy was homicided. See, that is why you got to wait to move the
body—got it?" Officer Marty saw Officer Dan perturbed and said, "Hey kid,
don't let it bother you. Let it roll off like a duck's bottom; like Bob Marley sings
'Don't Worry, Be Happy,' you can identify the body tomorrow. No worry,
they will peel back the face and wounds like a sardine de-fleshed." Many
homicides later, setting up a perimeter for the precinct detective unit and
crime scene detectives brought a certain hardness and a shell of immunity to
the complex traumas encountered over the years. You can say it also brought
some bad feelings and experiences, such as remembering a mistake Officer
Dan absorbed as guilt worthy. It stuck as a bad trauma will do. Well when
Officer Dan had more time on the job, he liked to schmooze and connect
with the citizens he served. He did his job well and cared about the young
folks in the hood he worked (NYC housing project). One such young fellow
happened to be an African American man about 19 years old. In the hood of
Bed-Stuyvesant in the early 1990s Officer Dan spoke with the young gentleman about his entering a career in the police department when finishing his
stint in the National Guard. They laughed and connected on a number of
points in upbringing and Brooklyn culture and nuances. The young fellow
laughed and said he would apply to the department, which offered a pension
and a way out of the projects, going to college, and being paid as a police
cadet. Well the local hoods thought he was ratting out some members of
the local gang, which he would not join. But the young man associated with
that local gang for protection, to survive other gangs in the hood. Like the
officer, he was shaped by ethological influences within the ecological niche of
violence, trauma, loss, and murder and identified with the officer, who also
offered hope in the darkness of poverty and limited options.

That night Officer Dan excused himself from the schmooze session. He
was called and responded lights and sirens to an assault in progress. Officer
Dan said "good" to the young man. Each looked at one another with a genuine connection and a warm handshake, as done in the hood. Officer Dan
hightailed off onto another call. Officer Dan, as typical, got another high-
priority call right after the past assault report was taken as a field report and
an open complaint.

He heard the high-priority call as "black male shot and down at XCY address of the same location he was at earlier with the young man." Further calls captured "multiple calls of male shot in chest and head." Glen, the young man, was hardly recognized with blood coming out of the back of the head, shot and reeling in confused chaos as some local folks were screaming at Officer Dan to help Glen. The sight of Glen was shocking to 27-year-old police officer Dan, who shifted into his comforter and rescue identity mode, offering comfort and help to Glen as he was dying and losing conscious awareness. Officer Dan and his partner carried this young gentleman into the patrol car and rushed him to the local hospital 10 blocks away. Upon carrying Glen into the patrol car Officer Dan shifted into his rescue operational identity mode, rushing Glen to the hospital. Regardless, Officer Dan believed he had failed Glen. It seemed surreal as he was functioning in full rescue mode and putting Glen in the bus (ambulance) from the patrol car "too slowly." Worse was his belief he "should have never schmoozed with Glen," which if he did not, he would possibly be alive today. The EMT who knew Glen also assisted in rushing him to the nearest hospital as the ER nurse and physician ripped off his clothes, tried to get the air passage free to breathe, and stop the bleeding! His breathing violently stopped, and they did immediate resuscitation as he died on the operating table. Officer Dan had to do the paperwork on Glen as the EMT placed the body tag on Glen's toe. Putting Glen into the bus (ambulance) and escorting the bus to the hospital full throttle, flashing turrets, and sirens blaring. This orchestration of noise, sight and mechanical movement drowned out the pain of emotional loss and shock with the pain of sensory overload in the moment of the rush to the hospital. The 95 tag is all that is left of this young man and the cop who liked this young gentleman. An affinity with Glen was established with a younger Officer Dan also brought up in a tough area of Brooklyn. He hoped to help him in his own way with his own hyperintuitive style. Officer Dan's confusion, anger, and anxiety are filed away as the precinct detectives take over the job. On goes the Bed-Stuyvesant tour.

Fast forward and Officer Dan has patrolled the concrete jungle another 2 years, with 90 more homicides in his Sam Browne belt and hardened street savvy. Loss and grief never expressed for Glen remained a shadow in Officer Dan's life as he gets to see one of the precinct's best detectives effecting a warrant on a very bad guy. Screams for help come over the air. He listens to the shots ringing out. Officer Dan hears his own siren and screeching tires and turret lights swarming like rainbows of blood and anguish. He can still see himself run up the stairs of the projects. He sees what he knew he would see—the best detective in the squad with part of his brain in his partner's hand, pushing it back in the skull and crying in rage, saying, "What do I do with my partner. It's his brain. What do I do man? Help! Get a bus here! Forthwith, central."

"My God this is not happening, Det. XY cannot be gone," he mumbles where only his fellow officers hear, including Officer Dan, also struck by the shock of the homicide of a brother officer hovering in the air. "Stay with me brother!" as his partner's brain in his hands is pitifully being pushed back in his skull, with tears of rage mingling with blood.

Well, what happens with Officer Dan's thoughts as he is traumatized but functions like all cops on the scene? He is doing well enough and does not act odd or allude to his loss. Officer Dan knows what everyone wants and expects, including his peers. At some level it is too hard for them to really deal with "it" as well. That is, except to just bury "it" with booze. Perhaps some extreme workout helps him feel as if he can control this. Ensuring his strength will protect this from ever happening again, like a tough street cop, a grunt in the USMC, or a hard-nosed firefighter/EMT officer. A sexy movie, followed by a zombie movie may do it. An endless cycle of stands with his girlfriend worked the last ounce of energy out. However, the harder shell of dealing with it through adaptive functional dissociation is followed by everyone returning to "normal." The flag is set at half mast and the inspector funeral passes in NYPD and NYFD dirges, followed by watering hole relief and choir practice. This too passes by and Officer Dan is still left standing.

Let's stop for a moment right now and do what I have done with many officers—even myself at first; after all, I developed my method of treatment. As my peer I ask you to please visualize me with a red cop doc (stop sign)! Let's go back and look at what happened. As oversimplified as Officer Dan's trauma was for purposes of getting out the chaos and the hit, you know well you have taken on the field of battle. What has happened here is good insofar as inoculation and immunity theory goes—think about a toughened cop as one who is likely to survive the streets. Likely to be tough as nails when dealing with the bad guys and gals. It helps you and me survive, and it helps you adapt to your environment, your beat, your patrol sector, your firehouse, or your ER room. It helps you understand what the spoken word means in your ecological niches of service. It helps you to gain a hold on what is meant between the lines. What is meant as toxic and dangerous, and what is and is not acceptable in learning to survive. The eco-ethological niche is layered in your community. That is when the community itself is ripe with problems of stereotyping you as an officer. How do you deal with the political machines and the ones who run the show as the muscles behind the scene? When the community you want to trust presses your very soul and compassion to your limits. It is not a real immunity when the community, as well as you as an officer, is taught to hide and deny your humanity and losses. When you become so traumatized you start to build another culture and a language that is not your own, but learned and distorted in the lenses of survival. Survival in an ecology of violence and terrorism, domestic and foreign. A community you also live and work in. Folks may say, "Well, the officers go home after the tour." Some do, and some do not. But even if you are there for the 8–4 shift, 4–12, or 12–8 tour of duty, you and I know that officers are on the job even when they leave their shift!

The Job Is Never Routine—Not a Moment: What You Do with That Reality Is Your Choice

Now perhaps you can agree the job is never routine and you do not become immune to the toxic effects of trauma. It is the trauma you may dread, and you likely seek at the same time, that can mess with the best and finest of minds and souls, including you as a public safety officer.

This is the beginning, and you need to gear up to understand the importance of the ecological-ethological existential impact of complex trauma first. Let's use an example of Officer Y, who is an EMT/firefighter whose responsibility it is to render first aid to victims of fires, accidents, terrorism, and any other domestic or foreign terrorist attack or natural disaster. Let's explore the setting on fire of a homeless man X in an abandoned building. Why is the ecology so important to understanding Officer Y's traumatic experience? Well, you are a first responder, and as first on the scene in doing search and rescue, you are oftentimes the first line of defense. Deep down, regardless of what anyone says, you know the fact is: "No one is left behind—no unit member—no matter what happens!" Yes, you are told to lay your life on the line; let's be real here—you will not just blindly die for the sake of doing that, and nor should you! Your life is sacred and not cheap.

Someone in a polished suit and shoes that cost more than a typical salary you make in a week tells you to have amazing courage and sacrifice—simply their line does not cut it. When a real public safety/military officer who has been shot at and been in the saddle gives a directive in the field, you pause and turn your ears and listen!

If I am right, when you see your partner in danger's way, you would almost to an individual cop, firefighter, EMT, or Armed Forces professional jump in and put your life on the line. If you saw a kid or an elderly person being abducted, you would jump in even if it meant your own death to save a kid or elderly person's life. The risk taking to "do the right thing" is at the core of who you are as an officer and what you do best. It is important to confirm that this is what helps you when you are challenged with your own mortality. When you witness another officer's life leak out of his or her body in a red line of anguish after being shot, hit in an accident, or in a rescue operation, your "ire" is up. You'll risk your life to protect the civilians you are sworn to take care of when they are threatened. The values you hold when you idealistically took an oath to lay down your life, if need be, to protect others are sacred. But you do not expect to die, and nor should you!

That is the larger culture, the larger than life culture: in your ecology niche and ethologically speaking, you do what you do because you love to do your job. The job then becomes identified with your partner and the unit you work with day by day. You also begin to hide the pain of loss you experience on the job. Truth be told, you protect each other and your own beats and your own unit's integrity. What I am presenting here is the grist of what you deal with day by day in your own beat. Now that is what motivated you to wear a shield; it is the ecology that means the very beat, firehouse, precinct, service area, or district house, or unit division, region, resident, or field office you "cover." That is a good and accurate word, *cover*, for that is what you do with each other and those under your care. Way before 9/11 I had seen many officers in very different public safety positions who did emergency rescue, negotiations in hostage situations, warrant executions, and recovery efforts and postcatastrophic response. They are all very unique situations, and officers who are also very different in who, how, and when they were impacted: as different as the colors in the rainbow. However, please stop for a moment and appreciate that you may be upset about some loss. Some loss processed by you uniquely in a way that is different than some other squad member, or the whole unit.

Let's look together at an event of complex trauma in an ecology that is physically and logistically from a tactical point of view the same. What you will see is ecological and ethological niches hold very different perceptions of losses. Differences experienced by different unit members. The unique meaning is very different for each officer: it is important to realize why these differences you are about to explore are so important. Respecting our own differences of dealing with losses builds healthier mutual respect. That mutual respect includes nurturing and accepting individual and unique differences you and other officers bring to the table as a unit. Units remain a cohesive team at the same time with purpose, direction, and meaning to be cherished and witnessed. However, each member retains his or her own personality and style of dealing with his or her own losses and trauma.

Appreciation of the complexity of trauma as you may experience "it," as well as the differences in your own peers, is strength, not weakness. In being vulnerable you realize your own weaknesses and then are able to create power by redirecting your unique strengths by sharing with others who have different strengths and weaknesses. The team effort includes your being vulnerable to losses as well as strengths. Without infusing your own layers of loss in trauma to being able to gradually share those losses as differences, no integration is possible in reality.

Different Eco-Ethological Existential Impact of Event(s) Not Considered Traumatic (SOP)

Let's open up the cases to follow with some context that will hopefully make sense to you as a unique officer. Please think about each officer that is presented and his or her unique experience of loss in the event presented. I will use one event that is not classified by the job as traumatic, but as routine. I trust you can look at this event for what it is and in so doing put in perspective the ecological niche in which it occurred. Ask yourself what that ecological niche may mean to you as a public safety officer. Another question to ask yourself is: What may be meaningful aspects of loss and strength if you placed yourself in each of the officer's shoes who were present for the event you are about to read?

Existential Empathy as Seen through Your Eyes by Looking through Their Eyes

There are three reasons why this breakdown is so important and why you should ask yourself the above questions. It will likely color your experience in the lenses you view it, not in a larger than life perspective, but your own—that connection to relating to the officer presented provokes empathy to feel what it may be like when you imagine being in his or her shoes in the moment trauma lands in his or her field of experience. In looking at the different public safety officers responding to the complex trauma event to follow, I share with you not only how, in the work of the eco-ethological existential approach, you can gain a hold of the different approach each officer shares with you, but also how differently the same complex trauma event affects each first responder. Differences are critical to learn. You may learn to appreciate what you possibly have glossed over in your own emotional, survival, and existential map. Self-knowledge may offer an understanding that will be novel in how you look at your fellow officers. Fellow officers include your partner, your unit, and the jobs you experience. When looking at the experience, it is complex because you as an officer uniquely pick up on information. Information important for scanning and functioning in your eco-ethological niche as an officer. That is, you scan information selectively in your own unique optimum functioning identity mode.

Understanding your own unique means of survival while understanding others' unique differences leads to the ability of being able to gain support where you are weak: also where you can offer support where others may need what you have to offer. That attitude is learned in the eco-ethological existential analysis. The attitude offers a dimension of strength rather than judgment. Egotistic behavior hurts you and the other officers simply because you may have been unaware. We have all heard the theory every person views a work of art in a different way—in my decades in this line of work, as in yours, we need to know why each officer has different experiences. Although it may appear each officer is dealing with the same identical situation, in reality no one is. Each officer has different keys that are molded by the most impact in his or her own piece of a complex trauma event that strikes home. It also offers reasons as to why "wounds fester" in different mental, physical, and spiritual ways. Second, the puzzle of how this is key to dealing in a way that is sensible to you and perhaps not the other officer you work side by side with is important. It is crucial for you to be able to empathize with and acknowledge. It is not novel to say, in fact, each of us is quite different, although we all connect at the gut and heart level. *But it is novel to understand with compassion in your heart of hearts and guts that you experience the existential pain the way you uniquely do in the context of your own public safety personality style. Why you do experience the type of existential pain as you do, and the focus you select in a complex trauma event, is critically important. It is critical for understanding what provokes you to dissociate with the greatest resistance and why. It also holds the key to the antidote to the existential pain you experience in large unsolved and accumulating losses. That is novel.*

Losses that remain hidden from healing are ripe for toxic effects. It is firmly my belief that it is likely your own losses and resistance to explore your own losses will never be revealed until you learn to understand your own ecological niche. Understanding includes your ethological influences that shape your own evolutionary defenses and strengths. These defenses and strengths, at the gut level of what was so meaningful, are actually worked through to the core. The core of analysis is what you experience as loss and why. One loss at a time fills the space of time with the weight of accumulating toxic trauma. Toxic trauma that shapes the outcome as it affects you as an officer and person is key. Owning your own outcome is what is the goal and redeeming. Redeeming your own gain in your guts and heart of hearts is a depth encountered existentially. The depth of losses can be filled with a renewed motivation, energy, and confidence in your own creative ability within the ultimate source within that remains hidden. Hidden in your own very losses behind your armor of evolutionary inoculation lies a strength that transcends the eco-ethological niches they were born in. It is the trauma of discovering what that armor is. What are you defending against in hiding loss that holds the strength you will regain and redirect in exposing "it"? The eco-ethological existential analysis affords naming "it" for yourself and identifying self-awareness and internal witnessing of well-deserved empathy. The eco-ethological existential analysis encompasses your understanding and needed involvement in your own treatment. Eco-ethological existential analysis demands using your very own losses to encounter the solution within your hidden strengths. You will see how this is done in the cases to follow.

Understanding Loss: Intent as the Bricks of Guilt, or the Window of Forgiveness

Before we move into the steps of prepping for an existential analysis, let's talk shop. If someone has done an act and it has horrendous consequences, if it is assessed as an accident, the person who may have caused "it" is given much support and comfort. But, let's suppose the intent is believed to be intentionally mean-hearted and criminal—then that person has the book thrown at him and gets the shoe in unmentionable places.

However, if it is simply accidental, the person is admonished at best with a chat about "you should have known better." You will likely go easier on him; even if an act is reckless, it lacks the mean-heartedness of intentional mean-hearted actions.

So here the fact of intent as you know is critical. Intent always is sought out by knowing the why and not the how as most important. In understanding yourself, you also need to dig deeper. Although it is more challenging at first, it is valuable for living your life to gain ground with deeper practical understanding. Approaching trauma also needs to be grounded in reality, which is your own reality! Your perception of what is real to you and why certain aspects are so critically important to you rather than others is more than interesting: it is crucial to you as an individual. So let's explore the event as different officers experience it in different ways. I ask you to suspend judgment for what may at first seem to be the same complex trauma event to you. I will show you, as I do in my other books (Rudofossi, 2007, 2009), that the fact is that in order to solve the complex losses in any officer, an understanding that is mutual has to be learned by the officer and therapist.

The goal is figuring out together what it is that blocks processing your own losses. I will take you and help you work through the losses you experience—and the losses you will likely experience in a long and meaningful career. It is as a public safety officer that you will go under a barrage of shots fired to assist your own brother/sister PD/EMT/FD officer. However, it is the "other" EMT/FD/PD officer that will assist you as an officer who is wounded by fire without wincing an eye. Why do you imagine you will risk all with a selfless act of bravery repeatedly? I imagine you do it because public safety officers are truly an extended family, and this is felt most when one is under attack. In this work consider that empathy and meaning, as much as survival, in an ecology you live in are never routine. While complex losses and trauma are not routine, neither are your reactions of anger, grief, and anxiety abnormal. Your event usually labeled as a critical incident is a large layered complex event that can burn out the best center and finest compassion in you. That is, it will burn out your core if you do not get a handle on the psychological and existential fire burning out within you. Unless you get dosed by stepping out and looking at it with different lenses as it impacts on you.

Brief Snapshots: Police Sergeant, Firefighter, and FD EMT—Unique Impact

Let's now move on and see for yourself as I flesh out composite cases. Meaning to protect the identity of any real officers, I have changed their identifying features and cases are joined. The meat and potatoes of what was done was not changed. The events are as real as the radio run received. I would like you to imagine your current command as you start your tour. Please see if you can connect to this job, which is considered by "the job" as not more than "a routine radio run."

The Radio Run: Routine as Quantum Moments Strung in the Space of Echoes in Time

Let's start our cases with brief snapshots to gain an understanding from the radio run from central command as it unfolds on a beautiful day in 1993 in NYC, Lower Manhattan. One of the Twin Towers was hit with an explosion; all units were mobilized that were not actively involved on other jobs.

Police, firefighters, and EMTs flew on their way. The central command was screaming out directives when the first responding units began to arrive. Right at that time Sergeant X was on patrol with Officer Y. EMT Z was on her way to assist a man down in her sector as Sergeant X was supervising the eight-to-four platoon.

Firefighters Z, B, and C were on their way to assist the citywide wide-priority call downtown. Sergeant X, Officer Y, EMT X, and Firefighter Z unwittingly and without any knowledge, save a vague intuition, will converge on the job that soon emerges unexpectedly in the hub of a citywide mobilization. This is not unusual for anyone on the job long enough. A sensible phase captures this synchrony of chaos as simply: "Expect the unexpected, and then there is no such thing as unexpected, got it—get it—good!" In the middle of this pandemonium a call of an unidentified anticrime officer is heard vaguely over the citywide mobilization on direct radio. Direct radio because the communication it is not on the major circuit.

Sergeant X's Unique Experience and Focus

The sergeant and his driver respond immediately. They are in the area of the direct radio call. Making out what they think is a location, they redirect toward said location. Out goes the bagel with cream cheese we all know about, that is, it is gospel—no jive turkey—there is some truth to the rumors about us all. The response is confirmation by the sergeant as he arrives on the scene to see one of the officers in his squad—screaming to him from an open window, "Get me out of here!" Plainclothes police are reporting they cannot find the officer ghosting the scene for a bust. She was not to be found and last was ghosting a bad grifter guy preying on homeless folks. Folks that were drifters and squatters in the rundown dusty musty tenements of alphabet city. It appeared what was in progress was an unrelated fire that ignited when a crack addict's pipe exploded. In the heat of the explosion downtown and the first terror attack on the Twin Towers the radio call was almost drowned out in the chaos. Police Sergeant X responding with his driver, Officer Y, to the scene arrived to see one officer running in the building and observed smoke billowing from the third floor. He stopped and immediately called in a loud command presence voice to central: "Have FD respond forthwith! 10-XX we have a member inside a burning building. Central, exact location is unknown, but it appeared to be coming from the third floor. Central, the member is plainclothes and she is possibly down with smoke inhalation and burns. We lost communication and she is in need of a bus [EMT/medic] forthwith, central! Put a rush on FD and the bus."

Within a heartbeat central reassured the sergeant as her voice comes back with FD on the way. Sergeant X says, "Central, make it forthwith, central!" In response, the central command 911 operator, in a reassuring lifeline voice, says, "That's a 10-4, Sarge: FD and the bus are on their way." The FD truck rolls up and in 3 minutes tops is in the mix. That beautiful red truck empties out with uniform firefighters each well equipped to handle the situation. But even so, most are aching to get downtown to join the larger call and mobilization. Within minutes the fire is under control and the anticrime officer is taken out with some smoke inhalation. The injuries and shaken officer look frazzled and roughed up, but the sergeant is told, "She'll be okay." It appears not to be life threatening. She is taken to the hospital in serious condition. Sergeant X has grime and soot on him that he brushed off along with the question asked of him, "Are you okay, Sarge?" He nods with a grin to the fire lieutenant of the battalion, "Sure, just a little smoke, not too bad. Take a look at my driver," he says without missing a heartbeat. His driver says, "I'm okay, boss, no sweat—take care of her," pointing to the officer on the gurney who looked frazzled and spaced out as the shock of smoke inhalation and heat was overwhelming.

A new call suddenly comes over by EMT X in the building, who calls for a medic as backup as the junkie in the building has very labored breathing. The junkie began to go into cardiac arrest. Defibrillation was called for. The dying person who was addicted to drugs, a junkie now is dying in the building—nothing is routine. The medics arrive. By the time they arrive the young man dies. He is pronounced dead on the scene. Sergeant X is back on the scene and notifications and reports are being initiated.

The young fellow who was called a junkie was identified by his Columbia University undergraduate identification card. He somehow ended up dead on arrival (DOA) in Alphabet City, NYC. DOA in NYC overdosed on dope and crack, which is called a speedball.

The medical examiner was called to the scene to rule out foul play. The place became a crime scene and the precinct detective unit was notified. That day ended a few hours later. Sergeant X, Officer Y, and EMT X all decide to meet at the local bar and get soused because it was such "an abortion."

Please stop, pause, and reflect as I ask you to take a deeper look at the sergeant's experience. The heat on the ground floor is excessive and intense as he slowly feels "hell's spikes digging into his Corfsam shoes." On scene he holds the metal-wood door open to let the good guys out as the drug operation is totally suspended. From the identity mode of apprehension and arrest supervisor the operation changed in seconds to a refocus on rescue, and not collars. Getting everyone out ok and safely without harm to any officers and civilians is his primary objective.

The sergeant's driver next to him slid in to the building to assist as the sergeant's distraction shifts and when he turns to tell his operator (cop who drives him) a directive, poof, he is gone. Sergeant X's shoes are almost on fire as the smoke is filling his lungs. Priority shifts and escalates rapidly like a bundle of straw with fuel and a Bunsen burner. The officer driving him shows up with a homeless person she took out in the chaos. FD comes out with the anticrime officer in a mobile gurney. It is a chaotic situation. The sergeant believes he is fine and needs to handle the next call. Sergeant X writes this up as another city-involved accident report. When Sergeant X sees the brave anticrime officer taken in a gurney, a deep painful feeling runs through him like a sliver of ice put down his back shirt.

EMT X's Experience and Focus in Loss: Ideal, Play, and Possibility

EMT X, who assisted with the successful rescue, is the one who in the fire being extinguished ran into the junkie dying. Perhaps by way of too much smoke inhalation, the junkie was so drugged up he could not do anything but just fall down. She figures as the on-scene EMT, he was overcome by noxious fumes in a crack room. The door to the crack room was semiopen and saturated with all the smoke with no window. It is there that fumes overcame him with whatever else in the concoction he inserted in his enflamed veins.

EMT X had to deal with the overdose complications on the scene and needed to tag the body after the attempted resuscitation failed as the medics shrugged and had to respond to their next call. The firefighter commander who took the fire call calls for his arson investigator. He demands a formal questioning about the scene be initiated.

Physical Facts Are Not Perceptual and Parallel Reality for Officers on the Scene

Please note an important point: each officer in the quartet of Police Officer Y, Sergeant X, EMT X, and Firefighter Z all experienced the same physical, geographic, and public safety radio call and event.

While parallels of physical facts exist in concrete reality, a different reality occurs for each officer in his or her own perception of the event. This perception is shaped by why different aspects of the event afford each officer different meanings. Further, what losses emerge in his or her own interpretation of his or her unique ecological and ethological niche. In other words, the eco-ethological niche of each officer is nested within each officer's differences of time on the job, status as boss or not, specialties and experience with this type of job, and attached unit.

Let's look at some questions as we review the complexity of the event and the way it is processed for each officer: Is it one event, many events, or one radio call with a different event for each participant? Are the FD EMT, FD medic, FD firefighter, police officer, and sergeant all dealing with one reality? Perhaps realities are based on different demands and what each officer feels responsible for in doing the best he or she can. If so, each in his or her experience may have striking differences in his or her perception based on his or her own viewing and perceiving lenses. This variation in perception is in part embedded in the intensity and novelty of the event itself. But hidden and compelling questions that are very hard to ask are as follows. Remember, I asked you to imagine being in each officer's place at the time of the event. For example, you may have asked yourself in private if it were you in the fire:

"What would you really do in the heat of the fire, if it were you in your professional identity mode?"
"Did you think if you were there you could say you did the best you could?"
"Did you do your job right, as you have been trained to act if it were you?"
"Did you meet your standard yardstick of a good job being done?"
"Did you feel that if it were you, you would cover your partner, driver, civilians properly?"
"Did you let your partner down when she needed you the most?"
"Could you really feel okay with what you did?"
"Even though you may not have felt okay with your thoughts, actions, and the event, would you also have kept it to yourself?"
"If you kept it to yourself, would you not tell a soul and solve the problem with drinking away the pain, or sexing away the pain, or amusing yourself to forget the pain?"
"Hey, you may as well fake it—till you make it—maybe you will learn to believe your own bull?"
"If you fool yourself, will you feel better soon, so you may forget 'it'?"
"Why bother? It is too much, right?"
"Anyhow, if you just stop yourself from thinking about 'it,' is that not the right thing to do?"
"No one can answer that question because you know you are a screw-up and you will never disclose."
"You think you messed it up and, even worse, you acted less than you should have, so you think you better be silent, right?"

Q&A: Question and Answer Sessions

What you will see is the resulting perception for each officer is as if each officer was on a different job. Each officer can recount the radio run as it came over central radio and describe the run as if it was responded to with accurate narrative in real time as he or she perceived it. Different narratives are told by each officer, and more startling than that difference is each is more than likely to be true. This truth needs to be identified by you, as it is not even part of the language within trauma and grief syndromes with police and public safety officers.

Yet, the fact of differences and the stories recounted are no less a language—a hidden one that is silent and yet potentially toxic if kept hidden from others, including yourself. I hope to change your viewpoint by bringing awareness to the ecologic niches and the ethological influences in your experiences that impact on you at the deepest level of your senses. The trauma that torpedoes your sensibilities must be solved by piecing it altogether. Silence about unconscious losses does not go away. Yet you can ask yourself if you do not do that, who will? What will you do with the questions that haunt you?

These questions may keep you chained to the losses of unidentified complex trauma, for you as an individual officer in your own skin under the armor you wear each day. Your armor may be a bulletproof vest as a police officer, a Scott rescue pack as a firefighter/EMT, or an ER nurse/ER doctor uniform that affects your choice of uniform and narrative, but not the fact you are absorbing losses and not expressing the toxic effects of such trauma.

Although the experience was quite different for each officer, each officer was on the same mission of public safety: this event may happen tomorrow with some variation in your own professional experience. Perhaps a way to make it real as we really know it is, is to say it is a different event each officer experienced. A different event based on his or her point of entry and mission each expected to perform. Further, it would make sense for you to think of each officer's expectation and even the differences of his or her personality as different. If you can please imagine being in his or her shoes as he or she deals with the fire emergency. Kindly think of the ability, skill sets, and experiences each officer puts to work. With this context in mind, you can now listen to each officer recount his or her story of what happened. Listen to how "it" impacted differently in his or her existential struggle. Listen as each officer faces his or her facets of experience in a way that is real for him or her with unique strengths, fears, aspirations, and perspiration about the job done well enough. Enough said; it is time for you to explore each case with your own psychological imagination to let go and imagine yourself in his or her shoes. In fact, you may find you have been.

Sergeant X: Brief Steps Backward into His Experience of the Potentially Traumatic Event

The first case is Sergeant X on the scene, who assesses within seconds of his arrival that one of the anticrime officers on his platoon is trapped in the building she was ghosting. Ghosting means being on the trail without being seen as a cop in deep undercover to observe a possible crack gallery. That crack gallery ID is also known as a lab, as most of you know. That lab is where junkies typically do cocktails of coke, dope, and maybe methamphetamine as users.

A runner brings the drug "goods," usually by using underage kids that are paid well. This tragic abuse of children is done because if they are caught, they could be released as underage.

In reality, Sergeant X was having breakfast with his driver, Officer Y, and eating some bagel with a smear of cream cheese and lox he loved to devour with black coffee. Out of the blue, central radio was inundated with calls of the World Trade Center being hit with a possible bomb. Sergeant X and Officer Y were already tossing out the makeshift breakfast as they had shifted into emergency mode for this major radio run. Sergeant X and his driver saw patrol sectors zooming by when he heard the echo reverberating on a direct frequency. Sergeant X and Operator Y picked up muffled distress calls. Sergeant X stopped and asked over direct frequency, "Hey, will that unit repeat? Was that a distress call? Please identify yourself. I need a copy on that call? Is some unit in distress?" He and his driver felt they got the address. Sure enough, they spot a plainclothes street crime cop outside waving to the sergeant as he quickly disappears in the brick rundown and semiabandoned building. Sergeant X quickly assessed a female plainclothes officer was caught in the crossfire of a crack room accidentally set on fire. Sergeant X rolled up to the scene as he got on the horn to central and in full loud command presence barked out, "Central, have FDNY respond forthwith, member down at location XYX and possibly civilians—put a rush on it."

Within less than 3 to 4 minutes FDNY are rolling up the street with full gear and ready to fight the fire. EMT X is on the scene immediately and ran in to perform CPR. This is done while other EMTs enter the side entrance by the cellar door. Pandemonium sets the scene for Sergeant X. His goal was to direct all emergency first responders in his shifting operational command presence identity mode. This identity mode is a hyperfocus of ensuring all civilians are okay. At the same time, Sergeant X ensured the danger to his crew was under control. Each member needed to be accounted for, and safe was his primary goal. It is daunting for the sergeant, who is responsible for his driver, his platoon, including FDNY firefighters' and the EMT crew's safety, the city case worker who was trying to help a homeless person planning to get hospitalized, and let's not forget his own safety. That picture is complicated. Let's not forget that the entire agency response of NYPD, PAPD, and FDNY was focused on the major emergency downtown at the World Trade Center (WTC) attack. In reviewing the sergeant's experience, remember he and his driver were on their way to the WTC terrorist bombing as he is struck by the cry of an officer in plainclothes whose whereabouts were almost unknown. He and his driver pick up her voice, which is in a shriek shrill that like a still frame frozen in a glimpse of time, was almost unknown. The sergeant and driver confer and figured in seconds she was a tenured officer or would not be doing the street cop detail she was active in. Sergeant X's troop's safety was all important, as was getting the plainclothes officer out of the unknown serious and dangerous situation she was in. He goes from operational identity mode of patrol commander to rescue identity mode. Sergeant X used his wisdom gained from his own experience within the ecology niche of his patrol command. Sergeant X's wisdom included familiarity with the building and the hidden places where ambushes occurred. (Remember, it was an operation earlier with some surveillance and preliminary intelligence gathering going on.) Upon arrival Sergeant X was hit with the gravity of the fire and smoke as an omen that flames were ready to explode. Still, the undercover officer was not to be found. He immediately shifted into his rescue identity mode from his operational command identity mode when he first called central to have FDNY respond forthwith. It was almost a drill of SOP for the sergeant to modify his voice to let all of on-patrol folks know he was dead serious! His call was urgent to get FD present. Still, he had to control panic being hinted at in his voice. Even when facing very threatening situations a command presence demands as much calm as possible. Please pause and reflect on how complex this so-called routine situation really was. Sergeant X shifted from relaxed to the highest threshold of adrenalin rush in a quantum moment. Sergeant X got on the scene and grabbed the entrance door and directed all troops out immediately while holding the door that was rapidly heating. That door got so hot he ignored the heat and placed his foot between the door undercarriage and the ground automatically. He left his foot there without daring to relinquish his hold: "Pain is pain," he said to himself. His troops exited with some civilian homeless folks. Sergeant X was trying to ignore the intense heat, smoke, and fire. He placed his flashlight beam on highest intensity as he called to his driver to wait for a second as he felt a tug on his foot. Sergeant X felt pressure against his body and when he turned, he saw his driver had gone inside. It was not Sergeant X's driver pushing him, it was the heat of the fire increasing in intensity and pressure. Some thoughts that will impact on the sergeant when alone at the end of the tour are as follows:

"I am really concerned I did not do enough. Why?"
"What if my operator [driver] got lost and hurt in the fire? I did not realize he was gone, and what if he did in fact get smoke inhalation?"
"How did this kid who turned out to be the child of a local minister wind up DOA?"

"Did I as a sergeant somehow fail to do enough outreach and how could
  I have done so?"
"A minister known for all the good work over years with his commu-
  nity has to deal with his son DOA. Why him?"
"Could my kid get this way? Maybe I did not see him enough? I may be
  a dad that is not there enough."
"How do I do that, without being called controlling?"

These questions bother him, but he soon hides it. He does not say anything to anyone. He buries his questions in a compartment he tells himself
he will open later. It is 10 years later he will. As we move on to the next public
safety officer, EMT X, please keep in mind her selection of what corner of the
complex trauma event afforded her focus. That is, why certain losses emerged
in her mind, thoughts, behavior, feelings, and emotions. Her losses emerged
as shaped by her ecological niche and ethological survival experiences, which
culminated in her own existential struggles. Her existential dilemmas were
clarified, as in Sergeant X's existential dilemmas, as uniquely deserving of
her own and my individual attention. That attention led to outreach as she
and Sergeant X opened up to accept both peer support and cop doc ambulatory intervention.

Officer EMT X: Brief Overview of Her Experience
of the Potentially Traumatic Event

Let us review the basic viewpoint of Officer EMT X, who upon arrival immediately confronted the junkie on the scene. Officer EMT X finds a room filled
with some light porn magazines and cigarette ashes all scattered around
one of the abandoned rooms. A room left as a smoking den. A young man
of attractive features, hardly noticeable, is hardly breathing. Invisible and
handsome, he is lying there before her. Initially in her eyes he was so pale
and sick with that halo of illness. Sick with labored breathing, he lay choking
on his own breath and heaving in a gagging manner for air. Officer EMT X
feared the young fellow was overdosing on junk (heroin and crack) in the
cocktail combo in the syringe infusing his enlarged veins. Poison lacing into
his heart, teasing its venom slowly without mercy. She pulled up his pants
legs, which was one of those baggy types used to cover his swelling from multiple tracks. Tracks marking his legs with swollen, small ballooning areas.
Areas of his leg turned partial bluish green in a hue reflecting gangrene and
its toxic effect.

The young man's heart raced as Officer EMT X was trying to catch his pulse rate, which she faintly felt. Pulse fading to emptiness as her head leaned into his chest. Officer EMT X was very concerned with trying her best to engage him in soothing and comforting words, in her comforter identity mode. She did not miss a heartbeat in her rescue attempts as she followed all the rules when her young fellow fell into sudden cardiac arrest.

Officer EMT X tried to get a pulse and called medics immediately. She tried to use safety instruments and started resuscitation. She hesitated without knowing why as she glanced in a deep quantum moment at his young face. Suddenly Officer EMT X felt a tinge of strong discomfort. That discomfort hit her as she counted the breaths into his mouth. Her shift from comforter identity mode to full rescue identity mode was startling. Her own realization of some hidden feelings emerged. The medics took over and he died after about 10 minutes of intense attempts to bring him back to life. That is a very long 10 minutes of attempts to get him back from death's door. The young man was pronounced DOA.

Officer EMT X silently and in a strange way felt a sense of loss when she looked at the young good-looking guy within in her mind's eye. Her silent experience surrounded by peers was stifling to her. She struggled to stop her visualization of a fantasy she had of walking down the aisle of life, love, and marriage with him. She found these unwanted fantasies very disturbing and even sick. She could not let go of this thought of why a woman her age (our EMT Officer X in her later twenties) was attracted to this young man. This was now fully blown, as he was slid into the gurney to be placed in the morgue's refrigerator later that day.

It is rough for this young EMT Officer X. Police officers and firefighters who were on the scene and putting out the fire unwittingly made some less than welcome comments. Comments that were annoying to her sensibilities, about the junkie. "It" felt like a failure. It ached as confusion and chaos for EMT Officer X that the young handsome junkie died. Especially because some politically correct agenda she read said she should not feel or think of any patient as a real man. She denied her own natural feelings, which she of course could not act on, but nonetheless were natural. Nature dictated different than any agenda. Officer EMT X did not act on her desires. But, that did not take away the fact that her fantasy was as real as the young man who tragically was now DOA before her. EMT Officer X's thoughts drifted naturally to him being her lover, which was firmly hidden in the mostly adaptive functional dissociative response to the event. "Hey, what a waste, X," says one of the police officers. One of the FD guys say, "Yeah, he should have done something with his life rather than become a skell junkie [dredge of society]."

Officer EMT X does not agree, and in fact she thinks the opposite way. She has very different feelings and ideas. But some hidden censor seems to push her to nod and grin as if she agreed with the others to fit in with her peers. Silently buried in her own thoughts deep in her bosom, she thought to herself, "How shameful a Columbia University undergraduate is lying there ready for his maker."

She watched as time stopped for a moment, as the moment became seared in her memory as the identification tag was placed on his toe. She remembers her scratch sheet for the property clerk invoice filled out with his demographics folded within the plastic envelope. Officer EMT X witnessed and scratched her signature on the fly sheet for the police officer on the scene.

Another thought sailed through her mind again, "Too bad I couldn't meet this cute guy before this happened. Hum... We could have been an item if only.... Well, who knows?" as she imagines a romantic hug with him and a kiss, as she looks at pallor settling into his face.

Officer EMT X is startled as soon as she awakes, as if to see he looks like a plaster model of a man. Still, he intrigues Officer EMT X in her silent fantasy. She experienced embarrassment for her forbidden thought. She moved on in her routine SOP. He is ready to be tagged by the medical examiner, as the toe marks him DOA with a 95 tag, which is all that is left of his life. She and the officer must go through the property to identify and list all of it. Officer X will go on to her next job very soon. Officer EMT X is affected and impacted by this trauma, as is true in all emotional memories imprinted in the brain. These emotional memories of trauma can be evoked in other situations. Even one in which she is soon to be in with her new boyfriend. She even has a flashback of trauma during a time she is enjoying intimacy with her boyfriend. The stirring of these associations, as you can well imagine, is not understood well and can intrude in the space of your relationships. These emotional memories are significant and can wreak havoc without preparation. More so, these memories come up unwelcome with disturbing effect. Keep in mind Officer EMT X's fantasy was not so weird. She felt the impact was weird due to her being silent about "it." In fact, daydreams are not so rare and are, at times, evoked when a public safety officer is doing a rescue operation. Further for Officer X, as for you, the complex trauma event discussed was not considered a trauma by the wisdom of public safety hierarchy. This trauma event was one of about 10 more Officer EMT X experienced that month in her life as an EMT in NYC. When asked by her cop doc about her thoughts, feelings, or reactions about this event, her first response, in almost exact words, was, "Oh Doc Dan, I am fine, shoe in and out. Doc, not a problem for me, SOP."

Briefly let's review how EMT Officer X goes from comforter identity mode, to rescue identity mode, to operational and administrative identity mode in a quick heartbeat of adaptive dissociation function. In EMT Officer X, realizing her ability to own her fantasies as desires but not her core self was immediately helpful. Wishes are aspects linked to dissociation that felt surrealistic to her. These wishes helped her realize the evidence was she was not crazy or even weird. She smiles and grins on cue with a wisecrack to mask the angst and anger by saying to her peers on scene, "Too bad he had a bad hair day." She wondered why she had said that. With working on it, she realized it was as if another person said that. In our work we explored how different identity modes such as rescue or recovery identity mode shifts serve superb sensible survival. They are not without exquisite purpose, including helping you function as part of a team. But without realizing their influence and becoming aware, you say things that you may find ugly at other times; you likely feel powerless, weak, and worse, mean-hearted. Trauma and losses can trigger that response in you as well. You may choose at this point to tuck that thought away and not go on with business as usual. First, you may choose to ease up on your labeling yourself or others. Second, please realize that becoming aware of influences takes time and effort. Time and effort, including a lot of work to yield durable results. Like all good results, time and effort are needed to achieve these goals; your understanding is a large gain, right here and now. Now let's move on and see what Firefighter Z felt as you take a corner of his experience through his narrative. You can see his unique existential dilemmas as you process his losses as a unique public safety officer.

Firefighter Z: Brief Overview of His Experience of the Fire and Overdose Victim

Let us review the viewpoint of Firefighter Z. He considers this a routine call that pales in the face of wanting to get down to World Trade Center bombing. He is itching inside to get out of this job he finds distracting to the major job downtown. No one planned this event or the major larger than life event of the bombing downtown. Firefighter Z is delayed from being able to respond downtown. He must deal with the arson investigator and the precinct detective converging on the scene. Firefighter Z, a fairly new member, was beyond rookie and less than a hair bag firefighter. Officer Firefighter Z was troubled as he was responding to the adrenalin flow beyond his control as a hyperexcited officer.

He was itching to go downtown and get to the big deal, not the minor job, in comparison to the WTC car bombing. Officer Z goes through what he considered a weird response in his thoughts, about a fire caused by a crack addict taking a blow in a self-made death sentence. He thinks to himself, "Could he even call this kid a crack addict, in this crack amateur factory?" He is bothered and speaks out with the following explosive statement to his peers, "What a loser. What a waste of human life, a shame, and this spoiled kid had it all. I couldn't afford Columbia University and to be such a skell and so spoiled. Shitty prodigal son!"

Yet in silent conflict, Firefighter Z reflects on a deeper level. Some real struggles within his head and heart gnaw away at his center, such as

"How could this spoiled guy be dying and dead? He had everything. Why was he so wasteful of his life?"
"I wish I was born with a silver spoon. Why did he drop out of school?"
"Why did his dad and mom let him turn into such a dredge of society?"

When Firefighter Z does the rescue he also senses a feeling of sinking in his gut and does not really understand "it." Why is he feeling upset about the death of this young man? He gets that feeling of sick revulsion when he is asked if he feels upset, or if it bothers him.

Firefighter Z responds when asked again, "Hey, the guy is a junkie skell. I couldn't give a rat's ass what happens." Yet when he is alone with his thoughts he feels sad, very sad, and figures in his self-talk, "I can't dwell on it. I really do not care less. Besides, this kid did it to himself. I have no responsibility to or for him. In any case, the high rollers who preach all that religious stuff really do not know reality. The solution is I will go to the watering hole when I am free and maybe pick up a good sexy magazine. Maybe even better, the cocktail waitress. Forget about 'it'!" In fact, Firefighter Z did what he set out to do with a resulting hangover and drag-out tour of duty that followed this multilayered event. Firefighter Z's pain was even more intense than his other peers', who had let go with their feelings to a higher degree of inner sight. But still, all were hardly aware of the impact this one event had. Officer Firefighter Z was no different than his peers.

Remember again that this event is not considered a trauma event, especially in the minds of the bureaucracy, and sadly even most of the chain and command of the respective departments.

Inner Sight to the Above Examples and the Question "How Are You Doing Officer?"

Well at this point, toward the close of this first chapter, you have inner sight: that inner sight is very useful where nothing is as it seems to you at first. You are likely thinking of my example from the front lines. Examples lighting up the fact that ecological and ethological survival are crucial to understanding the demands real trauma make in your own mind. By asking questions such as "Are you okay?" the likelihood is the same wall of defenses will emerge in you as did with the officers presented. When you are asked, "How you are doing officer?" you may answer something like "Fine, Doc Dan." I imagine if a civilian doc asks this question the chances of a deeper answer are about as likely as building Frosty the Snowman on a city project roof landing during a NYC heat wave.

That is why right here and now I ask you to trust the peer support officer. If you feel you cannot do that, then seek a therapist and preferably one who knows the culture of public safety. One who has been in your shoes as a public safety officer and will get you and what you are going through is the real goal here.

Secondly, someone who has worked within the culture and understands better than average what you are likely to experience is a good choice. But again, use your good public safety skills and find someone who is not in awe of you, not fearful of you, not in denial with you—but will help you say and ask yourself the right questions out loud, as I have thus far.

I have simplified the events here and have given you a brief snapshot. In this chapter you have learned some basic important facts of what trauma is: Professor Dr. Jack Kitaeff, retired major and police psychologist, lets us know, "There may be no single major trauma but the cumulative weight of a number of more moderate stresses over the course of the officer's career." The demands are all different, and the forces at play have everything to do with the ecology of where this complex event happened. Also, the impact of the trauma and losses as events is experienced in your own style of coping and history of losses. The defenses against those very losses and the coping mechanisms you have developed over time may have a lot in common with those of other peers. Some of those defenses, including peer pressure to go to the watering hole, are unusually destructive as well as tempting. Cop doc for three decades who has helped thousands of officers and a mentor to many cop docs, Dr. Dennis Conroy, retired sergeant of Minnesota police, lets us know, "It becomes difficult to handle all calls as they should be handled because of the extreme variation in importance and the differing levels of emotional intensity" (Conroy, 2008). How you handle what has happened is key in the eco-ethological existential analytic approach.

What to Do Beginning Right Here and Now: For Yourself, Peers, or Loved Ones

You may choose to do something different in processing trauma, including going to an AA meeting, a church, synagogue, temple, or other religious institute, or a community center. You may view a meaningful movie with family and friends. Cop Doc Conroy has shared with me at times "an ice fishing hole" or a "pier fishing spot" with a hot coffee (Conroy, 2008). The option of the all-favorite pastime that has destroyed at least one-quarter of all relationships is your choice as well. Choir practice in war zones in your concrete jungle is not going to quench your existential thirst.

New York State Attorney General Employee Assistance Program Commanding Officer, New York State Attorney Generals Office (EAP CO), Ace Detective, and brilliant cop counselor Professor Tom Creelman of St. John's and John Jay College lets us know with unusual wisdom that officer-patients' healing begins with a key:

> That key is writing a list of your blessings! Post your blessings by the grace of God. Even though you may have fallen off the wagon, or done something you are not proud of, look at your posted list of blessings day by day. Look hard and long at the list and realize you are ahead of the curve when you open your eyes in the morning. When you can say and hear your own name. Thank God and you are truly blessed and it only gets better after that. (Creelman, 2007)

Getting better after you acknowledge how many unheard strengths and blessings you have is an important key in healing. Healing begins with your owning strengths even when you are shifting into what appears to be different and complex changes in your identity as a public safety officer.

Identity Modes Are Not Scripted Roles: They Are Identity Shifts Shaped by Trauma

Let's review an important aspect of what you have heard me mention, and in order to not let you be left holding the bag, letting you know what I mean by identity modes. Identity modes are similar to what you hear peers say often, such as "Hey, I was in the mode." What that phrase really means is the officer was in pursuit, or ready to take down the bad guy and pin him or her to the wall with cuffs—tackle him or her to the holding cell door.

Your command and command presence matter a lot, as does your assigned unit identity. It is critical in the survival influences you learn over time in the ecology you work in.

Identity modes in this context is not a role—it is a lot more than that. It is motivated with the drive of life and death. As the backbone of public safety, patrol officers know that during a disorder control event you use every skill you have of being a streetwise diplomat. If not, you must turn into a lion ready to pounce when the dam of emotional control of the crowd transforms into a brainless mob. It is your identity that shifts into different modes in the way that your responses are learned and emerge in your own style and personality. This style you develop in your own personality is shaped by losses and defenses you use when you deny them. When you feel an event is surreal or you numb out over it, it is not the event but your own personality style that helps you cope during the crisis. Your personality style in part is composed of identity modes shaped by complex traumatic events shifting to protect you from being overwhelmed. Identity modes include the way you think, feel, and emotionally process events during and after the heat of fighting for your life, fleeing to take cover among other responses, for example, as if dissociative experiences. Identity modes like experiences of different locations are memorized in your brain just like those codes you thought you would never know, such as the 10 series of 10-4 and 10-13. These memories and codes are learned as clues you pick up in each event of trauma with the weight of life and death survival struggles. An example is when you are conducting a preliminary investigation of a fire, accident, or shooting. It is in part unconscious and in part a conscious process of responses in the behaviors you use when you anticipate and map out what you are going to do. You may think of identity modes as shifting responses in personality that help you effect a raid in a drug dealer's location, enter a high-rise fire and do what you must with little thought except tactics and logistics, or in responding to a citywide mobilization for a four-car crash with a tractor trailer on the highway.

I call the actual losses experienced in the moments that are not prepared for in your experience a quantum psychic moment. I use this term because these moments of heavy and intense trauma are complex as a meteor flashing out the heat of a flame thrower in the middle of a cool fall day. It is more than shocking, as you have no map for understanding what just hit you. However, this is not the full picture: it is the rapid shift back and forth in identity modes in the ethological context of complex trauma that is explosive. Explosive without you understanding what just happened and why. This contributes to why you experience trauma as surreal, as I have heard countless times, and if you think of it now, you too may have experienced this disturbing experience and may have even remembered using that term.

Let's Review Identity Mode Shifts and Adaptive Functional Dissociation

You may, like most officers, feel vulnerable at times, as if you can be hurt very deeply if you let out your true thoughts, questions, or feelings as you just witnessed for Sergeant X, EMT X, and Firefighter Z. Keep in mind you just scratched some of the ecological influences and the survival issues they iden-tified with and about. Being vulnerable as an officer is so feared as weakness that for you, it may be worse than suffering in silence. Accumulating multiple traumas, including the (ethological) survival influences that shape your own experience, has the surreal effect on you of dissociation. Reviewing identity modes for your use is to think of identity alterations that emerge in the context of trauma. The situation shifts and demands of your personality immediate changes in your response to those demands. Often these shifts in your iden-tity modes are not within your conscious awareness. These shifting identity modes and adaptive functional dissociation serve at least two purposes.

One is the satisfaction of what can be called instinct, or even more accu-rately, what is derived from your own natural aggressive, and even to a degree, sexual frustration. Second is an attempt for you to achieve a stable attitude, like a command presence, that helps you survive. The value of altering your identity modes is within the context of each shifting demand of trauma. Shifting demands that reach beyond thought alone, but into the realm of ethological survival. Each mode emerges in the ecology of your accumulated adaptation based on your own perception. Shifts in identity modes can often be so abrupt: shifts so sudden and intense can jar your sense of control and reality when you experience them.

Officer M's Ethological Object of Threat: A Hairbrush to a Firearm—Head Wounds

An example is Officer M shot a perp as he was moving to pull out a hair-brush. That hairbrush in the map in her brain instantly changed into a .25 automatic she perceived. She perceived a reality in an identity mode shift not because she was psychotic. Officer M was not as she was accused of being, an overzealous officer. In a politically correct nonscientific easy way that blindly prosecutes an innocent officer. Officer M, upon further knowledge of her his-tory, discloses her buddy, a detective in her precinct in a war zone, was shot in the face because he hesitated a second. He lost his life. The signal of the quan-tum psychic moment she witnessed left an ethological imprint. That imprint emerged in the streets when she shifted into a defensive and attack identity mode in which she felt threatened. Tragically, Officer M was not aware of this shift in identity modes as a dissociative process; neither was the ADA who prosecuted her.

This is one example of reality and one you need to understand as you move on in the text as you see ways to survive existentially when you are put in these very difficult situations. Another example is EMT Officer X. Her feelings were unmistakably sexual for a moment when she fantasized kissing the young man she worked on reviving. How sad she felt to be single and alone. EMT Officer X's fantasy is a hidden wish she kept silent. It was considered dead wrong and sick to have her thoughts. As a doc cop I can tell you that her wishes exist in many of us, as emerged later when her male counterpart, Firefighter Z, had a rescue fantasy about the female street cop he placed in the gurney and gave oxygen to.

Yet, another example of how the ecological context affects the officer is the deep-cover agent who is taking a beating to get deeper into the organized crime family he is infiltrating. The desire to turn on a dime and defend himself when the wise guy is "disciplining him as part of the standard operating procedure" is an enormous natural drive. His aggressive instinct is transformed into the feeling, "I am a good soldier cop and enduring this crap for a second-grade shield in the detective bureau."

Another example is Firefighter Z, who wonders if his need for perfection and making right out of wrong ensures disowning deep feelings of compassion under the surface of his angst. Firefighter Z learned feeling sad for "weak degenerates" is stupid and will in any case lessen his ability to be the best firefighter. The fear is he will get "all mushy and wimpy." But his need to defend against feeling what he is truly feeling is almost intolerable as compassion and empathy for the kid who died way too young. It is scary for Firefighter Z to fear he may express this level of compassion. Officer Z tells himself, "I really don't want to be here because it is a waste of time, so next job—full speed ahead." This need to get over any painful losses and challenges to his way of looking at his experiences helps him delay stopping and processing his existential pain. Pain over feeling the inability to have made a change in an outcome he could never change. Still, in his heart of hearts he really wished to rescue this kid in the worse way. He later disclosed he wished to be the hero to have saved his life. It is never as simple as all that! I guess you may agree that Officer Z gained the valuable wisdom that no, it is never as simple as all that.

So in reviewing the shifting of identity modes and dissociative process you will more than likely experience that surreal feeling, as if experience when losses are so intense. Pay attention to your own sense, intuition, and words you use that seem beyond your control or thought processes. Identity shifts you experience are ones you may not be aware of in the abrupt changes that take place unconsciously. The unconscious advantage is that if you can look at it from a public safety point of view, your inner perimeter, which is shut off from others, is your deepest and strongest and secret line of defense. That defense you experience is in part an adaptation by dissociation that serves to guard you against overwhelming existential painful awareness. Pain of owning feelings that are sexual and aggressive, which you may find very painful if you were fully aware of. That painful awareness without understanding why is hopefully starting to make more sense and is really more normal for your line of work. It is in line with your own individual identity modes in your personality style as police, firefighter, and EMT officers, soldiers, and emergency health professionals.

Finally, you share large and known symbols in your department on the gut level. You share metaphors in the soul of your work on the streets and buildings and region rules. It is in your unit that your own ecological niche and survival ethology are critical to understand. Most important is your own beat, sector, district you must survive in—is shaped by you as to what it affords for you to survive existentially and ethologically. It is what is afforded in response to what you learn, feel, and experience and adapt to in the process of life. Life with losses that surround and define each and every trauma you experience day by day. You have scratched the surface of loss in trauma with new understanding and tactics of dealing with the accumulation of losses.

Gearing Up: Transcending the Ecology and Ethology of PPS-CPTSD

At this point you have begun to look at complex trauma as a meteor that abruptly, without warning slams into your life as a public safety officer. Aftershocks move in multiple directions and in multiple dimensions. As an individual public safety officer you live and survive in an ecology defined through your unique experiences of one loss after another. It is the rip that losses force into your own unique attempt to push some sense out of these experiences, without looking at the eco-ethological dimensions and your own personality style. It is like trying to squeeze water from a rock blocked by your blue, red, or white wall of silence.

You are taught to defend against the vulnerability felt as a participant forced to witness the shock and horror of victims in each event. Still, without any choice of catching your breath or walking away even for a moment, if you ever have that urge, you are redirected to the next job. That shock and horror has to be placed somewhere. That somewhere is usually compartments hidden in toxic places. Toxic places that fill time with a deadly space where molding layers of dissociated experiences cannot be shed. These complex losses you experience are inner hidden perimeters of the outer complex of trauma. That hidden perimeter is where you can survive with toxic results hidden for many years until retirement, or a line of duty injury and disability marks the endpoint of your career.

The endpoint of the many creative ways and ingenuity you have used to hide your losses in your adaptive on-duty and off-duty personality style can be served. Served by transferring that ingenious self-defense into an openness to create new paths to your own strength and resilience. Your resilience emerges in existential analysis. I have committed my life to exposing these toxins so you can have a choice to responsibly identify, spot, and then figure out the options you may choose to change. You may also choose to live and suffer with them as best you could with some helpful suggestions to make them less toxic. Why would I say that to you? It is not politically correct to say what I just said: I do not want to be political and correct—I want to be real and effective in educating you. In educating you and supporting an understanding of why and how you are impacted by cumulative trauma and losses, it will be immediately helpful to you, your family, friends, and cop counselors and cop docs who will attempt to know you as an individual officer-patient.

Another lesson to learn for your use in the here and now, which you likely have intuitively learned, is that in my approach the unique defenses you present with make superb sense. They are emotionally and mentally strategic intelligence as adaptive responses where survival and instinct are constantly in motion. None of the officers need be characterized as abnormal, but rather as individuals who are attempting to adapt to a toxic environment that is sadly part of the human public safety ecology: terrorism, trauma, and losses are part of your life experiences. Damaging, abusive, politically correct, judgmental labels are too quickly and brutishly fixed on police, public safety, and military officers. Calling the officer stupid, brutal, mean-hearted, or cowgirl or cowboy without care for the public is simply ignorant. The truth in general could not be further than this prejudgment and stereotyping. It is unusually self-serving and politically motivated and psychologically damaging for all parties involved. A cop doc, Antoon Leenaars, has achieved more wisdom and skill in the understanding and treating of suicidal folks in general, and specifically public safety officer-involved homicide/suicides. He shares with us all the critical importance of being aware of the individual behind the final choice of suicide/homicide. Dr. Leenaars has fought hard to get officers and clinicians to not broadly sweep the brush of simple problems and narrow solutions to major complex issues like trauma and grief, reducing the plight underlying such tragic decisions officers make; suicide/homicide, once done, is too often, and dead wrong. I will not apologize for being politically incorrect because I am like you, a public safety officer in heart and soul, and I promised you to be real! In my own biased opinion, being real means I will be helpful to you and your family: that is my dream in writing this book for you! Let's now move on to more case examples and how we begin to do and understand what I developed as an eco-ethological existential analysis in the next chapter—one officer at a time—that is you!

When you recognize you, your partner, or family member or dear friend, you may choose to stop and land. When you land, let's see if you can spot your own place and make sense out of some behaviors, ideas, and feelings that at times have seemed weird and displaced that you may have suffered with in silence. Silently suffering is where you need no longer stay—that is, as you have begun by now to realize how sensible many of your responses are. What appears to be a lack of response may be the impact of silent suffering to the very real losses you have endured surrounded by toxic trauma. Our flight will lead you to being better at reconnaissance than you ever imagined while covering the ground of your own inner sight as well as your peers: so stop to pause and reflect as meaning is resaddled in Chapter 2 in your own Sam Browne survival belt.

Complex Trauma, Terrorism, and Loss

2

Ecological and Ethological Survival— Saddling Meaning into My Own Sam Browne Belt

Overview

Let us pause for a moment and reflect on the lessons harvested in the first chapter: I introduced some new ways of looking at what I have investigated, assessed, and treated for a decade prior to the terrorist attack on the World Trade Center, and for another decade post 9/11.

Today a lot more is known about trauma than two decades ago. Significant understanding illuminates some pressing questions about trauma. Yet, many questions about public safety trauma remain unanswered. I believe my approach and some colleague cop doc guides I recommend (see Appendix B) offer significant understanding. Being straight with you means you're offered a handle on the why, how, and what to do when complex losses in trauma strike home base. No book can accomplish what the tough road of therapy and insight can provide you. Newly gained understanding put into action, thoughts, and communication—in your day-to-day life—will affect the necessary change in deed! New concepts in this chapter help you navigate through your own difficult and painful losses. Each event not worked through and processed sits as active and silent memories hidden in the audience of your own mind. Painful hidden experiences do not get swept away. Rather, like dust in the closet accumulating until even your own breathing labors for the lightness of air. You gasp and cry out to a peer "SOS" when it has gotten out of your own self-coping methods.

Memories may reignite in your own mind, heart, and soul at a later time when the dust of a trauma experience has settled. Suddenly your view may be struck by the clarity of time that demands your attention, try as you will to avoid working on your traumatic experience. In Chapter 1, it is key to realize

55

that the most neglected and unusually harsh experience on officers emerges from unacknowledged losses.

Losses vary from changes in duty status, mobility, and skills. Losses related to work status become shadows in your past left unused, unappreciated, and sometimes beyond repair. Losses may also include being placed from full duty to restricted and modified duty status, and in some cases without firearms. Psychological losses also include believing you may not have done your best with an aided case that went south and DOA on you. Or recovering a victim's body parts, such as a wedding finger without a body, as yet another loss for a trained rescue officer. Psychological losses usually carry a load of guilt and often self-punishment. That self-punishment may be done with your awareness, but not your full awareness.

Often you may not be aware of your own tendency to pay yourself back for what you perceive as shortcomings in standards you have self-legislated for yourself as a public safety officer. This type of self-payback or self-punishment is largely not within your direct awareness. For example, you will see time and again the reason why you may be drinking too much, or having multiple partners for sex, or gambling away your life with other high-risk behaviors. In part the reason may be you control that path to take charge of your own suffering/punishment. Tragically, faith is vacuumed away from what you believe, is suffering without any sense and beyond your control— despair sets in: despair can lead to the most constricted of choices, including ending one's life.

"It": Barricading Your Own Guilt, Self-Punishment, and Hidden Losses

What I have found as a fact is most officers are their own worst self-critics and suffer guilt and self-punishment that is so often unearned: couple this sad truth with the fact that you may be too ashamed to speak about "it." "It" is the center of chaos when losses are hidden deep inside an officer and not allowed ventilation, or expression, and "it" implodes—or explodes.

What that "it" is, is expanded in this chapter, and for the rest of this guide.

"It" is hidden from you as you try as you will to bury it as part of the past and not important enough "to dwell on." "It" is covered in layers of muddied shame, decaying delay, and stoned denial that capture losses into silent tombs in your mind: "it" may also be buried in your existentially unconscious memories. These hidden compartments of existentially unconscious perceived mistakes, bad behaviors, and wrongdoings are not a function that is healthy. But as unhealthy as these unexpressed losses are, the denial

serves many purposes. Some purposes of denial, hiding shame, and delaying expression are highly effective in the short term. In fact, that short-term
effectiveness that denial serves helps you function very well as an officer. A
common statement I often hear is, "Hey Doc Dan, I have no time to really
think of 'it'! If I do dwell on 'it,' I will be stuck in the pain of it all."

When I share my concept of adaptive functional dissociation (see
Chapter 1) I lean my big ears to the right and hear the expression of many
losses. Losses are let go of and expressed in the therapy hours that fill that
empty feeling that so tortures the officer left to his or her own devices.
Delay and denial work foot in mouth to hide your losses in denial. Delaying
expressing "it" helps you tell yourself that you are not really denying "it."
But, you will save "it" for later. By later you mean when the rush and intensity ends. Guess what happens when you delay and deny your losses? Well,
you put off expressing and understanding the complex traumas you keep
banking on expressing later, just another year later, or when you retire
from the job. But, it does not end when you retire from the job. In fact, with
almost full certainty "it" will return over time with a vengeance that hits
you with the gentleness of a boulder in your shoulder holster. That is, unless
you speak about "it" and release your trauma with a peer who can listen and
support your expressing yourself.

What you experience when you hide your losses is a predictable process.
Hiding your losses due to shame and denial is like hiding milk that spilled
on the carpet. That milk processes into cheese under the carpet you covered
it over with, by putting it away for the while. For a while "it" remains hidden
from view. But sooner than later "it" will reemerge exposed. Even hidden
under the carpet you and others smell the stench as you inhale the mold. Like
milk hidden under the carpet, an implosion will blast its aftershocks under
the snug rug of your own denial. Denial of losses in trauma is taught as a
strength in the larger culture, and with subtle rewards in the public safety
ecology of trauma.

No matter how many cop docs/clinical police psychologists and other
medical mental health professionals desire to help you, not even the best will
be able to get it out of your mouth—if you remain in denial, delay, and are too
ashamed to talk about "it." Keep in mind you are not abnormal for feeling
shame, living in denial, and delaying working through the losses. But now
you have an option with your new understanding to disabuse yourself in
your choice to step over and shed your delay. You can commit now to begin
the process of opening up and expressing your own losses to a trusted peer
support officer and cop doc.

You can choose not to go further than your own shame, denial, and delay
unless you absolutely insist on putting yourself as worth it. Realizing the
reality of doing it right here and right now is self-liberating. Taking the first

step of making one call, and you know who that call is for, and who you can trust, you begin recovery and healing.

Peer Support Team Members: Allies for All Seasons

Trust is a big issue for you, as it was for me, and all public safety officers. Fear over what will remain confidential is a real issue and serious as it gets! Nowadays more so than earlier in the history of intervention model programs for police, public safety, and military units the incredible work of peer support has improved to higher professional standards than ever.

Peer support is offered in many departments, agencies, and administrative and military units. Peer support team members are the best professional officers you may seek initially. But you may ask what if the problem is deeper and still remains? That problem is that often when trauma accumulates, it does so in hidden compartments. That situation of hidden losses is not so uncommon as believed. That belief extends even to many peer support officers and mental health professionals in denial themselves of how many officers suffer from complex trauma and complex grief syndromes. Peer support officers are critically important beginning steps but are not the final analysis in most cases. Eco-ethological existential analysis looks at the officer as an individual and as a public safety professional and never preassigns or prescribes treatment drawn in the sand of politics and economics.

A Politically Incorrect Truth to Be Aware of: A Tsunami Is Not a Bleep on the Radar

Another often unspoken about problem is when police and public safety Employee Assistance Programs (EAPs) are directed as managed care, by non-public safety professionals. Non-public safety professional administrators who never saddled up as real public safety officers require extra scrutiny: in fact, after that extra scrutiny, many can be adept—more non-public safety EAP administrators are not. Those that are unadept manage the EAP with accounting principles contracted out as exact formulas, with one-fits-all standards, no matter how politically pleasant. Their message, in spite of pitching different agendas, is all public safety officers are of one personality, and assessment and treatment follow that logic. Platitudes do not cut it, and in bureaucratic inefficiency the bottom line is the sinker coupled with insecurity drop a ballast of hot air. Hot air rises when what is needed is an anchor for you as a public safety officer. Cop docs trying to effect change are as tied up as you are. In reality, outside of nicely packaged mission statements the fact remains these wonders of bureaucracy have never been in the saddle, and yet talk as if they have been in the saddle with you. Their experience is being bureaucratic watchdogs for their agency's fiscal department—not for the humanity and mental medical health of their participants. While you and I both may continue to hope that uniform executive public safety chiefs rid themselves of less than scrupulous contractors, internal hired watch keepers, the responsibility lies with you to check into your quality of EAP and services offered. The most notorious of these hazards are issues related to disclosure and service. Nonmental medical health workers making decisions that ultimately affect your mental/medical health by putting a stop gap on the number of sessions needed is inexcusable.

For you the simplest, humane, and scientific solution is also the most cost-effective: appointing public safety professionals who are also mental health professionals as both internal EAP and psychological services administrators (Conroy, 2008). The history of this practice is proving more than effective; it is proving preventive as well. Having said that, it is sadly still your own responsibility to ensure the credibility of your medical-psychological services section, EAP, and peer support response unit.

Another issue for you to wrestle with is payment for mental health service. Sometimes your insurance will take on the majority of the bills, and sometimes it will be your own burden. That being true, consider the fact that your own mental health is part of your overall medical health. Your mental health is paramount for your well-being and healthful recovery posttrauma and grief experience. Motivating yourself is critical, and if you do not work on your own issues, they will within time most likely overwhelm you: being overwhelmed, you may find yourself landing in the "burnout zone."

Terrorism, Trauma, and Losses—Officer, You Have Landed in the Burnout Zone

Let's stop and look at the problem of trauma and the losses that color the impact of your accumulating traumas. You need to think of a few factors that kind of hold together like glue. Some factors to consider are essentials of what is meant by your own way of dealing with terrorism, trauma, and loss. One factor is your own strategy of coping with trauma experiences as the holding glue at times of challenge and crisis. Times of challenge and crisis will vary in quality and intensity. One example is a threat to your own life. These threats are delivered in different situations, such as the following:

"Officer I will take you out when I get out of the cell!"
A rescue operation where the trolley you are hooking up to suddenly
    freezes in midair
Body tag situations where you are recovering contaminated DOAs from
    a biological leak
How you react when you are in an enclosed area like a subway cellar
    during a terrorist/fire rescue (as British brother and sister officers did
    indeed on July 7, 2005)

Survival is a very important motivation. Survival is rooted in the eco-logical niches you live in and map out as members of a unit. Stop, pause, and reconsider you are a human being influenced by what motivates you from an ecological and ethological survival perspective. This fact of your awareness of the eco-ethological sensibility makes a lot of difference in how you process any trauma. Meaning that once you rethink what you perceived as surre-alistic/twilight zone experiences, they are slowly redirected and processed with your new vision. Your new vision includes being able to focus on the eco-ethological context, which frames how and why you may have acted and processed a trauma event in the way you did.

You come to realize gradually that no matter what your behavior and strategy, the outcomes on the front line you wish to control are, in truth, out of your control. More so, although you may not be able to effect a change in terms of certain heartbreaking situations, you can now under-stand that in fact any reasonable peer also thinks that same event was surrealistic.

Still many questions remain. Let's try some questions on for size:

What tendencies emerge in your own self-understanding of your own
    strategy to survive and the map you have laid out in the ecology and
    niche you work in?
Do you notice your own unique mode of survival strategy emerges
    almost without your own thinking and planning as if it is in an auto-
    matic mode of tactical alertness?
Did you ever wonder how and why your responses to terrorism, crimi-
    nal activity, or catastrophe emerge and wrap around each stored
    memory of similar experiences you seemingly forgot?

Maybe after a terrorist attack, including being ambushed, or betrayed (domestic or foreign) with criminal activity, or emergency rescue or recovery efforts you are left with as many questions about the event as answers.

Rehearsal of Possible Outcomes: Real or As If Surreal—Attack, Regroup, and Recover

Perhaps you rehearsed again and again with your unit possible outcomes of terror attacks. In your many rehearsals you planned in your own mind, as most public safety officers do, to act in a certain way if such and such situation occurs. But what happened in real time and space is incredible in comparison to what you did in real time and in deed during the space of the event you are looking at. "It" is as if it is surreal!

You drilled in role-plays, you laid out a plan of action and inaction toward dealing with a catastrophic event happening. Suddenly, guess what? That very event happened. It happened as if what you visually or mentally anticipated about some event happening happened!

Worse in your own mind, you had also planned all you would do and said what you would not do. Now after everything went down you have no clue as to why you acted contrary to the way you anticipated, rehearsed, and with full intention planned on acting. Perhaps you felt as if the event was déjà vu. Perhaps you thought you acted in a less than brave, noble, heroic manner according to your own standards in comparison to the department guidelines. What makes it so difficult to deal with right here and now is not only are these questions left unanswered: the follow-up is you are unable to let go of your own thoughts of self-doubting your actions in the field. What can you do to relieve yourself of this gnawing pain of self-doubt and uncertainty about your field actions?

One solution you and probably at least a third of all officers have found quite within your control and choice is cooling down the heat. The way many officers cool down the heat is dipping into risk taking, depression, a bottomless well, addictions to jump-start mimicking control, or acting out regrets with some wild behaviors. All these cooldowns, rather than confronting your losses and trauma experiences, fan fires within that cannot be extinguished from without. In your own self-imposed punishment, which at times is not fully conscious, you believe you will forge a new start and self-forgiveness. Yet, in spite of attempting your own way of letting go, you are deeper in despair than an elephant in quicksand. Let's move from quicksand to understanding the higher ground of solid context.

What Is the Context of the Impact of Your Losses? Even More Questions as Guideposts

Contexts are very important in shaping losses. Contexts in part are shaped within the location and geography of where you do your job. What are the demands of your own ecological niche you have selected in the many behaviors and emotions you allow and disavow in your night-to-day work? For example, are you working in Beverly Hills, California, or in Brooklyn North in a domestic war zone where roll call is marked by shots fired? Was the context of your work area where bad guys did their firearm practice at the times your own roll call occurred with a cadence of exact timing, whether you are an EMT, a police officer, or a firefighter?

Are you a Chinese American special agent working in a 400-square-foot area in a foreign country where American, British, Israeli, Chinese, and Italian soldiers are hated with a zeal? Are you overseas and feeling homesick for your family and friends and anything that even slightly reminds you of home, as a Hindu Indian American. While on a redeployment in Kabul have you heard murmuring of being a traitor because you are simply an American Indian in Afghanistan?

Are you in denial trying to make it through day to day as if it were a marathon achievement? Do you feel no one can understand what it means for you to exist and survive in the foreign war zone, or the domestic war zone right here in the United States?

Are you a child porn investigator and feel your soul is shattered and cannot believe what you are dealing with in reality? Your reality is filled to the brim with exploitation, cruelty, and perversions beyond what you believed was possible by any human being. Is it really happening as you see day in and day out?

In an interview with an honest reporter from the *Washington Post*, Del Wilber (Wilber, 2010), I was asked about the impact of child porn investigations by the detectives responsible for tracking such criminals. I shared with Del Wilbur that it was hard to go back to normal life and erase the fact that an adult exploited these children as if they were toys for perversion on display—left in infamous perpetuity as victims in celluloid perdition for an eternity. The evil twist in ironic injustice is hard to process in the healthiest of officers, which most must be, even when investigators understand the illness underlying this sick and disturbing behavior. This sick and disturbing behavior shatters the souls of those who must descend to the lair of the depraved and heartless exploitation and then relate to their own significant others as if "it" never happened.

More cases of existential challenges accumulate, for example: Are you covering fires that are started to gain claims for insurance that ended the life of your brother firefighter? You now cannot get his loss out of your head. Perhaps a tree collapsed on the body of your newbie firefighter trainee and you had to drag him and thread him out of the forest fire area as he slowly died in the process, as you reassured him, in the same ecological niche you must return to night in and day out.

Are you an Italian American Jewish police detective in a criminal investigative unit attached to the U.S. Army who has worked on the case of a synagogue torched because the occupants were Jewish. In your investigation of this terrorist act, a network of Parisian radical Islamic anti-Semites who have a storefront of peace and refuge meets you. In addition, you are a son of a Holocaust survivor who, like many Jewish survivors of this horrific complex trauma, lost two-thirds of his family. You are having nightmares about concentration camps as this same terrorist front denies the Holocaust ever happened.

Are you an African American special agent attached to the U.S. Department of Justice who has to investigate a hate crime against a Baptist Church reverend. That compassionate reverend was a warm and charismatic minister who was called ethnic and racial slurs and left beaten for dead in a bias motivated crime. As a survivor of intergenerational hate crimes that targeted your family based on race, you have a memory where you remember hearing about a lynching of a relative African American cousin during Sunday dinners. You are reminded to believe in God and maintain your own faith in spite of racism you felt was left behind. Your own chaplain tells you to try not to feel rage and harbor resentment.

Well, you once again may ask me, "Hey Doc Dan, why are so many questions necessary before you get to the heart of what to do?"

In part, the answer is laid out in knowing what ecological context exists and what survival demands that ecology niche has on you as a public safety officer.

The contexts highlighted in the questions bring us to answers that otherwise are missed. So keep asking them and you are in good company. The famous philosopher Socrates developed a method that uses questions that become links to figuring out many puzzling events in life. Most investigators use this method unaware they owe thanks to Professor Socrates, another public safety leader. All public safety officers use questions and seek answers: the answers to good questions lead to more questions and eventually to truth. Truth is culled out like a juicy morsel hidden in a bone's marrow when the paths are narrowed to a solid answer in the Socrates method of analysis. Truth is healing to you and is in part sown in your choice of what you decide to focus on.

Perspective in Your Own Focus: Thoughts, Feelings, Behaviors, and Soul

Let's look at what I just described as cognitions (thoughts) about the event, feelings you process or do not about the event (emotional responses including none that you can consciously feel or express), and in fact the behaviors you do to cope better with your feeling of being overwhelmed (avoidance and withdrawal).

For example, your own feelings and emotional reactions to trauma may be an addiction to "it." You may not yet be aware of how addictive a behavior pattern is when that addiction leads to immersing yourself in similar situations again and again, rather than your decision to end the addiction. Without rest for the weary your own energy level may be drained without realizing your own losses. Energy drains really do have a cap on how much energy you can use day by day without exhaustion and collapse.

Perhaps you have discovered your own style is very different from the addictive style. You may be attracted to ambivalence as a style of coping. Ambivalence means you have learned to just go through the motions. Without really expressing an expected level of distress or excitement you may go through very challenging situations, including trauma as if it is not anything, but an "it is what it is" outlook. An example of ambivalence is when you act as if a homicide or fatal car wreck is an issue of getting body bags ready to be processed for the morgue or makeshift hospital triage center.

A psychological meaning of ambivalence is broader in scope and means you feel intense feelings and have different levels of disgust and attraction that in the final expression you present as if you don't care and could not be bothered. For our purposes let's see ambivalence as psychologists and psychoanalysts see it: in other words, you do care but cannot express your disgust, attraction, or agitation at a traumatic loss. The reason is because the experience is too overwhelming at present.

You may even respond in another stylized manner of ambivalence. That stylized manner is as if an idea is fixed in your own head as "whatever—whatever!" It is kind of like an odd experience you never really accept and place in perspective, but you do not let go of either. You go through the motions of trying to imagine different layouts and meanings when you are alone with "it."

Meaning like the fictional character Monk or even Sherlock Holmes, you cannot let go of an idea until every option and solution is fully explored, whether you express this process or not. Finally, returning to denial, you may have the style of "the least I do, the better." You may think that by not even being noticed by your bosses, you can "wing it" by moving through this maze of life and living by withdrawing to the landscape of minimal involvement as your own haven for survival. Your style of avoidance is another way you do what the bare-bone minimum requires. The key here is to remember the ecology influences helped shape your perspective and focus in your experience of learning different styles in synch with your own personality. The experiences you have accumulated over time have hardened into patterns in which you think, feel, and act within your own motivation to survive and how to survive ethologically.

Sworn Officer: Stripped of Civilian Longings and Strapped for Public Safety (SOP)

The person you envisioned yourself being and now becoming when you were sworn in as an officer is not who and what you are now as a person and officer.

I say this from my experience with almost 97% of the officers I have worked with: who and how you process trauma and special moments in your career and the way you do is in change.

That change, as many officers recall, almost always includes their loss of all innocence. It is the reality of dealing with losses that is so complex and intense over time that strips you of innocence. Cop Doc Conroy puts it this way, "You may even experience a loss of your own humanity. It may become extremely difficult to be gentle, caring, tender, and nurturing. These feelings create vulnerability, forcing you to feel the pain of those you work with" (Conroy and Hess, 1992, p. 91). That pain is so difficult to feel, and at the hub of that pain is once again losses.

In fact, choices you exercise are still within your power to make. Perhaps your choice is to read on and not to go to any cop doc or cop counselor. You may feel it is too overwhelming to tackle some of these issues at this point. Your options are fine as long as you hopefully think it through before acting on any choices of the many you have to make. Taking what you can out of this guide for yourself may mean you want a better understanding of your experience of loss and trauma. That is good enough for me if it is for you.

Self Help Is Better Than Not Helping Yourself at All

Even if you never choose to go to a police counselor for your losses and integrate inner sight and behavior changes from this guide, your achievement is solid! You will gain an incredible validation of why you may have felt, thought, and even taken in a lot more guilt, anger, anxiety, grief, and angst than you needed too.

How will I continue to assist you further in this guide without being physically present with you face-to-face? Well with difficulty, but let's start here by asking yourself how aspects of guilt, perfectionist super standards, and the 24/7 cop, firefighter, and EMT/RN mentality, while not as healthy as you would like to acknowledge, are your choice. But your choice is shaped by your ecology, ethology, and cultural learning as influences that are forceful. Forceful as influences, they are not as powerful as your individual will to change your own path existentially! With this fact of power of your own choice over forceful influences many of you will move on to meet a local cop doc or cop counselor. That cop doc you meet ought to be right for you and your own style of relating to others.

Choosing the Right Cop Doc/Cop Counselor for My Own Public Safety Personality Style

The therapist you may choose to work with should not be a random choice out of the Blue Cross and Blue Shield book, but someone who has a background in working with police and public safety officers.

One of the best choices is someone like you who has been a firefighter, police officer, special agent, or emergency medical technician. Why?

As most of you need not be told, having a connection to what you are going through is easier if he or she has been in "the bag" and in the saddle, so to speak, just like you.

However, regardless of background, the key to healing is working with the therapist you are most comfortable with. It is crucial to not give up on therapy if the therapist you have worked with makes some very human mistakes. Even if he or she did not get who you really are—right away. Patience works both ways: patience helps you sort out if your therapist has the capacity to actively hear what you are saying to him or her. Actively listening is being responsive to you.

Second, you can also test if your therapist is having an impact on how you are feeling and thinking. Even if he or she is a highly recommended therapist, but you are not feeling differently after a few months of therapy, pause and be alert. Please talk about the issues you think are blocking the therapy from working. Be a participant fully and with passion.

Do use your active listening skills to intuitively listen for yourself and see if a viable reason exists as to why you and your therapist are not connecting. You should feel validated and not on guard for being a public safety officer: if you are feeling you have to legitimize your existence as a public safety officer, please end that relationship. Do not give up—please take your time and invest in finding a competent therapist.

If your therapist repeatedly does not attend to your trust issues where you feel safe to give a good cry, leave the relationship.

Why go over these steps of ensuring the right therapist fit for you? Because it is that important to not lose out on an experience that can be life altering. Another reason emerges. That reason is that while you are expert at serving others, here in therapy, redirect your reality to accommodate you: you are the one served and attended to in the haven of therapy. Meaning you may be asked to clarify, challenged to change some thoughts, and even confronted on some very difficult behaviors or thoughts existentially—that is good stuff. You may just be listened to— even if your therapist is just a great listener—that is okay: nothing less is acceptable.

Red Flags—Red Alerts: Exit Doors from Trauma and Grief Therapy

If your therapist minimizes or denies your losses with you too easily, then realize you are likely sinking good time and effort into bad ground. At this point, if you choose to be the victim and rebury all your losses, that is not good common sense, but silly nonsense. What makes sense is to move on to better grounding with a new therapist. Simply put, not all therapists are equal, and some will connect and some will not. You are savvy and know how to get to the real deal. Take your time asking peers on the job that have sought help. That is, ask someone you believe. Some peer who can appreciate where you are coming from.

Your Responsibility in Counseling— Resistance and Working Through

It is important to understand another concept as a public safety officer that works in a superb way on the streets. That method is getting to the bottom line: but in the counselor's office, it may lead to a premature withdrawal from a cop counselor. In other words, understanding and helping you work through the grit and metal of your losses and the shell of trauma takes time. Time has hardened your shell of denial, unique ambivalence, and odd self-soothing perhaps, hyperfocus, and overly sensitive intuition skills you've learned to deal with your losses. It takes time and mutual effort and investment to go over these bottom lines in the sands of your trench of defense, so please give it the time needed.

That grit and metal that help you deal with trauma situations on the street also have a harder surface approach, and are captured by a word meaningful to you and the counselor you are working with. That word is not a million dollar word: it is *resistance*!

Resistance is a very good and natural defense, and it is important to really process this fact; otherwise you are bound to resist what I am exploring with you in your own odyssey of working through the losses you have experienced. If that happens prematurely and without taking the time and energy with me, you are likely to ignore your losses. In burying your losses too soon you will likely replace your own inner sight with more toxic accumulation of pain and guilt. Pain and guilt fester and grow inside by leaps and bounds if unaddressed due to a lack of trust. Exposing losses with your therapist is not only important; it is crucial. Think about it for a moment: Could you go over a case without being able to trust your public safety partner? Well, here your therapist is your work partner, and the work to do is exposing, grieving over, and placing your losses in your life history. What is meant by placing your losses in your life history is a gradual process. A process where you learn to own your losses is healthy.

Understanding your own growth, challenges, and getting unstuck from a place you no longer want to be. By becoming aware of your own losses, rather than hiding them in a hidden compartment that festers denial, ambivalence, and excessive worry in endless solutions of acting out destructively and in your unique addictions, you work through them.

You can achieve the needed mourning and grief work, or you can numb your feelings out. You can also adapt and function while in a dissociated state of mind. But all these options of denial will help you put the losses away in a compartment of resistance, until the pressure explodes, or more often implodes. Imploding is no less than seeing a building that explodes internally. In your own way—whether an explosion or implosion—the end result is tragic. It is this tragic moment I deal with a lot. At times even what is sometimes called an emotional and mental breakdown is the final result. But in therapy resistance, while natural, is not your best ally. Resistance needs to be exposed to you. If not, resistance will lower the effort needed to put your sights on the real losses that grate, eat away, and at a deep level torture you.

Public Safety Officers and Therapy—A Revolver Needs a Holster—Alliances

The promise of an alliance with a therapist regardless of where you are when you seek to gain understanding into yourself is best served by your willingness to explore issues. Exploration ought to be within the beat of your own cadence with someone you can let go with gradually, as need be. Why you are experiencing some troubling symptom such as not sleeping well, having recurring flashbacks, or just not feeling right may and can be shot down by investing in and beginning the hard work of trauma and grief therapy.

Counseling is a joint adventure, like working and choosing a police, EMT, or firefighter partner you work with and bond with for survival on the streets. The survival motivation here is one of meaning. Existential meaning transcends the ecological and ethological influences so crucial toward effective counseling. Why go through the hassles and the deeper stuff to work through your losses—aren't you functioning okay?

Truth be told, no argument here: probably you are functioning okay and you will continue to do so for a while, until one day. That one day will come when you just cannot muster the strength anymore and your energy reservoir is done to the pit: empty and with no juice to go on. Time to get open and real, and make that appointment.

Don't Play Doctor: Go to a Doc You Can Trust: In Therapy—Honesty Is the Only Policy

But accepting the wisdom of your doc to assist you in understanding what is going on is reliant on a crucial aspect of all counseling and therapy. That crucial aspect is trust, meaning you must be able to listen to your own words without blocking what is said. That is, as best as you can, open up by trusting and letting go by being fully honest. If you can't be honest and trust over time, there is no alliance and your own resistance will block any real work from happening. Without your own real disclosure, no real change can take place in therapy (Kitaeff, 2011; Leenaars, 2010).

Why is it so important not to present yourself in only your best and most favorable light? Perhaps you are thinking, "Well, it is to humble you."

Maybe it seems it can stop you from having too much pride, as "there is pride before the fall." Well, maybe in part if you choose to look at it that way, but in the seat of your saddle the answer is no!

Honesty and trust are so critical because only by letting go of the wall in therapy can you and your cop doc begin to unravel the layers of resistance you used in surviving the streets as a cop, EMT, ER RN, or firefighter.

By understanding the ecological context of your own words and the tendencies you present honestly, you need to trust to open up in therapy. With trust in the process of therapy you can give the therapist some context as to how you deal with trauma and loss underlying your symptoms. Honesty and trust can help you and your therapist work on understanding that will help you express grief that otherwise may never be released. Grief can have a very toxic effect by being hidden in you and left unexpressed like a virus that implodes. *It takes your honesty and trust in partnership with your own cop counselor for the mission to be accomplished.*

That mission to be accomplished is to understand the why and how to place your losses and let out the necessary expression of that loss we call the mourning process. It is this mourning and healing therapy process that is helped or blocked with the two best keys to use or misuse. *These two keys are quite simple to express and hardest to do: being open and honest in communicating your losses and trauma, and trusting your therapist with that sacred experience.*

If these two keys do not exist, there is no alliance. With no alliance and a need to stay guarded you cannot let go and begin the difficult process of grief therapy and the mourning process. What the father of all psychologists, Dr. Freud, called the mourning process—"working through." You know when you hear some public safety officer use the phrase "I'm on the job" what that means. Working through being on the job takes courage, commitment, and a can-do attitude.

Resistance from an Ecological-Ethological Perspective: Working through Being on the Job

You have touched on the problem and benefits of what is really at essence called resistance. It is the resistance to looking within yourself in a deeper way where you understand what is in essence maladaptive behaviors, maladaptive ideas, and maladaptive emotions that help you on the streets. On the other hand, resistance hurts your ability to adjust and adapt in healthier ways off duty. Dr. Kevin Gilmartin, retired police lieutenant, called this process emotional survival and the many cognitive aspects of how you may sabotage yourself in policing by shooting yourself in the foot. You may do that by being too stiff-shirted when you leave the job. You may be on duty too much. Cop Doc Gilmartin's book is a gem and opens up many police officers who are stuck in a being on the job mindset (Gilmartin, 2002).

Another of the best hard-core and effective guides exploring the reality of the streets for police, medics, public safety officers, firefighters, and correction officers is written by Cop Doc Conroy.

Dr. Conroy assists officers at risk grabbing for a quick fix washed away in blood, sweat, and tears and offers real hope and options (Conroy and Hess, 1992). Exploring your options is key in understanding stress, burnout, and the struggle for survival.

The Eco-Ethological Identity Survival Modes

The ethologic perspective you are tackling is in part that emotional struggle of survival on a human animal level within an ecological niche. That ecological niche that you have evolved in and will continue to do so includes earlier to present assignments on the job. Resistance is in part unconscious and set in the context of what you have forgotten before you even had a chance to absorb what you really had experienced in trauma. The speed in which you are struck by the quantum moment of trauma does not allow you to stop, pause, and reflect on what just happened. The quantum psychic moment allows you to shift into automatic gear and move onward to your next job. Your adaptive functional dissociation forwards you with key functional effectiveness, while time, and all around it ethologically, is frozen in that ecological niche in space. In order to get a feel for the importance of this psychological effect, an example will help you put the quantum impact of trauma in perspective. Let's use an example that is not far removed from what you have learned is simple and routine. Simple and routine may be re-viewed as complex and not so conscious after you do the following exercise. Take, for example, the steps of driving a bicycle to the more advanced government vehicle you drive. Sit for a moment and do an exercise with me.

Exercise on Your Own Conscious Awareness as a Public Safety Officer Operator

I would like you to write out the steps of riding a bicycle. After you do that first task, follow up with how you drive a car in detail. Please include what each step in the process means and why each step functions the way it does. Focus on how and when to use each function on the bike or car the way you do and include why these functions operate the way each does.

Experiment in Assessing Conscious from Unconscious Awareness: Results—What to Do?

I am reasonably certain the evidence you have witnessed for yourself in this exercise is difficult to understand at first. In other words, as simple as it seems, it is not so simple! What made it seem so simple in your recall initially is you have been able to drive a car and no doubt a bicycle for so long with ease. In the process of being able to drive effectively and function with expertise, you have forgotten how complex becoming the expert driver you are today was in reality. Think of it this way: when you do anything too often, you lose contact with the core experience of the basics that got you there in the first place. If this is true of riding a bicycle and car, then stop, pause, and reflect how deeply unconscious the impact of the crater of the quantum psychic impact of your first complex trauma must have hit you. Hit and then buried in the entombing of unconscious denial and resistance in your own mind toward becoming conscious.

Think of the first experience in your own ethologic resistance against trauma and loss within your own ecological niche of resistance. Your expertise at learning to deny losses and horrid scenes of terror without processing what this experience really means in the higher levels of your own existence is at many levels: it helps you understand how powerful learning is and what you are expert at, such as driving—largely in part done as a complex task—remains largely unconscious. It was once conscious and intentional. It is now guarded within your public safety culture from disclosure—the blue PC and correctional wall of silence, the red FD and EMT wall of silence, and the general culture of the bottom line. It is also your own need to protect those you are most intimate with by not allowing anyone into what has become the shadow of experiences best left buried and forgotten (Conroy, 2008; Creelman, 2007; Kitaeff, 2011; Leenaars, 2010).

Pause and think for a moment with fascination at another level of this experiment: what you actually do on many different levels in your identity modes as a public safety officer is similar to learning how to ride a bicycle and official government vehicles (OGV)/radio motor patrol vehicles (RMPs). First, let's review the evidence taken from your experiment. Once you review the evidence, you can return to the comparison in your own identity modes and the unconscious shifts that occur. These shifts and identity modes allow you to function with effectiveness as you move from one trauma to another in the field of operations without your own awareness.

The evidence is you are not likely to be able to sit down and write down the basic steps of driving a car, listing all its parts and operational functions. What about your recall of firing your first .38 caliber revolver, Glock 9 mm, Beretta .380, M15, or shotgun, and how to do it safely and with maximum effect and firearm control? What about stripping it down and cleaning your firearm on your own without your training officer present? The answer is it is likely complex, learning you cannot do any of these recall exercises with ease on a conscious level of awareness.

Ask yourself the following questions: Were you a lone operator trusting in yourself to ride on your own while evading the cones in a tactical operator's course? Let me ask you an even more elementary question: Did you learn how to ride a bicycle and later your first motor vehicle, and then department vehicle, without guidance? More importantly, were you able to achieve this highly complex skill of coordination and thinking and emotional attunement by yourself? How about without trust and confidence in not only you, but in your training officer or mentor? With reasonable certainty, your answers are almost always about 97% no!

Why am I asking these questions of you? Because again, the fact that trust and confidence in your cop doc or cop counselor is that important to be able to get to the unconscious influences that impact on your working through "it": working through is a two-way thoroughfare because here you are going to learn along with your cop counselor aspects of yourself you may not be aware of. The first goal in working with your cop counselor or cop doc is getting to know what you may not be consciously aware of in your own police personality style. The second goal is understanding your own unique survival motivation within your eco-ethological niche, and why you have repsonded in a specific style of defenses against your own trauma and losses within your eco-ethological niche. This is followed by a third goal of discovery—how you may choose to make some differences in your style as a unique public safety officer. Fourth, she will seek your own unique history of losses needing expression and integration in your own healing. What will be crucial to understanding for both you and he or she in a guided journey is your motivation to emerge and be the best you can be as a humane public safety officer on duty and off duty. Now go a step further and think of the unconscious process of learning. You have forgotten some of the very basics, and only when you are put to task to see how much of learning has become unconscious can you let go. In letting go, please realize a lot of what was known and learned was once very novel to you. Your knowledge and experience of this fact is humbling and important to keep in the back of your own mind. Think about the process of faith and ideals you have believed in. Is it possible some of your own existential faith in your source of courage and your own moral compass has also become unconscious?

Think of the complexity and ability not only of public safety officers of your own unit, but also of other types of public safety officers, from police and corrections to firefighters and medics and EMTS, to ER RNs and MDs and PhDs.

This insight may be humbling as well as something to be grateful for. Your attitude of gratitude will help you be more open and tackle down resistance while respecting its sensibility as an officer who is likely to be judged and mislabeled. The wisdom of knowing you still do what you do with professional integrity and human error as best as you can is not fully conscious or unconscious—it is both. It is like all goals and achievements—gradual and a complex learning process—as is your understanding of your own experience of trauma and loss.

Becoming the Finest—Humane in Being— You: Questions and Your Own Answers!

The existential questions we looked at in the first chapter now have a deeper context by preparing you for the journey of understanding resistance. Now you can move into the existential soul of the matter of resistance and its connection to existential meaning or the denial of that meaning in your own life.

On one hand, some resistance you may have encountered is your own blocking from awareness the cumulative losses you experienced, such as the following examples:

1. You have taken down a bad guy, who suddenly died in the arrest process.
2. Your rescue operation did not work in spite of your full commitment and dedication.
3. You had an accidental firearm discharge as a range officer.
4. You are accused of medical malfeasance even though you followed EMT SOP.
5. After a major trauma you used a chemical substance you would never use otherwise.
6. After a severe loss, you acted out sexually and impulsively.
7. In a moment of anger you reamed out a civilian and now have a serious complaint.
8. A malicious and corrupt complainant accused you and you are innocent.
9. You accept abuse by your boss, and you do not know why you do not stand up for yourself.
10. You have been falsely slandered and you cannot disclose the truth due to department regulations.

So let's pull it together here and redirect your attention. First, if you read these behaviors and thoughts and you immediately reflect what a sucker I am or have been, tackle that thought to the ground of reason and survival ethologically. The reason that the above cumulative losses are so resistant is that a harder than normal exterior shell exists to block your expression: in the public safety culture, drilling into your mind is the reality of your own survival being contingent on the very painful lessons, as follows:

"Hey, Officer A-Z, let the crap roll off your back and learn to duck the BS."
"If you want to survive the job, learn to get a tough exterior and don't blabber to everyone!"
"Keep a low profile and do what is needed without getting noticed. Got it, get it, good!"

"Hey, we all felt blue at first and then it gets easier."
"Enjoy the thrill of it before it gets old."

As you evidenced earlier, most of you may love to eat Peking duck, but eating a duck is hardly becoming a duck. So you refuse to hold and believe in what is sometimes in ignorance called distortions, distractions, or brainwashing. Why not? Is it not brainwashing, distortions, and distracting to tell yourself the above thoughts and the ones preceding them?

At a fundamental and simplistic dummied down view, yes, it is. I am not giving you a dummy guide; you are not one and neither am I. At a deeper level in your training, the self-talk and thoughts of denial of losses and trauma above have been taught and learned well for your survival skills in the street. Since these words and self-talk helped you in being more efficient tactically, they are not completely dysfunctional, distracting, or really brainwashing. Even the play on duty and wild play off duty reinforce the learning process for you to survive the streets. But, these thoughts are not healthy all the time, and in fact, when you put yourself down, you are likely to increase the likelihood you will lose the changes you seek. Losing the changes you seek quicker than you as a firefighter trying to use a jammed extinguisher. Losing the desired relief you seek as an EMT, medic, or ER RN, ER PA, or ER MD with a stethoscope without acoustic percussion cups to hear your traumas relieves you with echoes of your own silent wounds. As an officer trying to use the same script of these lines, what you have learned to rehearse and use in combat will help you like a crack in your .38 cylinder revolver, which goes round in revolutions as an officer moving through the revolving doors of criminal justice.

For now let's reflect that only God is perfect: all public safety officers, no matter how competent, responsible, and decent, are prone to error. This is the first step toward actually embracing reality. That reality includes realizing you are error-prone as a human being and officer. You picked upon some very important unwritten rules you learned in the academy, field training, and the street experiences in your units, respectively. Some of the learning made superb sense, and if you did not learn it well, you would not be reading this book now—you would have gone flatline long ago.

Now the reality of healthier coping begins with you understanding that the learning of these self-statements was not only sensible, but helped and may still help you survive on the job and off duty. So if you try to erase the self-talk above by saying you were brainwashed, think distortions, or are distracted, you will believe a lie. That is, a lie that suggests you are not so intelligent, not so clear, and not realistic in thinking. You will easily fall into depression, anxiety, and addiction as avoidance of reality, which demands adaptations to changing and shifting events. The most pressing of those events are losses in trauma.

Let's say for your purpose you may tell yourself with passion how adaptively intelligent you really are: how well you learned evolutionary demands in an ecology of trauma and ethology of survival in very challenging and complex loss-filled niches. Ecological niches are beats you live and work in and adapted to over life and death experiences. Then reflect out loud or privately with passion for the next task at hand, covered in the next section.

Reload and Redirect the Cylinder of Your Eco-Ethological Beliefs to the Barrel of Your Existential Purpose as It Is Developing Now

How can you reload, redirect, and barrel to existential purposes is as follows: you will stop, pause, and redirect your own self-label in which you call yourself a sucker, failure, stupid, or a zero for any of your mistakes in your thinking.

For example, you may be saying to yourself, "I am a loser because I did not see the wound in the aided persons back" or "I had an accidental discharge; therefore I must be a keystone cop."

Look at the evidence through a simple and effective question you may ask yourself right now, "Can I prove to anyone, even myself, that because I may have even made an error in my human behavior or thinking, like having an accidental discharge, or even not seeing a problem accurately, that I am an all-time, all-place loser, zero, or incompetent 24/7 and always will be?"

Can you take one of a thousand experiences and because you made an error in one of these situations, now must fix a nonsensical label like calling yourself a zero? Can you stop and let go of this self-defeating label as ineffective. In fact, the evidence once again is that you are actually defeating yourself by your own self-abusive labels you are choosing to fix on yourself.

Let's Reload the Ethological and Ecological Cylinder Further by Asking "Why?"

Question: Why? The answer to why the question "Why?" is so important is one we covered in Chapter 1. Let's start with "Why?" comes as natural to any public safety officer seeking to figure out intent and meaning behind any preliminary investigation, recovery, or rescue event. Could you imagine ever doing a report or investigation postintervention as an EMT, medic, firefighter, or police officer without looking at the question of "Why?" Well, you may ask the doc to be more specific as to what he or she means when he or she asks, "Why?" Okay, good question again. The question of "Why?" someone died is as telling as what intent or lack of intent was involved even in a medical situation. It is doubly true in a police or emergency medical/psychiatric situation. It makes all the difference in the world. Let's say Mr. X just took an intentional overdose, or did he? Why did he really take the overdose? Did he accidentally ingest the wrong medication? If he did, you know the next course of action is critical as soon as he is stable. It means involuntary hospitalization, or treat and release. If the little girl Jane slipped and banged her head on the floor, or if she was beaten by a peer in school, or if she self-inflicted the wound, the difference is an accident, a criminal action, or psychological/psychiatric care.

"Why?" is a hot question but of critical importance in my approach with public safety trauma and losses, including any of the 10 examples highlighted as cumulative losses you may have experienced above: the why question helps you understand the impact on you and why these losses make superb sense in terms of ethological influences within the niche you have developed your unique style of being a public safety officer. That is, what you tell yourself is not so much irrational, but a process of survival tactics that in part may have become maladaptive over time. What has shaped your thinking and understanding is in large part the answer to the sensibility as to why you may accept many things civilians do not. If you revisit the 10 cumulative losses as examples, you may have encountered in an ecological niche where being a good soldier was the payoff. It is drawn in as part of your experiences in learning to buck up and shut up! That buck-up and shut-up philosophy is extended way too far into your life and way of thinking. What was meant to teach you how to survive on the streets has spread to an automatic response in many more situations.

In terms of survival, this makes great sense from an evolutionary point. So when you look at your thoughts, behaviors, and emotions, reflect that they are in part an aspect of your surviving in an ecological niche where you learned how to modify your unique style to survive as an officer. How you learned consciously and unconsciously to defend against the existential spiritual aspect of that crushing quantum moment of psychic trauma exploding into your life.

You, or anyone else: stop, pause, and reflect. In stopping, pausing, and reflecting about why you have learned to act in a certain way, many answers are fleshed out. One such answer that arises is survival in the front line. Survival in the front line requires self-restriction of your natural responses ethologically and constriction of those emotions that can interfere with your own existential meaning and life beyond being a public safety officer. What you learned to do and think helped you sensibly develop your unique personality style within your unit. So now if it remains and has become intense, even if it is maladaptive, this does not mean you are sick, mentally ill, or weak in character. Such labels are grossly judgmental, self-destructive, and stupid, even if uttered by politicians and social critics with equal dispassion.

In response to how you label yourself, I will begin by saying to you that you may learn to say to yourself that you are an intelligent, competent learner. *In learning how to survive ethologically and within your ecological niche, you learned all too well how to survive ethologically—without understanding the very process of why you changed.*

Second, I may say as you may say to yourself, some behaviors and thoughts you have kept up make superb sense now because those patterns you learned have helped you survive. Let's look at survival here, by example. Your survivor ethology and ecological niches shaped your patterns of behavior and tactics in a way that is natural in the foundation of the personality. You entered the gates that promised "Enter to learn and exit to serve," or some variation of that.

Survivors of Land and Sea: Lions, Dolphins, and Navy Seals, PD, FD, and EMTS

Let's now move to that example of natural shaping that exists in a dimension you have in common with the lion and seaworthy social survivor, the dolphin. Is it not true the lion learns to drink and survive next to the mighty crocodile and the dolphin next to the predatory sharks? In the lion's and dolphin's ecology, do they not adapt to harsh environments by learning tactics to ensure living by their prowess? That prowess translates into very complex behaviors. So let me ask you, why is it so hard for you to believe that you did not learn in the same way to be a survivor on an ethological level in an ecology where life and limb are threatened? Lions or dolphins do not express their courage or losses in the way we do, but they also suffer from grief ethologically and at their level of conscious awareness.

We have a much more complex way of thinking and feeling losses and with more intensity than we can express tactically and strategically when we use lethal force, counterterrorist attack, and arrest and apprehension of criminals. First, I would like you to process in the context of your survival identity modes is the force of trauma and loss and how it impacts on how you view the reality of your evolution as an officer. I also want you to think that just as the lion or dolphin cannot express its losses, you can potentially communicate your losses. Second, you can learn a language that can help you reach that path to express yourself and, in doing so, control and manage some of your emotions left unidentified until now. It is also possible to place experiences in a conscious context and understand why you may have acted or judged beyond reasonable expectations why you may have acted badly, weakly, foolishly, and now may think and act quite differently.

Third, you may say to yourself, "If it makes so much sense to feel, act, and behave the way I do, then why is it my choice to still persist and be so hard on myself?"

Why should you insist on labeling yourself rather than working on accepting what you now know. What you now know is how and in part why your behaviors, thoughts, and feelings about losses are so difficult to process and how that complexity needs time, patience, and attention.

Would you realistically expect to clean up a crater that was left by a meteorite in your own backyard overnight? If so, I heard there is someone trying to sell the Brooklyn Bridge with a 401K plan. Go easy and gentle with yourself is key to moving through harsh terrain. If it works, you may choose to keep patterns that are not healthy for you now. You may also choose to work harder at investing in change through inner sight, behaviors, and even more. Try reaching your heart and soul where a better way of thinking, acting, or interpreting your life experiences lies open to change.

In terms of letting go of your own judgment of yourself, you can start right here and now by admitting you are not God.

You Are Not God! You Can Say to Yourself, "Let Go: Let God!"

You need not worry about changing the bad guy's culture or even your own culture. Since the public safety culture is ripe with trauma and losses, and the terrorists' culture tries to take you down a notch—resist! Resist taking on the impossible goal of changing a whole culture. You can work on making the best you can of you. You can do that by doing, thinking, and believing deeply that since you are influenced by surviving and suffering the hits of losses in trauma, it will not be easy but you can make meaningful changes. Changes begin by saying to yourself that your deepest beliefs include valuing your own unique self and personality. That lesson is what existential psychology is all about, and so am I as an existential analyst. By default, if you change your self, you will reach and likely have a positive influence on many more, including and beginning with you.

Uniquely Me: Choices, Responsibility, and Compassion Begin with Yourself!

You may ask again, "Why me?" "Hey is that not self-centered?" "Is it selfish to think of yourself first?" No! The reason no is so strongly asserted is that in your own center, being loved and respected begins with yourself and spreads to wider extensions of your own center, expanding to many more lives. It is both self-preservation and self-love that truly allow you to affirm what is important to you. By your ability to stop and explore for yourself what you value and love, your own love will extend to another significant person. Self-respect follows self-love and is not for sale. Loving yourself is not for compromise, it is your genuine center and the center of the universe—you!

An ancient Hebrew wisdom where all major religions begin states something along the lines that the "world was created for you—imagine that!" Professor Nachmun suggests what is critically important.

It is true when you think about it—the mission you accomplish is unique. Being rebellious by finding your own center in a universe slowly wrapping around itself in losses is inspirational. No one can quite replace you or the unique way and style in which you do your own job. Think about that. When you really take the time to reflect on it, someone may replace a position, but who can do what you did, and as you did it? So even looking back in time you can choose to fill the space of your experiences with a powerful redemption of self-valuing and release of false guilt.

Let's look at the importance of being uniquely you through another perspective. Anyone can put a pen to paper, but only J.F. Kennedy could have written *Profiles in Courage*. Only Dr. Martin Luther King Jr. could have delivered the "I Have a Dream" speech. Only Modigliani could have painted the canvas *Bride and Groom* in 1915 as his masterpiece. Professor Einstein was meant to develop his theory of relativity as only he did and could have (Einstein, 1954). Dr. Sigmund Freud let us know about the unconscious mind in a way that only he could have. Only Dr. Charles Brenner could have taught the world the compromises we form (compromise formations) in the way we land on our conscious feet in covering the unconscious mud.

It is important to pause and think about each of these people and the fact that each added an important contribution to life and living.

Public Service as Artistic Expression: Creativity and Compassion's Shield against Despair

I may receive a question from critics such as, "Doc Dan, why are these historic figures who all are of genius caliber so important and relevant to public safety officers? Isn't the bottom line important! Isn't that bottom line to get to the meat and potatoes of trauma and loss?"

Great question. I have an answer for you to think about with me in answering your own question: "Why not?" Yes, and you finally got an answer as simple as all that! Why not open up to a strength within to withstand the assault from without!

In fact, let me ask you another question, which may further answer your own question. Since I do not agree with any bottom line and since you are not fishing the bottom of the bay, let me ask you: Are you not a wonderful and complex public safety officer with your own style of doing your job in the style you do perform your own duties in?

Is your own style and your own way of doing your job as a public safety officer not cause for internal witnessing of what you know in your heart and soul? What you know at times is nothing less than remarkable! Imagine the unique power you have achieved on the job by how and why you affect others in ways you may have hardly noticed. Further, use your psychological imagination in reflecting on how many regular folks you help and you do care about (even if silent to everyone) as "you do the right thing." That is, you do the right thing with the personality style you were born with and in a complex way only you could do, as only you do it. Together, right here and now, you can begin affirming your own unique actions, thoughts, and reflections as a masterpiece of artistic creative expression in your own life.

I invite you to redirect your perspective to include what a masterpiece means here. A masterpiece may be including how you have affected or are affecting someone else's life: influencing their world by doing something uniquely courageous in assisting him or her in a tragic moment.

Imagination is a powerful tool. I would like you to use your own psychological imagination. Meaning what? Meaning the following working definition of your own psychological imagination: imagine that your influence and power to be as you are includes valuing your own courage and your own voice while serving the public. That voice of courage within you is a source of power to heal others. Healing power not only in helping others, but also you as well!

If this thought is novel, I ask you to at least try it on and see where it fits you. Does this attitude of psychological imagination grab you in part or whole? Can you use your own psychological imagination as a thought for life and living in the ecological niche you have survived in as a public safety officer? Psychological imagination in how you may shift your perspective in the public safety world you will be seeing. Imagine the power of a re-vision within a new perspective of valuing your ideals, your myths, and your existential values within the context of very real eco-ethological stresses and strains endured. Power of your ability to work through and at times transcend those very challenges. Challenges that are never perceived without taking into account the complexity of your own personality style as a public safety officer.

Personality Styles as Different Styles
of Expression and Process

With the hope you are considering my suggestion, let's sample some differences that highlight your own personality style as an individual officer. By using your own psychological imagination, you can look at aspects of you that distinguish your own from other officers' personality style as unique creative expressions only you can fulfill.

For now, let's move back to that officer who may in fact in some way be reflective of your own unique style and experience. Some questions that follow will help you redirect your understanding of your own style here:

> Are you avoiding any real challenge on the job? Suppose you are more avoidant in your personality style and think to yourself, "Hey—why reinvent the wheel when it works so well. I will just do my quotas, keep my head low, and get my job done well." Your focus is an attitude of low profile: after all, what you care about is collecting a paycheck at the end of the biweekly cycle.

> Perhaps you are the officer who cares about being the first to arrive at the most chaotic job. You love to run in and tackle down the bad guy, kicking butt, and making collars. Your goal is getting your gold shield eventually. Deep inside you want to be the best first responder and a cop's cop, a firefighter's firefighter, an emergency medical tech to EMTs, the best of the best ER nurse or doc—all this regardless of personal risk.

> Perhaps you are the officer who needs to do your job with 25 parking tickets, 2 felony collars a month, with a sprinkling of 5 misdemeanor collars. All exacting goals you have made for yourself to ensure you will receive no more than exactly 10 hours 54 minutes 36 seconds overtime for the month. You get the point here: you put Monk to shame and that's hard. You follow projects with exacting precision. That is, you must get your goals met with precision, or else you feel as if you let yourself, your boss, and ultimately the world down.

Now hold on to your memo book, for we have not exhausted the personality styles yet. For example, what if you are the midnight squad watch commander and you are the consummate bachelorette. Say you also love sci-fi films, and secretly you are into watching the old outer limit series and *Twilight Zone* reruns as your accountant boyfriend dresses up as a cowboy with you. You and your boyfriend play rodeo cowboy and girl when off duty. You love being a detective squad commander where your intuition and ability to be what we shrinks call an empath is what drives you. You are unusually on the money when you do your job, but off the job your love life is one big mess. You have a very adept hyperintuition and may even look at yourself with a sense of humor as quirky. At least you have been told you are idiosyncratic and a bit more passionate and sensitive about the work you do at times.

In all the examples you just reviewed, stop and think about the fact that different types of tendencies in personality styles that include behaviors, thoughts, and emotions would disappear if no reinforcement was motivating their continuity. That desire to survive as best as you can on a conscious and unconscious level that is not giving you some reward, even if unconscious, would end on a conscious or unconscious level. Responses to loss in trauma can include healthier adaptation, resilience, and effective accommodation. The therapist mobilizes and enhances these healthier responses with you, depending on your willingness to effect changes in your own life. A solution without giving in to pessimism, and cynicism that dehumanizes you in your professional career. On the other hand, enhancing your life outside of your career in your personal life and identity as the unique you—becoming the balanced healthy you is in part the tragic optimism necessary!

The task of therapist and patient, without applying simplistic labels, is to work together on accepting the limitations of the work to follow. I will be real with you in this book as a peer: this, at the heart and soul level, is what you are!

The impact and work of partial understanding and change are well worth the effort. That understanding is partial, subject to error, and is the heart of the therapy work both of you face in the mission you are both geared to accomplish right here and right now.

But even if right here and now you want to put any type of counseling on hold for the while, realizing the differences you see in your own style with your own inner sight and that of your public safety partner or family member will go a long way toward self-acceptance, which brings self-respect and compassion to the most important person and public safety officer—you!

Working through being (and in all our cases becoming) on the job is what makes it more tolerable, a better job, and service to all. Let's now move on to seeing the differences as we journey through the depths of working through together.

In working through, let's return to the basic ecology of what shapes—like a sculptor—what behaviors and ideas become so important in your day-to-day work. Attention is redirected here to your command and even more importantly, your unit.

Your Unit as the Ecological Center That Shapes Your Identity Survival Modes

Your unit is a center that in part shapes your own identity as a unit member and skills. However, in turn, your own developing identity and specialized skills shape your unit as well. Your internal journey of how you internally witness your own actions, thoughts, and emotions in the field of your own eco-ethological niche of your unit is crucial to how you evaluate and think of your actions. It is in a union of the ecological niche where you as an officer learn the culture of the community you begin to identify with as an officer. Identity modes, as we learned earlier, include why your tendency to select certain special solutions to problems in your own special way is key toward self-awareness: looking at it another way, when you are baffled as to why a certain behavior, idea, and tendency is so appealing or distasteful to you, and to another officer the opposite effect occurs, this is critical to self-awareness. Your personality style is shaped in part by the ecology you work in. The shaping of your personality is also drawn from survival demands you encounter on the job—these same influences can stifle and limit your ability for off-duty adaptation. Your own desire for adaptation to living in the civilian world can become blurry as your adaptation became rooted in ethological demands within your public safety eco-niche. However, survival is not only on an ethological dimension, but is nested in the existential struggles we all experience as individuals and members of a unit.

The goal is finding out your own unconscious existential needs within your own unique personality style, which at times although not apparent, emerges as conflicts. These conflicts are hidden within an even unconscious existential dimension. Together, if you work with a therapist as a facilitator using an eco-ethological existential analytic attitude together, you will discover self-awareness. Your own hidden existential core often is teased out of the center of the quantum psychic moment of your experience of complex trauma.

We psychologists and psychiatrists call it the "aha" experience, or the moment of truth. I call this frame internal witnessing when you select a component of complex trauma as the most impactful crater in your wound of losses. Losses are at the very foundation of the healing process, including self-awareness of hidden resilience (Rudofossi, 2007).

Internal witnessing is your ability to learn, your "owned" courage and resilience to other experiences you have of trauma. It is a means in which you can learn to soothe yourself in the knowledge you have done your own best and been courageous in your own moment of challenge.

I need you to listen to what I am about to say very carefully: when you express in your own voice what is meaningful to you within the specific trauma event you experienced, stop and pause. Let go and focus on the ecology of what comes to mind in your own experience that is so impactful. Quantum psychic moments of trauma impact your thinking, feeling, and believing with a force that caves in your sense of time. The time of the trauma becomes frozen in the ecological space surrounding that event. Please listen to what I just said, once again: that force of terrorism violated your personal space with violence at a force so great that the event surrounds and freezes the space it happened in. Along with the space, time is frozen and kept secure with the symbols that surround it and keep it in place. That is the psychological space you now occupy, and is what brings back anytime those symbols unique to the trauma. You may even be brought back and again to what you perceive is a trap, a prison, a twilight zone, and it truly is that at some level of perception. It is within an eco-ethological existential analysis that you learn how the surrounding ecological space affords meaning with a numbness and frozen feeling: the feeling as if you are trapped in your own psychological prison. Your own unique style of resilience and courage to adapt in a healthier way is forged with energy and momentum regained with your own inner sight.

Internal witnessing begins with your own understanding and relearning the ideals and values that made you a public safety officer in the first place. That first place within the space of your own time of being sworn in as a public safety officer is powerful—against the force of trauma. Motivation and creative energy lie as a spark within the chest/breast of every public safety officer. A spark that with the right resources will enflame your soul with passion to work through and reignite your own strengths. Strength used in transcending your own losses in trauma, terrorism, and burnout as a public safety officer.

Overview of Understanding the Eco-Ethological Existential Analytic Attitude

Your initial goal is to understand your losses occur within an ecological niche. That ecology is not just a passive niche, but a niche influencing you and of which you influence. The force of survival and its driving forces of adaptation and maladaptation are part of this ecology.

Ecological niches include another dimension that is more than just surroundings with biological substance. Ecological niches are also subject to your sense of meaning, values, and ideals. In other words, a mythology you create in interpreting what happens, happened, and may happen in that context in which you not only work in, but also live in. Live in because you must rely on being the best you can be in surviving and overcoming challenges. Those challenges include threats to your existential survival as a humane being with compassion, empathy, and intention in the direction you choose. *This distinction is what sets you apart from a mercenary or terrorist who is an automatic self-detonating fanatic. You are an officer with passion and reason in a balance that is uniquely within your center of choice and responsibility.*

In overcoming your challenges some ideals, values, and meaning shift. These shifts complicate matters in what I have called and we looked at earlier as identity mode shifts. Your task here is you keeping in mind that trauma you have experienced can be reexamined, reinterpreted, and redirected. Your own ability to recognize your choices in interpreting the trauma(s) experienced brings to the urban and concrete jungle of war zones too stabilized peaceful zones—a sensibility and compassion. That sensibility and compassion for your own work and identity modes are likely to have never been felt before.

Your view of your own resilience is key to healing. Your leap of faith in meaningful suffering is where unavoidable losses do not lead to despair. Rather, your faith helps you bridge tragic loss with powerful resolve. Self-change in place of the quicksand of guilt buried in losses left unmourned is delivered in embracing your hope, courage, strength, and faith hidden in those losses.

What those losses meant to you and mean to you now is crucial as an individual officer.

Internally witnessing and embracing all these components of the impact of trauma and healing are tools that work together. They are as important to healing as bacitracin is in cleaning an open wound. Your duty belt toward survival existentially on domestic or foreign fronts is aided by mourning. Mourning your own "tragic past" and "present losses" that have been denied in your own unit, your own department/agency, and perhaps even culture at large. As suggested, it is your own task to work on identifying your resilience and meaningful choices you have taken. Choices you have taken with your own inner strength, including the promise of your future. The language of experiences you may choose to attend to with intention as an officer-patient may open doors. The doors that lead to the often neglected ecological and ethological context of your own losses hold open windows.

Communication Works in Three Directions in the Eco-Ethological Existential Analysis

The three directions are with you as a participant with your therapist, who is also a participant and observer. Communication is also your openness to tolerate your own unique experiences of losses in trauma with honest disclosure and motivation to work through them. The flow of your joint communication with your therapist is the final direction where the losses are retold in a manner that is made existentially sensible, together.

Therapist's Attitude: Engaging Your Partner in Working through Complex Trauma

Joint communication is critical, and in asking questions you find the right answers. One such question is: How can you choose the right therapist? Another question is: What are you looking for in your own therapist in working through trauma and losses experienced? I suggest many otherwise effective techniques fail to reach public safety officers such as yourself because you require motivation in the face of human cruelty and evil.

Terrorism (Domestic or International) Is Not Diplomacy by Other Means—It Is an Act of Evil and Cruelty That Should Never Be Whitewashed Away in Platitudes

You as an officer-patient, no less than a person defending his or her right to survive terrorism, should not be labeled as being too aggressive. Using your power to stop terrorists' force while being human and living humanly at the highest existential dimension is a legitimate use of your authority.

Your Highest Existential Dimension Is Your Own Unique Courage to Serve

My theory and therapy of complex trauma as a cop doc boldly asserts blaming the victim makes one a co-conspirator with the perpetrators: when police, public safety, and military forces (domestic or foreign) fight terrorists—whether homegrown serial killers, violent gangs, Hamas, or the Taliban—the courage to call terrorists evil is not antipsychological—it is honest.

Speaking honestly, evil is beyond doubt a unique and tragic choice of some humans to act violently and murder without conscience: terrorists use excuses so that their victim somehow deserves to be destroyed. They project their own murderous hatred on the victims and blame them. As George Orwell said, "Political language is designed to make lies sound truthful and murder respectable and to give an appearance of solidity to pure wind" (Orwell, 2005, p. 62). What implication for meaning does trauma, death, and brutality hold in this general context where the Holocaust is denied, and in fact terrorists claim their political goals legitimize murder? How can you not interpret these acts of legitimizing terrorism as "pure wind" released from a growing mound of manure as a seasoned officer and returning veteran dealing with radical

Islamic fascism in Iraq, Afghanistan, or Pakistan? Pure wind against your own courageous fight to uphold the very society you are protecting and serving.

Your therapist must understand this basic premise of trauma and grief therapy with police and public safety folks without you needing to educate him or her about how tough it is to just be the "walking wounded." A therapist who desires to gain your confidence and motivation needs to speak honestly, without apology, and start by calling evil, frankly, "evil"! If he or she cannot, then you may have him or her seek the exit door. Why am I suggesting that you adapt this stance as a public safety officer?

First, it is consistency. I have informed clinical mental health profession- als of the same advice if they desire the privilege of working with you. Second, is if clinicians cannot call sweeping evil and madness what it is, how can they possibly understand your own losses in living and working in a place where human life and values of human decency are being rapidly washed away? When human beings have been reduced to the rubble of mean-hearted cru- elty where "might makes right," is it really a big difference whether it is an individual murderer or murderous cells? Indeed, they are never less or more than what they are, that is, murderer(s).

That said, let's move on to finding a competent public safety mental health professional. A number of skills and beliefs you can place on your radar screen follow.

Competent Public Safety Mental Health Professional Attitudes

1. She can tolerate and listen to the violence of trauma directed at you as an officer-patient.
2. He will not tell you to leave your firearm with the secretary. He will not ask you why are you wearing that revolver on your hip—pro- vided you have told him, for example, you are a firefighter marshal, a special agent, a police officer, a corrections officer, or a courier public safety security specialist.
3. She will not tell you that's enough of the gore and blood. She will not follow up with, "Okay, now let's get to the real business of ther- apy, not your profession." She will tolerate the intensity of your pain and losses.
4. He can understand and relate to you as an individual person who values your identity and history regardless of other factors as a pub- lic safety officer.

5. She will know it is not you who caused or causes death, brutality, and trauma. She will not suggest to you that you are a latent authoritarian or control freak. She will not give you the line that you are the exception to the rule. That rule includes a belief that police, firefighters, EMTs, and other public safety officers are (fill in the blank) _____, that is, stereotypes that do not work with public safety officers as individuals. (She who labels you this way cannot see you for who you are, that is, the individual, what makes you who you are with all your issues, problems, strengths, and unique and hidden gifts. This seems commonsense, but sensibility may not be all that common.)

   For example, as one seasoned detective informed me, a therapist asked her, "Why don't you choose another line of work?" Another asked within the first 15 minutes of the first meeting, "Do you get the connection between your core aggression and people responding with rage when you pull over someone simply because they went through a stop sign?" My suggestion is if this happens to you, do not try to repair your therapist—take immediate action. *Your suggested action is to politely check out and find a competent public safety therapist.*

6. Actively engage your own listening and intuitive skills to ensure your therapist's responses to your own losses are delivered with a compassionate understanding of what you have endured in the battlefield.

7. Use your ability to size up a person and sense if you feel comfortable to work together in bridging an alliance and rapport with him to work through your own complex trauma. (If not, do not pass go—let go! Find another competent public safety therapist.)

We are now ready to enter the approach developed to work through complex trauma that is geared toward you as a public safety officer. As you actively listen to Sergeant Z's trauma, you may gain understanding to rehearse how to work in achieving healing through your own losses.

The Eco-Ethological Stance toward Public Safety Complex PTSD

Ecological and ethological insight offers awareness of the dynamics of why and how trauma has influenced the shaping of your own thoughts, behaviors, feelings, and meaningfulness for life and living. I suggest that in understanding the impact losses in complex trauma have on you, an immediate gain is made. That gain is your partial freedom from self-denigration, the fear of being labeled crazy, weak, and experiencing overwhelming guilt and anxiety.

Your task here is to achieve understanding the ecological and ethological demands trauma forced on you. The most hidden demand is your need to survive. That sounds simple enough but is not. Understanding your original adaptation to trauma in different contexts demands survival skills and modifications that make superb evolutionary sense. How can understanding your behavior is shaped by demands on your own survival in an ecological niche influence your own minimization of losses that impact on you? Even if you learn how survival demands shape your denial of losses, how can this understanding help you stop labeling yourself as crazy, weak, or feeling so much guilt or anxiety?

Well, let's stop and pause for a moment again. You may ask yourself, "am I acting in ways that I would never imagine I could perform?" Putting behaviors, thoughts, and values that spiral out of control may be shaped by an ecoloical niche you must survive in. A catch-22 of sorts you have become stuck in that pits your own needs to survive against your entire value system and your own personal desires for life and living. Is it not possible that you are trying to adapt your thinking to an ecology that can never fully be controlled, rational, or even responsive to meeting your own needs? Are you weak or responsible for a system that is under siege?

Perhaps your own actions to preserve life and liberty within the limitations of your own human strengths and weaknesses are all you or others may ask of you?

Energy that you used to turn in overly harsh self-judgment is now energy that you can use for your own personal change. Personal change once the inner sights of your own responsibility to yourself and the choices you can always make, including your own attitude, emerge triumphant!

How is that challenge I am suggesting to you successfully achieved?

A realization you can now embrace is that your pulse of grief is mourned in your good time. There is no deadline to make here. *The line drawn in the sand of time that says you must mourn your losses in a certain timeframe is better buried in the stillness of myths. Myths not to live by, but that are ineffective illusions at best, and toxic delusions at worst.*

It is this fact of self-care and patience with yourself that will help you own your unique losses and begin your own healing process.

Eco-ethological existential analysis is a fundamental therapy and is based on a theory that you are being educated in. By that affirmation, I mean it stands as a foundation in which you as a participant are responsible for exploring together with your therapist. This does not exclude the fact that there are many other established approaches outside of my own that increase your own meaningful insight. For example, you may have gone to a therapist who practices logotherapy, rational emotive behavior therapy/cognitive behavioral therapy, psychodynamic/psychoanalytic psychotherapy, Eye Movement Desensitization Response (EMDR), and configurational analysis, among others. Using one or more of the above approaches or using the eco-ethological existential analytic approach as a sole trauma and grief therapy remains your own choice. A note to beaware of is that any therapist or EAP professional that blocks either directly or implicitly any type of psychotherapy, for example, EMDR, logotherapy, or Rational Emotive Behavior Therapy (REBT), is one you likely want to leave go of. You are next going to be led through the step-by-step method illustrated with case examples of participants for your understanding of how an eco-ethological existential analysis is processed.

Understanding an Eco-Ethological Existential Analytic Approach to Police Complex PTSD

Your approach is achieved in part by moving through five phases that will enable you to begin working through the losses you have experienced. This process cannot be sped up; it can only be pursued within the context of your own individual experiences and style.

With that said, you are offered the eco-ethological approach that will help you discover meaningfulness in your own life. You are challenged to sustaining meaning in your own life. Whether that meaning is taken from your own spiritual, religious, existential, and philosophical beliefs. In place of these beliefs, more often than not, substitutes that may be unusually toxic and destructive in your life include alcohol, gambling, volatile risk taking, and impulsive, short-term hedonism. In many cases, losses that are not acknowledged, as we will see, may lead to that feeling of surreal numbness. Overwhelming feelings of guilt and despair over what you had once viewed as brutal events have become tolerable, but only at a high personal cost. Much of your own extraordinary courage goes unnoticed as your own traumatic losses pile up into heaps, left unmourned. That is one part of the picture.

Your counterposition is another. You bring into the sphere of "working through" your passion, and confidence in your goal of healing. In turn, you will be led to valuing your own reservoirs of unrealized resilience, courage, and commitment. Meaning may be rediscovered through joint exploration to identify novel means of mourning losses, while accepting the reality of trauma, and harvesting your own hidden resilience. Reservoirs of optimism are framed in one's unheralded courage, commitment, and resilience only if it is brought to awareness to counter the despair of what has been called the existential vacuum first coined by the famous Dr. Frankl (1978, 2000).

Existential despair is the giving up of hope, courage, and faith to the individual's surrender to addiction, depression, and aggression. Frankl said suffering pain, loss, guilt, and death without any meaning is the existential vacuum.

Cop Doc Antoon Leenaars, a leading authority on suicide and its prevention among police and public safety in Canada, coined the eclipsing of choices toward hope and optimism in life "psychache" (Shneidman, 1993; Leenaars, 2004, 2010).

Transcending the losses, overcoming the existential vacuum, and confronting the psychache you are liable to as a public safety officer is a core of your own healing.

Meaningful growth is not just mourning losses you have left in the underbelly of the armor you wear day by day: growth lies in the field of opportunity where you choose to frame your own optimism by learning what is left hidden and buried in losses unmourned. That is, healthy tragic optimism where courage, faith, passion, and creative bravery are buried in cynicism is now used as fertile ground for growth. Growth that is priceless and of unmatched value in life—your unique style in service to others and yourself!

I want you to participate in going with your own hunches and feel, observe, and listen to your own responses to the cases you review. Think and use your own newly gained appreciation to shape changes in your thoughts, feelings, and meaning from past and present events with an eye toward your own future.

Keeping these few suggestions and qualifications in mind, let's move on to the five tasks of the eco-ethological existential analysis. On the surface it will appear that the five tasks have some parallels to other trauma interventions: it will become obvious as you explore the case example in this chapter that my approach is as unique as you are. The goal is focus and simplicity in making the complex trauma and losses understandable to you.

The Five Steps of the Eco-Ethological Existential Analytic Method

Step 1: Express Your Most Distressing Traumatic Event as You Define It in Your Own Words

There is no right or wrong way of presenting your thoughts, feelings, and the actions you took or did not take in your own words. This is doubly important when getting out of your own head and putting down in words what both you and another person may understand about your history. When writing about a traumatic event or a complicated loss, this task is more difficult than you may at first think. Why is it difficult, or any more troublesome than writing a routine patrol, emergency medical report, fire incident, or military action against say a terror cell or unit? Because here I am asking you to write about your actions as you perceived those actions at the time of the event.

Ideas, feelings, and emotions as you feel them in the here and now are equally important. Honesty, meaning letting your own thoughts flow as they emerge. As they emerge without censoring them is not only challenging, it is crucial! In doing this you will see the evidence for yourself as your thoughts (beliefs) about the event begin to change and your interpretations become more intense and passionate. You will see that your idea of being helpless to the scourge of addiction, depression, aggression, sexing out your conflicts, zoning/numbing out, and anxiety bouts begins to make sense. That sensibility, among other feelings, ideas, and behaviors, that results from heaping losses and trauma no human being was made to experience, but you have in reality. You will learn to be more gentle on yourself and others as you begin to realize aspects of your actions, deeds, and even thoughts that are significant and remarkable. What was often viewed with grave error as routine is simply not routine, but unusually sensible from an eco-ethologic perspective!

Getting back to basics now that you have a broader picture in place as to why you may choose to express your experiences of trauma and loss, the question remains: How do you actually begin to do just that? While to some public safety officers this may appear obvious, you simply write it down. But that is not the only way to account for your experiences. Another way you may express your losses and trauma is by speaking it into a recording device of some kind. In that way you will have in a well-hidden place your own oral history, and if you'd like to, you can share your record with another person at a later time. Whether you write, record in a tape, or just have another person you trust, including your peer support officer/clinician, listen, you have expressed your own story.

The ecological context will also lead you to understand the ethological shapes of your need for survival within that niche you survive in. In the retelling of your history you will gradually possess the very history needed to jointly re-create the antidote. That antidote is in rough outline in this chapter. Remember, there is no right or wrong way of expressing your own experience, save communicating what comes to your mind.

Another way you may achieve this task is by sketching what you can. Remember, you do not have to formally be an artist but just willing to experiment. That experiment and mastery in drawing out your own pain, suffering, and death you witnessed is empowering. That pain, suffering, and death may have been in a rescue, recovery operation, or analysis of a crime scene post-event. You can then write down notes as they emerge to fix as sticky post notes or on the sketches to express reflections on your creative work.

You may also choose to create a copy of your own file of papers that capture the job, if you have copies. For example, a closed case with complaint reports and follow-up reports of a homicide/suicide, fire investigation write-up, bombing and crime scene, or aided reports of a person down, such as a "space case." Now you can attach separately from the flip side of the page a brief write-up on the investigation, action, inaction, or closure of the case. Of course, from a practical level, do not do this if the case is active and under investigation at present.

I suggest that while you may be able to express yourself well in writing or feel comfortable to work this out with your therapist directly, you also may not be so comfortable. Choices are up to you as how you will actually do this first task. To repeat, there is no one better way than respecting your own individual differences as a key in your effort to work through trauma. You may also have some other creative way of presenting your own experience of trauma not listed in this step.

You note details at this time. For example, you may observe what your expectations were when you experienced the trauma. Do you remember the cues or clues you were responding to in your own ecological niche at the time of the event? How intense were you relying on those cues in helping you prepare for what was to follow? For example, were you doing a canvass of a building or a transport escort of a dignitary. Were you then ambushed/injured in the line of duty by what appeared to be out of the blue? Were you expecting a certain outcome and everything fell through hard and fast without any room for preparation during an aided case as an EMT, or when trying to intubate a patient as an ER RN or ER MD? Were you fighting a fire with your battalion when the stairs caved in unexpectedly? Did another crew run into a stairwell when a backdraft wiped out three members of your brother and sister fire-fighters/EMTs? Your expectations based on earlier similar prior experiences you had, if at all, within your unit are important notes to remember, that is, the expectations you believed were expected of you. Also, what were the identity modes and positioning you can identify at the time of the event? The cues you may have felt intuitively are important as well. For example, did you have an intuition that what happened was to be played out before the event? The physical layout in detail as you are likely to recount is not incidental. It has meaning in how and what you remember and in what manner you express what you remember. These details are windows into the castle of your own trauma history.

The task you have is to write, speak, draw, or express the accounts you have as suggested above. This is so you can see the "quantum psychic moment" of the trauma and the impact it had on your ideas, feelings, emotions, beliefs, and meaning to you. You're looking at your own experience of trauma and loss and formulating a hypothesis at this point. A hypothesis is your understanding as to how and why complex losses in trauma have affected your thoughts, feelings and emotions, and behaviors.

The way you are affected may include withdrawing, immersing yourself in more events that are similar, or acting indifferently. How your thoughts, feelings, and behaviors are shaped by complex trauma is as much your responsibility to understand as that of the therapist, peer support officer, spouse, or other significant family member or friend in your own life.

Step 2: Take the Experience of Trauma and Losses You Expressed and Shift Your Focus to the Details You Remember about That Event

Details here mean the ecological and ethological influences as you recall them. Pay particular attention to the aspects of life, death, numbing out, anger/rage, anxiety/fear, relief/aches, and discomfort.

By focus I mean that you attempt to express your emotions (the adrenalin rush, rage, fear). Emotions are the biologic aspects of your behavioral and thinking processes to survive during the event. They are not totally involuntary and not totally voluntary, meaning that emotions you experience are in the context of not only survival as in life and death struggles, and not only fight or flight. Ethological emotion includes numbing out, zoning out, dissociating, and other automatic impulse-driven shifts. For example, you may feel the need to jump in and take down a bad guy. At this step expressing each aspect of the traumatic event as it emerges and as experienced is critical. Your focus also includes your expressing feelings such as relief, anxiety, sadness, deep loss, and blues. Remember that it is not only one feeling or emotion, as you will see in many case examples to follow. More often than not, conflicting emotions, feelings, and thoughts emerge simultaneously. *Some emotions and behavioral impulses you feel so strongly will collide with other emotions and feelings you are almost compelled to act on at the same time in opposite directions.* An example is emotions you experienced at the time of the event may have focused on tactical defense postures against life-threatening dangers while you simultaneously attempted connecting with care and compassion with the same victim, emotionally disturbed person, and with more rarity, the perpetrator. Your existential experience, for example, over the ethological rage triggered by the perpetrator and sadness denied, unexpressed, or numbed out over the loss of life, including that of the perpetrator, is deeply impactful. Certainly some expectations weighed within the ethological force never came to reality, some did come to reality, and some did not come to reality as you trained for, rehearsed for, or left to chance. Again, keep in mind that the emotions, feelings, and thoughts you have, if not examined, will simply not go away on their own. By your taking the time and effort to express your own history now as best you can, you are laying the foundation for later work. That foundation will include growth that may not seem possible at present.

Shifting into feelings you now own as your losses, into what you feel in the here and now, is allowed expression. That expression allows your feelings such as anxiety, anger, grief, and depression an outlet that could not be let out during the event. Actions you may not have ideally taken. Actions you have taken that are different from what you desired or expected you would do are expressed in this step. Some other important questions you will answer in this step are

> What are your current ideas about the trauma event after working on description?
> What are the geographical aspects that jump out at you?
> What are your sensory experiences?

Sensory experiences mean what reminds you of the event when you smell certain places, things, or even objects of clothing, or physical things.

Ask yourself the following questions:

Does your memory have a photographic quality to it?

Does that photographic quality return again and again in your visual memories?

Do the smells trigger a nauseating and body experience of feeling like vomiting?

Do you feel drawn to that event as if it is occurring again and feel a need to reexperience it?

What noises do you hear that may startle you at any given time?

What tastes remain in your mouth, for example, after the first fire, or after the shoot-out?

How and what do you do to counter that taste, feeling, smell, and hearing sense that haunt you?

Do you notice certain phrases or choices of words you realize you are saying repeatedly?

Are you aware of similarities to the original event of trauma as new, similar situations trigger your avoidance, or need to seek the senses you first experienced, or numb out right after by destructive behaviors?

Do you hear certain words you repeat in specific contexts as if you are lost, confused, disoriented, agitated, overly excited, or withdrawn?

If so, I would like you to explore the answers with your therapist or peer support officer. If you can, explore the answers to the above questions with yourself as to how you feel about what you selected as most distressing and see a pattern that is important toward the best understanding of yourself.

How you now feel about aspects or items you expressed in recounting your own experience of trauma is very important. That is, items (physical or geographically located items) that may symbolize important aspects of what you experienced as loss.

What meaning do these selected items have within your own ecological niche and your status, such as rank, and the assigned mission(s) you do?

Let's make this understanding more concrete for you. For example:

Are you a patrol officer in a high drug interdiction zone, or are you patrolling a very well off area of the city?

Are you a lieutenant commander in charge of sex crime investigations, or are you in charge of administrative quality assurance in headquarters?

Are you a fire marshal doing suspicious investigations of insurance fraud claims, or are you a private investigator doing fine art theft cases?

Are you an ER nurse manager dealing with intensive care burn patients, or are you part of a mobile team responding to citywide calls of distress?

Are you a medic responding to serious calls with emergency management teams, or are you a medic working in a private hospital with private cash-paying patients?

As you can see, these differences in status, command, and specialty as public safety officers are very important. This importance is not only in sharing your own duties and responsibilities. The importance is in understanding your own thoughts, emotions, and feelings within the survival demands that ethologically or biologically lead in part to your own behaviors. That importance extends to your own expectations, ideals, and stresses you may accept or challenge about your own experiences. What you are paying attention to in cueing in on items that are meaningful to you? Express what these items are and what, if anything, these items mean to you. Are you feeling intensely about these objects without realizing why?

Items can be highly significant to your own losses. These objects may be played with, or kept as private reminders, without any apparent context you can see at first. Objects may be inanimate but have much meaning in what they represent to you. Objects are links at times between the ecological niche and symbolic meaning you have invested in it, the survival connection between both and the myths you live by in connection with it all. Objects may be representative of what your expectations prior to the traumatic event meant for you in your own private meaning. In the method I have been illustrating, objects you remember or feel sad, anxious, or angry about are never accidental and certainly not nonsense. It is nonsense to simplistically downgrade the meaning to you simply because it is as complex initially as the trauma you have experienced.

Step 3: You Can Now Express Your Thoughts and Feelings about Your Actions, Deeds, and Your Own Quality and Intensity of Emotion and Experience as Meaningful to You in Your Unique Interpretation

The quality of how you feel about the trauma and your own intensity of that event may include your focus on a specific aspect most meaningful to you.

It is important to realize that in identifying your own emotions after experiencing a trauma event that fear, disgust, hate, and loathing may not be easily expressed. These emotions are not just expressions of feelings but are biologically motivated in the ecological niche of your survival. From the public safety ecology nested in that culture you have been taught to block these emotions from expression.

Happiness, sexual feelings, and even pleasure may also be hard for you to express and own as your personal experience. However, your immediate reaction to block these emotions from expression is far from meaning they may never be expressed.

For example, initially you may be able to express the intensity of your feelings through a response on a test given at your counselor's office, or through a formal department questionnaire, perhaps in your physician's office.

A more specific look at your blocking the identifying of your own emotions that may be very hard for you to express at first, for example, is rage: instead of reporting you are "very angry" you may check off "slightly angry" when responding to being personally assaulted. Yes, you may have written a brief narrative expressing the injustices of the criminal justice system. Perhaps you had even taken the time to express that being kicked at and punched in the face was no more than a mild inconvenience: "par for the course" as a cop, EMT, or firefighter. But when you are in with a peer support officer and cop counselor you finally get to express how angry you really are about being assaulted. You may fear legal repercussions of letting it hang out. But letting it hang out in a safe haven is what you need. That same approach may expand the use of identification of feelings that come out when you do get to see how certain thoughts become associated with denied feelings, including the sense of loss and fear of expressing that very loss you experienced so painfully.

You can use what you hear and gain in feedback with another peer, or better yet, with a counselor when you listen for and acknowledge contradictory feelings when you express your own losses. Contradictions can be enlightening, and may help you understand the context in which they emerge through the series of sessions you have with your therapist.

An in-depth example to consider is the case of Officer-Patient Q. Officer Q is an assertive, dynamic, and highly intelligent professional with a great deal of charisma that eclipsed when she suffered the sudden double loss of her partner in crime stopping and husband—best friend and lover all in one sweep of history. Space froze in the moment of time's unpredictable handle; she was told simply, "Bad stuff happens—deal with your losses, and move on."

Officer Q's husband was a public safety officer who died on duty of a medical condition. Officer Q expressed fear of her emotional distress being visible to others. She felt weak and like she was really losing it over what she considered an exaggerated response to his death over 2 years ago. In reality, she was suffering from complicated grief, not abnormal but complex traumatic loss. The eco-ethological approach helped her understand and make some sense of what appeared to be nonsensible. Officer Q had become concerned over her symptoms of grieving. One of those symptoms she was distressed about was considering herself as possibly going "crazy" after experiencing spontaneous crying bouts.

At times Officer Q expressed that "without a clue, and for no apparent reason, I just don't know why—I break down and cry." She and I observed with more attention the situations when she would break down and cry. I established a connection with Officer Q, and that connection was through her own unique observation, "When I saw loose rounds [bullets] I had placed on the night table, I would just erupt in tears."

A comment is due here. Typically, not only an officer but a therapist may fail to look at such behavior or discount it as not important. However, in the eco-ethological method this behavior is critical in understanding losses. For example, the arrangement of the rounds afforded her some solace in keeping her connection with her dead husband. Officer Q's husband was a public safety officer. The rounds being placed as they were led to some significant insight under a very difficult process of our discovery. That discovery was achieved by her letting me in on a crucial fact that her bond with her husband was kept alive through the way the rounds were laid out on the table. The rounds, though inanimate, left her with an animate sense of illusion. It helped her feel his presence in the transition forged in the space between them through life and death. Her surviving his death was a guilt that delayed grief in this space they had created during life. The rounds, unfired and kept in space laid out by her, remained under her control, transcending death itself, sort of cheating death's angel with a wink along with her beloved deceased husband. After the death of her loved one, loose rounds became a link to what was now missing day in and day out. The loose rounds became a representation as a shared ritual through its apparent and hidden meaning.

If you note with me that meaning is at the core of opening up the existential analysis. In part, as in this case, it helped cop doc and public safety officer understand her unique meaning hidden in the ritual that had become so special in her heart of hearts. That hidden ritual she defended against understanding also kept Officer Q stuck in losses: left unwept for and unacknowledged. Separate loose rounds, left in one way or another, symbolizing different meanings, were kept alive. She would leave the rounds on the table she arranged as different fantasies. Keeping his shirt, she smelled and held so as not to close his casket forever as she released streams of tears in letting go of some of her hidden pain and shame. Expressing her own associations, as difficult as it was, with what came to her mind, Officer Q was able to associate the loose rounds as aspects of her sexual life and creative shared dreams. Dreams disrupted by the sudden death of her husband: his abandonment. In our work this ritual that may have been left alone in most other approaches led to other insights. A shared dream of Officer Q becoming an assistant district attorney, and he a squad supervisor. That dream they shared would lead to retirement and a change in her career. The roles both she and he lived, shared, and labored for, and the shared meaning of these rituals were now gone.

That loss on multiple levels remained hidden from Officer Q, as did other losses. Once she understood these losses, while unique, were not abnormal, "freaky," or for no apparent reason, she opened very painful losses toward expression. It put into focus a process of acceptable emotional grieving within a context that made sense to Officer Q. Prior to our work Officer Q had been unable to express the pain and anguish over her husband's on-duty death due to a medical condition. She had been unable to express her anger at his death, as she eventually was able to express as his betrayal by abandoning her through dying. Officer Q believed—as would many therapists—that she was avoiding grief with intention. Her avoidance may have been wrongly interpreted as evident by incorrectly interpreting her crying over rounds left a certain way on a table that was disrupted by death as meaningless distractions. This evidence was used to suggest her losing a grip on reality. This is no light matter, as peers and administration responded as they did initially about her being "a basket case." Nothing was farther from the truth.

But, worse without our work she may have remained stuck in her false belief about her sanity being lost in her "abnormal response to her husband's death." In our example, Officer Q and I gradually rediscovered the symbolic meaning of the loose rounds that were placed in a specific location as a hidden symbol of her husband's perpetual presence. A habit of leaving these loose rounds in a certain way on the desk made sense as Officer Q gave me the privilege of sharing her own internal view of her world. That internal map was nested in her ecological niche she made with her peer husband and as his playful lover. Our exploration revealed what was significant in her own ecological niche that she and her husband uniquely forged as law enforcement officers. The placing of rounds and how they were arranged had eco-ethologic and ultimately strong existential meaning. Rounds were symbols of their bond on and off duty. In their shared symbolism the rounds were so much more than a few rounds.

Officer Q broke into tears as she began to express how much she missed him. Once she realized the symbolic meaning of the loose rounds, his death was made real in a very special sense. What seemed for no apparent reason to be causing Officer Q so much pain was given all the reason in her own voice, in her world, and within her own unique meaning in the context of her eco-logic and ethologic niche. Of course I am only offering you a snippet of the work Officer Q achieved as she was allowed to mourn other losses associated with his death.

Remember, the ecological-ethological approach helps you own your own insight into behaviors, emotions, feelings, thoughts, and your deepest hidden beliefs as you gradually feel open enough to express them with less toxic self-blame and toxic self-guilt. As in Officer Q's case, she achieved in this second step a beginning. That beginning is her desire to hide her loss and what she considered as abnormal as being sensible in her own ecological niche, evolution, and sensibility. That meaningfulness became clearer over time until she finally was able to rid herself of many negative self-thoughts and toxic beliefs she was made aware of in her own inner sight.

Officer Q achieved through this opportunity existential and psychological insight into an otherwise unapparent expression of emotion. Without ever asking the question "Why?" she may have suffered silently and without grasping the meaningful relation to the current ecology and ethology of her own losses. Not knowing then leads into the existential issues that you might find yourself stuck in as you read more cases or even Officer Q's. As Officer Q put it, "I break down and cry." But now, in your view, as with Officer Q, her crying has a very different meaning. That very different meaning in my approach as a cop doc and yours as a public safety officer includes her being able to allow herself the freedom in the safety of an eco-ethological existential analysis to let out of mourning a complex grief that remained hidden from her and all others.

As with Officer Q, the next gain is living the first three steps in a manner in which you can return two steps, and go forward again, as you are able to in your own pace—achieve the first three steps. Let's move in gradually within your own timing. In rarer cases you can reach the fourth step as a process of self-gain. Your gain will emerge from the pits of complex trauma and grief—to the summit of inner sight—within your own scope of vision.

Step 4: Meaningfully Separate Your Adaptive Thoughts, Beliefs, and Behaviors That You Have Learned from the Maladaptive Thoughts, Beliefs, Behaviors, and Destructive Interpretations to Motivate and Navigate in the Here and Now of Life and Living as a Public Safety Officer and Individual

This fourth step will give you coordinates to map your own future motivation. It will also help you tread gently in looking backwards and forward.

In that separation between adaptive and maladaptive, the context of what really works for you in the field of survival and motivation becomes important without labeling. Labeling includes self-labeling, where you may have defined yourself as ugly, bad, or toxic. Labeling has been relearned as being shaped by forces that you were unaware of. Realization of those forces that were unconscious is useful in your attempt at your present adaptation. An adaptation now that makes a superb sensible foundation of behaviors in a forest of drives. Drives for survival and control where the sensible paths of evolution and life supplied energy. Your knowledge and action now is altered by attention to transcending by placing these influences within the ultimate meaning and unconscious, which is your own individual potential as an officer and being humane.

It is here that your knowledge of your own unit and status at the time of traumatic loss helps shed light on the context of your own personal identity and development. The validation of your experience in the field actions you have achieved is key to nourishing your own motivation. Rank, status, and assignment are very important in understanding yourself in the eco-ethological perspective where analysis of existential meaning emerges.

The reason your status as an officer, your own prior expectations, and investment in your desires to perform in a typical way that works for you are again nested in the branch of how you are present as the unique individual you are today. For example, some officers' styles suggest remaining status quo is the best fit; for other styles, moving up the ranks of ambition is their best fit; for others, specializing in a certain assignment and skill may be their tendency. It is not only a personal preference, it is one's ethological shaping in their own ecological and cultural niche. Perhaps your "calling" places your perfectionistic tendencies toward achieving both public safety excellence and some other professional calling. Valuing as part of this process where you are right here and now is healthy. So with that in mind, you can proceed with cautious and healthy optimism.

Adaptation must happen after the impact of what we defined earlier as a quantum psychic moment; some aspects of that adaptation, as we have seen, turn south and come around north. Understanding your own psychological influences that impacted on your own adaptation at the time of the quantum psychic moment the violence of trauma impacted, consider some factors. Some such factors are the importance of whether you were off duty or on duty. Did the event follow with immediate disciplinary charges pending against you, or being threatened against you, directly or indirectly? Was there a divorce or breakup with a significant other after the event, or perhaps imminently preceding the event? Was your boss supportive? If you are a boss, were the chief administrators supportive or were they leaving you holding the bag? These considerations ought to be kept in mind as these ongoing situational influences are unique to you and they are indeed part of the stress and strain you are affected by.

Your responsibility in the unit, the selected demands of the public safety event and what expectations were set for your role, and the consequent losses you experience are, in part, products of your rank, duty at the time of the event, and the way you perceived your role to unfold during that event and what you perceive really happened (see Rudofossi, 2007).

Peer support officers, cop counselors, and cop docs no doubt will offer much understanding here. The mental health professional that cares enough to understand not only the culture you live and work in but you as an individual officer. For example, if you return to Chapter 1, remember the patrol officer who is assigned as the sergeant's driver who now becomes responsible for gathering information by interviewing potential witnesses door to door. That gathering of information can involve dealing with guilt displaced onto the officer by some of the homeless friends of the young man who died of an overdose. The impact of grief related firsthand by witnesses to a crime as they are questioned now becomes an existential burden. The sergeant challenges his driver's competence to get a simple notification and interview process done. The officer who felt he could have done more at the scene absorbs his guilt on top of the displaced guilt from the folks he interviewed. Now the officer is feeling overwhelmed and never gets to speak of it to avoid more perceived berating.

Another example is the officer on community patrol who may be responsible for an entire small community and has intimate knowledge and responsibility for ensuring the safety of seniors. In one case, a community patrol officer recounted the rape of a senior citizen at a community center. That officer was particularly fond of that senior, whom he knew quite well. While anger was acceptable, a feeling of loss was not; the feeling remained unspoken, and more so unidentified.

In yet another case, a duty captain responded to an off-duty police lieutenant who was driving while intoxicated (the first time in her life). The captain had neither choice nor discretion in processing her arrest. The police lieutenant sustained minor injuries and began to express suicidal ideations. The lieutenant now discloses that she and the captain were academy recruits together and had remained friends. To complicate matters, the lieutenant is up for promotion and is married to a detective in the captain's command. The captain had to face incredible stress over his command decision.

In the few examples I barely outlined, you can see how and why rank and the eco-ethological influences are so important. Your expressing and placing the specifics makes all the difference. Your understanding of your own ecological and ethological dimensions of status, rank, and expectations and prior adaptation within your own unit and what it afforded you is key in centering your experience for your own healing.

Relating your understanding to your peer support officer, and if possible your public safety therapist, may be the thread that binds. Bear in mind, that thread will become ropes over sessions where trust and commitment foster insight and trust in yourself and the therapist you work with during the upheaval, as Cop Doc Al Benner would suggest. That is the upheaval grief work invariably entails. This step in the eco-ethological approach is to help you see that your own adaptive and even less than adaptive behaviors were and are sensible human responses in the context of your status as an officer and unit detail at the time of the event. This is an important distinction you need to be aware of. When you not only know this but believe the impact of these influences on and in your life, you will truly embrace your own remarkable sensibility. Another key point is important here, and again you are best served with an example. For instance, a lieutenant detective sharing a current trauma with me may be more impacted by an original trauma that occurred in her first year as a detective.

In our work she learned part of her motivation to do such a difficult job was overcoming her losses experienced as a police officer on patrol where she witnessed a horrific crime against a child. She hid that loss and the fact it was experienced so early on the job. Her hardened exterior was presented in order to give her the illusion of conquering all fear on the job. Together she and I observed many hidden strengths, including resilience and abilities—not despite trauma experienced but as adaptation to trauma.

What usually will come out as if it was born in the darkest of moments is what has been largely hidden by your own existential blind spot. That spot, as I call it, consists of behaviors you may never have even considered as a helpful contribution. By discovering what has eluded you, you encounter your own strength as it evolves. What is so meaningful is you are not inventing what is not there but discovering what is already there—in the frame of your own experiences of trauma. What is potential for positive growth is provoked to growth.

Step 5: You're Able to Retell Your Own Eco-Ethological Reconstruction of Thoughts and Behavior Related to Your Own Experience of Trauma

From the perspective you have gained you are able to take your new wisdom and apply it in the center of meaning for your life and living both on and off duty in a healthier path chosen. Here is the final step in the process, and some may not be able to fully achieve it for one reason or another. But achieving it in part is doable. Your involvement and expanding conscious awareness of your own personal resilience, your own adaptation and courage at varying levels, will transcend the ecological and ethological and biological shadows of guilt, shame, and perfectionist standards.

Moving beyond your own ability to function while still experiencing dissociative states of mind, by using your own existential insight gained in my method, you will be able to embrace your own unique meaning that emerges. Meaning that emerges within the specific framework of understanding of "how" and "why" your own eco-ethological niche developed as defenses against your own traumatic losses. I am not inoculating you against trauma but helping you build the natural immunity you possess deep within the core of your center essence. Your choice, responsibility, and active involvement in living become core targets of this step. It is the basis for your own empowerment as a humane officer and person. You are able to more clearly look at yourself in the actions you do in deed—not dream of doing in this world. Grounding in yourself is made tangible in a new mode of adaptations as you see your vision of your identity as a public service officer in the lenses of reality. As will become apparent, part of this fifth step is achieved in part within the beginning of your work and comes full circle at completion of trauma and grief therapy. One focus of this grounding is your new skills in identifying maladaptive strategies that deter you from reaching new areas of social support, changing self-doubting beliefs and harsh evaluations of your behaviors to using newly gained inner sight toward reinvestment in recapturing meaning in your own life.

Trauma is no longer a series of hidden and shameful episodes. Trauma is no longer answered by more intense choir practices and war stories that suck you in deeper to drink more, outsex yourself, and escape in other endeavors of addiction, aggression, or depression. No more turning away from your soulfulness. Your soul and your ethological self are united in the ties that merge your humanity as the captain of your ship, when you say, "There go I but for the grace of God," you mean with the gift of God's grace. God's grace for who and what you realize you were, are, and will be within your imperfect and noble self.

The war stories remain in your own narrative but are placed with the dignity and respect "it" undergoes in becoming an event in your own life experience that helped shape you as an officer. Your own life history becomes experiences with power that transcend and remodel your own path to return to healthy adaptation. For most officer-patients in my experience, this achievement necessitates the retelling of the loss in their own words, and within their own sense of meaning. At this point, while shame, humiliation, and guilt may exist on some level, thus far it is hopefully much easier to see the other side: you are not as guilty, not as much in denial, not as self-judging as you were when you first picked up this guide.

"It" has been the harsh and painful losses that you have experienced. "It" is a defense that helps make your own experience of trauma distant from "its" toxic impact on you. What I have done with you thus far is actively involve you as an individual officer in daring to use your psychological imagination. You have proactively rehearsed your own effective assertiveness in response to the types of trauma encountered in the center of your life. That is where your soul sits as a public safety officer.

The acceptance of the fact you have experienced losses and trauma changes the earlier need for denial and minimizing the pain and anguish of these earlier losses unheard, unidentified, and unacknowledged.

This fifth step involves the following specific objectives being achieved by you:

1. Disabusing yourself by not owning up to guilt, shame, and avoidance of your own identity as a public safety officer.
2. Developing a sense of meaningfulness in the choices you have made in becoming and remaining or having been a public safety officer. If you realize that the profession is not for you any longer, then your objective is accepting your choice and acting on it. If you are retired or disabled, then your objective is to redeem what is of value and use to you as a point of strength and continuity in living and growing regardless of age or condition.
3. Choosing to assert your own ability to choose, and not dissociate from the moments so important in your own trauma history.
4. Accessing your own strengths, not self-accusations, from the experiences of gains and losses you have worked through more than likely with a cop counselor or cop doc. Realizing your choice and responsibility to stay with a healthy attitude encompasses resistance in the face of conformity, terrorism attempts to deter your strength and integrity, and reduced meaningfulness in your own professional achievements, actions, and interpretations of each trauma.
5. Choice and responsibility empower your own reaching out for social support, including nontoxic relationships, expression of your own

inner existential voice, and achieving the acceptance of limitations as strength.

6. Resolving phrenophobia (fear of going crazy) by replacing your thoughts, behaviors, and feelings that were not adaptive with your gained sensibility that eco-ethological influences in your unit and detail provoked losses being denied. The key is mobilizing your own higher tolerance of all the shocks you have absorbed with kindness that begins with your own compassion toward yourself.

7. Active involvement begins with your own rewriting, sketching, or expressing into some record the outcome in the here and now as challenging, active, and evolving.

An achievement of this phase is evident when you are able to retire, change assignment, or stay on in your unit based on the meaningfulness you have found through personal choice.

Trauma and loss worked through is never without pain and suffering, and perhaps never fully worked through. Meaningfulness may entail your choice to realize "the job" as your own "calling," absent excessive guilt, suffering, and pain of unmourned losses. *It may be said that your being able to reach out and give voice to your own pain and suffering to another significant person may be the critical factor between your own mental health and illness, between immunity and susceptibility to serious illness, and between life and your choice to end it.* If you are able to conquer your hidden losses in your own trauma history, then you are more likely to be that significant person in a peer's life as well. That is, a fellow peer's life on the ledge with the edge you are now acquiring: you at this fifth step are most likely to be that significant person. For you, it is an awesome responsibility, choice, and ultimate reward in nontangible and existential growth. That point of reaching out and helping yourself extend out of the five tasks of the eco-ethological existential analysis. You cannot afford to be passive in your approach toward working through PPS-complex PTSD, for it is anything but quiet when it strikes so hard with force! Complex trauma breaks silence with violence and noise. The goal is not to avoid rage, violence, and noise, but to commit to dealing with it. Committing to deal with the ongoing chaotic and at times violent and unfair aspects of the profession, without succumbing to emotional and mental burnout, helplessness by withdrawal, mental hopelessness, and spiritual despair.

Now that you have reviewed the general steps of the eco-ethological method, let's move on and see how it is done in reality. The best style of teaching how and why you can put my therapy to your best use is with a case example.

Prelude to an Eco-Ethological Existential Analysis of PPS-Complex PTSD: Final Hours of Suicide by Public Safety Officer—Deadly Contagion Contained: The Trial

> The lesson I had to learn in three years spent in Auschwitz was the awareness that life has a meaning to be fulfilled … uncounted examples of heroism bear witness to the uniquely human potential to find and fulfill meaning … we must never forget that we may also find meaning in life when confronted with a hopeless situation when facing fate that cannot be changed. For what then counts and matters is to bear witness to the unique human potential at its best which is to transform a tragedy into a personal triumph. (Frankl, 1978, p. 37)

Taking heed of Dr. Frankl's exquisite humanity is encouraging. It may be helpful to resonate on digging your heels into the depth of losses that left their tread marks in the path of your life. Like you and me, he was a public safety professional who guarded his fellows even when placed in the bowels of the worst war zone imaginable without ever losing his humanity.

How you go about enhancing meaning within the poverty of death, violence, deception, betrayal, and cruelty aimed at you is not sugar coated in the case to follow, and in fact without apology lets you and those closest to you understand the stress and strain of this good officer-patient's experience. Reflecting as you are actively listening and discovering the quantum psychic moment of Sergeant Z's trauma's violent assault is hard as the hell it is placed in. Yet you will see how finding motivation lies in the existential meaning of his pain and suffering. In part, achieving motivation means understanding why Sergeant Z's guilt, rage, depression, and anxiety are not only overwhelming, but a self-imposed prison. A trap of denying the trauma and the mortality faced as hellish—not his to own—and not constructed by his actions or inactions.

Gaining a different perspective of the same situation, Sergeant Z is persecuted when he shifts from step 4 and step 5. You can pause and listen with me as Sergeant Z's redemption of strength, resilience, and courage through inner sight and internal witnessing is achieved in our dialogue. Passion and reason are wed in grieving his losses. Losses accumulated over time and left ungrieved are toxic to healthful living: losses are poison in trauma. Left untouched, they remain preserved in timeless tumors in the walls of any officer-patient's life. Gaining insight for Sergeant Z is facilitated via healing the toxic loss by understanding what Lieutenant Colonel Grossman discovered and called the virus and epidemic of killing (Grossman, 2004). The virus of killers some may decry as being politically incorrect, but I am not into the politics, but the correct truth. That truth is as real as the concrete you pound on your beat. Professor Grossman opens that concrete in his theory and approach to helping public safety officers regain ground lost in his works on killing and what it does to officers who are put in the line of fire. Lieutenant Colonel Grossman asserts three very important gifts to give warriors by family to communities: "understanding, affirmation, and support" (Grossman, 2004, p. 333). He explains these three gifts are not the usual meaning, but listening and affirming each warrior's piece of wisdom brought back from the field of experience. In his indisputable wisdom, Professor David Grossman educates the warrior within all five styles to be presented. That truth extends to all warriors in public safety, including EMTs, firefighters, and of course police and soldiers (Grossman, 2004, p. 361):

> You have the mission, the authority, and the responsibility to stand up and say, "Friend, neighbor, brother, sister and buddy … are you looking for a safe place?" And they will say, "Yeah." So you tell them. "Then get behind me, because I am a cop—because I'm a soldier because I'm a warrior—and this is as far as the bastards are going!" We are all called to protect our civilization in this dark hour. It's about preserving and protecting. It's about serving and sacrificing. It's about a dirty, desperate, thankless job, every day of your life, to the utmost of your ability, because you know that if no one did that job our civilization would be doomed.

Human freedom to choose another path that ought not to be passed over is critical. In this case Sergeant Z's choice in gaining the antidote against self-destruction and suicide is a conscious choice. His conscious choice comes from his willingness to confront his tragic virus with courage to work though "it." He will mourn unspoken losses in tragic circumstances beyond his control. I will share with you what I have shared with therapists for years as the following truth: "In my clinical judgment, putting a timeframe on the process of grieving is like putting a timeframe on any fluid process: It is illusory at best, a shared delusion at worst" (Rudofossi, 2007).

By returning to the pain, suffering, and human anguish of trauma, there is much unacknowledged in the police culture, specific unit and community, that highlights what was done right with courage, responsibility, compassion, and humanity by the officer in the face of very harsh losses. That task I will illustrate in segments of the dialogue of Sergeant Z and me: that task incorporating the five stages of discovering the courage, humanity, compassion, and resilience of Sergeant Z to mourn his tragic losses of suicide by cop. At the same time, I facilitate motivating his own creativity in the real personal level of encounter and responsibility in the eco-ethological existential analysis. The task of therapist and officer-patient becomes visible through identifying and validating the courage, resilience, and ultimate humanity of Sergeant Z's experience with his own trauma. What may be most helpful in an age of terrorism is your taking from Sergeant Z's example an existential attitude to grab meaning that humanizes him, the therapist—Doc Dan, and the therapy process.

Sergeant Z's hidden resilience now exposed provokes his own redemption of courage and meaning from past trauma in a self-initiated rediscovery of renewed commitment to his mission. Sergeant Z's courage enhances an ability to tolerate tragedy and maintain his own sacred optimism: not in spite of terrorism, but in the face of terrorism inspiring more strength and resolute commitment. Sudden and unpredictable trauma is a dimension of terrorism trauma experience that puts you as an officer into a position similar to that of brother and sister military combat veterans, which may include you as well. You are forced, as the case of Sergeant Z will illustrate, to make quantum judgments in response to quantum moments of unfolding traumatic events. These judgments carry consequences that radically alter the landscape laid out by your prior expectations afforded in your ecological niche and ethological influences.

For example, your attention to the event itself is well worthwhile to connect to. Also, Sergeant Z's shifts in identity modes and adaptive functional dissociation that follow the event unfolding. Anticipations of how things unfold will shift into intense complex emotional and mental memories. The boundaries of each dimension of trauma are not cut with a razor's exactitude. In fact, unheard and disenfranchised loss emerges. The motivation of redemption is sweetest in the bitter dessert of losses left uneaten, and tasted at the end of a marathon well run as by this ESU sergeant. It is in the peril of your work and the heroism you achieve that you can hear the echoes in your own internal witnessing. You validate the meaning of your work. An example of a Spartan razor pithily applied as a historic moment of timeless value appeals to officers nowadays.

You do not have to be Greek to appreciate the genius of power standing up to the force of brutal might makes right. Taking solace when the public safety leader exemplar Leonidas of Sparta challenged by terrorist tyrant Xerxes World Domination by force stood his ground is a shining example of losing the battle, does not mean losing the victory. Leonidas is a great example for the age of terrorism, fascism, and human bondage. The tragic loss of King Leonidas's life and the Spartans that "stood their ground in the Battle of Thermopylae" is a legend that all Public Safety Officers can gain a sense of heroism and solace from: The Persian or curfently Iranian geography is telling as the terrorist tyrant named Xerxes who had attempted World Domination. Although death martyred the Spartans lost in battle, their death marked a turning point in mobilizing a divided Greece into a formidable power to resist Tyranny. When King Leonidas was threatened with terror monger Xerxes' threat, "The sky will be blotted out with the stream of spears and arrows," he did not bow to him as a gesture of subservience, hence ensuring Greece would be second-class citizen slaves. Within miles of the light of the historic marathon (no pun intended), Leonidas, with equanimity of a true leader, stood his ground as a public servant, not a demigod along with his 300 special agents/soldiers: "If your spears will blot out the sky, then we will fight in the shade." He estimated in action and in deed that the shades and shadows of terrorism, loss, and trauma are temporary. Unlike Xerxes, who held to hiding behind his mercenary troops and having them slain like sheep, Leonidas stood with his ideals, heroism, and rational belief and understanding: losing battles are never in vain, when they are fought in public trust and security. If you can, savor the dessert of your own courage and resilience at the end of battles that seem lost, victory is at hand: it is not in the battle lost but in the ultimate victory that healing is achieved.

I use this analogy for public safety officers because as you know, many battles can be lost when a bomb explodes in a suicidal and cowardice action against innocents. In fact, not every job is won with success in the field of battle. But, the courage, resilience, responsibility, and will to meaning in the moment of trial fought with dignity hold ultimate meaning. That ultimate meaning for you, as a public safety officer, can never be stripped from you. It could never be stripped from Leonidas and the heroic soldiers who gave their lives on the domestic or foreign battlefield. This is a voice most civilian psychologists are fearful of espousing up front.

Not I, nor you, in taking our cue from the noble public safety and service doctor Dr. Frankl (1978) as he quotes Einstein, who summed it up well: "The man who regards his life as meaningless is not merely unhappy but hardly fit for life" (Einstein, 1954). Professor Dr. Frankl elaborates on Einstein's point:

> This is not only a matter of success and happiness but also of survival in the terminology of modern psychology. The will to meaning has survival value. This was the lesson I had to learn in three years spent in Auschwitz and Dachau ... it is true that if there was anything to uphold man in such an extreme situation as Auschwitz it was the awareness that life has a meaning to be fulfilled ... *uncounted examples of such heroism and martyrdom bear witness to the uniquely human potential to find and fulfill meaning even in extremis* ... we must never forget that we may also find meaning in life when confronted with a hopeless situation as its helpless victim when facing fate that cannot be changed. For what then counts and matters is to bear witness to the unique human potential at its best which is to transform a tragedy into a personal triumph, to turn one's predicament into a human achievement. (Frankl, 1978, p. 37)

No hell is as vivid as war with its dehumanization, death, and losses that heap upon a never-ending pyre—no matter how legitimate—the combatants never remain unscathed. Except for war fought in one's own backyard as additional shock, disgust, guilt, anxiety, and depressive effect that you as a public safety officer deal with.

Clarifying That Truth with You Is Healing for It Validates Your Own Truth and Experience

What is timeless is military and cop docs unapologetically confirming the "terror" in the terrorists' attempt toward terrorizing and agitating you as a public safety/soldier-officer. An internalized witnessing of your own resilience and redemption may motivate you toward a self-initiated renewed commitment to public service. That renewed commitment can enhance your own ability to tolerate tragedy and maintain your own sacred optimism, triggering other areas of growth and healing.

In assisting your process of my method I will present a real case example of trauma and loss to guide your odyssey. The inherent challenge in this process may be a motivation for you, as it was for me. Each session becomes an evolving renewal of moments of opportunity for encounter. I learned from each and every officer I have worked with. It is my hope you will share that wisdom with me. Wisdom gained is a gift each officer gave me. One qualification, again, is the identity of Sergeant Z as presented here has been intentionally altered. That altering is to give a composite case example that is not identifiable. The content of the trauma is not altered, nor is the clinical material presented. The case follows.

Case of Sergeant Z: PPS-Complex PTSD: Experimental Traumatic Neurosis

Biography

Sergeant Z is a German American first rescue responder. His background includes being a veteran of the Iraqi war with two tours under his Sam Browne belt. His wife is an emergency room physician. Although an intimation of *folie a deux* related to a craving for excitement and hyperstimulation may exist, intimacy and love in this couple have sustained the relationship. Another dynamic here is that both are highly committed, no-nonsense professionals who share a goal of work as the *sine qua non* of meaning in their life. Both have a hyperfocus public safety personality style (see Chapters 3 and 4 for details on the five personality styles) toward achieving their common goals.

Predictably each also helps the other when there is a crisis.

Sergeant Z expressed one problem he had in his mid-forties. He believed "life is too unpredictable after so much crap on the street, I cannot commit to marriage."

This fear of commitment was related to intense worry about loss. That fear of loss through the repeated violence and death he has witnessed has kept him from expressing the love he felt for his girlfriend. He delays marriage for fear of loss. In place of this love, he will allow expression of overprotectiveness for those he considers significant in his life: his longtime girlfriend, family, friends, and the officers in his elite unit. He also exhibits a hypervigilance (Gilmartin, 2002). Hypervigilance is a way of thinking. Dr. Gilmartin coined this way of thinking as police-oriented cognitive schemas of constant guardedness against non-police-oriented culture and perceived outsiders.

Sergeant Z's major complaint was sleep disturbance. He wrote down his dreams in a log as per our plan of understanding, identifying, and changing his behavioral patterns. He reported "feeling bored, unappreciated, and upset about a lot of things on the job. Recently 'it's' caught up with me."

Paradoxically, Sergeant Z focuses on doing a great job: "I will be one of the best bosses in the department. I loved being a cop. I will be a great boss as a sergeant, too." Over 7 years Sergeant Z responded to an estimated 300 emergency situations involving officers and civilians in dire straits. This is likely an underestimation. He presented me with multiple letters indicating risk taking and bravery. He achieved being the great boss and cop he dreamt of. But Sergeant Z was not foolhardy, and did not run in without caution.

Sergeant Z is a highly trained and skillful police supervisor. Sergeant Z expressed "loving the mean streets and the excitement from rescue calls." Yet, Sergeant Z has expressed exasperation with these same jobs. He "demands perfection or nothing"; this highlights his hyperfocused style of public service. More evidence is his need to present many achievements and commendations and training certifications that required a great deal of savvy and increasing sophistication. He remained highly evolved and involved with officers who worked for him on and off duty. His drive and ambition were second to none in achieving his service record accolades. He collects his achievements, which lay out his sense of security. They advance him to his goal to be the top-of-the-line commander. While I was taking his trauma history he described what one of the worst events was in his career.

Sergeant Z's Account of His Most Traumatic Event

About seven years ago I responded to an emotionally disturbed person (EDP) job in the confines of Precinct X. Upon arrival we were informed by the sectors on the scene that there was an EDP in the house, possibly with a gun. The male involved was at the window shouting at the police. I made contact with him by telling him my name was Sergeant Z and I that was here to help him. I do not remember exactly how he responded. But I do remember it was with viciousness. For about 130 minutes I tried to talk with this male and establish some kind of rapport and mutual trust. No matter what I said, he would not respond directly to me. He responded only with hate toward the police, including me.

Because the radio run said he was armed, I came in armed with an automatic weapon. This made him even madder. I tried to explain why I was armed. He didn't want to hear it. No matter how I tried, and I really tried to give him a pitch, it failed. He would not have a dialogue with me. During my attempts to talk with him he would leave the window, come back a short time later, and then back and forth. After waiting a while, we tried to talk again, but he would get that look of hate, then pain in his face, then hate again.

The last time he came back with a gun in his hand. Before I could say anything, I saw his face and eyes filled with extreme hate. He looked straight at me and said, "Let my blood be on your hands." He then put the gun into his mouth, and blew his brains out.

I remembered a short time later he was lying on the floor, with his brain matter all over. I wondered why he did this. I did not understand. I still don't understand. I remember we were all getting our gear together. We were then called to another EDP job. I didn't have any time to talk about this. I do remember going home and wondering all night, "Why did he do this?" I had a lot of dreams. Why couldn't I reach him? I didn't ever discuss this, until now with you. This was one of the worst things that happened to me in my life. I just feel this can never go away.

A Trial and Error Reconstruction of PPS-Complex PTSD with Sergeant Z and Dr. Dan

Sergeant Z's emotional and mental memories have an almost photographic visual intensity in absorbing what he has seen. Sergeant Z has a more than average awareness of emotional expression in others (i.e., hate, viciousness, and fear). His brilliant perceptual skill is likely biological, and as we know, ethologically learned and shaped by survival demands in his repeated experiences within his ecological niche as an ESU sergeant.

Sergeant Z's behaviors and thinking strategies are influenced by evolutionary demands. As with evolutionary demands, they are constantly demanding responses to changes that are sudden and intense.

Sergeant Z's survival depends on being correctly attuned to severely disturbed folk as well as violent offenders at times. Sergeant Z's experience with the situation demands calm responses under the most intense threats of fire. Ecology shifts in trauma are mini-episodes one must respond to and track in the field of operations. In that field of operations volatile and uncertain risks emerge without warning. Anticipating the unknown as possible hypotheses without knowing how long the timeframe for any shift in behavior and emotion will last is expected of public safety officers. Learning that what is unexpected is probable as a strategy goes against human/animal nature. Many studies highlight what uncertainty and violence do to animal as well as human health (Rudofossi, 1997, 2007, 2009). It is doubly so for the ESU officers who respond to these situations when other officers are endangered. In this trauma together with Sergeant Z the eco-ethological survival demands opposing and violent collision of forces simultaneously. In other words, identity modes demanding contradictory goals shift rapidly in response to the unfolding event. A suicidal/homicidal officer Sergeant Z had no real control over. Sergeant Z tried to use every imaginable skill and tactic in the field that shifts with amazing speed and complexity. The complex losses in the experiences of Sergeant Z's identity modes shifting end with the suicide by cop of the emotionally disturbed person.

Sergeant Z's experience of complex trauma fit the core dimensions of what I have discovered and call police experimental traumatic neurosis. For a thorough study and support of this syndrome, see Pavlov (1941) and Rudofossi (1997, 2007, 2009). For now I will briefly review the dimensions that include intense contradictory and simultaneously experienced situational demands. Demands on the officer forced in uncontrollable life and death struggles for self- and civilian preservation and protection. Apprehension and takedown operations that shift in quantum moments of trauma when rescue operations with the offending party pop up intensely. Finally, the last component is the potential of extreme violence or nonviolent resolution potential throughout the event.

To these extreme ecological demands, the infusion of motivation for Sergeant Z's own survival is framed in rapidly changing identity mode conflicts Sergeant Z is forced to make as commander (see Chapter 1 for identity modes defined). Let us review why this is so. In Sergeant Z's own words, his existential conflict over what he is forced to suppress his own personal need for survival by trying to assist this severely life threatening emotionally disturbed man from harming himself and others. The almost intolerable pressure is holding back his own need to fight or retreat from the ongoing hostage situation.

Experimental traumatic neurosis is usually done by forcing an animal to choose between desired outcomes that are mutually exclusive and in fact oppositional. One may be food and the other danger involved in obtaining that food item. It is done when an animal needs to survive by eating and at the same time must overcome a puzzle or a fear condition it will have to face for the food. Coupled with that are conflicting perceptual cues that can trigger confusion and contradictory feedback. Contradictory tensions for approach and withdrawal create psychological terror and stress in the animal otherwise healthy and alert.

In looking at the experience of Sergeant Z, why do I choose to help him fix a label on the syndrome as police experimental traumatic neurosis?

Well, first in reviewing the situation, remember no matter how well trained Sergeant Z is, he has no control over any of the shifts the EDP is forcing him to respond to. Attention is intense, and on high alert. Secondly, Sergeant Z has many different identity modes he must yield to in split seconds. Sergeant Z is forced to become active, attempt to engage a person who has defied attempts to reach him while taunting the expert police sergeant's honest attempts to connect. Sergeant Z holds back natural and simultaneous internal responses that are cornerstones to this syndrome. For example, Sergeant Z is unsure of what will come next for 130 minutes. Yes, 130 minutes! The stimulation is as intense as it gets.

Think about having a psychotic man threatening to kill himself and possibly Sergeant Z, and anyone who gets in the way of his maddening objective. This person is attempting to place responsibility for his destined outcome on Sergeant Z through unrelenting and extremely unstable behavior. The situation is about as complex as it gets. The possibilities make it a situation that demands the utmost drain on Sergeant Z's emotional and strategic intelligence. The strain on Sergeant Z's ability to inhibit his own ethological arousal toward self-defense while simultaneously increasing provocation toward confrontation is exhausting. Sergeant Z's emotional and strategic memory absorbs these toxic threats and their chemical releases in his brain. Toxic tracks that lead to imprinted memories in complex ways that will remain for life. His memory imprints become part of his ethological memory triggered in similar ecological niches when cues trigger intense trauma. These cues are highly likely to generalize to other traumatic situations he is likely to experience. It is critical that Sergeant Z understands the impact of this hidden event almost buried until in his work with me we uncovered "it." Complex wounds defy simplistic Band-Aids.

Let's review at more length and depth the intensity survival demands on him as it thrusts him into an event beyond his control. Yet, pause and think of how media pressure, internal affairs, and external legal review contribute to superhuman expectations. Sergeant Z's performance will match his desire to achieve superhuman standards of success. Coupling cultural and ecological demands on Sergeant Z's compulsion toward perfection is the exquisite storm of experimental traumatic neurosis. What is stimulated with certainty is a collision between two opposing forces—inhibiting his desire to take down a dangerous potential killer and excitation in talking him down and rescuing the EDP from his psychotic rage. In other words, acting out of rescue wishes and fueled by his hyperfocused personality style, his own natural tendency for self-survival is turned on and off by the EDP's actions. Suicide is an enormous series of losses when put to existential analysis. Here is a reconstruction of that collision into four parts as follows:

1. The inhibition by Sergeant Z of ultimate physical force is achieved in the ecology of the pursuit/attack and confrontation identity mode consistently provoked by the armed, barricaded EDP.
2. The EDP is exhibiting "a cry for help" as Sergeant Z perceives it. I believe Sergeant Z's read is almost certainly correct. Sergeant Z picks up the EDP's cry for help through his unstable actions of hate and extreme rage gestures and behaviors. The words spoken by the barricaded EDP betray a possibility that communication may be bridged. Sergeant Z is attuned to his own voice of conscience to effect his custodial and rescue identity mode.
3. The oppositional conflicts above are both physiological and psychological. These conflicts are complicated by yet another collision in the existential realm. That conflict revolves around whether or not confrontation might result in potentially lethal identity mode stimulation. Great personal risk to Sergeant Z and his troops is increased when he inhibited action. This inhibition is risked in his attempts to persuade the EDP to drop his firearms through hostage negotiation techniques. Taser or not is the question that may make all the difference in the world for Sergeant Z and his troops—to be or not to be taken down themselves. The moment of choice is between life and death. For Sergeant Z, and his troops who are forced into this dance between the threshold of life and death that pivots on the eye of a mentally ill violent man.
4. The existential dimension of Sergeant Z's compassion and mercy toward this disturbed person is intense. His investment in success as a rescuer and his investment in his own idealistic goals are enhanced by the highest standards he has learned as a member and executive commander of his elite unit. That is his adaptation within his

eco-ethological niche. While the result of his intention could very well end in his own loss of life, he is not naïve nor ignorant of this choice. He chooses to place himself in the front line and to resolve this event at great personal risk and uncertainty. What remains unclear is how much neurological, ethological, emotional, mental, behavioral, and spiritual aftershocks will reverberate in the trauma syndrome that follows Sergeant Z's traumatic experience.

What we are certain of at this point are Sergeant Z's supervisory responsibilities. Second, his conflicting and opposing demands within identity modes. Third is the conflict that is laid out in an unknown timeframe. Fourth is the chaotic demands that emerge within an extremely unstable field of operations where a barricaded and psychotic person is armed, suicidal, and homicidal.

To begin to appreciate Sergeant Z's experience, an individual perspective enhances understanding his own thoughts and reflections as the humane being he is.

First, he seeks out excitement and the challenge of his detail. However, unlike the officer who may be addicted to trauma, as with the hyperexcited personality officer, he appears to get little pleasure in being the first in the line of fire. Rather, we will now touch on his style of being hyperfocused on achieving ideals of perfection in his work. Specifically in this trauma, Sergeant Z's hyperfocus includes success as he sees it unroll through his maps. Maps of what he sees unfold in the layered multiple events in his complex trauma experiences. Some conflicts involving the identity modes of pursuit, confrontation, arrest, custody, and rescue.

Elaborating on what we do know, Sergeant Z still is a sergeant and evaluates his sense of self and identity with his successes on the job. Being a boss on the job is not being a little Caesar—it is safeguarding your troop's welfare with your life. Recall this original trauma was experienced 7 years ago. Sergeant Z called this hidden event "one of the worst things to happen to me, and what I did not discuss, until now." The hyperfocus afforded by his elite unit's value of rescue and survival complements his perfectionism. His eco-ethological niche affords the specific development of PPS-complex PTSD. While the psychotic man did not succeed in getting Sergeant Z to shoot him, Sergeant Z did not get a chance to Taser him. The EDP unconsciously used a form of hooking Sergeant Z into absorbing his toxic hate, torment, and anguish from the initiation of the first event until his suicide. The suicide triggered the emotions of guilt, uncertainty, and doubt. The personality style of Sergeant Z suggests his vulnerability to absorb these toxic attempts from the EDP who fully attempts to inject Sergeant Z with his own psyche pain and existential vacuum. The EDP's suicide infuses in Sergeant Z a sense of failure that likely stems from a dominating parent who the EDP is punishing—along with a society that failed him. His recreated dramatic enactment is measured with malice and illness at Sergeant Z. That toxic hate and guilt hit their mark in Sergeant Z's heart and soul for believing he failed the ill man and his troops. Without intervention the risk for suicide may dramatically escalate in Sergeant Z.

Let's review another aspect of this trauma from Sergeant Z's experience: the different identity modes that were being triggered simultaneously in the ecology of situational demands could have unfolded at any time and in many different ways than they did. Sergeant Z was keenly aware and hyperfocused for 130 minutes.

We know Sergeant Z had no chance to debrief, moving on to the next job. A critical factor of the shock and loss after intense investment is that his experience was disenfranchised. Meaning he was never allowed full expression. This is true even where formal programs exist; sadly most officers do not use them. Seven years later his impressions have gone through many changes through a series of subsequent traumas.

Sergeant Z's extraordinary courage was not acknowledged in the least. The reality was his bravery was considered a failure by performance standards. He did not prevent the suicide. While no one put him down, no one acknowledged the magnitude of this trauma either: adding another to many losses Sergeant Z experienced. As a sergeant his existential angst motivates thoughts that provoke anger, hopelessness, guilt, and self-recriminations for what he appraises as an unsuccessful conclusion—suicide. Every time he was successful in a barricaded situation after this suicide by cop he garnered proof he failed in that moment. Gathering what others may look at as subsequent and former successes, he used them to measure against the one exception with precision. Condemning with similar and violent toxicity he absorbed by the EDP, he was debasing an incredible exceptional performance "when it really counted." The personal toll emotionally, mentally, physically, and existentially is excessive. This type of trauma is what officers deal with as chronic, overwhelming, and extreme strain in emotional shock that is inescapable.

Eco-Ethological—Existential Analytic Intervention with Sergeant Z

Let's review the anticipation and expectations in Sergeant Z's strategy. His goal was establishing a relationship and reaching this psychotic fellow emotionally. His attitude was to hold and contain him to stop a very likely deadly confrontation. Sergeant Z's investment for a successful outcome was heightened as more time in negotiation was established: the anticipation in his mind was the outcome of disarming, taking custody, and rescuing the EDP from his own violent nature. At the same time his role as a supervisor demanded personal safety perimeters for his troops and himself for containment purposes. These demands weigh heavily on his tactical apprehension and arrest identity mode. His ethological motivation was to defend himself and others with the full weight of personal survival weighing him down.

Existentially an intense desire for rescuing and connecting through his exquisite empathy is countered by the situational demands of confrontation with an armed and seriously disturbed man. Tactically, Sergeant Z assessed three possible and radically different outcomes:

1. Arrest and custodial identity mode with all the tactics in anticipation of a nonarmed struggle ensuing, including Tasering the psychotic fellow. With potential lethal effect looming over the event as well.
2. Custodial and rescue identity mode if the person surrenders to assistance (this man's injuries are undetermined).
3. The ultimate confrontation identity mode if the EDP moves into an assault mode, entailing a full-blown firearm life and death struggle. At this point release of firearm control to stop the EDP shifts into maximum use of lethal force.

These outcomes are dependent on the situational demands that unfold in relation to the EDP behavior, the ecology, and Sergeant Z's intuitive and tactical response. Each outcome demands radically different approaches in terms of safety, action, or refusing to take lethal or takedown action. In reviewing the potential outcomes, the investment and response to any outcome involve risk to life for all involved. Sergeant Z has not dehumanized the EDP, and chooses, as far as he can, desperate attempts to preserve life at extreme personal risk, to establish an encounter. He has the following identity modes simultaneously active and in extreme contradiction to each other:

Sergeant Z has activated the identity mode of strategic pursuit: Following every move, tactic, point-by-point intention that the aggressor forces on Sergeant Z as an emotional dance with unconscious and conscious awareness of hate, rage, despair, and excessive anxiety.

Sergeant Z has activated the identity mode of arrest and custody: Following every opportunity to capture this highly emotionally disturbed person without effecting harm and using the necessary force to accomplish this goal, including the Taser gun. What this entails is uncertain throughout 130 minutes.

Sergeant Z has activated the identity mode of confrontation: The moment he tried to encounter the emotionally disturbed man with a possible deadly weapon. He has anticipated whether he will, and how he will, use deadly physical force if necessary to stop him. He has also no doubt anticipated his own death if he is shot point blank.

Sergeant Z is constantly monitoring the ecological opportunity to end the barricaded situation with the least harm to all participants. He no doubt has fully activated his unconscious existential voice to creatively effect a successful outcome: idealistically conflicting with ethological demands for his troops and his own survival.

Sergeant Z has activated his rescue identity mode as the most desirable: It is the most difficult in the face of all the other contradictory and oppositional roles. He anticipates gaining an inroad to lessen the strain and stress of the emotionally psychotic person. This person thwarts each attempt with extreme rejection. Sergeant Z is painfully aware of the desire of the psychotic man to either commit suicide or attempt to kill Sergeant Z.

Factually, these identity modes are all activated, and in fact, in seconds of one another and at times even simultaneously each potential outcome is lived over again with me as if in the surreal intensity they had taken place in. Our specific understanding is clarified through the following facts as we reconstruct the trauma with Sergeant Z: Sergeant Z led the work of his unit with this EDP barricaded person who threatened suicide in an escalating ultimate confrontation through potential suicide/homicide. Hateful emotions and vicious expressions were picked up as invariants that Sergeant Z learned to pick up accurately as affordances in his ecological niche as an emergency first responder. There is communication for 130 minutes. High-ranking officers are controlling the outer scene, as yet another factor of escalation and anxiety are added over how he performed. Perimeters of safety are set, and established preparation is forged for contingencies where he is at the soul's seat of piloting negotiations of life and loss.

The Pit of Piloting a Psychotic Storm with Sergeant Z: A Hell of a Ride with No Exit Door

If you have flown on a plane that has turbulence and felt tension, please use your psychological imagination and magnify that tension a 100 times. In doing so, please do not limit thinking being on board for 130 minutes of extreme turbulence. Imagine being the captain of that plane with no known coordinates and needing to keep your staff and the passengers calm and safe. The internal perimeter is highly charged. At extreme levels of sustained attention for Sergeant Z, the emotional intensity and mental exhaustion are overwhelming. Sergeant Z's communication with his unit, his bosses (superior officers), the sounds and cues of his environment, and general communications are all in addition to his communication with the EDP. Keep in mind, action and outcome are uncertain and unknown. The extreme all-out combat situation is established tactically. Sergeant Z adapts by what we reviewed in Chapter 1 as adaptive functional dissociation due to the sustained attention the situation forces him to adapt to.

Sergeant Z is running the equivalent of an emotional marathon. The EDP's pattern of leaving the window and coming back and forth heightens stimulation for combat and inhibition of combat. Moments of uncertainty clash with peaks of combat readiness, and stopping of Sergeant Z's own fear and anger. Escalating rage by the EDP is in striking opposition to Sergeant Z's strategic counterinvestment in establishing nonviolent rescue.

Keep in mind that this suggests Sergeant Z is confident in the success of his approach. Sergeant Z is left with the print of traumatic shock and loss when the involved victim commits suicide, setting the fertile ground for delayed complicated grief within complex PTSD. With the clear understanding of how significant this trauma is, my approach is not to force change for Sergeant Z. That choice is ultimately Sergeant Z's. Our choice is first to understand the toxicity together; that alone is a success at least in part, as he no longer denies or thinks he is crazy for his memories of trauma. I structure understanding within Sergeant Z's personality style and the specific event in mind. I would be remiss if I did not end this chapter with a snippet of a beginning of the working through between myself and Sergeant Z, whom I was privileged to have worked with in the moment of time. Time ripe for intervention between both of us, and plucked while ripe enough. In the following case example (a snippet of our work) I will skip ahead to the point where he and I have worked together and where you may enter. Please understand Sergeant Z and I have already established an initial alliance. I have begun working with Sergeant Z's hyperfocus on how he perceives his failure as a sergeant when the emotionally disturbed person as described in this chapter tragically committed suicide.

Sergeant Z's self-blame is very harsh and his guilt is overwhelming—he expresses feeling he messed up. Sergeant Z also believes he will have to pay for what in his mind is moral weakness. At this juncture you are invited to view my initial clarification of his nightmare, which is a gift he presents begrudgingly to me. A gift that is one of trust in helping him open up our working through his experience of complex loss in his traumatic experiences as an important aspect of the eco-ethological existential analysis. Remember, this is a snippet to illustrate some points for your own motivation to seek the same intervention with a therapist. Perhaps you will use Sergeant Z's insight gained to improve your own into losses you experienced.

My specific task in this piece is to help Sergeant Z express loss he has experienced in the complex trauma while valuing the highly courageous, intelligent, humane person that makes up who Sergeant Z really is at his soul's core. He is made aware of this reality.

Sergeant Z: Doc Dan, I am not having any real nightmares, you know what I mean? [Sweaty and wiping brow of forehead] I mean I am just going through some weird type of stuff at night. But, I am fine. Really, I am not really seeing anything weird like images of dead people or anything weird like that. I mean, it is really nothing anyhow. You know what I mean. "It" is just one of those things. I mean stuff like seeing DOAs. Hey, how are you feeling, Doc? [This is a way of diversion I will answer and immediately redirect our attention.]

Dr. Dan: I am fine. Thanks, Z. I may be wrong, but it seems like you are having a hell of a rough time around some very intense dreams at night. Talk to me, Z. Why do you think you needed to look away and give me a whole pitch as to why you are okay and not seeing anything weird? [Sergeant Z looks away from my eyes and looking downward wipes his mouth.]

Sergeant Z: [Pausing and looking at me with his head tilted and with a slant of his eyebrow] Maybe I could have gotten the guy to drop the firearm and connect with him. It was a while ago. I never failed like that. I was worried the job would get my own throat cut, maybe even demote me. I know I let my guys down; they could have been killed. But I could have tried harder to get him to look at me. I could have gotten him to drop the piece and let me take him into custody like XX. Remember that one I told you about, Doc? [I nod a yes, staying silent, allowing Sergeant Z time to express his thoughts as they emerge.] What is happening is I guess I am paying for a kind of penance for my allowing a guy who couldn't help himself to kill himself on my tour as the boss. It is okay, Doc, as I tell you I am really not upset at all. I mean he told me I have his blood on my hands. [Silence for a few moments] I am not sleeping so well. I need to hit the gym again. I've been getting a real belly. Hey anyhow, what are you doing for New Year's?

Dr. Dan: It is hard, real hard to tell me. I imagine you are feeling guilty as if you caused this guy Henry's death. His name is Henry right? [Sergeant Z nods and turns away.] You are blaming yourself. [Stopping and looking Sergeant Z in the eyes] Sergeant Z, did you see Henry in your dreams? Is he ghosting you? [Sergeant Z, teary-eyed, face becomes flush and looking away. I gently and in a very subdued voice turn again to engage Sergeant Z.] Talk to me. I am listening with my big ears…. [Silent and intuitively feeling and sensing extreme discomfort, I respond with my own intuitive sense as a cop doc.]

Sergeant Z: I am not seeing him exactly you know, Doc; I am kind of visualizing him in the moments and feeling very weird. Look, it is really nothing and you got other patients. This is not that important. [Sergeant Z hopes I will be distracted. Yet on the other hand, Sergeant Z counts on me pursuing his grief and fear.] Is it really that important?

Dr. Dan: [Without missing a beat] I think it is and I think you really want to let me know what you are going through at night. But you may be worried I may think you are ready to be put in the psych unit. What do you say if I tell you it is not abnormal to see an image or flashback even when you are alone in the room at night. [Although I have repeatedly shared this before with Sergeant Z, I never tire of letting Sergeant Z (as is true of other public safety officers) know it is safe to share their fears and traumas with me.] I am all ears. Take a look at my big ones, I am listening Z. [I incline my ears to really listen with more attention than even usual.]

Sergeant Z: [Looking away but moving toward eye contact and moving forward to gain security and connection with a peer cop doc, he is expressing a willingness to trust and be vulnerable.] I had a really freaky dream, like he was going to take me with him. I felt I could not wake up from my nightmare. When I did I could not breathe. I awoke screaming in the night. I was awoken finally by my wife asking me if I was okay. It was humiliating. It was that I could not rid myself of his presence.

Dr. Dan: So Henry is present in more than your dreams. Does he sometimes appear in your waking vision or just in your sleep? Do you ever speak with him?

Sergeant Z: I am not crazy, Doc! I am no shrink like you. But, I do know I do not speak with him. I kind of see him at least sometimes at night right before I sleep.

Dr. Dan: I wonder if there are certain times you tend to see him and do you remember him ever telling you anything?

Sergeant Z: Do we have to do this, Doc?

Dr. Dan: We are here and I am interested in knowing what is going on so we can approach this together. Yes, if it is too painful we can stop. But, I would really like you to help me understand what is going on in your mind because that can help us figure out how to lessen some of the pain you are in.

Sergeant Z: The dream is very vivid-like. When I told you he is in my dream, he is in my room and cuts into his arms in front of me. I tell him stop. "Please, it is okay. I am here to help." He says you cannot help me! No one can. I look on in terror as he just [pausing while his breathing is labored but hardly heard and Sergeant Z's eyes avoiding mine in shame and fear] ... he does not care at all that I am there. As if I am not real, he just starts to cut into his flesh again and I see blood. It is very painful and he looks at me and lets me know he is dead and says, "Why did you kill me?" I know I am dreaming but I am not able to wake up. Doc, I wake up and will not allow myself to go to back to sleep. It is hell for me, and I do not know what to do. I can't take a pill for it. I know you think it will help, but no, I can't anyhow; it is just a dream. But anyhow ...

Dr. Dan: [Staying on track and not being distracted] Do you think you still killed Henry, or has our review of the incredible catch-22 and the tension between your own survival and your need to act as a boss by backing up your guys, maintaining a perimeter, needing to be armed yourself and ready to shoot to stop him, gain custody, deal with his being extremely dangerous, mentally ill, and psychotic, and at the same time you were trying to let him know in real time and real space you cared and tried your very best to save this man's life and protect your troops as well, seem like superhuman expectations? Let me ask you, who cared and protected Sergeant Z, and allowed him some slack? It is amazing that you hold a standard for yourself that is superhuman. Do you not see that standard for yourself as impossible to fulfill when we witness the incredible bravery and wisdom you actually fulfilled in the field? Let me ask you one more question, Sergeant Z: Who willed himself to die, Sergeant Z, you or him?

Sergeant Z: I don't know! You know, Doc, please help me get rid of this nightmare and stop seeing this guy.

Dr. Dan: Tell me, Sergeant Z, please help me out here. Will you?

Sergeant Z: How, Doc?

Dr. Dan: By answering the question I just asked you. That very hard question, which is very hard to imagine. That question is: Unless you were the Angel Gabriel, how could you have possibly saved Henry when he had planned to do himself in and commit suicide by cop? Yet before you answer now, let me ask you another question, okay? [Sergeant Z nods yes.] Do you remember the breakdown of what we both learned together as to your courage and will to believe in being compassionate to a person who could not even be compassionate to himself, as was tragically true with Henry? What does that compassion in you really mean as to who you really are? Who you really are at your core, Sergeant Z? Tell me, can you answer that question as well?

Sergeant Z: [Silence and sadness in tone of voice, teary-eyed, no expression for a few minutes, a deep sigh. All these wonderful gifts of his trust and allowance for his own humanity is about to let go in a healthy release.] It is very disturbing, like the feeling I told you about. I remember now. I did not cause his death. I could not prevent him from doing it. I tried hard, real hard Doc. I did care enough—I guess like you said—I put myself in the front line like any boss would, including you, Doc. You were a sergeant, weren't you?

Dr. Dan: I do not know if I would have the superb courage you did when called on to be as courageous as you were in the moment you were called to act as you did. Is it possible you could allow yourself to revisit your incredible ability to stay with it when most people would run the other way? Can you accept your only being human, even if at times you take on superman human tasks that only by the grace of God can they turn out as we may wish? It appears you did the best you could and in this case it is tragic Henry died. Agreed! But you did not cause it! In fact, my dear Sergeant Z, you gave him every opportunity to retreat and surrender. Z, he already wrote his own script to die and attempt to put his own tragic choice and his own responsibility on your hands. Is it possible to pray for him in your own way and forgive yourself for an act you had tried to help avert and had no responsibility for?

Sergeant Z: I know you are right, Doc! It is hard to believe after this I truly could not have done better for him. I mean, I know what you are saying is true, that Henry wanted to kill himself. But why out of the blue?

Dr. Dan: [I will explore that question with Sergeant Z later in the session; in the here and now I will not miss my opportunity to further make solid his gains. Gains he made in realizing even if only in part, and for now, he is not a failure and he in fact has the power of compassion and courage.] Sergeant Z, it is clearly because Henry had not sought help, or perhaps could not have accepted help without hospitalization. It is easier in the short term to avoid the painful work of being vulnerable to therapy, and I do not have the wisdom as to why he needed to kill himself then. I do know he was very ill, and as we discussed Henry tried to drag you into his hell by lying to you and blaming you for his own death. It is very clear to me, and I wonder if you ever pause as we discussed and reflect real deeply as to how you care so much. Even after 7 years your compassion is so intense you are worried you may not have superseded the angels. For God himself gave free will, and it appears you did everything humanly possible to save this tragic man's own self-destructive choice. What do you think, Sergeant Z? [This intervention helped Sergeant Z realize through an existential level of experience his innocence.

He realized his self-blame at its toxic trap was set with superhuman standards many officers with a hyperfocus hold with bulldog
tenacity when events that are out of any human control fail, as they
invariably will in fact at times by that superhuman standard.]

In the work you just witnessed, Sergeant Z, with my assistance, relearned
valuing his pain and the loss underlying his experience of loss. I supported
a powerful reflection for him to use for internal witnessing of his existential
nightmare. A nightmare he did not cause. Beyond that nightmare a window
opened in our shared commitment to work through, step by step, in taking
away his nightmares and self-abuse. Self-abuse about guilt, fear, angst, and
anxiety for outcomes he never caused. My intervention tends to be helpful to
Sergeant Z, as he incorporates our work in his own internal witnessing when
he is long done with our work in therapy, as he continues in his response below.

Sergeant Z: [A slight expression of relief that is genuine] I mean I am sorry
      Henry died, but I did not cause his death. It is this crazy job; that
      is what it is! Imagine, a young guy killing himself? Over what,
      Doc? Blaming me when I put myself out for him. That's crazy. Why
      would he hurt me—it is crazy, isn't it? It's not me, it's the shitty situ-
      ation and I did do the best I can, right?
Dr. Dan: No, it's not you! Yes, it's been hard to allow yourself permission
      to express your compassion, which cuts like pain, as you're doing
      right now. It is important for you to realize that. Yes, Henry was a
      very sick man who tragically lost his life. Lost his life in his illness
      and rage in the face of the remarkable efforts and decency you tried
      to give him, and in fact did when you were placed in a crazy situa-
      tion that you never created in the first place.

Our work continues; the intervention worked well in this session. Many
more revisits will create the web of strands that create a bridge. A bridge to
healing for Sergeant Z in his own unique eco-ethological niche with soulful
motivation. There is a lot left to do. But this example hopefully gives you as
a public safety officer a taste as to how complex trauma is. It also hopefully
illustrates how durable trauma and grief is for you unless the commitment
and the wisdom is generated toward lighting the fire of passion to understand what is toxic to you. Taken as a whole, I hope this case example serves
a tentative outline toward understanding public safety-complex PTSD for
you as an officer. I also hope it has helped in understanding my treatment
approach for your practical use and the theory behind it.
    Doing your work requires challenges to your own intellect, and more so
to your passion and the existential meaningfulness you invest in your own

work and those with whom you work. Yet, that is not an impossible task, but one where patience and curiosity support this attitude in you as effective. To achieve your task, learning the reality of demands in your own ecological niche is your own investment to combat your surrender to becoming another demoralized participant. Demoralized participants go to the other side, including some who with full tragic loss opt out of the journey of life.

Once you are able to express and work through your losses, all your training and experience is put to the best selective advantage in a world of increasing terrorism, both domestic and foreign. Remember, as in policing, firefighting, and medic work, a world increasingly anchored to limiting therapy to "briefer as better" is really dummying down your losses into a quick guide that one fits all—and that attitude just does not work. As I have used the metaphor before, which fits your working through your own trauma, like Sergeant Z, when you meet the needs of a goldfish, you can use a bowl. But stop and pause; when you need to meet the needs of a blue whale, you had better be thinking expansion. That blue whale is trauma being hidden in your bathtub, your locker room, or the local bar where you try to wash it away—something's got to give. I suggest that grasping this reality deepens your own inner sight. This reality boosts realistic strategic healing in working through complex PTSD as you are likely to encounter as you step into the next chapter. The next chapter will provide you with a basis for an expanded understanding of your own personality style and that of your peers as your own healing advances.

Healing advances, as in the case of Sergeant Z, who in my estimation, like Leonidas of legend, put himself in the front line of defense and leadership. His heroism was unsung, unheard, and unacknowledged until he redirected his attention within an eco-ethologic existential analysis with me. Like Sergeant Z, you do not need to work with me, but with a competent and caring cop counselor and hopefully, if possible, cop doc.

Many of you at this point have come forward with the dysfunctional myths we discussed. Some of you may be green with idealism, some of you may be tarnished with the gray of pessimism, and many more of you may be soaked in the red shock of war wounds—as so many tattered rags on the war fronts. In the conflicts within your psyches and souls existential meaning is invariably personal and relates back to validating your own way of looking at the universe. To infuse the wisdom of the ancient philosopher Hillel, "to save one life is to save a world," if you prevent your own, or a peer's suicide, you have saved a world, not only your own—but the world at large! Please do so! With that said, the world begins with the most important person—yourself—taking into account your own personality style is critical to working through trauma. Let's move on in your increasing understanding of your own personality in the context of your own trauma and loss experiences!

Prelude toward Understanding Your Own Public Safety Personality Style

3

Overview

Complex posttraumatic stress syndromes are nested in your own biological, psychological, and spiritual expressive self: all revolve within what is known as your personality. Extraordinary events are interpreted by you within what can best be characterized as your own specialized style with the depth of your own personality. Personalities are stable over time but are also affected and affect human-animal survival influences (ethology) within your ecological demands of your unit. The eco-ethological influences create an impact where psychological wounds sear into your psyche, as well as soul. Your own active shifting identity modes as you witnessed with Sergeant Z emerge during your experiences of traumatic losses. Over time your wounds leave scarring, and each scar leaves tracks leading back to the original wound. It is those tracks that I make it my business to understand and to learn anew with you and each officer I work with.

Your unique personality includes your own style of defending against losses developed over the space of repeated trials and errors with each trauma event you experience. Your own trial and error experiences are what shape the tracks leading back and forth in sudden and intense shifts in demands placed on you. Like a locomotive without a conductor who is aware of his back cars falling off alignment, collision awaits to happen.

Collision of demands placed on your identity is often contradictory and within short time gaps. As a human being in part ethologically motivated (animal instincts/drives) and in part psychologically aware (psyche), and in larger part capable of being existentially (spiritually) powerful. Being aware of your own human condition and the ability to transcend tendencies you are born with and learn in the eco-ethological niche of trauma and loss are critical. You are even capable of creating a change in the ecology loops you live in. Transcendence is not leaping over your losses—it is shielding, deflecting, and then head-on confrontation and transformation when ready.

Existential power in your will to maintain equanimity as a balance between meaning, pleasure, endurance of pain, and active defense for your own survival includes faith. A leap of faith to continue when all else feels as if losses have anchored you in quicksand: courage, resolve, regaining lost ideals, and sacrifice are grounded in your own desire to redirect your vision. Communicating your losses and how you do is in part framed in your own unique style.

Your personality style has emerged as a unique adaptation. Adaptation ensuring your survival and functioning as an officer in niches psychologically and physically shaped.

Wounds denied, or salved with the ointment of increased risk taking, or delay will create losses festering in internal infections tracking back to original traumas. Wounds of the soul and psyche left untreated shift from infection to toxic shock.

Psychological and existential wounds are surrounded by boundaries: boundaries flexible enough to engulf more losses become stronger as armor forms defenses over time. Defensive boundaries become enflamed. Left trapped and enflamed, wounds do not heal: gaps left open fester.

Festering gaps that are in part unconscious leave traps where other losses slip into pits. Pits close over time. Numbed emotions may be looked at as volcanic; they are not inactive as most experts suggest. Numbed emotions are quite active under the erupting surface. Toxic losses not removed constrict your growth—and remain walls that were once boundaries. Boundaries created in the illusions of denying loss now become red, blue, and white walls. Walls that hold your losses within your own self-constructed prison. The screaming holler of trauma's silence takes on new meaning—enclosed in walls without windows.

Full-Filling Losses in Someplace: Losses, Options, Solutions in Closed Spaces

In part it is reasonable to say each of the five different styles of personality shape and in turn are shaped by the wounds inflicted. That shaping of personality is sculptured by the psychological impact on you, which includes ecological and ethological forces. Your own individual style is nested in your personality as each wound reshapes and interacts with each new one leaving a deeper scarring. That is, until it is full-filled: *Full-filled is not an error in spelling; it is meant to impress you with a fact about losses.*

A loss from a wound aches to be filled at someplace it may rest and no longer feel empty. Think about a metaphor of water being saline tears. Water seeks to find its level by flowing into the lowest place of gravity until it rests. What that place full-fills is becoming the water's eventual resting place. It may also replace what was lost in reality. It can also change into a place of transformation. Water is a great analogy if you have been thirsty, or have been in a desert. You know well that water can present itself as illusion: That is, water may be so wished for when you are very thirsty it presents itself—even when it is not really there. Water may also rest when it hits the deepest place hidden from all onlookers. A place frozen in space where the energy needed for real growth closes in on itself. A locked place away from anyone else's sight where tears fall in your silence without wetting your eyes—as denial and withdrawal tax you. The lowest level at times is really the deepest inaccessible level to your eyes' vision. Water seeks to rest somewhere it is naturally inclined to move to based on its unique style of escapes, defenses, and walls. Directed without a set course, tears held in follow a direction with the least resistance as the most convenient path.

It is usually the inconvenient and difficult path initially unseen that leads to an underground water aquifer or well. That well takes time to uncover but holds a deeper source of natural resources where water is full-filled with minerals and fresh air for context and perspective. Peers support and cop counselors offer that context and nourishment to the well. More often the convenient path stagnates and festers in a pit with no new source to replenish and clean the water. That is left alone with your own devices of denial, aggression pitted against yourself, and owning what is not your own as your burden to purify. Water as tears unreleased is left in a tomb hidden in time, which becomes a toxic pit. A pit is illusion and may feel as if it is a haven to escape to. It is not! It remains a pit in the bowels of denial. Alone and without being heard, air to breathe new hope becomes despair. A pit may seem as if it hides you from the elements, is warm and protective like a stout drink of booze: perhaps a bet where you can win enough material to escape without losses. Perhaps one sexual exploit after another where if conquered will ensure you a place where you can look from a peak, with an eagle's eye: it is not—it is an eagle's bluff! A pit is where Joseph was banished by his brothers when he was shunned and cast down with vipers for daring to dream of lofty visions. If you are like almost all officers, regardless of their eventual public safety style, you also dared to dream your own ideals when you donned your police, firefighter, or EMT shield. Ideals with your own vision of how and why you were going to change the world of public safety you worked in.

Illusion or real, a pit is a place where losses remain unfulfilled in abandoned dreams. Dreams deceived, betrayed, and abandoned in the cold thrust of reality. Dreams, lost in the trauma of shock, overturn your expectations with violence into a pit: quantum trauma psychic moments strike fast and hard and send aftershocks. Tears like water falling seek any place to full-fill wounds. Wounds such as betrayal after investment in ideals you held sacred, lived by, and gave significant aspects of your life and commitment to are lost with violence! The deepest well within yourself is not a pit of risk, addiction, or denial but the source of that hidden well of faith. Like water, tears seek their easiest place of rest, which is in part sought in common within your eco-ethological niche. Complicating choices is the illusion that someplace appears to be under your perceived control. This makes superb sense, for you are taught to control every chaotic situation you are thrust into. It is the loss of controlling a traumatic outcome that provokes you to seek regaining the control that was lost. Regaining that sense of the deepest inaccessible psychological state of loss provokes a no less natural tendency to reach its lowest level. The lowest and stagnant level, like a cave without any source of nutrient, may be thought of as the pit of existential despair.

Existential despair in a hidden pit is an effective metaphor. A hidden pit remains outside of others' vision to assist you: but, like the biblical Joseph's tears, wept losses of betrayal in a hidden pit out of sight, not of ultimate redemption's sight.

Full-Filling Losses with Something: Toothache to Psychache: Options and Solutions

Fulfilling losses is not good or bad. At least initially your choice with what to do, how to fill a loss, and with what makes all the difference. Increasing your options by exploring your increasing knowledge and wisdom about trauma and the pain of loss is crucial.

Learning by example in public safety culture is unusually sensible. An example is one that is common and one that involves choices made responsibly when loss is experienced as pain. Pain can be a sensation that something is off, surrealistic, fuzzy, shaky, or some such experience that things are not right inside you.

Using your psychological imagination, let's check out another concrete loss almost all people experience. A cavity seems like a good example of such loss. A cavity is a physical hole in your tooth—a wound of sorts. It is reasonable to say you are likely to feel a cavity as a gap in your tooth. Painful sensations such as an ache when you have something to drink or eat that is too hot or cold is a sense of something being off. At times your cavity will feel better when you chew gum, eat meat, or cheese. These fixes of food allow the hole to be filled with something.

While I am not a dentist, I am assured by colleagues in this specialty that the temporary solution of meat, cheese, and even gum will satisfy the sensation of "full-filling your wound." Full-filling a hole in your tooth no longer gives you an empty sensation. That is the sensation of being empty. Like a cavity in the space of your expectations of your own behavior, and what you actually perceive as your public safety, shortcomings may habitually be full-filled with addictive behaviors. Addictive behaviors fill the holes in your bite on life for moments when you unconsciously seek that lowest and darkest level of despair. In fact, as reported, they create an effect psychologically and physically as if you have filled the emptiness in your heart and soul. You can choose to fill your own existential pain with some immediate gratification of pleasure: quick fixes make sense like a donut tire in your hidden trunk in the back of your car fixes your flat on short trips. Your need for quick fixes, short trips of escape, and excitement suggests the *addictive hyperexcited personality style.*

But, you may have a very different style and approach to your toothaches and cavity. You may seek options when you realize there is one best approach, and you commit to it. You realize replacing your toothache's cavity as a loss in your tooth with temporary solutions is a quick fix. Quick fixes you think are never a permanent bridge—no pun intended. You do have a good sense of humor, even if dry at times. All these temporary solutions leave a pit in your mouth where the hole was, leading to more pain. In caring for yourself you choose the best and sensible risk of thinking and acting on ending any further loss by gum infections. Seeking a lasting solution as the more difficult but effective path, you immediately have the cavity filled. That lasting solution you realize is immediately painful in the here and now. Your solution is you seek a dentist and she fills the cavity for you. Temporary pain of "working through" the cavity helps you envision the other options you can choose responsibly to act on for your own behalf. Your approach here suggests you have an *adaptive resilient personality style.*

You may also have another approach where you attempt all kinds of methods where you can delay the pain, and the cavity wound in turn will not deepen. You tend to delay treatment until a threshold is reached. Having reached your own threshold for pain, you seek help from a peer. After enough pain and persuasion you go to a dentist. You feel avoiding the solution of going to a dentist will result in a costly, painful, and worsened loss of pulp. Yet, you ignore your own good sense from the beginning. You act as if you are compelled to try all options you can before closing the deal of asking for help. You are drained and exhausted, finally calling out for help. You plan from A–Z: you check out every possibility with caution and deliberation before making any "leap." Certainty is something you do not leave to chance. Ingenious planning is overcast with all options. You have lost much energy by the time you decide to go to the dentist. You likely have a *hyperfocused personality style.*

You may have a different personality style as you wait until it is too painful of a cavity loss to deal with. At that point of experiencing the maximum impact of aching pain—extraction of other teeth being infected as well as gum procedures—you frantically call, "Help!" At this point hospitalization and very complex procedures are likely. Little choice is implemented for your own rescue if allowed to reach this severe level of infection. You do not lack intuition—quite the opposite. It is more often than not that the boundaries of losses in trauma you experienced have grown so weary that you stubbornly choose to ignore your own wisdom. You experience the outer limits of endurance you lay out in your own idiosyncratic path. You do not like seeing anyone given too much control in your life. You are used to doing things in your own creative *hyperintuitive personality style.*

Finally, you may be taking any ache as a mild and annoying sensation for a warrior. In your own way the aspects of gaining strength through your own suffering and even that of others who deserve it is welcomed. You were not paid to be sympathetic or weak. You are strong and need not allow others in. They will simply take advantage of your being vulnerable. You do what you will do, and as you like. If need be, you will remove the damn tooth if it gets that bad and endure a fever. It is your way or no way. Aches are ways you get stronger, and if it aches too bad, you can, if need be, end it yourself, but you will never seek help. You truly believe seeking help is being weak in your own *hyperaggressive personality style.*

Existential Despair and Psychache: Suicide Is a Forever Solution—The Pit of All Illusions!

As you may recall from an earlier chapter, Dr. Antoon Leenaars, a cop doc in Canada and a worldwide expert on suicide, expressed the ache in one's psyche (and soul) when psychological stressors are felt as so overwhelming they crush: like a vice on the officer's chest, they crush the breath right out of your passion and motivation. At the point the "psychache" is so intense you have intensive peer support and psychologist's ambulatory interventions. However, depending on your own personality style, you may not see your options in this situation of psychache as our officer with a bad cavity ache. Like the officer avoiding, denying, and substituting addictions for his cavity now infected, you too may choose a course of action in your very constricted view of complex trauma. Narrowing down your option to choose to dig a ditch, you may be on the verge of jumping in. Like water seeking the convenient path to its lowest level, you fall under an illusion. An illusion that burying yourself in a pit of despair is under your control, and so is the power to change. An officer feeling trapped and enclosed as if denying oneself help, or delaying it, or jumping into the hopeless and helpless mode leads to the pit of self-destructive options. At the base level of these destructive options you, as any officer, may be led to suicide. Suicide is the worst-case scenario, where the officer chooses to end all options: it is then totally out of anyone's control, including the officer who commits suicide. Death is permanent!

Existential Analysis in Eco-Ethological Analysis Is the Head of Your Own Myth to Live By

Let's return for a moment to options that are there for you to act on. It is apparent most folks fear dentists, but I have no doubt how many officers equally fear going to therapy, especially to psychologists and psychiatrists. But why? This fear is too serious to ignore: "A journey of a thousand miles begins with a single step," Lao Tzu suggested in scaling the Wall of China (Moeller, 2006). While you may not have to scale the Wall of China, seeking help may feel as if it is insurmountable as your own Wall of China. Calling a therapist may begin with calling up a peer support officer and opening up with thoughts of burnout, despair, or tortured anxiety: your first stepping up to the plate is a leap, and only you could effect that leap.

Please think about the options open to you within your power of choice and responsibility beginning with the most important person. The center of the world of public safety is you! Pain experienced now is temporary, and gain is immediate when you begin the slow and hard job of working through your losses. In full-filling the wounds with the compassion and insight you need to start healing within. Full-filled is your key. The full-filled experience is only achieved on a dimension that is spiritual or existential in terms of meaning, attitude, and willfulness to transcend what cannot be changed. On the other hand, it is also being able to face and change what can and will change with your own effort and trust in one other person. What happens to your losses that accumulate over a long period of time?

Well, you have seen how intense the impact of an emotionally disturbed person's (EDP) suicide was on Sergeant Z in Chapter 2.

This important question is a crucial one: if not answered and understood, this question leaves a wide, gaping hole. That hole impacts on you beyond what you have rehearsed in the role-plays, field experiences in training, and what you may never have been prepared for happening to you. The horror has hit the fan and "it" has happened. That hole is usually both physical and psychological. It is nonsense to speak of trauma without loss; in almost all cases it is physical and psychological.

Trauma is defined in the Greek language as "wound." When you have a wound, you have a loss—a loss that is not filled with understanding needs to be addressed. If the loss is not addressed with conscious awareness, it will remain under the surface of your awareness but with no less forceful effect on you. Finding meaning in your own attitude and your own stance toward the here, the now, and the future is where the existential analysis comes into play. Existential analysis challenges your own courage and willfulness to journey within—to explore without. Wounds are not only the losses but also boundaries you need to understand. Why wounds have seared so deeply and how to soothe them within the comfort of your own existential compass. I know you may, along with many of my peer officers, say, "Doc Dan, I hate you for adding the existential analysis in the fray." I almost guarantee your hate will foreshadow what any challenge yields—that is love. Love of yourself when you reach the endpoint of your own unique journey. That endpoint I have seen in my work with all of five personality styles of police and public safety officers. The same connection with complex trauma as you have seen in this guide is loss wed to trauma. Until the losses are healed in a way that meaning full-fills, gaps trauma rips open will remain toxic within you. Loss always occurs in terms of a context for you as a public safety officer with a unique personality style, which includes one of five discovered.

Sudden Strike: Shock, Loss, and Shield—Personality and Ecology—The Armadillo Effect!

Quantum moments of trauma rip into vulnerable humane sensibility within each officer with such force that defenses are aroused that circle your own vulnerability with closure. This closure, in a circle that protects your vulnerability from being overwhelmed with fear, loss, shock, anxiety, and rage, is a superb evolutionary shield. It also is a lock and snap-shut, steel-clad suit that suffocates the humane being within. Circles are sometimes more oppressive than linear lines that may alter courses where circles can loop around head to tail—and the tail of two tails remains one where no head is to be found. For example, as one patrol officer, P, on the beat now pounds away day by day on patrol, he remembers witnessing a mom with her kid in a baby carriage. Suddenly and without any preparation the carriage was swept away and hit by a careening car. Streaking across city hall as mother and baby are ripped apart in a quantum moment of trauma. Mom is holding the blanket, which witnesses the transition between the tattered body and mangled steel. The carriage holds her real baby wrapped in the wheels as Mom is hurled frozen to the ground in shock. Officer P reviews every possible trajectory that could have prevented that tragic death and then applies the harshest view of how he should have, could have, and would have saved the child. He uses a formula of self judgment against a super-human as well as super-police standard of professional performance. He displaces loss, shock, and trauma, is invested with figuring out every which way he could have and should have acted: that is except stop, pause, and reflect on expressing his pain and grief over what he could not prevent. Well, save being the son of Jarrel, that is, "Superman in red uniform," rather than an officer in blue. He understands his tendencies are that of the *hyperfocused officer* style as we work on his quantum psychic moment of complex trauma.

Ecology and Ethological Dimensions—Shifting Impact: What Unit, Detail, or Mission?

Let's now just look at some events without knowing the personality style you may have or, as you're reading the former examples, may be hinting at. Again, please use your psychological imagination and place yourself in any of these public safety officer missions.

Perhaps you are a deep-cover officer. You are for all purposes an unknown operative infiltrating a radical Islamic terrorist organization and just took a beating going beyond your role of comfort as an agent, and now you feel like debriefing, but with whom? What can you really disclose?

Perhaps you are you a firefighter working in a firehouse where buildings and the structures you deal with as part of your ecological niche make a lot of difference. For example, are you dealing with a forest fire, an industrial fire, a vacant lot, a high-rise housing project, or a hotel in midtown Manhattan?

Are you an EMT, medic, or ER RN public safety officer? What disease are you dealing with? Is it an ambulatory case where you need to stabilize a patient that is not responding to the code red protocol? Is it a possible bioterrorist outbreak in seeing a similar sudden onset of symptoms in patients that usually do not cluster together as they are now?

Are you a police officer working a midnight tour in a war zone in the inner city, or a reconnaissance soldier going into safe terrain, or ripe with mine fields that may go off? What motivation in terms of survival (ethology) is at stake here, and are you aware of the impact these influences have on you and your loved ones?

Without context and without motivation no conflict would ever emerge: fundamental to life is struggle, movement, and change—without these components of conflict, life as we know it would cease. The lack of change and movement signifies death. You are active and conflict is the context in which the trauma occurs for you. What "it" means to you as a public safety officer within your own public safety personality style is what you and I are going to tackle together.

The Most Crucial Questions Hardly Asked and Most Important for Field Duty!

Offering a healthier outcome for your work mission is necessary. Healthier by you gaining inner sight into the layers of personality you have developed as a style. Your personality style shaped and molded in an ecology of losses is nested in the ground of complex trauma. Questions emerge such as "Why have certain events impacted on you the way they uniquely do?"

The question of "Why?" is of critical importance to me as a cop doc, and while many colleagues in the mental health field are placing this aside in the world of managed care, I insist it is one of the most critical questions and with good reason. Well with no pun intended here, let's take a look at "Why?" why is so critical from your public safety culture perspective. Let's look at a four-alarm fire where three firefighters, a police officer, and two EMTs lost their lives, a forest fire where a squad of firefighters lost their lives. It is in these truly tragic cases that the question "Why?" it happened is so critical. Without knowing the cause of the fire, which is asked by the "Why?" how can the responding units know what chemical agent to use to take out the fire? The why here is fundamental to knowing what to do with the fire itself. Still critical is without the "Why?" you have no cause that is known. The fire marshal, a cop-firefighter, needs the "Why?" question answered. The unknown task of investigating a major catastrophe includes seeking accidental cause, negligence, reckless behavior, or worse, malice involved. The why determines many outcomes, such as whether she can charge or not charge someone with the major loss of human life.

From another perspective why disease emerges in a location is crucial to figuring out the cause and the cure: Is it or is it not contagious? Is an endemic ready to shift into an epidemic? Could it be bioterrorism, or is it rather a natural caused incident? How the EMT on the front line and the combat medic respond is contingent on this knowledge as soon as possible. Say you are a patrol officer arriving on scene and see a serious injured participant with second-degree burns on his arms. Why it happened is crucial for how you will respond. Did he accidentally burn himself in a barbeque, or was it a reckless act of horsing around by the participants, or an intentional assault with a red-hot iron? This sorting through is complex and will determine how you approach each respective party. "Why?" answered results in closing, opening the case further, or effecting an arrest and emergency response.

In other words, even from this brief review we can see together "Why?" why is so important to ask, and seek answers in your respective ecological niche. The evolving ethological survival motivations you live with night in and day out. Nights lived in your beats, districts, houses, and fields of engagement. Unnecessary labels that are self-imposed or imposed by others who are simply not aware of the complexities of your work and judge too quickly and swiftly will fall away like a scab. As you know, no situation is near the same for any officer on the scene. How can one mental health approach protocol assist every officer as if he or she is the same, and regardless of detail, unit, ecology, and ethological experiences not withstanding your own personality differences?

Yet the problem is clear when ready-made protocols and reactive judgments internally work on the premise that as long as officers are taught how to deal with a situation, who cares about the "Why?" for the individual officer? This brings us right back to you! To me as a cop doc, that is a poor question and an ever-narrowing destructive answer. Why assert that point in this guide? After all, large clinical questions are not really public safety officers' and their family's questions, right? Wrong!

It is an incorrect assumption of intent and outcomes in a culture and ecology and ethology folks who have not been in the field make. Those who know the field well know the power of knowing you as an individual is what counts. So do you! Simple solutions for complex problems hardly are effective in the long and even short run. It is with this in mind that we may bury the uncommonly destructive ignorance of ignoring the question of "Why?" and almost always seek the answer in the trauma and grief therapy work you are ready to encounter. For that matter in all humility—you need to learn how to identify influences that impact on you as trauma and losses within the larger picture of your own unique public safety personality style.

Mapping Out Your Public Safety Personality Style: Prizing Your Own Uniqueness

Let's think of trauma as disrupting with violence that which has been laid out in a map of how you think and form a strategy for survival in an ecology that is ever evolving. A map is a very comfortable concept for most public safety officers, as it gives you a sense of outcome and direction as to what to expect in a given situation. That outcome and direction are what constitute your expectations for experiences you may anticipate happening in your lives as public safety officers. It is the layout of that map that you get used to in your day-to-day existence and what, how, and why you feel a certain way and the meaning you get out of your own existence. Your own unique existential stance is related to values you place on overcoming or transcending your own ecological and ethological influences and repositioning them. Once you gain understanding of these eco-ethological influences on you, confusion as to their impact surrounding the evolution of your own life is less likely. Well, you may ask as a cop, firefighter, EMT, ER nurse, ER MD, or infantry professional, why time is so important and how does time become fixed to losses you may have experienced? The motivation is to find out in the context of your experiences and development as public safety officers—the critically important questions hardly asked out loud in public safety culture, such as:

How has trauma affected you?

What events are specifically more difficult to deal with on the scene and afterwards, and why?

What component of that specific trauma event leaves you feeling sensitive, and why?

Why does that one trauma come back to you in nightmares or abrupt flashbacks?

Why do you have memories that come into mind without any seemingly known context?

Why, in spite of trying to erase those memories, do they return to you without invitation?

"In fact, to be honest and real with you, Doc Dan, the funny thing I cannot control, no matter how hard I try, is even more present when I attempt to hide or push away these events! 'It' comes back stronger and harder with a vengeance, why is that so?

Events you closed successfully are now reemerging in your thoughts and dreams. Why is this intrusion of trauma events important to you? "After all, you know what, Doc Dan? I can drink it away, or block it out when I am out having fun, or amusing myself. Why should I bother myself about 'it' so much?"

Let's assume right here and now you do believe and know "it" is bothering you. Let me ask you a question: Is it possible that your partner you work with in the field may be secretly bothered as you are? Is this possible even though she may have a different focus of what that trauma event means to her, and why?

You may ask me, "Hey Doc, is it possible she may be hiding the intrusions of her losses and trauma?"

When you ask her, for example, how she dealt with "it," and she says, "Fine, a piece of cake," can she be lying or not even aware of the impact it has had on her?

Cop Doc to Public Safety Officers—Important Q&A Session—Right Here and Now

My task and your therapist's task is to tackle these questions above with you, and we will begin here. Let's begin with an answer that will make sense to you by saying no trauma is just an incident; it is complex and also hits hard on many levels of experience. The levels I am talking about with you beg certain questions you likely have, such as

How do you think about the complex trauma event?

How do you feel about the complex trauma event?

How are your behaviors different after the intensity of the last major trauma event you experienced?

Why is one event or part of that complex trauma event bothering you so much?

Why is that very same event not bothering your partner on the job as much as it appears to bother you?

Is it possible your partner has cornered a different aspect of his or her experience of that very complex trauma event that makes it feel as if he or she has experienced a different event from you?

If so, take a sigh of relief. As you realize now, a partial answer that makes superb sense is she may have a different set of experiences. Meaning her way of looking at her mission within the unit detail, what expectations she has entered that experience with, and her own reflections as an individual officer vary from yours.

What is the difference between your own perception of the same event of trauma compared to your partners? Sometimes the different ideas, feelings, and painful losses you experience are so striking you are left wondering: Did we both experience the same traumatic event? The answer highlights the individual differences as altered perceptual experiences.

Remember in the first chapter how even being in the same public safety department may mean different perceptions. Differences based on your own tendencies for outcome and rescue or recovery efforts that lie under the shield you are wearing. Your heart and soul are what lie under the shield and uphold it.

Is your perception different than your partner's as a result of the differences in you and your partner's unique experiences of what and why those selected differences are so painfully distressing?

Once again, sensibility starts to emerge from her personality that may be hyperexcited and alert to be the first in a rescue of an aided case. This hyperexcited style has been your partner since she was a rookie. Unknown to you, she remembers arriving on scene a few moments too late for a robbery in progress where the perpetrator escaped and the aided victim died. Your partner blamed herself for being too slow to save the victim's life. Hidden from you, she vowed to never be second on the scene. That vow was made to herself and she will keep it with the motivation as if her life depended on her own sworn oath being full-filled. On the other hand, you may have perceived you did all that was required and in your own style that makes sense to you. Your own tendencies are collecting the paycheck and doing your job without a complaint. That is your main goal. In your view there is no need to be the first on the scene for every emergency, and definitely not at all times.

Are these differences in part also a result of your own selection of etho-logical motivation for survival rooted in your experiences of what works? Second, is why it works for survival in your own map distinct from your partner's? As you may have already figured, the answer is yes, in part, as all answers are never complete or exact. Your own growing wisdom of how trauma and losses are sown in a context of ecological, ethological, and indi-vidual differences affects you and your partner differently. How and why the effects are different exist here. Why should they not? Is this mapping, so to speak, conscious or unconscious as well? Well, the map you form is not only of thoughts, feelings, and ethological-emotional motivations, but change in ways you are aware of, and even more so, largely unaware of.

Existentially speaking, that unconscious map is largely influenced from your own compassion, empathy, and sense of suffering of others you connect to on a less than conscious level. This is largely unconscious, but can become much more under your intentional awareness.

Is your perception a result of the differences in your unique experience as to what and why selected differences in the context of the ecology you work in develop over time?

Yes, in part the unique ways you interpret and experience ecological niches and survival influences shift in time. Also shifting is how your denial, avoidance, and delaying these influences impact on your sophistication in how you experience losses or defend against them. Maladaptive experiences or healthier and increasing conscience change over time. That is, your own effort can affect the outcome on healthier perceptions and strategies you gain. Are the demands of your unit for survival and the meaning afforded to different aspects of your own experience of meaning a two-way street? Meaning, insofar as perceptions held by others of you, are your own ideas about your identity as a unique public safety officer and person at odds?

Without doubt, as you have seen and will see in more detail, the per-ceptions you hold of your own identity and others' impressions of you may shift over time. These two-way streets can change with motivation toward empowering you as you understand your strengths and weaknesses in your unique personality style. Is it possible to change your own perception of the eco-ethological influences of loss? Yes, loss that is shaped within ecological and ethological influences is made more understandable. With understanding you can shift from hiding losses to mourning these losses. In more cases you will also learn to disabuse yourself of unwarranted guilt, self-judgment, righteous rage, anger turned inward, and wounded professional pride. Is it so hard to change what is your own unique public safety personality style?

It is not your own personality that needs change. What may need tweaking is your adaptive functional dissociation that has worked so well. In place is full-filling the wounded existential meaning and path in your own life. The answer is complex trauma lies on its foundation. Understanding of losses is the first part of this survival guide, but this guide goes beyond it in this second part. You will get into the real grit of personality, and why and how it impacts on you for life and living. Not just for getting a glimpse, but a larger picture of you! It is the first guide of its kind, and it is meant to help you help yourself first. The survival guide spreads to partners you work with and your own spouse, and other significant people in your life. That is hard and difficult work. Another answer in part is as follows: you and I are peers at a deep level as public safety officers. That fact remains true regardless whether your auto is blue, red, or white. Near and dear to my heart and soul is the importance of understanding that complex in complex trauma and loss is being used with dead serious impact. Why?

Your trauma syndromes are seen, understood, and influenced by your experiences. But, not without the knowledge that illustrates why your personality style is what makes you a whole and unique human being. A human being for better and worse in your relationship to you, others, and the world. Meaning what, Doc Dan?

Meaning you are an individual public safety officer with very important differences from your partner. That is whether you are getting along grandly, in constant conflict, or are okay for now. Those differences distinguish you and other officers from one another. That difference is also the glue that makes you a good soldier and not a paid hired gun, regardless of your public safety profession. You do what you do for the reason you do. That reason varies in important ways that distinguish you as being a unique public safety officer with your own calling and mission. But even so, Doc Dan, why bother understanding these differences—as you say yourself, we are brother and sisters in red (FD), white (medical, ER RN, medic, EMT), and blue (police, special agents, special forces supporting a perimeter or a police-military reponse). In the field of battle and service all differences wash away, don't they?

Well, again you ask good and tough questions! The answer resides in your question. When you respond to an event—as in my first part of this guide—I illustrate you experience different identity modes. In the emergence of those identity modes some are in conflict with one another, and some in fact contradict one another with great intensity as collisions. Yet you function well in the field. At times the shifts in your identity modes are so sudden, shocking, and intense—in ways that are so opposite: when you stop, pause, and look at your behaviors and thoughts, you feel as if your personality has split into many different identities at times. That experience of dissociation is not far from the truth. In fact, I call it police and public safety field experimental traumatic neurosis, as you observed in Chapter 2. So the answer is not only do differences not wash away after the field of trauma is experienced, but different experiences you encounter do not touch on the differences between you and other officers. Officers side by side with you on that very same front line where complex quantum psychic moments of trauma struck may process the event differently.

That surreal experience of adaptive functional dissociation may continue, but you may not be the victim of this experience. Understanding an experience helps make you by choice become a survivor. You may in fact gain understanding of the sensibility of how your personality has been shaped and evolved by influences greater than ones you can control. You can regain the meaning lost in the crack in your expectations. By knowing the differences and understanding your own personality style and others, a natural empathy develops for peers you work with. Another gain is upward or downward appreciation of those who are bosses, and the troops on the front lines develop. This appreciation in my treatment is not by washing away differences, as much as one cannot wash away culture and religion, but by valuing the individual officer. Appreciation of differences is complex to learn. But giving you a line that you know is untrue, for example, rank, unit, detail, and experience and personality must be forgotten, is an impossible complexity beyond reality. It is so because it is simply trying to bend what is untrue in reality into truth! With that truth said, let's view a real case of loss as Officer Mary and her partner Officer Greg process loss differently.

EMT Officer Mary's Personality Style of Handling a Homicide: "Being Dissed"

EMT Officer Mary brushes off her feeling traumatized about being involved in a case of a victim stabbed with a Sai sword through the eyeball. She arrived on the scene of a man who was lying in his own pool of blood. Why? Because he dissed his neighbor's wife, who complained they were playing music too loud. The fellow upstairs felt dissed when he spoke to his wife in a dismissive way. Because the victim dissed his murderer to be, that man had a Sai thrust threw the occipital part of his brain that was punctured from within the left eye to the outer perimeter of the back part of the right side of his brain. Mary, upon arrival, shoved people aside and ripped off his shirt while attempting CPR. EMT Officer Greg screeched on central command for EMT response forthwith and the boss to come immediately. He tried to help, but Mary had taken command presence with him doing crowd control while assisting Mary as he could while the victim died. In Greg's self-evaluation he did very little in his own perception, except to help Mary move the victim as she was doing CPR.

EMT Officer Greg soon plagued himself with questions. Questions such as when Mary acted as if the death did not bother her. When he asked Mary about her feelings about that event she said, "Greg, hey, that was a few days ago sweetie. It was a piece of cake. We did what we could and don't let it bug you—bad stuff happens, get over it!"

Officer Greg thinks to himself, after Mary with ease washes away any sadness or shock, "Why did I even mention it?" He reflects to himself silently, "Perhaps Mary is not openly as bothered about the shocking gruesome aspects of seeing the man with a Sai through one eye and out of the back of his head on the opposite side." EMT Officer Greg is anxious about Mary being bothered by how that xx-yy-zz killer got away with murder. Mary felt the bad guy got off with manslaughter when he whacked the guy without any mercy. Greg felt overwhelmed by the fact he arrived after this murder, was unable to do anything to prevent or change the outcome, and did not do the CPR like Mary did. Mary felt that Greg was being too sensitive and complaining about the tough facts of life. Mary did not understand her anger at Greg being more empathic openly, and her aggressive approach and style of judgment covered some of her own experiences of losses.

Hidden from her own insight, which later emerged, was Mary's belief that she did not do enough in getting the police enough evidence to support a murder sentence for the perpetrator. Greg's style of anxiety was about what he believed was his inadequacy and guilt that he did nothing to assist the man down. This self-abuse was fueled by his feeling that Mary had no appreciation of his feeling so shocked by the murder scene. These hidden losses provoked anger, guilt, and anxiety mushrooming into unexpressed resentment at each other. Grievances were collected in a pile of unspoken resentments under the boundary of losses accumulating. Ignorance of their feelings and distorted perceptions of one another labored their communications. Over time, the different personality styles fell out of synch. This disharmony had little to do with stereotypes of how male and females process violence and death, but had everything to do with the officers' distinct personality style. Greg's hyperintuitive and Mary's hyperaggressive personality style, if better understood, and without judgment of one another, would have led to a complementary balance in their field of trauma and losses. Instead, a death knell for their partnership resulted in a disaster in the making waiting to happen. Greg's and Mary's experiences created images and memories that stay fixed in their memories and the dissolution of their public safety partnership. What happens to these dark memories swept under the locker room at the end of their tour of duty?

Intrusive Images and Hardwired Memories: When Will They Leave Me Alone?

Mary and Greg had unique aspects of complex trauma haunting them. Like them, you may experience images of victims, the crime scene ecology, and the objects you remember when no one is around. Intrusive images and memories may linger for a long time. They can provoke questions you have and never ask out loud. Such as the ones Greg had in relation to the homicide, and his thought he did not do enough. Other questions emerge: "Am I really sane?" "Am I faint of heart?" "Did I act cowardly or weak?"

These questions do not go away easily and may bother you intensely and without stopping until you get some answers. Worse is these questions may not emerge at first. I have witnessed many officers having questions such as these hit them when they are quite older than the time that event happened. Sometimes 20 years can pass and telescope backward to that original event without warning with the intensity as if it happened today (Rudofossi, 1997, 2007, 2009). Whenever "it" raises its ugly head of self-doubt and self-downing thoughts about what, why, and how you acted in a certain way, it is unusually intense. You will understand in the context of the tendencies that make up who you are, and why you may have acted as you did, that you are not blameworthy as you may believe you are now. Understanding these questions within the layers of your own personality is very important.

Why you as an individual with a certain personality style act, think, and feel some losses in trauma more than another officer does will be helpful to you. It will bring understanding and sensitivity to you, as well as your peer's responses. Perhaps as you read Greg and Mary's trauma event you perceived lack of sensitivity. Now you may be remembering other officers or even your own responses as callous to losses you felt deeply in your heart of hearts. Understanding helps normalize the trauma and losses you have endured as a public safety officer in the field in which you live and serve. In other words, you will not feel as if you are weak, less than perfect, and even worse when you appreciate the shadows of your own losses. In the wake of your own unique contributions hidden from you, the realization that only you could have made choices and actions as you did will be drawn into focus.

Public Safety Personality Styles Are Not Disorders: An Important Distinction to Understand

When we look at the problem of trauma and the losses that color the impact of these losses we need to think of a few factors. Factors that hold together like glue. Such as what are the essentials of what is meant by your own public safety personality style? What tendencies emerge in your self-understanding of your personality style? For example, some tendencies may emerge as follows in the course of the day and with the work you do, or you may be a firefighter arson investigator that has a pile of papers on ongoing investigations. Suspects are catalogued with accuracy with five different categories you placed in color shades from likely to unlikely perpetrators with pinpoint accuracy. You are more inclined to note and count the times your suspect taps lightly with his fingertips, rubs his eye lashes, and avoids eye contact every time you ask about the fire started in the workplace.

You are the "facts only" investigator and believe that other stuff, including your own intuition, is for the birds. You may not say it out loud, but you think to yourself, "Yeah, yeah, hunches are fine but only solid evidence is acceptable. After all, the only thing the ADA or U.S. attorney wants is hard core evidence, not flighty feelings and intuitions." You monitor yourself a lot and deny other types of stuff like hunches and what you consider wild speculation. Your approach indicates a likelihood your tendency is toward a hyperfocused personality style. Your hyperfocus style is a strength that allows you the skill to eliminate the innocent from the guilty with exquisite relish.

Let's check out a different stylized approach you embrace. When a suspect talks about allegations weighed at her, you deeply rely on your own sense, that is, intuition, to guide your investigation. That is, whether you pursue your investigation, or whether you make notes of that fact or not. Are you the type of investigator who also gathers details but in a large picture you piece together a profile connecting each with your own special intuition, such as smelling out a bad guy or gal? You look at the finer details like: Is this suspect frowning? Is there a wincing of her eyes? Does this suspect look down whenever she talks about the insurance policy on her husband who was gunned down by an unknown assailant? You use your hunches to frame a working hypothesis to seek the bad guy. Your unique skill of sensing and using your empathic mind's eye creatively is the strength of your hyperintuitive personality style.

Perhaps you kind of use both methods and explore the problem when conducting an investigation regardless of how innovative or kind of run-of-the-mill preliminary investigation you conduct. Whether you are an EMT, firefighter, or patrol officer, you and I know the paperwork must get done. Right? Well, yes we all know the forms required must be filled out and understandable. But please hold on a second and let us pause and take a look at what your tendencies tell us about your personality style: For example, are you the officer that does not do your paperwork on time, but kind of the last thing you want to do, and in fact do? Action is where it is at in your style of doing things. You are the firefighter that must always jump in first to kick in the door and break the windows—even when you and I on the QT know it is not needed. Or you are the police officer that loves to tackle with the meanest bad dude and take that extra risk off duty? If there is even a whiff of a good collar, almost nothing can stop you from the rush of taking down a bad guy. Your hyperexcited personality style assists you in making the grade most of the time with flying colors and accolades in the street and pinned on your shield holder.

Perhaps, on the other hand, you love to do paperwork and write to your heart's content and even be creative with the content. Are you sensitive about how it is perceived and to any comment about your work that is not perfect from A to Z? Is your tendency to get the paperwork done by the recorder as your police or EMT partner you work with day in and night out? Is your own preference to get the paperwork done day in and day out shifted to your partner? Is the working relationship you both established a focus on you being the operator of the Radio Motor Patrol (RMP) and she being the recorder of the units you both make up each tour of duty? Both of you find you really like doing the driving and pursuits, and your partner always does and even relishes doing the paperwork, which you could leave alone with a 10-foot pole. You may have the hyperintuitive personality style and she the hyperfocused style, which has evolved to a synchrony of a complementary relationship. It is the intention that is given to one another's differences that leads to a collision, or a mutual exchange of strengths, in place of an emphasis on each other's weaknesses.

Intention, Attention, Focus to Refocus: Arteries to the Heart of Personality Style Flow

Personality styles press tendencies and intention you use to avoid, embrace, or distance yourself and others from losses or talk about them or reminisce about them in war stories. A key ingredient I would like to bring to your attention after we have scratched your intention is the focus factor on the traumatic losses you experienced and how and why you have processed them as you uniquely do.

Even if you have denied these losses and even if you have spoken about them with buddies, this does not mean you have worked though and placed these traumas in your life. You may not realize the impact they have had in your lives. The compass that you use as a public safety officer and an individual is intentional with attention you can learn to refocus as your own direction. Why is knowledge of your own personality style so important? And why do I insist on clinicians learning your style as well as you do? My first two works (Rudofossi, 2007, 2009) address clinicians in learning about complex trauma and the five police personality styles: as the saying goes, save the best for last, for in the cream of the dessert is the best and finest taste. That is the treatment of the eco-ethological existential analysis.

Another reason is because in my studies and clinical work with your peers I have seen time and again surface interventions do just that. In other words, surface intervention guides help no doubt, but they scratch the surface. My mission is to get to the core of what is plaguing you as an officer. Getting you to work through your losses in the heart of your soul is what will free you to be you. That core lies deeply inside your self-image, self-perceptions, and in understanding your unique public safety personality style. By your understanding the how and the why, you can refocus on working on what, when, and which way you can deal with your own losses. In doing so you will navigate and improve your own processing and placement of losses. Hopefully seeking help for dealing with and an improving your own life as a public safety officer and as an individual human being will be achieved. Change may take place through different means, but the one of interest here is beginning a process. That process begins by keeping in mind how losses and trauma have shaped and are reshaped by your own personality style. When you refocus on the demands of your unit, your own identity modes, and situational demands, an eco-ethological insight of your perceptions of losses will emerge. For example, your own beliefs about how you acted, why you did what you did, and when you did what you did will be reassessed with your new vision and coordinates. That re-vision will assist you in confronting and encountering new and challenging situations where survival psychologically and existentially will be empowering. Joint exploration of what you are going through today is a hard mission, but the payoff is great. You can only enjoy your pension if you live long enough and with the quality needed to enjoy your time meaningfully.

My task is to help you understand how the shadows of ungrieved losses are so hidden from the light of today within your own personality style. A good clinician will want to know and explore with you a better understanding of stable and consistent patterns, and features that make you an individual officer with your own unique personality style. At this point I ask you to accept your own self-worth and value as unconditional simply by being the public safety officer you are! The strength of your own public safety personality style is highlighted to maximize your own inner sight. That inner sight helps you with your ideas and the meaning or lack of it in different experiences and behaviors you do, as well as avoid doing. It is key to not give up hope while maximizing your own improvement in dealing with your feelings and emotional expression of loss you experience. I will offer very close snapshots of my work with fellow officers to give you examples. These examples hopefully will guide your own exploration, clarification, and inner sight—helping you get ready for self-reflection and change.

Asking questions and bringing out an understanding of your own motivations and tendencies is a strength, not a weakness, in the world of therapy and counseling. In dynamic and existential analysis such as the work you are doing, disclosing strengths and weaknesses with the trusted professional is necessary. It is crucial as the stuff you work with together on "the job of working through together." In the presentation of the five personality styles to follow, the individual identities and integrity of each participant will be fully protected. This is done by realizing each personality style I will present in the next chapter is a combination of many participants—this ensures personal identities are protected: you will learn that you are not abnormal when you have learned maladaptation to an abnormal environment filled with multiple experiences of trauma and loss. Your resistance to understanding aspects about yourself is normal in almost every human being and certainly every patient I have met, and that includes me! But that does not mean you are powerless to these influences and resistance. What will become clear as you examine personality styles in Chapter 5 is strengths to be developed as you gain inner sight to your own personality style, including your own hidden courage, decency, meaning, and faith unheard on the sidelines of your night-in-and-day-out behavior as a public safety officer.

I have spent my life and will continue to serving you as a public safety officer, who serves, served, and may continue to do so. I am sure one way of serving you is your own understanding of valuing your unique work and your unique impact on others in the personality style you were born with, developed, and will develop further throughout the process of life and living. With that wisdom let's move on to the final chapter to enhance your understanding the force of loss and trauma with peers that is likely to match your own public safety personality style.

Living Well with My Own Police Personality Style

4

Tough Questions to Ask and Answer: Finding Your Own Police Personality Style

Working through being on the job makes your personal and professional life more tolerable, healthier, and even meaningful. Becoming healthier is achieved by gaining insight into your own unique personality style. Recognizing strengths and weaknesses you bring to the shelf of public safety offers you many opportunities. One such opportunity is based on your newly gained insight where the veil of your shortcomings is drawn well over by the shades of your courage to change what you can. That responsibility you are fulfilling emerges in unique encounters only you can fulfill. The encounter for change begins within yourself. Changing the moments you transcend feeling stuck. Feeling stuck can range from feeling as if you are wading in illusions of mud to "no way out of self-constructed hell."

The range you feel from being stuck in the rip via quantum psychic moments of emotional despair is challenging to the best of you. Trauma hits you at your core.

Despair is suffering without meaning, as Dr. Viktor Frankl suggested after living through the terrorism of fascist Germany. Living with faith, even in the war zones, whether on the domestic front or the foreign front, is what Frankl called tragic optimism.

Why tragic optimism in the context of police personality styles? Experiences you experience in public safety often are tragic moments. Moments in the field where anguish and despair are sown in furrows slipping through cracks. Cracks where human evil is tilled. Seeds of inconsolable losses tilled from cracks in the shells of your broken dreams. Inconsolable losses are the worst moments that you've witnessed victims, peers, perpetrators of crimes. Hidden losses within concrete losses webbed in strands of failed innocence, idealism, expectations of trust in the job to protect you from evils, and ethological tactics—gone awry. As with all tragic experiences, imprints of meaninglessness are where your tears well up in closed screens.

Like a well that can stain your soul in dreary colors of gray death, and ashen white of failed rescue and recovery efforts.

But, there are other wells within you that are colorful. Colorful wells that await drawing color as passion, reason, and redirecting wisdom only you can cultivate in your own field of trauma experiences. Making a small step, even the most minute move toward wisely embracing tragic optimism, may be viewed as a major artery cleared of plaques. Plaques of despairing tragic moments reside in the heart of your experiences. This chapter offers tools of insight and suggestions to prize your own unique personality style with tragic optimism, not tragic despair. Optimism in your tragic moments has a certain meaning suggesting your abiding faith. Faith that even the tragedy of suffering, pain, and death is redirected by your own moral compass. It is crucial to redirect your lost chart to a map in deed. In my existential analysis I do not suggest you passively accept being stuck in a world of chaos, rage, and violence—quite the opposite. The redirecting here is learning to witness your own actions of bravery and courage in the healing place where you regain order in chaos: order in purpose and intention for your own direction where you understand the ethological and ecological forces and with intention empower your ability to transcend despair, and embrace the tragic optimism.

Only you can embrace meaning and values you invest in yourself. Values of how we nowadays deal with suffering, pain, and the ultimate losses in different varieties of death. It sounds like a closed drama: "It is what it is." Rather than a closed drama, let's open up to a heroic epoch within your own life history.

Discard the cynic answer of passive acceptance of suffering without meaning as a badge gone tarnished square and with the stain of pain. In its place spit-polish different thoughts that move you to modify a cliché of "It is what it is" to a value such as saying to yourself:

> It may be that it is what it is—in its present form—but how you deal with "it" is your own choice and responsibility: Regardless of the pitch tragedy furrows in lines across my naked back, I will not break. I can engage my own courage, will to connect, and transcend despair with my own faith and pace.

Your new value is a coping statement for motivating you as you move on with me: *"It is what it is"—for a moment, but life holds promise for ever-changing moments.*

How you deal with any trauma can be done with gentleness on yourself by holding on to hope. Letting go, letting God transcends your own limitations and knowledge. Ninety-five percent of all public safety officers believe in the ultimate meaning in life and that there is a creator of the universe: there is no apology for being real here. Public safety culture and beliefs herald faith and spirituality! Regardless of your own religious or spiritual beliefs, how you choose to look at losses in your trauma experiences is crucial.

You will observe in the case examples that follow once and again how strength in your attitude, values, and direction can impact on how you see and integrate your experiences in a healthy way. The ability at any point for you to regroup and redirect your own path is within your reach. In learning a new sensibility that is brought into awareness with your own vision and style, you learn to place the target V for victory, in the scope of your horizon and beyond. V by embracing your own limits and contracting boundaries of losses in silent suffering!

Universal Doors to Perception: Creativity and Destruction Are Borne in Worlds of Words

Words are important: words you choose to tell yourself and others on a practical level make the difference between a commendation and a civilian complaint. You think in concepts expressed by words you tell yourself. Words direct your own thoughts between narrow corridors of success in the most volatile events. On the other hand, words can disconnect your wish with those who you may most relate to. Take the example of the police officer on patrol responding to a call for a disorderly group and possible injury on the midnight-to-eight tour with an EMT officer on a "routine call." Nothing is routine in your line of work, only the wish that it may be so.

So here you are; there is a large crowd and a minor injury of one of the partying folks. He refuses medical care, and may even be okay. Besides his injury you have a noise and crowd situation. Well, you make a decision to put on your diplomatic outfit as you generally try to adjust to difficult situations with a potential for escalation. You keep your moral compass tuned up. Your thoughts and words reflect minimizing harm and enforcing the laws within your discretion. You are able to put your own emotional impulses in check and use them when you need to if it is called for.

On arrival your goal is to assess the situation, keep the heat down. You realize from experience that any party harbors a crowd mentality. That crowd mentality can ignite like a keg of dynamite without much provocation. Diplomacy and ensuring safety are the major desires obtained for all parties involved. It is your goal to ensure safety is accomplished, noise control is maintained to acceptable levels, and you go on your way.

As an *adaptive intuitive officer* you are reasonably assured you can get the situation under control. The objective is to get folks to lower the volume and intensity by schmoozing a bit. You arrive and after assessing the person hurt (aided case) has a minor cut from a slip, you then move and identify the alpha party leader and in a firm and friendly style tell him, "Hi sir. Hey, sounds like nice music and some good people you know [smiling]—it's a bit loud. Could you keep it down, sir? We have a busy night and I know [you pause], believe me, I know having a nice time is needed after the busy week. But please ensure some guys don't make it too loud pal. It's cool hanging out. But, again [with serious look for a moment and eye-to-eye contact] I really don't want to come back—you know what I mean." The head leader nods with his head up and down and says, "Yeah officer, I will keep it down." You say, "Thanks buddy I sure don't want to come back. I know you are having fun, and if you keep it down, keep on having fun. I prefer chilling myself and having a coffee and keeping busy dealing with real bad guys, which I know you're not." The fellow at the door says, "Chill officer, enjoy that coffee. I will keep it down and sorry for the trouble." You say, "No problem, sir. Have a good night and have a nice time. Thank you for being able to ensure compliance with the noise issue."

But what if you are a *hyperaggressive officer* and love the heat of being a gang buster. Let's be honest, your goal is to put some defiant punk in his place while the music is blaring. You don't blare music after 11 p.m. You think to yourself that you know the rules and follow them. Why should this punk and the gang he rode in with make so much noise? You work hard as a cop and are not putting up with nonsense. You may say to your partner, "Who the hell does this dude in the slick sarcastic grin think he is? Looks like some overgrown delinquent." You then go into hyperaggressive mode and itching for "this joker." You begin to get psyched up, saying to yourself, "Hey, it is my makeup to be a tough cop. I'm not a pushover cop." You turn to the guy in the showy clothes and you say, "So you're the cheerleader here guy. Well let me tell you, it's midnight. Can you see the time? Look at your watch. Can you tell time, man? Anybody ever teach you the ABCs and 1, 2, and 3? This crap is over! Right now—end this noise! I am the police—not you—see this shield [you point at it and lift it for him to see]? This is not a Cracker Jack toy! You and your gang got about 10 to close it down, or guess what? I will! You got my drift. I don't want to repeat myself—I am not playing with you. Ten seconds guy—and don't try me! [You then begin to count down while you tell yourself if 'I give an inch, they take a yard; I give a yard, they take a mile. Tough sh_t, I am just doing my job. Simple as that']." I am with you. At least in part, as your sensibility is in synch with your personality style. I understand as a cop doc you have been working the mean streets for quite a few years. But here we may look at your words to yourself and your readiness to kick butt that may give you a lot more heartache and pain than you bargained for. Looking at the situation from your perspective, let's stop and pause for a moment. No matter how right you may feel in the moment, the real danger and conse-quences can come back at you with a fury. A fury as hot as the red hot anger you feel, legit or not. We will revisit your options as well, and how we may lower the gauge without giving up your ship as captain.

Let's look at it from another personality style, you are a *no-nonsense, con-trolled, hyperfocused public safety officer* and you know the rules of the patrol guide by heart: although you know it is not the bible, becoming boss is key. In your mind you follow the rules and procedure with whistle-clean precision. In your heart of hearts, as long as you do your duty as a good soldier, you are covered by the job and the bosses.

You arrive on the scene and you assess the situation with precision. Your breakdown is as follows: you have a bona fide crowd, a civilian injured non-city involved, and need to file both an aided report and an ECB summons (Environmental Control Board ticket). The rules were broken and you will be polite and professional but issue a summons. Going beyond the pale is not your thing. You are a by-the-books cop. You say to yourself and you remem-ber as a good student at the academy and in roll calls, it is good to not let your child get hooked. The instructor taught: it is not good to be parental with the group. It is good to identify the leader and deal with the situation as a disor-der control event. You sort out and pick the group leader as you try to estab-lish a rapport and communicate adult to adult with him. You objectively seek his name and write out a ticket, you issue a warning, and inform him if you return, it will be necessary to effect an arrest, "as simple as that." The boss will be happy if you issue a summons, and you like to get a pat on the back for a good job well done. You pull aside the leader and pull him to the side. You did this even though it appears impractical, as it is with a crowd situation, but you kind of override your sensibility. Why? Because rules must be followed. Rules and thinking through of every possible option help you gain a sense of security. The general rule is separate the leader. As you do separate him, you use no humor and he gets more guarded. You see some of his guys moving close; nonetheless, you tell him very politely and assuredly in the correctness of your command presence you need to receive a driver's license. You make copious notes on your scratch sheet and get all the proper ID lined up. With command presence you assert effectively, "Sir, you are in violation of the law and I am going to issue you an ECB summons. What this means is you are not being arrested; this is not a misdemeanor but a violation. Sir, in order to effect this summons properly to its conclusion, you must appear on XYX date and time and pay 316 dollars and 22 cents, which is payable in U.S. currency. You may bring an attorney. If you cannot afford an attorney at that time, one will be available to you cost-free. This summons is not personal or against you or your friends. It is simply my job to ensure a quiet environment. If I am called back I may have to arrest you subsequent to Penal Law XYZ Code for such and such offense. I am hopeful this summons will serve as a warning and you will not commit this violation again." It all seems to go well and you hear some snickering under the breath of the fellow who got the ticket and he says with a grin, "Officer, you take care of yourself. I will definitely not do anything to violate the law anymore."

As you leave you feel you were almost too matter of fact and he is laughing under his breath. It is hard to know what people really think of you at times. But you reflect you do your job well, and that is what counts. In one half hour you head back as the crowd is as loud as ever. You are wondering: you did the job by the book and this should not be happening. How can it be: What did you do wrong? This is not supposed to happen—why you?

Let's look at another style as you may be the *addictive hyperexcited personality* style officer. You are itching to get to this job. Your goal is to jump in and check out what is going on. You love the excitement of the job and getting into it. The job is boring as hell. Issuing a summons, especially the paperwork of an aided case and worse an ECB ticket, is nothing but a royal pain in the you know what. You got a plan in your head, a quick one, as you have a tendency to work things through in microseconds and worry about it all later. You tell yourself, "I am going to get there and give them one chance—maybe about 5 minutes." Everyone better be dispersed. Guess what? If not, it will be show time—you take no crap. A crowd is an oyster field waiting to be culled for juicy morsels of potential collars. Collars for dollars: collars for time is well worth it. You say, "Maybe I'll toss a perp and get a good gun collar. Hey, who knows? Maybe some joker with a serious warrant—you never know." You go on in a personal review of the situation, thinking you don't want a BS collar. So if it is nothing, then hey, it is what it is—but you are ready to rock and roll if not. You flip on the turret lights and sirens on your way; although no emergency, you love the adrenalin rush anyhow. You need some more collars and OT. Besides the money or time, you figure you will never make a gold shield if you do not go over the board of the boring lackluster routine. Truth be told, you can't wait to get promoted. You also know full well you hate those BS ECB violations, so if it is not a good collar you will warn and admonish and be off on your way.

You arrive on the scene all psyched up and ready for action and get ready for tackling the crowd, and you even surprise yourself by what you say. Hey, sometimes you got to do what you have to do and you do it. You spot the leader and walk right up and tell him, "Hey buddy, I know that you know that this crap has to stop, okay? [You stare deadpan into his eyes.] It's late and I am not here to hold your hand and dance with you. Keep the music down. It sounds like real weird stuff. But hey man, whatever floats your boat. You know man, I could not give a rat's ass about what you listen too, and do. But it is my job if I get bothered with these nuisances calls. You know what I mean buddy? [The leader is about to respond and you look at him with a grin.] Hey, don't even try to get in my face, or you know we are going to get down and dirty. I am just telling you, man, nothing personal, but you are not going to win—got it, buddy, or what? By the way, I am giving you 5 minutes to clear out. If you don't, it's curtain time. Curtain time for you and your bros. So, let me know—what will it be?"

This officer gets a response from the gang leader like, "You can't talk to me like that. I have rights too. Hey officer, this is rap music. I'm not listening to weird music." Skip ahead and before long a 10-13 call goes off and the troops are down. It is not a pretty site; however, you do have a collar, including resisting and disorderly conduct. Yeah you do have a nosebleed, and in fact a gun collar was made by one of the responding officers. In part your goal and need for excitement and even the "trauma drama" are met, but at a high cost. You have a line of duty injury, IAB investigation, and CCRB complaints. It will need to be resolved before you can receive your gold shield. It is worthwhile taking a better look at minimizing the damage to you, other officers, and civilians at risk.

Finally, let's look at the event from your *idiosyncratic hyperintuitive personality style*. Your goal is to see what is really going on as a gathering of hidden agendas. Is it perhaps a simple group of dudes. Dudes with nothing better to do. Perhaps it is a front for a cat house—in other words, a brothel for men. Perhaps it may even be some cover for murder that could happen anywhere. You never know; after all, you are a sleuth even without a detective shield as of yet. You may have to make a collar and you will do it. In reality, as you see it, you really don't want to make a collar here. Why? Because truth be told, you're a compassionate fellow and can relate to a party situation. You'll take no abuse, and will try to straighten out what is going on. It is a bit exciting but unnerving for you to go on this job. As usual for your style, you pick up on a lot of information and sense a lot of stuff. But of course you'll keep it on the QT. After all, you are not the first officer on the scene. While you are full of courage when you need to be, you are cautious enough, but let's be honest with yourself—you feel very deeply. You can and do figure things out in unique ways and do that so well. You use your sixth sense. You are very attuned to many aspects of experience. You fit in well and then, on the other hand, you really stay aloof by not participating with the unit in playtime, choir practice, or other such activities. You are ready to use your skills and tact and find out what is going on with the noise complaint. You also await the EMT officer arriving. It is almost fun and exciting for you to ferret out if the injury was a slip, an accident with some touch of reckless behavior, or perhaps more is going on than meets both of your eyes. You are on the call for about a half hour and the music has gone down a bit. You think to yourself the music is still somewhat loud. You get a second call by central for a disposition and you say you will get back to her. You approach the leader and in a very engaging style communicate with him, "Hi sir, what is your name? No, not your last name—your first name. Hi Jerry, well interesting music. Jerry, when did you start to listen to postmodern jazz and who is on the saxophone? Gee, it sounds like an interesting combo of rap and jazz—cool stuff. [You and he engage at a level of sharing stuff while the background starts to get louder.]" Central command gets over the air and asks again for your disposition code. The desk officer has called for you to go back to the base after you finish the job. The EMT officer who has a personality style akin to your own also gets a call from his central command and duty EMT captain. Central for both you and the EMT officer is carrying a past assault over the air. You tell the nice fellow, "Hey Jerry, please keep the music down. I dig our conversation, but you know there are calls in." Jerry responds to you in a smile that looks genuine enough, leaving you with a nice feeling inside, "Hey man, take care and be safe. Sorry, for the noise."

Well you go back and the boss says, "What happened, Julius?" You tell her what transpired and Teresa K.O. gives you a lecture about doing the job; she grins and says to you, "Officer, try to not be the nicest guy in the world—nice guys finish last." She winks at you and smiles and you go off, wondering what she really meant by that. Did she really mean that you are a really nice guy, or is the joke on you, or with you? Anyhow, you go off to the next job and smoke a cigarette to release some steam. No further complaints from that incident are made. You receive no other calls to return. You say to the other patrol car, "Whatever, and whatever, no sweat." You are asked by the other team, "What happened?" Saved by the bell—the boss just called you in.

Let's Understand the Complexity of Differences in the Five Police Personality Styles

We have just again looked at one event handled, perceived, and assessed very differently by five different public safety officers. The crucial factor was the personality style each officer brings to the table of experience and why and how perceptions and thoughts are different. It is key to not judge. Whatever your style is, you can use it for your advantage as a public safety officer, your unit, those you serve, and your family and friends.

The key is each of the five officer personality styles is a part of your natural ethological motivation, and then again, it is a part of what you have learned ecologically.

The level of awareness and selection of certain aspects of the event or ignoring of others are nested in the personality style of each unique officer.

There is really no right or wrong aspect of your personality. Accepting as best as you can who you really are and what traits you may want to work on is critical to good mental health. Enhancing, decreasing, or learning to accept with reason and passion are critical toward both working through your losses and achieving your gains in resilience.

Let's review important compass points to navigate why and how your public safety personality style developed, as it did. *Becoming* is a word to keep in mind in this chapter. Where you are now does not mean where you will be tomorrow: the crap you are feeling overwhelmed with right here and now is not what you will be dealing with and feel overwhelmed with tomorrow. In other words, your attitude is yours to own as to how you can look at anything. Ask yourself: Is my attitude toward this situation working for me on the job? Is my attitude working for me off the job? Perhaps on the job your attitude may be the best way to behave. Off duty that same attitude you have learned so well only harms your chance of success. I am here to present a consistent approach that can work both on and off the job within your own personality style. How you may understand yourself with gentle coaxing rather than hammer down on your shortcomings—or imagined shortcomings. Shortcomings may be made quite sensible by the demands on your need to survive as a public safety officer.

Love Is Not Tough or Soft! Love Is Passion, Compassion, and Ever Resilient—Like You!

If it is not on and off the job that your attitude does not work for you, then we may need to look deeper and with a different approach that is gentle. Love is not tough: it is compassionate and gentle. You need to love yourself. Gently relearning your tough attitude toward that which thwarts you toward the goals of love in your own life and living. Becoming has a lot to do with my existential analysis, which at the core focuses on who we are in the front line and moving beyond what it is—to what it can be and may be. May be if you dare to take the initiative.

I have no doubt as you read this chapter you may be in the shadowy place of feeling depressed, deep into harmful addictions, and even acting out by blowing up. I am not going to give you a line of warning that will make you feel even more blue, angrier, sadder, and more anxious in the mire of your losses and self-doubting thoughts and behaviors. No tough love here!

Despair at what you have suffered, are suffering on the job and off the job, or anticipate suffering is the target of our analysis as well. I will not white-wash your suffering away—as it is part of the human condition as an officer for you and the folks you deal with night and day. You likely suffered some heavy stuff that can shadow the best of us. I have witnessed and heard my own losses and trauma: my losses as a cop doc include betrayal, dealing with domestic terrorists, seeing police partners murdered, divorce, and working like a bull-street cop and studying like all dickens to earn two doctorates. What motivates me to write this book is, like you, one of the police personality styles fits me. Ultimately I learned, sweated, and fell and got up again to become the adaptive resilient officer, as you will if you work on it as I did. By what means did I succeed? CPR:

Compassion to see yourself through forgiveness for betrayal, injury, and shock to your system

Passion to be what you know you really are in the full-filled place where your heart and soul reside

Resilient skin that sweats with openness and vulnerability where you shed the dry and callous layers that hold you back

Cynicism, labels, and numb passive acceptance of internal slavery by drinking, sexing, and eating yourself to death in what seems "as if" you are wrapped in the invulnerable armor of tough love is too heavy. Let down the suffocating armor for messy love. Messy love, including the original love for yourself, and the unique complexity of your own nature. It is here that I can say that your core self and your vulnerability to those worthy of witnessing your suffering may be celebrated as compassionate witnesses—the rest who judge you too harshly can be shown the back door: compassion need never be too tough, and should never be mean-hearted, or cruel-spirited. Love is not tough, and is not full of demands—it is open to responsive change, and the ownership each person individually needs to accept. Accept to make it worthwhile. It is the ones who try to hoist tough love that may be in most desperate need of love period—in their desperation they keep their loved ones in perpetual dependency. Overindulgent, underinvolved, and overly controlling family members sadly and tragically perpetuate that pattern until understood. It leaves both controller and controlled subjects of their own games of checkmate.

Private and Public Self-Invincible Myths to Discard: Naked Badges for Real Shields

Plowing through the core of who we really are is a private issue, on the one hand. However, you and I would be surprised to know how many of our friends and family and especially our peers on the job pick up what is going on in you—that is, even when you may think you are hiding that information with a shut mouth and blue, red, or white brick wall.

Again, we are taught for good reason "not to be open books" and "keep them guessing" in the "us versus them mentality." It is our culture's wisdom that "keep them guessing" and suggest "not to be open books": outsiders from our culture say that is really narrow-minded and must be changed as stupid, bad, and narrow-minded. Is it not true, Dr. Dan?

Well, let's look at that question. Let's not base our answer on the authority of some expert from the outside looking in. Let's stop and pause and examine the validity, or the lack of validity, with sensible eyes. Eyes that can wrap around reality for public safety culture. Let's get to the heart of the matter by getting a real police, EMT, firefighter, RN, or medical uniform mental health professional for suggesting a tentative answer: ask yourself if it is really narrow-minded to hold your own vulnerability and personal feelings card close to your heart? Labels narrowly applied to you by people with a political agenda, such as "stupid," "bad," and "narrow-minded," may be a reflection of labeling public safety officers too soon and way too narrowly.

Looking at the evidence, whether you are an EMT, police officer, fire fighter, RN, or ER doctor, you are given discretion and a lot of power in your command decisions. You are also judged very strictly if your assessment or your powers of discretion are interpreted as inappropriate. In fact, you can find certain political and interested society initiatives that directly narrow, thwart, and stereotype public safety professionals. To complicate the issue, a demand for automatic compliance with extreme and sweeping reactions to interpreted bad behavior is thrust on all public safety in reactionary form to follow, enforce, or integrate with impulsive immediacy. Standards of operations at times disregard the wisdom of our own more conserving culture. In needing to comply as a sworn officer, you do not relinquish your own ability to think critically. While embracing your own freedom to conserve your unique self, the frame of your own unique personality style and your peers will set the stage for how you act.

Peer Support Officers and Cop Docs—
Complementary Teams!

Our culture has links for you to reach a competent and culturally aware public safety counselor. In thinking about an effective and compassionate assistance officer, you may not have to look farther than your own precinct, service area, firehouse, medic sector, and field house for triage. That assistance officer is likely to be one of the finest professional public safety officers. A peer support officer is trained and voluntarily has chosen to put herself or himself out there to understand who you are and how to help you. Helping you in the thick of losses and trauma you are dealing with. This fact is true whether you are on the streets, the firehouse, the EMT base, or the clinic where he or she will be able to listen actively to you. A peer support officer is likely to be present during the initial crisis and may have gone through his or her own trauma. In the heat of searing pain, a fellow officer who understands and respects the unit and complexity you are working with is the crux of cultural competence. All peer support officers are paraprofessionals who are there for you in your worst moment. A peer support officer is a sworn public safety officer who ideally is supported and trained by a cop counselor or cop doc!

A warning to take heed too is sad: not all peer support officers are created equal, nor are all peer support team leaders unfortunately. Bureaucracy sails in again with saving corners without any real public safety experience save an appointment in these opportunistic times where non-public safety career bureaucrats have taken over key positions. Knowledge is your best aid and assistance. Most peer support officers in the police departments have certain exceptions to disclosure, and some also are required to disclose information: please check your agency's policy. A licensed mental health professional as cop doc or cop counselor will not disclose what is called privilege. Privilege is a great check to cash when you need to ventilate: but before cashing in, let's explore the meaning of *privilege*. First, privilege belongs and is controlled by you, not your doc or cop counselor. The privilege is yours to disclose your treatment as the officer-patient in a legal proceeding. Confidentiality is protected by your state and federal law.

Let's move back a moment and look at the peer support professionals where officers are here to provide you with support and outreach and connection to the professionals who have expertise in the area you can benefit from. Without a doubt, I have seen PSOs who in 97% of the times move in with expertise at defusing and debriefing and giving me all the information I need. Great crisis intervention begins on the scene of the trauma. Still, peer support is not counseling or therapy, which is of a different quality, frequency, and approach. This topic is too complex to fairly cover in this section. Peer support is critical and available for any 10-13 you have. You will come across the finest and bravest of peers one can hope to genuinely encounter.

Let's now return to your own distinct personality among your peers that makes up who you are.

Overview of Personality Styles in a Nutshell:
A Finest Kernel of Inner Sight and Health

In each officer's public safety personality style the ecological niche you work in and how you perceive that niche is as unique as you are. Your need for survival and adaptation shapes and affects your personality style. What is stable in your character and traits is answered by "Why?" as an individual your survival and adaptation to an ecology and ethological beat area makes superb sense. That sensibility as to why you have developed a certain personality style is established at young adulthood: that age in which you were recruited was no accident.

Personality as a concept can be challenging even to the trained psychologist plummeting the depths of what that really means from a scientific view. In this chapter we are not going to get into the science of public safety personality styles, but how they apply to your survival and meaning in your life situations. In doing so, I will lay out the sections to follow as well as the importance in understanding your own personality style as different from some other officers'.

If you are interested in the scientific clinical guide for clinicians in understanding the personality styles of public safety officers, then you may want to get a copy of both clinician's guides to complex trauma and grief (Rudofossi, 2007, 2009). For now, I will break it down for you and other peer police and public safety officers and your family members to identify and understand the personality style you present with for your own use. Major subheadings for each public safety personality style will follow this outline:

1. What Motivated You Toward Swearing Your Own Oath as a Public Safety Officer
2. Psychological Survival Defenses within Your Own Public Safety Personality Style
3. Framing Your Moods and Emotions in Your Unique Public Safety Personality Style
4. Existentially Relating to Me, You, Others: Ecologically and Ethologically Speaking
5. Your Personality Patterns: Ecological and Ethological Sensibility: Why You Act So
6. Our Personality Style Peer's Most Traumatic Event in His Own Quoted Viewpoint
7. Impact of Traumatic Loss in My Own Unique Personality Style: On Duty and Off Duty
8. How Your Public Safety Personality Style Is Different from Other Public Safety Styles

9. Initial Inroads to Lay Out Your Own Map for Trauma and Grief Therapy
10. Let's Get Real: Your Public Safety Personality Style: Officer and Cop Doc's Corner

The importance of the why with a how to achieve change in my eco-ethological existential analysis will frame your outline of what you may do. You may embrace meaning in the context of multiple losses experienced in the complex trauma you've experienced—resilience within is sparked and will build to a balanced passion lit as a flame in the seat of your own soul. Suggestions for getting to therapy, problem identification, solutions, and achieving meaning for each profile are offered in the last three sections, but are also layered in the other seven sections as well. These suggestions are placed to increase your chances of a humane and rational dialogue for growth and healthful living. In a closing section I will offer you the summary of highlights and inner sights specific to your own personality style titled, "Let's Get Real: Public Safety Officer Personality Style: Officer and Cop Doc's Corner."

I will offer aspects of your style to be aware of as a public safety officer and why and how you may rethink, redirect, and where it seems more sensible to work on the fact that your own tendencies are not fact. The fact is with choice, compassion, and strong passion you can make your style work for you without throwing out the Sam Browne belt you have styled and wear. The cases finally bring home lessons learned in thousands of effective therapy sessions taken out and polished as speed loaders, medic, Scott packs, or hose clips you can use when you are in the field, and within your own unique public safety personality style. With that said, let's move on as we open the windows surrounding the five public safety officer personality styles.

The five public safety personality styles are presented in the following order:

Addictive hyperexcited
Hyperaggressive edge
Idiosyncratic hyperintuitive
Controlled hyperfocused
Adaptive intuitive

Ports of Personality Styles: Titles Are Metaphors for Substance and Change

Before you enter the portals of each personality style a comment is necessary. The descriptive title of each style highlights understanding of a service focus and identity: for example, when you hear street crime officer, emergency service officer, community relations officer, or internal affairs investigator, different images and expectations come to your mind.

When you hear emergency medical technician or field medic or practical nurse, different images and expectations come to mind.

When you hear forest firefighter, forensic fire examiner, city firefighter, and emergency fire rescue, very different images and expectations come to mind as well.

Keep in mind titles I use, such as addictive hyperexcited, hyperaggressive edge, idiosyncratic hyperintuitive, hyperfocused, and adaptive resilient personality styles, all have different meanings, images, and expectations as well. My hope is the key to different inner sights and tailored approaches bring home quite different results that are highly useful to you as a unique humane being exploring your own style. Being aware of others is great information to use. Personality style is used, not personality disorder. This guide is written to assist you and not judge you or your fellow officer. It is the first written to help you be the best you can be with very individual differences in mind and heart. As you can see, the word *hyper* constitutes almost each personality style. Why? Well, for a darn good reason and redirection, as it is well within your own motivation to make your challenges your very strength. As my recently deceased dear friend and mentor Cop Doc Al Benner, SFPD captain and U.S. MC air wing pilot, would say often to me:

> The underbelly of your weakness holds the best strengths with in you. Public safety officers have one over on being on the good side. That fact you must never forget and never let them forget as a real deal cop doc. Not even in the worst of firefights!

Cop Doc Allan Benner's wisdom holds the test of time as truth. Think about it—that is, if you are willing to look within, and not without, for your own unique style and how to live with it. Living with yourself includes being on the side of the angels, and not the underbelly we all have. But any underbelly is visible. If you think you can hide it and try as you may to tuck it under the Sam Browne belts, it will eventually emerge without any hesitation unless you confront it in your own good time. No better time exists than the here and now to do what needs to be done.

Now! Let's set our ignition key into the cylinder of the first public safety personality style.

Addictive Hyperexcited Public Safety Personality Style

What Motivated You Toward Swearing Your Own Oath as a Public Safety Officer

Classic examples of officer quotes are as follows:

> "It seemed like an amusing idea at the time."
> "Something different to do that would provide excitement instead of work-
>   ing in an office or desk type job. By the way, the benefits aren't bad."
> "I always wanted to catch the bad guys."

Psychological Survival Defenses within Your Own Public Safety Personality Style

Your personality style may be loosely called bold and brash. What has shifted is a change in your orientation toward danger. When you reflect that you are stuck in what has become a once adaptive belief of tackling danger, you now have begun to embrace an invincible belief in yourself. In turn, you seek the most dangerous situations. Hyperexcitement has served you well. The heightened excitement that is biologically conditioned and psychologically exciting helps you function with a valuable trait. That trait is a sociable connection with a lot of folks in the military setting of a public safety command. It feels like you have an immediate savings bond to cash in. That savings bond covers gratification and attention seeking. Your goals are met with bravery, excitement, and being honest with yourself—deep in your gut—a flare for the dramatic. Your performance and supervisor evaluations are often above average in the sheer frequency of arrests and summons, or rescues and commendations. You are intensely involved in chasing after bad guys, and being the first firefighter or EMT on scene for rescue and medical operations. You do have an exquisite ability to tolerate frustration in the streets, and war zones in the naked city. Your tenacity is like a bulldog: enduring more pain while putting fear aside. In fact, you complete many police, firefighter, EMT, ER, or combat tasks with matter of fact excellence.

The flip side is when it comes to delaying strong desires for pleasure—overindulgence is a good lay of the landscape—regardless of what seeking you are doing. It may vary from going to the tracks and placing bets on horses and dogs, to risky behaviors on a whim, to alcohol and other types of addictive behaviors. In tune and key with your need for high excitement, relationships repeat a pattern of impulse and romantic fire brightly lit, but soon dimmed in an abysmally low toleration of discomfort. As an officer in your personality style you are likely to put yourself in the center of all dangerous operations as standard operating procedure. You enjoy to the point of craving being called by your peers "a cop's cop," "a guy's guy," or "a great street cop cow girl." What is puzzling to you is that you crave a deep desire to relate to others: you do this in a way by doing whatever you feel is called for, and if we use the million dollar word, we can call your way of showing it *action empathy*. Your compassion is achieved by doing for others, not offering strong emotional displays. Offering strong emotional support is called emotional empathy. Action empathy entails taking great risks that are selfless toward your own safety, especially when the well-being of others is at stake. Your extraordinary level of heroism is set with a trigger point balanced on a strand of hair. You are without doubt the quintessential heroic figure. Trigger point heroism means running into situations of grave danger at times without really being cautious and without really thinking about it. At times you also kind of stop and think of legal guidelines; you then sprint ahead and stretch the formal rules to get the job done as a police officer, firefighter, EMT, ER RN, ER PhD, or ER MD.

Collaring the bad guy is as simple as that—without worrying about any of the consequences too much. Some behaviors are driving 90 mph on a city street the wrong way to catch a bad guy, or volunteering to effect a warrant on "Insane Mary" or "Crazy Joe." As a firefighter you know that past the 10th floor great personal risk is likely, still undaunted you are first to leap into an inferno. As an EMT you will try to rescue the aided even in a highly volatile situation before the police or firefighters get there to stabilize the scene for rescue.

In asking yourself "Is this really me?" please realize that there is a wide variation in what is presented here and what truly resonates in your heart and mind in general. It is not what you may or may not say aloud, or confess to your peers. Your need for peers and supervisors knowing and acknowledging your courage is very strong as a desire, even if you never say you need to hear it. The feeling your need for attention by the brass and the team is never fully met is disappointing no matter how much excellent performance and meritorious commendations you have strapped up and down your ID plate.

Framing Your Moods and Emotions in Your Unique Public Safety Personality Style

Dissociation, as we learned in earlier chapters, occurs in your style more often than most others and what we even call *fugue states*. Fugue states are like spacing out—except you temporarily do not know where you are and doubt reality. Because it is like you have lost your sense of perspective when you started out on a trip. For example, you may not remember going en route to someplace, and then awakening as if in a trance, and wondering where you are. Not so rare is an amazing state of mind and mood that you may experience as if you are going through altered states of consciousness during police, firefighter, or emergency medical trauma events. Sometimes it feels like your mood is expanding with some really tweaked highs. You may find it hard to describe, but you know it when you go through it, kind of like being on a roller coaster. You experience that high, when you talk about war stories or other heavy jobs. Let's look at an example that highlights the process of some officer with your style working through this altered state where a craving to be on a high of excitement is itching deep inside.

Officer Z: Hey, how do I feel? Well, Doc, I'll tell you—great and excited. Yeah, that pursuit I felt elated. And you know what?" [I stay silent and wait for him to let me know what, I am not disappointed and he tells me.] Not for nothing, well for real—Doc Dan, if you ask me truly … [he pauses].

Dr. Dan: [Straight shooting I tell him] I do truly want to know what's on your mind Z. Officer Z, tell me, please. I am all ears, and I have two big ones.

Officer Z: [Looks at me straight and with no hesitation shouts from his hip straight as an arrow] Doc, I feel a need to stay high most of the time. I am on a rush from these jobs. It wakes me up. It's like having the coffee you're drinking—you know what I mean. You've been on the job.

Officer Z went on and gave me his accounting we had worked on. For example, post 9/11 he informed me he was exhilarated by that "awesome event." The involvement and the excitement being expressed channeled his low-grade depression into a distraction on one level. On another, it helped him feel needed and have a sense of belonging. He felt that the job as of late was slow, which by all accounts was far from objectively being slow, but his perception is not a matter of my assessment, but his. This need for excitement by Officer Z to an addiction to trauma may in part be a result of the following:

1. A distraction from low-grade depression due to losses he had never expressed
2. A more biological and psychological tendency for addiction and a craving for trauma
3. A continued condition of working with heavy and intense trauma that reinforced his need for excitement and became gradually and biologically supported in the brain-mind combo

Existentially Relating to Me, You, Others:
Ecologically and Ethologically Speaking

You know you are truly at some level impulsive. In other words, you will take on a dare in a heartbeat: chase a bad guy at 90 mph without a blink of an eye. You love the thrilling adventure of saving someone else's life. You seek out high-risk experiences and feel the rush of high excitement when dangerous situations just happen—as they do on the job.

You also love schmoozing with others, but sometimes that impulsiveness leads to wearing your heart on your sleeve. After wearing your heart on your sleeve you think to yourself, "Why did I take that leap of trust?" As bright as you may be, and good as you are at what you do, personal judgment, risk taking, and jumping in to the mix leave your self-preservation wanting. You love the zombie movies, high-drama police and combat movies, and you know you have indeed become addicted to combat zones. Let me give you an example again that you can connect to here. An example of your thinking and action-oriented "can do" response in attempting to solve a problem is as follows: A fellow detective left his keys in the office. In response, being a cop's cop, trying anything to assist another officer, such an officer may choose to climb onto a ledge three stories up, crawl in, and let his peer in. I used some questioning to understand and gain a sense of whether he had thought of safer alternatives, or if he judged the serious danger of his risky behavior. With serious bravery and lack of self-risk, he answered without hesitation, "I needed to save my pal from shame, so the boss would not think of us as keystone cops."

All of life is a risk. No sweat. Standard operating procedure, man, just SOP.

However, let us understand what is going on here as we know in the case of police and public safety officers. It is the urban war zones that mold and perpetuate what is what we can say afforded in your ecological niche. If this sounds like you or a peer you know after working in a heavy house, and it feels like a compulsion, it likely is. In other words, once you have been in the bag of a war zone you have a lot of pent-up energy. You need to let that anger or agitation loose during heavy operational events. Events such as a four-alarm fire, car and tractor trailer accident, or riot disorder control event. Without reflecting on by-the-book tactics, or thinking through first what may happen and going over your options before plunging into action, the song "Born to Be Wild" truly is the beat of your own tune.

You can honestly say your style is "do it first—then think about it all." While this is not supported formally, as you know, we are all told to use safe tactics first. It is just something that is not natural in the way you think and act when the heat of action is stimulated and you are in the identity mode of pursuit, rescue, or even recovery. You believe deep down and maybe not so consciously that you are truly invulnerable. Meaning you are not open to real serious injury.

Yeah, you know there are risks, but you know what you are doing and the bad stuff just ain't gonna to happen to you! At the core of your deepest beliefs you do believe in the perfect hero ideal, and a demand that your peers and CO of your unit approve. Constant energy and risk are invested and spent by you to be the top dog in your unit. Anything less is not acceptable. The risk taking in any conceivable situation follows your belief "I am able to act in survival mode and will survive. I must be the first to break through to the victim and nail the bad guy, or dose the fire."

That of course does not mean you are not a team player—you are the best, but regardless of being a team player, you need to be firstm whether kicking in the door to a raid, first in a four-alarm fire, arrest situation of a cop killer, or rescue of a hostage-barricaded victim. Being last on the scene is a large crater in your need for being a top public safety officer. That is a severe blow not to your ego, but to your entire way of being a cop, firefighter, EMT, soldier, or ER nurse or doc. Your own self-image of who you are and how good you are revolves around your career identity mode as a police, firefighter, EMT, medic, infantry, and emergency responder. There is little reflection on your personal life identity except as it relates to being an officer of one administration, agency, armed forces, or department. In your way of thinking, kicking butt or threatening to do it is and will remain for now an acceptable means of survival. Truth be told, you are more likely than not to have experienced war zones in an ecology of trauma. If someone gets near being in your face and stepping into your personal space, an almost automatic response is your physical and psychological armor is aroused. Your personal space is violated and you will be respected as the officer—simple as that!

Your Personality Patterns: Ecological and Ethological Sensibility: Why You Act So

Being protective of boundaries makes superb sense from an ethological view. This guardedness needs to be understood first and foremost by you. Even before peers and family and civilians, and sadly certain internal units that may have a tendency to assess your level of protectiveness as brutality. I have argued for the past 13 years, since I published my first doctorate on my studies on loss and trauma on police and public safety, that an almost automatic response is not an officer being brutal—whether police department (PD), government agencies, firefighters, emergency medical technicians (EMTs), medics, or certainly not soldiers fighting terrorists of a domestic or foreign type.

The word *brutality* is an automatic and reactionary fixing of an officer in the zeal of labeling and finding a target to fix an uncomfortable truth about policing and public safety officers.

Brutality, when waved at police, firefighting EMTs, and military personnel when tackling violent criminals (domestic and foreign), is not only destructive to you as an officer, but it diminishes society's right to defend itself. Labeling you as a figure of brutal authority, when you are legitimately defending the public trust, can lead to those who foolishly do this as identifying with the offender. Of course brutality does occur in rare circumstances and needs to be addressed in many ways. Brutal labeling and unjust judicial practices against police and public safety officers are seldom discussed. Why? Because political agendas to correct what the public might see as bias eclipse open education and forums. Officers are seen as brutal when partial and selective videotapes capture pursuits and takedowns. We all know biased videotapes do not capture the ambush, and the physical violations of the officer's need for his or her own space.

In fact, in my work as a cop doc we witnessed one out of four officers of the NYPD over a 4-year period subjected to assault with injuries ranging from minor to line of duty homicide/suicide against officers. In more than a rare case I witnessed a survivor/victim public safety officer labeled as brutal without an allowance for understanding the in-depth ecological and ethological influences and dissociation that adaptive functional adaptation provokes.

Let's look at it as a street cop, including myself. I had spent time in the historic operation pressure point, and in Bed-Stuyvesant and Fort Greene Housing Police on the midnight tour patrol force. The moment you are being challenged your reaction is a stop gap. A provoked ethological need for survival and defense surrounding your ecology where life and death choices coexist with addictive highs of intense response to emergency calls. The map that every public safety officer rehearses in his or her mind is set in his or her unique ecological niche with the motivation of ethological force. Brutality implies a sadistic state of mind: to act without care and inhumanity with a goal to hurt another human being by misusing your authority with cruelty. This is not your case, hardly ever. Even in officers with the one profile that may have hyperaggressive tendencies it is not usually being so cruel as to be indifferent to human suffering. In other words, you may be labeled when you receive too many civilian complaints and IAB investigations. It may be you have a problem connecting with civilians in a civil way, but outside of a puberty-stricken idealism or very immature perspective it is more than a written record. Often the realities of your own personality collide with the eco-ethological niche you work in. It is likely you do your job as best as you can—you do your job with passion—and doing it all too well has created this ironic distortion.

On an ethological (animal-human behavior) level, when you are in an ecology of a war zone or say a slow house in which a war zone emerges with a terrorist threat (domestic or foreign), your natural tendency will be to select the best possible survival course. At that point you are likely to be as forceful as needed. Couple this with the adrenalin rush that with other chemicals kicking in, such as cortisol and pheromones, provokes healthy defensive responses in you. Looking at this push into survival identity modes over time changes from soft wire into hardwired as your attack and arrest identity modes are activated again and again. Your tendencies at a heightened level are a full combat and apprehension identity mode since you are likely to be an alpha officer. Thankfully, far from always but in general usually the use of force employed is within legal bounds. The higher risk you face is you often find yourself in situations that are an immediate danger to you. The irony is I know as you do that your hyperexcitement seems to add energy and charisma to make you the best public safety officer in the eyes and hearts of your peers and the public.

Supervisors vary in their reactions to you: Authoritative supervisors usually are likely to appreciate the heroism of your action and will still give you a lecture at the end of the day for such high-risk taking. Lenient supervisors will enable your style and kind of go along as long as your activity holds no major situation that hits the fan. When the risk taking hits the fan, your lenient supervisor likely has a metamorphosis and winds down the shaky road block. Finally, no-nonsense street bosses are likely to encourage you— even when you are aware you have gone over the top, for example, in a fire rescue operation, or an aided intervention in a volatile crash all aflame, or a violent warrant execution.

During the most intense public safety and police confrontations as an officer you take the highest risks and are unusually successful. You learn to maximize a real reward that makes superb sense ethologically where success breeds a feeling of being a cop's cop, a firefighter's firefighter; an EMT's EMT, an emergency unit responder's takedown man, or a task force operative or deep-cover operative. I am not implying you are a reckless officer, but rather you know your gig and your territory (ecological niche): having the edge and the rush drives you deeper and deeper into getting a fix of a rush at confrontation and takedown or rescue stages (ethological) as a firefighter, EMT, medic, or ER nurse. Your risk taking in rescue identity, pursuit, and arrest identity modes, as the first on scene, that is, shootout on duty, to off-duty incidents of rescue involvement, at times no matter how noble, is unhinged. Without waiting for backup by on-duty personnel you are at fault. These high risks, including putting yourself at the front lines without assistance as your priority, hint to having this personality style. This is a pattern and not a one-time situation. High levels of civilian complaints and allegations of use of excessive physical force are usually related to your frequent involvement in pursuits, and calls for assistance from other officers. This is not precluding you may also be in a specialized unit where this is the norm due to revenge tactics. Revenge tactics by organized criminals, that is, drug dealers, ambulance chasers, and haters of police, public safety, and RNs and MDs, and their sordid attorneys. Off-duty activities are built around the subculture of high-risk behaviors and excitement, that is, addictive highs, including alcoholism, illicit substances, gambling, and indiscriminate one-day sexual relations, including orgies, prostitutes, and extramarital relations experienced as conquests. Perhaps you achieve your high by speeding at 100 mph and Russian roulette. Intoxication to dissociate your own feelings includes self-soothing attempts through addictions that are often destructive in more than physical risk. There is also an enormous psychological and existential risk to you, your loved ones, and peers. Most of this addictive behavior is done in subgroups with cultural, ecological, and ethological release of the tensions you encounter on a day-to-day basis.

The great police writer and real-deal Joseph Wambaugh's (1987) "choir practice" was not made up in an ivory tower, but LA's seedy parks. A great place to release some of the horror of day to night losses where all traumas can be fixed in "booze, bets, or high-risk addictive behavior, and guys and gals."

Your appointment and promotion to specialized details include achieving high-level commendations. You survive high-risk exposure to dangerous events that are noted by superior officers and supplemented by civilians who write and advocate for you as their hero officer as a superb adaptation. Your passionate impulse to respond to emergency events at times becomes so hyperexcited you can override constraint—with tragic consequences. At emergency events your expression of empathy for victims of crime is genuine, empathic, and protective: you do not shy away from people knowing you are a cop, firefighter, EMT, ER RN, or ER MD—you thrive on that identity as the rescuer/hero. You relish the rescued victim's warm thanks. However, conscious manipulation and exploitation are something you do not do. In fact if asked, you genuinely despise, at least consciously. The other side of your style is at times you may overstep boundaries with flirtation and beyond. Even so, you never lose your essential depth inside at your core being to genuinely and protectively really care about the job you do, and the people you service. As an officer, while you do care a great deal about victims, you are not really aware (as of yet) of your own unconscious motivation into some high-risk taking and self-sabotage in your approach. At times your impulsive need to rescue civilians off duty who may not be as benevolent as they present themselves to you. An unusual liaison may quench your urges to conquer danger, and place you in its grasp.

Our Personality Style Peer's Most Traumatic Event in Officer Z's Own Quoted Viewpoint

On 0X/0X/0X the Y Precinct had our annual canoe trip. We had a great time. A lot of drinking, a barbecue, and plenty of laughs. During the bus ride home the fun continued. About four blocks from the precinct the bus pulled over and a sergeant said he had an announcement to make. He then told us that P.O. X was killed that afternoon at xx hours. The bus was silent as we continued to the precinct. We exited the bus and went directly to the bar across from the precinct. The old timers helped the younger guys. About 2 hours later, I was drunk and went to my girl-friend. I felt the need to be close to a woman. I was filled with all kinds of feelings, one minute it was anger and then sorrow, then I was fearful and then became guilty. I felt I should have been there and prevented this. I wanted to be there to help. It was hard to understand how a day that was filled with such happiness, laughter, and so much fun could end in such an unexpected way. After this incident I became somewhat hardened. Not so much shook me up after that as a rookie. Before I was a cop, I never drank. I wanted to fit in and be one of the boys. I started to drink and after a while I got used to drinking. We forgot about all the things on and off the job.

When I had about 5 years on the job my partner and I shared an apart-ment in the Bronx. He was promoted. The night of his promotion he asked me for a ride. I was tired and wiped out and drove him to his own car. He drove right under a truck and was killed. I never can forget him, the wild stuff we did together, women, drinking, and all kinds of adventure; most of all that night he was standing in the doorway asking me to wait for him. I was so wasted I forgot and just left. I killed him by leaving him.

I started to drink more heavily. When I would wake up in the morning I would drink a full glass of vodka. For 6 weeks me and another officer drank together and talked all the time about how much we missed Officer YM. During this period I would cock my gun and put it in my mouth or to my head, but just couldn't pull the trigger. Then my friend, who hung out with us 3 weeks later after a tour of duty ended, was killed off duty. I saw him that night, and I realized I was joking with him and kind of rough, and it was the last time I would see him. As I said earlier, I don't blame the police depart-ment, but it was too much for anyone to handle.

I just boozed and went to women for comfort. As my career went on I became very frustrated with the constant way perps got away with all the crap, and the court system and situations I felt were controlled by politics and the press, not our welfare. The one that sticks in my head most was Tompkins Square Park.

When I was there I felt I did my job and did it well. If it came down to me having to use physical force on a person I also arrested that person.

I felt that the public looked at us as one, and not that out of a large number of police officers who did what we had to, only a few made mistakes and were wrong. I also became very prejudiced toward any young guy who would mouth off and disrespect us. It changed. I went from having fun and excitement to getting all out of sorts. I just didn't even like or know who I was. I started to cut myself with a razor, go to bed with women to ease the pain, just strangers. It wasn't like the roulette; it was not to kill myself, it was just to stop my fears, my missing my buddies, and focusing on something else. The excitement keeps me going.

Impact of Traumatic Loss in My Own Unique Personality Style: On Duty and Off Duty

Loss is acceptable in expression for someone else. You know what is meant when officers say, "That guy is just projecting his bad stuff on me." What we really mean to say is that the shock and tragic losses are too hard to swallow: "I am feeling the pain of loss so I will convince myself I am okay period, simple as that! Leave me deal with 'it' alone."

The not so conscious part is you most likely are shell shocked with what you see in how callous others can be. I have uncovered in countless hours with officers an incredible lack of belief that other human beings can be so vicious and cruel to others: violence, whether shooting, stabbing, batting someone, burning someone else alive, and bombing others, is too much. You learn to tell yourself, "It is so surreal," meaning it is so horrible. Meaning reality cannot really be so cruel. It must be a scene out of the *Twilight Zone*.

You then tell yourself that if you let go, and let yourself mourn your losses, you will be a basket case. Everyone will know you're weak and not able to deal with it. You figure it is better to distract yourself with any amusement as escape. So even though you know deep inside that your losses would bother any living being, even a maple tree, you are tougher. After all, you've heard yourself say a thousand times over that you're a street cop, a kick-butt firefighter, or a no-nonsense EMT, ER RN, or ER MD, and if anyone can deal with it, you can. You can deal with it. You felt you had no time to have a pity party, so you let it go. Simple as that!

That dialogue is true. In fact, you suppressed your pain just as the officer recounting his many losses in his own words. He is a fine and decent officer and yet the pain of losses, the guilt of surviving, is enough to numb even the mighty lion, pushed aside as he plows ahead as the walking wounded. By putting it onto the next fellow or gal, you project or toss your own losses onto them and say, "Yes, I understand losses for Mary, Joe, Dan, and Sue, but not me!" It is no different from a street survival mechanism you have learned in tactics and operations, but here it is not so conscious at all until you face how many losses you have really buried. Unburying these losses in this guide, or any other, is only a beginning of awareness. Fully working through is possible only when you can work with a competent, public safety-trained "with it" therapist. Think about it for a moment: if asked by a shrink if you suffered losses or trauma, the blue, red, or white wall of silence comes up and you may say, "Well, you know that homicide or burn victim who pleaded to me to help who was beyond rescue certainly would bother Joe Q or Mary Q Citizen, but not me—I am a public safety officer, ER nurse, or ER MD."

While I am not a green ivory counselor wannabe cop, but a NYPD cop doc, I have still heard one answer a thousand times when I ask a peer support officer, delegate, the partner of an officer, or the officer herself, "What are you thinking of, or how you making out?" after experiencing an event that would traumatize a bull. The response is almost automatic, "Me, I am okay, really, Doc! I let that crap roll off like a duck's backside. In fact, I couldn't care less. It's just my job, no sweat, no problem."

Well from your perspective that is true. It appears so because it makes sense from an ethological sense of survival and an ecological sense too. After all, being a street public safety officer, especially with this personality style, means you are able to handle anything. You believe in your gut most likely that you will rise above the fear and anxieties regular folk must deal with.

You may even be able to express feeling some loss. Perhaps you make some token gestures in grieving an innocent victim, but when it comes to the officer in the example of this personality style (you read in his description of significant losses), his revolves around what I call a sacred victim. A sacred victim is another buddy officer downed in the line of duty and then another off duty: shock and anger emerge, blood will be given for blood, taken one way or another.

Loss and grieving is put off and your guilt for being alive swells like the undercurrent in a riptide hardly visible even to you as you are swept away. Deep inside, guilt can turn your world upside down and inside out. If it is a bad guy that gets his just dessert as the official line, you can call him or her a profane victim: no loss is expressed or guilt allowed. Rather, a feeling of satisfaction, such as "Hey, I did my job, another bites the dust. It is what it is. A good shooting, or a good use of force, it's good work." Typical is a comment like, "Detective Mary, one less bad guy to screw with innocent victims. Great job! I'll take you as my partner anytime."

Well that may be true, but it takes away nothing from the reality of Mary living with a decision she had to make to keep herself alive. You see the untold story was the guy who was being attacked with a car door being readied as a makeshift deadly battering ram into this poor Joe's head had to be stopped. So some small-time numbers runner now caught by the collection guy assigned the task to make him a lesson for all small hoods. After all, in the hood it makes street sense since the bookie owed profits made on time, but did nothing to pay it off. You came in on the attempt almost executed just on time. Time that you, like Mary, may have made a decision to take a life. Taking a life is never free to the taker, even when justified. It is a very painful, gut-wrenching choice, awesome responsibility and loss. Yes, loss, even the loss of your innocence. The loss of the security that you never had to kill anyone: now you did. The fact you cannot express the loss adequately and publicly, as family and friends you believe will not understand. With the accolades you are bound within our culture to further shield losses. This armor also occurs when you do not succeed fully in a collar or safeguarding a prisoner, "I am a loser because I let the perp get away." This thought is one that is taught to prevent you from ever letting this happen, the same with an accidental discharge. It has now happened. In a way you may lean toward acting impulsively off duty as on duty. The reason for that impulsivity in part allows you to maintain a sense of personal power. Power of being you, and a rebellion from being controlled, especially in the military culture you live in.

It also in part fulfills a wish to be absorbed in the drama of trauma as a heroic officer. You are not alone in this drama, where myth and metaphor of the hero are as ancient as Homer's *Odyssey* and Hercules' seven tasks. It is the heroic ideal as romantic that leaves your sense of being indestructible wrapped around your Achilles' tendon to your head.

It is sometimes enlightening to know that when you are running from being controlled, you are usually trying to escape from a hidden secret within yourself. That secret is so hard to acknowledge. I find at the root of that secret a fear. Your fear in part is a fear of death: by conquering that fear you embrace the very behavior that you fear the most—a sense of being immortal. In other words, your sense of being indestructible is forged by you being the first responder a cop's cop, firefighter's firefighter, ER doc's doc, ER RN's RN, or EMT's top medic professional. It is hard to let go of proving yourself as invulnerable. This myth served your gaining an eco-ethological edge in your unit and helped you overcome your own fears. The reward in your unit with gold and silver medals does not fade and lasts the test of finite time with eternal honor. Commendations delivered by chiefs addressing you with honors reinforce the ideals so deeply engrained and shaped within your profession—and remain. This heroic myth and metaphor also serves an existential gain of meaning. Meaning that in part is genuine, and in part a very real danger within your personality style. When the rush of heroic ideals and risk taking stops, you are suddenly and existentially left face-to-face with your own mortality.

Self-realization and letting go of your own need to control danger and death put you right in the viper's lair with no psychological antidote. In many cases you can displace your own fear of death to all the victims you rescued: rescued victims are recipients of your heroism that give you evidence that if you can rescue weaker folks in need of your help, you can certainly cheat death itself. Your rescue identity is supported within public safety culture. A culture that is supported within many communities. Without stopping to reflect on the impact of death and its denial, many misconceptions about anxiety and fear of death emerge. Not letting go and letting love is a major side effect. Without the letting go of the armor of invulnerability, you cannot let go and let love be learned and emerge. The result leaves two parties struck with emptiness when all is said and left undone.

I want to bring to your attention another aspect of your style as an addictive hyperexcited personality officer. You are there for other officers during a time of crisis. But, it is likely your behaviors are high risk and stretch to the maximum elastic band of brother- and sisterhood. This stretch of boundaries in many cases leads to the borderline of self-destructive to nearly suicidal tendencies. Survival guilt is also an enormous loss that needs to be filled as your peer's example at the beginning of this profile. In fact, your survival guilt is likely to be acted out in a variety of addictive ways without you being consciously aware. It is a lot easier, so it seems, to take a bottle of booze, take some risks with a random pickup person, and sleep with the opposite sex to gain some relief in ecstatic rites. Perhaps you do something to just get a thrill that can ease the feeling of loss and shock from the trauma, by even shocking yourself. But is it really relief? You can slow down that craving for relief, right here and now. Think about that question as it affects you, your loved ones, even if you have by now lost many of your close friends, and family. You can choose to stop, pause, and reflect to yourself in this moment with me: it is never too late! Hey, where there is life, there is hope—and the ability to change! It is not that easy, but you can begin by owning you have an addictive tendency. A tendency learned in part, in part biological and psychologically part of your nature, or traits you were born with: you learned to select what made sense in your adaptation to an ecology of trauma, and in filling in your losses ethologically. In a unique way choir practice is worthwhile to read again and immortalized in your style, which includes earned special privileges: it is highly adaptive, on one hand, to be a star player in a unit as a key to your quest in dealing with overwhelming losses that give you the power of being one of the immortals—the invulnerable hero! Legends and public folklore perpetuate the idea that "heroes do not really die." Heroes go off and become distant memories. We all need to call up other strengths when the real blues hit the fan for you. It is a lonely place, and one in which you get all the attention until that curtain goes down. You are left alone. Alone with yourself. When that alone time with yourself occurs, you may wake up to a homecoming of rejection and being cast away. When something goes awry, panic may set in alongside of obsessive thoughts of being rejected, and suicidal impulses.

Your relationships may be romantic and short-lived. Relationships may be subject to the same type of sabotage with stretching boundaries with people you come into contact with. On and off the job you take major risks. Stop, pause, and seek counseling for the repeat losses and risks. Another danger is your own dissociation and anger are projected into the domestic situation. It feels as if you can never trust your loved ones to appreciate what you have been through. I would say in some situations that belief may in fact be correct, just as all officers are not the same, the same is true of families, and their dysfunctional styles of interaction. Your crisis regardless of social support at the moment can lead to change, growth, and trust. Trust you may never have had the opportunity to learn or experience. Left unexplored until now, the possibilities of growth are large. Explored in therapy, you may choose to not turn against a loving relationship, and even with a dysfunctional partner you may choose to work on change together. In rarer cases you may simply choose to end the relationship.

For example, a male officer may tell his wife she does not understand the police lifestyle. This usually is not due to a shortcoming on the officer's part. It is usually a fear of being exposed to his own fears and anxiety, which he is terrified of confronting. He likely has been taught well to protect himself against being vulnerable, as Cop Doc Gilmartin calls mindsets and schemas within public safety culture, and Cop Doc Conroy calls officers at risk, and I call shaping within your ecological and ethological niches of public safety within the nest of your own hyperexcited personality style.

Another result of these losses is more likely in your response to loss (and something meriting more research): the victimization of many officers by choices of mates. If your choice seems like a slate of romantic flings, your own attention is needed. This pattern is an important response to losses not mourned. You may be needy without your own awareness. By rescuing your prince or princess type, who in turn is not likely to view you as the unique person you are. He or she is likely to look at you as a public safety officer and provoke you to rescue him or her and you're geared to do just that. The problem with the fantasy is the wish is a lot deeper, and when you fail being his/her perfect hero/heroine and your rescue fantasy cannot be fulfilled in a perfect ideal way, you will likely be rejected. Your spouse/partner's loss is your own. You cannot fulfill a gaping hole of losses with all the love you bring to the ditch: your natural tendencies to take risks, be bold, and confidently take on all challenges make you exquisitely ripe for exploitation. Exploitation where you eventually become victim when you fail to make the grade. A grade set so inhumanely high. In part, your tendency for being a hero leaves you vulnerable to select mates who are truly hostile and exploitive: measured seduction can leave you clueless when it strikes your heart and leaves your soul gasping for meaning now lost. Since your identity is so infused with your being a hero, you fail to see you are the ideal mate for the confidant woman/man. With your confidence and feeling good about yourself as an ambitious public safety officer, you are like a flower for these highly flirtatious mates. Mates who like a busy bee pollinate you with charm, promises of forever love, and other seductive wishes. Wow! It does sound good. So does happily ever after. I have seen and witnessed the dance more times than I care to recount. A dance where a hyperexcited addictive public safety officer has fallen again with the sting of betrayal. Broken promises and betrayal are the worst psychological pains and hurt so bad when marriage equations of love leave you reeling in excruciating psychological pain. Your tendency to find a mate in quick fashion and flirtatiously falling in love is as quick as he or she may swallow all your assets. As quick as the sand of a dune, she may say you just do not make her happy as quick and frivolously. If this sounds like you, it is important to seek a cop counselor and immediately protect yourself. A choice is not rushing into the siren of quick-fix marriages—like Las Vegas endings. It takes one bad throw of the dice.

The other type of mate you are vulnerable to will want to possess you completely and project that need on you. The sign is he or she is jealous of everyone that comes near you, especially the opposite sex because you are so idealized. Idealized lovers will turn on a dime. You become the bad guy as soon as the well runs dry in your ability to perform as exacted. This tendency in part may be acceptable due to your own need to fulfill losses that have become so ripped open by traumas. Open wounds left to fulfill may be susceptible to others who need you to fulfill their own in cash cows and bulls. The tendency is you fall again and again in your own willingness to participate in this dance of self-indulgence. A never-ending need for rescuing the damsel, or prince in distress. This dance of dysfunction may be stopped. Stopped by pausing right now and realizing the good news is you are not alone. You can choose to work on these issues—where tendencies are not fateful conclusions.

Another path in relationships falls into your own ambivalence—meaning both good and bad feelings in different shades of desire or withdrawal from your partner. In fact, you have likely distanced yourself from choosing mates that match you well, when doubt colors your clarity of experiences that are meaningful. War zones you shift into and moan about, night in and day out, leave you with a feeling of why bother—good is good enough.

Think about it, you have seen one crime after another in an ecology of violence that leads to a loss of hope and optimism in a real and meaningful way: you start to believe love that holds all the different colors and flavors is not for you. It is BS awarded for civilians in la la land and Disney—not Brooklyn North, Baghdad, Chicago, or Detroit.

The peacetime/wartime (night in/day out) in an urban war zone may be too intense a break and repair to go through every day. Your experience slowly peels off your interests as you shift from being a civilian whose physical space cached too many real losses in human time. Too many traumas you have been through, or care to remember. Defending against having other officers see you expressing fear and loss openly—when compassion for victims is quickly stifled: but when a peer or yourself is injured badly or murdered in cold blood, it is okay to get outraged. It is okay to use a legally appropriate use of force. But between you and me, "it" still boils down to hostility for yourself or peers expressing loss openly while safely being redirected at perpetrators. In other words, pause for the moment and consider your own fear of loss may be redirected into outlets where little if any emotional expression of loss is allowed ventilation. That memory that comes back, say when you are on 46th and 8th Avenue, where you had seen your peer shot dead is "dead space." That space is frozen and stuck in your mind at one level of your own experience, and on another it is dissociated from your own experience of losses and trauma. Since you find it too hard to allow admission into your mind, it makes superb sense to maximize your own chances to maintain a sense of control and self-soothing. Self-soothing absorbs your attention and redirects "it" away from the shock of another officer hurt or killed. Your own hurts channel into addictive and exciting on the edge behaviors. Substitutes redirect attention and give intention to a sense of control in your hand and will.

From a medical psychological view your repeated experience with trauma, heightened anxiety, and the release of chemicals in your bloodstream such as endorphins and epinephrine give you a hardwired high. When you experience your high peak of excitement it is self-reinforcing.

Meaning the behavior that is addictive needs to be satisfied longer and more intensely until it becomes hardwired repeats. Repeats where thrill seeking to reach that level of excitement is reinforced. Rewards for being an "alpha officer–top dog" are heightened by shared emotional highs and higher status in your own eco-ethological niche. You may get a wink in a unit that is in high gear and intensity that may have a CO like yourself or of the hyperfocused personality style look at your work product as excellent. That eco-ethological niche is a culturally and psychologically legitimate outlet for you.

It is not unusual if you are retired, recently transferred to a slower house, have been injured on duty/off duty/in the line of duty, or on restricted duty and you are feeling like a fish out of water. You may even feel like a Siamese fighting fish in a bowl, not a tank: you are ready for action but stuck in a bad way in a constricted bowl making circles without an exit sign.

Still another aspect of your style may exist here; that numbing effect persists in you, perhaps a reported lack of feeling, including fear and sadness, for your own suffering.

Well it makes sense as well since you were trained as a public safety officer. That training meant you have witnessed and learned that being unemotional is a rewarded status. An officer that can let all pain, loss, and fear roll off his or her back helps mobilize you for pursuit, arrest, and custody. Your confrontation identity modes are so highly valued and rewarded—as long as all goes well. Not expressing losses and trauma emotionally includes male and female officers. In part, your responses are shaped by a unisex approach to training, socialization, and exposure to trauma in public service culture. The formation of your public safety personality is shaped in evolutionary influences and ecological niches larger than your own awareness. Becoming an officer occurs in the formidable years of late adolescence to young adulthood. Shaping the blocking of your emotional expression of fear, guilt, and loss is in part the ecological and cultural dimension of training. In some ways you learn how to block losses and trauma in your unique style in the unwritten shaping you experience in your unique eco-ethological niche. Your armor of defense against losses on the job is achieved by numbing out through adaptive functional dissociation over time. Numbing your reactive feelings of fear, and loss through projecting onto others their fear, while accepting your own acceptable emotional aggressiveness makes superb sense ethologically in terms of survival value. For example, an officer-soldier that weeps out loud instead of in silence awakes the sadistic onslaught of foes. The officer-soldier that weeps in silence eventually echoes a perimeter of indifference with an impression of invulnerability.

That impression serves survival physically while existentially leaving you with the echoes that reflect away from your own insight and act as projectors onto others. It stings when you realize the only service it does on an existential dimension is leave you alone. Alone in a glass room with smoking mirrors. Those smoking mirrors have no respite in your public safety shield where the pad of your own self-imposed but sensible survival motivation leads to your own bondage, so to speak.

Another catch-22 you are stuck in for now: the exit door with a large sign you can choose will be offered soon enough. One such door you have used as an exit from danger physically is the training you have received as a recruit. That method is role-plays and rehearsals that teach you the real risk of death and serious bodily injury and how to avoid these dangers. You learn that as long as you use the tools given correctly, you will remain above the dangers and rewarded with department awards. The reward for being a public safety

officer with your hyperexcited style is in the larger culture highly contradictory. Let's look at why. On one hand, the very award of public commendations
along with rising up the chain of command or being appointed an investigator or a member of elite details such as ESU, aviation, mounted, swat, medic,
and fire rescue emergency responder is a major reward for taking high risks.
These high risks offer major payoffs—if all goes well. If all goes well repeatedly, it makes superb sense that your sensibility is attuned to an increasing
belief in your own invulnerability, or simply feeling superhuman. In a way,
when you are faced with situations that would make most officers cringe in
the moment, at least for pause, you run in, full throttle. What happens here is
important to realize. Your numbing and functional dissociation is not consciously within your awareness—it is your ally and comes into play as a role
you live and you become repeatedly exposed to. Think about it as a function
of what you were once aware of consciously, and no longer even think twice
about. It is now fully automatic, and unconsciously hidden within your best
defenses. On the other hand, nothing is said about the damage being done
with each new increasing risk, which raises the probability of an accident,
against the existential cost in your professional life on one hand, and your
personal on another. Your ideals and beliefs about invulnerability collide
with the reality when all hell breaks loose and you are left vulnerable. The
cruel irony is you did or do all you can humanely do and are left with a pile of
human tragedy. A tragic series of losses even a mythological superman could
not clean up. In a very important way your own fear of loss becomes less and
less conscious. Replacing your fear of loss is increased aggression toward the
perps, arsonists, or at times reckless causes of fire. This relationship is like a
seesaw—the more you have weighted down in investing in being superhuman, the less you have balance on the other side of tragic reality. The more
you have weighed on tragic optimism as meaningful, the less despair sets
in on the other side of paradise for you, here on earth. Boundless optimism
without realistic appraisals of tragic occurrences leads to the hills of despair.
Yet, if you hold on to the tragic in mind at the outset, you will not have the
passion to deal with the unstable, uncontrollable, and extreme intensity you
are confronted with existentially and need to endure in marathons you are
thrust into: again, through no fault of your own, and even worse through no
intentional fault of the department you work for, reality happens. In real time
filled with the space of toxic events, your normal response to toxic and genuine danger is replaced with more and higher levels of risk taking. Objective
fear and healthy caution go out the window as the door to achieve being at
the top of your game increases exponentially. Why? In part, it makes sense
to say the public safety culture no less than the media gives heavy reinforcement to the benefits, honor, and illusion of mastery of death with heroic
actions. Mastery becomes symbolically associated with altered states of

consciousness via identity modes where you become highly functional with increasingly high risk to danger, and your physiological and psychological state of mind reinforces this state of mind and being. The cost of risky activities on the job becomes the quest where it now makes sense as to why off the job the finest of the finest, the bravest of the bravest, and the strongest of the strongest sabotage their own life goals of stability and living off the job. What is happening in many cases is you're striving to repeat symbolically what you experience in the saddle of the job, and that tragically is likely to have been set even earlier in life as to your own tendencies biologically and in family dynamics. Said another way yet, you are trained as a rodeo rider, and when you get off duty it is normal to want to shift onto another saddle of excitement and increasing addiction.

So let's review why there is a continuity of your own hyperexcited addictive style when you as an officer are off duty. Your addictive behaviors off duty have likely increased with damaging effects shaped, and in turn shaped by your behaviors in an ecological niche you have re-created, where excitement and turning off the losses is set in amusing distractions.

First, let me qualify to you a choice to look at your tendency in a negative way and label you exist—this would be not only a narrow-minded view, but also almost worthless in helping you: it would be conforming to a dishonest attitude that blames what is real and sensible within our culture and in the deeper shades of your personality. Being real with one another, I will not do the label game or blame game. I hope you will not play that game as well. In fact, in a very creative way you can appreciate an ingenious conscious, and in part unconscious buffer you created within your field experiences and personality style.

This happening occurs because your direct experience of loss dissociated from the objective danger and harm was redirected by you in accomplishing becoming the best in your professional specialty. In doing so, many rewards symbolically and in reality have been achieved by you in the ecological field you work in. The needs you express are in turn satisfied by the recreational highs sought by you off duty. These sought-after highs mimic your own biological and psychological highs experienced by your actual complex street trauma and loss events on duty.

How Your Public Safety Personality Style Is Different from Other Public Safety Styles

While you are superficially similar to the hyperaggressive edge style, which we will look at in depth below, yours is quite distinct. Like the hyperaggressive style, you thrive on excitement and getting into the heat of rescue and response. The hyperaggressive edge style, however, has a different approach when dealing with the civilian population. The key here is motivation as well as intensity of certain behaviors as goals in and of themselves. The hyperaggressive style seeks getting something out of every interaction as the norm: where frontal confrontation of any person who gets in the way—whether on the job or off the job—is no problem. In your own hyperexcited style it is the public folks that in and of themselves are in a way intoxicating. Meaning folks that are civilian unusually reinforce your own ideals—as victims rescued by your interventions. The civilians mirror your own heroism and investment in your own wish for being to a degree invulnerable to the very losses they suffer.

This does not mean you are not genuine. You likely experience a genuine satisfaction as well as addiction to this immersion in your rescue and recovery efforts. Doubly so in law enforcement, arrests of the most dangerous perps, fire rescue operations that are most risky, and medical operations that lead to near miracles in novel techniques applied. While you have a true concern for other people, especially victims, and not just a shallow reaction for their pain and loss, you likely will not allow your own loss to be expressed. The way you deal with this loss is sensible in a culture where expressing loss is okay if it is for "them" as victims or even the sufferers, not you! Deep under the covers, so to speak, your genuine feelings of guilt and self-doubt exacerbate even more high-risk behaviors. Risky behaviors to overcome a circle of dangerous and costly physical, mental, emotional, and existential damage. That layered damage covers over an armor, so to speak, that you have developed over a long period of immersion in war zones, high-risk assignments, and daring missions. These specifically may include infiltrations and reconnaissance objectives you have sought, seek, and will continue to do.

Similarities abound in what we shrinks call borderline tendencies. This I believe is a pseudoresemblance, meaning for our purpose it reflects an image but not a reality. The development of your hyperexcited traits emerges in an environment of constant danger and persistent patterns of survival as resistance and defenses against loss. Eco-ethological dimensions are powerful forces in all human beings, but honed to a perceptive genius in public safety officers.

Hyperexcitement may help you gain what sensibly in the context of your experiences makes good sense as an officer-patient. Meaning you gain in rescue efforts and being protective of innocent civilians a cover for the deep pain you feel for others. Let's look at it another way; you have heard the saying "One hand washes the other and both the face!"

I agree with this statement, but with an added understanding. A good way to think about washing away the stuff you would like to rid yourself of—the one reality you can never wash away is your own stuff: while you wash so many others faces, hardly anyone in reality washes your own dirt and grime away! Why?

Because the armor that protects you also shields you from being vulnerable and that is what your craving is all about: filling the losses you witness night in and day out in rescue and recovery effects.

When and Where Do You Let Out Your Own Private Losses of Public Tragedy?

The watering hole is where you can wash over losses that ferment in a barrel rounded in the circle of thrills and excitements of another night out with your peers. Repeat performances where you get no chance to stop, pause, and reflect on the "traumas" in your own circle of life.

Being a hero public safety officer is another truly noble craving; at its core it is an addiction, and at a very deep level your losses are forgotten and unattended.

Risk taking is also a roller coaster you may never exit and helps keep you on an edge where the real you is buried in helping everyone else save one. Until crisis of meaning hits home plate, we all know ground zero sits within the breast that holds your shield, which works both ways and has two sides: one spoken and the other silent and unheard—your own.

As a cop doc that's what I am all about—you—the hero left unheard in your own pile of losses unsung in ground zero!

I ask you at this point in reading to stop and pause: I need you to now think of you and your needs! Slow it down right here and now and look at your own losses to see what may be done to help you cop-in. Copping-in and working through some options include remaining stuck in your road block, selecting a best route, or the longest path.

Initial Inroads to Lay Out Your Own Map for Trauma and Grief Therapy

In your style it is likely you feel displaced and likely to resonate on the happenings of the day when things finally cool down and all your losses in trauma are experienced as extremely painful. Think of the early example of a peer sharing his odyssey with us. Go back and reread his own words of the process of change when he first learned on a beautiful outing with his peers that a peer officer was murdered in cold blood! Was it easier for him and perhaps you to go to the watering hole and numb away your pain of loss and fear? Perhaps he said as you may have, "That can happen to me—what to do?" One thing you are expert at doing is frankly taking more risks to be the first inside the doors of physical danger. Why? Again, it makes sense as you can now conquer more of your fears, and while not sitting with your losses in a seesaw relationship with the more risks you conquer by surviving, the less fear of loss. Also, with the three addictions of booze, bets, or addictive sex, the higher your tolerance of high-risk behaviors and temporary satisfaction gained in each. Addiction, depression, and aggression all spiral down to the internal enemy of extreme prejudice against the best ally you have—you! It may be more likely when you are injured in the line of duty or off duty with an illness or injury that the busy and hurried crashes to a sudden halt! Perhaps your memories are as vivid as ever and rise to awaken you. They may be ever present and cannot and will not be ignored. It is like the debt collector—if you do not assess your damages and pay up front, we all know what happens in the final analysis: no joke intended—it is not a laughing matter here—you pay on the tail end of retirement, or a tragic accident to confront what has been long denied. Your choice!

It is important to consider another aspect of how and why loss likely dissolves in toxic concoctions of addictions where peacetime can be a repetition of wartime for you. Keep in mind what is happening is the chaotic aspects of your street experiences are reenacted, often with tragic results at worst and more dysfunctional relationships at home with significant others.

In some cases you may place your husband or wife as a victim waiting to happen and may not so consciously be overprotective (or controlling, including with jealousy) toward loved members of your own family and even friends. Why does this pattern emerge so often in a style where you take so many risks on the job?

Well, one is the danger experienced on the job transfers to situations at home and your need to be the rescuer and hero cop or other public safety officer, and in being too excited over your loved ones' welfare, you can cut off the support you need and desire most. That support is the one you live with and love most; the irony is tragic and if it was not so sad, it would almost be comical. That irony is being a very active and protective officer you may exact a rigid boundary, which may in protecting your loved ones, push those you love most away. This situation can lead to relationships where misunderstanding shatters your desire to protect—you are perceived or rather misperceived as being overcontrolling. This state of being less than clear on your love and need to shield your loved ones from danger you experience in the eco-ethological niches is no less than what you do with your partner on patrol or emergency response. Since the departments do not understand this phenomenon, they have not set up training to help you with it. This tendency to create niches of protection that excludes outsiders is an "internal affair" where a sacred trust and bond on the job turns astray in your home life. Put another way, your desire to shield loved ones from what you see clearly as a dangerous situation provokes a command presence you have learned works on the mean streets. You take lessons learned in the streets and bring them home, which is natural and can be unlearned over time and effort. But chances are when you are misperceived and labeled a control freak, you feel rejected and let down for doing what brings so much praise and accolades in the public safety field, especially "war zones"—command presence and being protective of others. Looking at it from a deeper level and also in terms of your eco-ethological niche, you have learned that without command presence no officer could do his or her job effectively. It just will not snap into place by wishing it will. The daily reindoctrination you have undergone is to a different set of subtle, symbolic, and sacred rules distinct from the world of nonpublic service culture. Let's take a look at another experience that is very hard to balance and that is working in urban war zones and peace zones, say as an EMT/firefighter or ER nurse or MD all in a day's experience. A day quite intense, abrupt, and similar to combat soldiers on the front line in a transition zone.

For tactical patrol officers or street crime officers, as is true with doing deep-cover drug interdiction and ghosting bad guys/gals, we see a parallel with soldiers in foreign constant combat for time-limited events.

In public safety/service this is exacerbated when there is no transition or planning for healing and habituation—even less cultural and ecological transition support at the time of off duty to on duty. In fact, if most officers are asked they will say, "Hey, even when I am off duty I am on duty. Once a cop/firefighter/EMT/RN/MD/PhD on the frontline, always one!"

The solution at minimum entails law enforcement agencies using a systematic program of rotations out of urban war zones; this is true of foreign war zones. I would like you to consider how much of the losses are left frozen when they are not defined or accepted as real losses.

The ecology of addiction and risks with self-harm and even self-endangerment becomes more human and understandable, not only for you but also hopefully for your own spouse, or girlfriend, boyfriend, family, and friends. Reaching into your own honest accounting enables painfully recounting a safe place, as did our fellow officer in the case above. In his own words, his repeated experiences are presented. He was able to transition from seeing a peer support officer to a cop doc. His outcome was positive and he healed over time from the cumulative losses worked on. It is important to realize that in reading about your style you may have made a choice to go about a plan to work on some addictive behaviors by reducing the harm they are causing you. If you can start changes, you are succeeding in the purpose of this book. Redirecting yourself, as follows, includes asking: Why can't you allow some expression out loud about loss about the death or serious injury of a young person in an accident? Can you attend and participate, or even sit in the back of an AA or rational recovery meeting? When you feel the high of a pursuit, can you step back and try some other natural high?

For example, why can't you get an iPod and do some running instead of acting out? Can you visualize letting go of your need to rescue? Practicing for at least moments off duty and exercising can help. Another thing you can do is make a list of all the amazing rescues and recovery efforts you did, or attempted to do, and how incredible even failed attempts may be as an achievement where heart and motivation counts.

How about more examples:

Make a list of some consequences that happened when you have attempted and may have actually reduced your tendency toward high-risk taking behaviors on or off duty.

Can you think of any gains you have made in terms of changing the way you think of taking less risk taking and valuing your own courage and commitment without extending the boundaries to a place where the risk of serious injury or harm is exacted by you?

Can you look at this life-altering experience as a gentle act of love that was perhaps a wake-up call to your own inner worth and value as a humane being?

Can you dare to accept yourself as worthy of all the love imaginable?

Perhaps, crisis has just shattered your perspective on life: you were involved in an off-duty and even perhaps an on-duty driving under the influence arrest as a subject—do you feel you cannot ask for help? Well now, right now, just do it, and call in to the union or department assistance programs and ask!

Perhaps you were infected during a medical intervention or rescue with a sexually transmitted/infectious disease.

Maybe off duty you had taken some risk behavior with a person you did not really get to know and now have a sexually transmitted disease.

Did you receive an injury during a dramatic rescue, and now have legal difficulty as a result of heroic action taken?

Has survivor guilt after a peer is injured severely or murdered in the line of duty hit you hard?

It is important once your own safety and self-care is established with a peer support officer who genuinely cares to further your own longer-term goals. As you see, your longer-term goals are to take out the scratch sheet in the back of this guide and fill in the sheets and make copies of these sheets as needed for each question above, and the event associated with that event. Make some assignments for yourself, including the "to do" lists of actual behaviors, and goals you can establish right now with commitment and realistically. Fishing may sound good, gardening even better, and cooking a nice dinner with vegetables, protein, and some fresh fruit superb. The beer and chips will be there, but give it a break first.

Start by reducing the alcohol, caffeine, and nicotine intake as self-initiated interventions. They help in the moment, but in the turn of time they each weigh down and hit you with one strike after another. I now ask you to answer some questions, hopefully with a peer support officer and even better, a cop counselor after some time. Following are some questions you may find helpful:

> Why do you insist on giving assistance to another cop without hesitation but that standard (I agree with) does not apply to you, but only applies to any other cop?
> Do you have a double standard, one for you and another for the rest of the mere mortal officers?
> What would it mean to loved ones if you really did die in the line of duty taking the high risks you do night in and day out?

Let's Get Real: Your Public Safety Personality Style: Officer and Cop Doc's Corner

One Fellow Public Safety Officer: Different Venues—Similar Windows—Different Exits

Rethinking Extreme Risk Taking—Let's Reduce the Risk of Harm Not, Your Heroism   Officer A is a young police officer on the job with a hyperexcited public safety personality style. He is a bright and caring officer who takes high risks in doing his job. The most recent was chasing a bad guy who took some shots at officers on the midnight tour as he took off in heavy pursuit. His car careened into a pole, and luckily he was able to walk away from his injuries. His realization he needed to talk about it with a peer support officer led him to my clinic (flirting with death/ unconscious suicide or invulnerability). Note: I would like to ask you to use your psychological imagination as I work with an incredibly brave and yet risk-taking officer to reach an understanding that will hopefully illustrate how you can also make a choice to learn as he and I did. Learn as to why and then how to lower the risky consequences with doing your job as an expert professional, that is, less likely harm to yourself and perhaps others.

Dr. Dan: You know we have been here before and it seems like the risk taking is not a big issue. The consequences are: like, who worries? I'm not going to be a statistic? Yet, you and I have also figured out, if let's say an accident occurs, and things do not go as planned, then what? Take, for example, when you stormed into a street robbery off duty. It could be a disaster waiting to happen, huh?

Officer A: Yeah it could be like [expression of a thousand-yard stare away]. I said you've been a dinosaur and have not been on the streets for a long time. You know if you want a gold shield, you've got to work your tail off. I have no hooks, no uncle who is a chief. You took a lot of risks when you started off.

Dr. Dan: [I did. While some were risky, it is important for Officer A to stick with his issues at hand.] Well, let's get to the heart of it. I want to help you prepare for experiencing what may happen. For example, say you get shot real bad or hurt in a patrol car accident. After all, it seems you ought to be able to experience some preparation beforehand. So why don't we go there now and bring it to you? [Hesitation in his eyes and facial expression] Stay with me, do you trust me?

Officer A: Yeah, of course I do, Doc.

Dr. Dan: Good, I want to help you actually figure out just how high of a risk you would like to take with your life by doing a brief experiment. I am going to ask you to put your trust in me. I will need your cooperation to follow my instructions to a tee. How does that sound?

Officer A: Okay, Doc. Why the hell not—what do I have to lose?

Dr. Dan: Exactly, what the hell do you have to lose? Let's start. [First, I get Officer A to relax, put his feet up, and ensure a state of calm. I make a direct request for him to close his eyes. I go on informing him to place stopples and his fingers in his ears and hold them (I set the second timer). Then, I am silent, turn off the light and surrounding noise. It usually is within a range of 1 to 4 minutes before his eyes open and his fingers drop from his eardrums.] I noticed you opened your eyes, and removed your fingers from your ears.

Officer A: I didn't know what you wanted me to do. Nothing? With no instruction, it's strange, Doc. Don't you think?

Dr. Dan: You mean strange in how you felt? Let's say "slightly" is 1 and "freaked out" is 10.

Officer A: About an 8, real strange.

Dr. Dan: So, your eyes were closed for 108 seconds. Why open your eyes after only 108 seconds? Why did you also immediately take out your ear stopples?

Officer A: It felt like [blank stare]. Hey Doc, I just didn't know what to do.

Dr. Dan: So if I got it right you were so uncomfortable without hearing and seeing me, after only 108 seconds, you felt an urge to break away and gain your own sense of control?

Officer A: Yeah, it felt like I was suspended in the air, without anything, nothing there.

Dr. Dan: You mean like loss of control—silence with full consciousness—no contact or communication with any other? [We then see negative effects, anxiety, anger, and confusion. What is very interesting is to see how Officer A realizes he is gaining no control when he places himself in high-risk situations—he is eventually highly likely to lose control in a way that he cannot repair if an accident happens.]

Officer A: It felt like hell. I mean, like really just strange. I felt I had no control. It got to me.

Dr. Dan: Why hell? It's almost a likelihood if you keep taking the same level of risks that you will get your goal achieved. For example, you may receive a traumatic brain injury, loss of sight and hearing, even loss of full consciousness. Imagine, if I have it right, and I may not—so correct me if I am wrong. [Officer A just nods his approval I am correct.] Well, for only 108 seconds, I timed it. At 108 seconds. Within 2 minutes "it" felt almost intolerable to lose control of what you can know, do, feel, or experience within your own will, so to speak. The evidence is even in a comfortable setting being relaxed and with me, whom you trust, that your urge for control was overpowering. What do you think about life support or being left conscious if one of your high-risk choices puts you there?

Officer A: Yeah, it feels as if I am in prison within my own mind, kind of a zombie without any real ability to do anything. Just do what is done to me. [Officer A looks concerned and is breaking a sweat. After a pause and some reflection time Officer A continues in a strong and well-thought-out understanding with me.] Hey Doc [I nod a yes gesture with my head and eyes with attention], it spooks me out, like all hell. Like that movie *Coma*, or the *Twilight Zone* series. It would be hell.

Dr. Dan: I imagine you are right, Officer A. It is clear you do take risks that are well placed. But sometimes you have realized that your desire to do the right thing can be done so well and with so much passion that reason goes out the window. Your courage and risk taking become very dangerous.

Officer A: Well Doc, do you mean I am not caring and reckless at times, which would mean I am not much better than some bonehead kid who races his car?

Dr. Dan: No, Officer A, you are a police officer and doing your job with passion. Knowing yourself and learning about your tendency makes superb sense. It is key to choosing your behavior and also to a degree increasing your chance of survival. Does that make sense to you?

Officer A: [Grin and also reflecting on the exercise] Yeah, it does make sense, Doc, but you know being a sergeant when you are in the mix, ya have to get your Irish up and trail down the bad guy without play-time right?

Dr. Dan: Absolutely, A. But like yourself, I know traveling down a one-way street on a midnight tour in the dark at 90 mph is very risky and you can wind up wound down in a coma for a few weeks, as you witnessed happen to one of the finest. You made it through okay, but as we have seen—many do not. A chase can happen the next day and be continued when it can end your life and civilians'. Your own invaluable life and others entrusting their lives to your own. When you kick in to your pursuit and apprehend identity mode, try to remember you are in the mode and for your sanity reflect safety and arrest, not just arrest and apprehend.

Officer A: I see your point, and the fact if I crash, I lose all control if I am dead or in a coma. But how can I live with myself letting the bad guy get over, Sarge Doc Dan?

Dr. Dan: Great question. What do you think is the real answer, you know, in your Corfsam heals and your Sam Browne tools, as we rehearsed?

Officer A: Doc, you know. [I remain silent and wait; Officer A grinning but in serious thought.] I can tell myself it makes sense to get into the iden-tity mode and pursue the bad guy. But what good will it do if I react purely on my animal side without pausing. I mean, when I sense I am getting out of control I need to even in the rush just think out loud, "Safety, visualize Dr. Dan's stop cop sign," and see me making a conscious effort to think consequences while doing my job as best as I could, and it will likely end up as good as it gets. Is that right, Doc?

Dr. Dan: You tell me, Officer A. Do your own words make sense to you? You know you slow down long enough to gain perspective in your sights as a task force officer. Slow down before taking action that can cost the most important person to lose all control to some orderly in a hospital, heaven forbid. That is, before you even get a chance to gain all you have and are working so hard for as truly a cop's cop. What do you think, Officer A?

Officer A: Zezz, Doc, give me a break. But ya know, you are right and alright in my books. I guess I can still be me and take risk to get the job done but just not without using my noodle to stir the soup first. I'll try your suggestion.

Dr. Dan: Yeah, Officer A, our wisdom, if it makes sense, is I am confident you realize right here and now by the grace of God you are okay! I am okay too since I know you are a man of your own will and choice to get the job done without embracing your own worth and life!

Officer A: Thanks, Doc, I will keep in mind this exercise. Hey, I will tell you truth be told, and not for nothing, Doc, it is one hell of an experiment. I got it and me! I do not want to give me away to anyone. Thanks, man!

Officer A's experience in risk taking led to certain very important points in learning how to deal with his tendency of high risk without self-downing, or stifling his style. Officer A appreciates his tendency for hyperexcitement but has willed reducing harm to himself and others in doing the remarkable work he does. His work serves others as one of the finest officers. Working through is a distance between two points: Officer A has embarked on point 1 alone and I am privileged to worked with him to point 2.

A positive inspirational note of risk within a measured frame comes from a nonfiction writer of note. Professor William Zinsser (2004) suggests good thoughts to comfort moderate risk takers:

> All writers are embarked on a quest of some kind, and you're entitled to go on yours. My purpose in this book is to give you the permission and the tools. My method is to take you on a memoir of my own—to tell you about some people and places and events in my life that still amuse and often amaze me. Many of these events changed the direction of my career because I gave myself permission to not take the road I was expected to take, starting with not going into the family business that would have been a secure haven. Risk has been my ultimate safety net.

As the great scholar King Solomon said in Proverbs: everything in moderation except anger and lust. Moderation needs to be taken into account with equal measure in consequences before leaping; the costs unmeasured are too complex to ensure simple outcomes.

The Hyperaggressive Edge: Public Safety Personality Style

What Motivated You toward Swearing Your Own Oath as a Public Safety Officer

"To be a boss, not a subordinate."

"A 20-year pension with not having to be under some pinhead square-head boss."

"The power of being an officer."

"To teach my mother what a woman of the 21st century could do, kick butt if need be."

Psychological Survival Defenses within Your Own Public Safety Personality Style

Your personality style is the rarest of all five in police and public safety officers. However, many strengths you possess are invaluable in the world of public safety.

You are unusually in need of benefiting from the most therapeutic help, but it is equally very difficult for an officer with your personality style to accept help. You lack no confidence in your presentation to other officers and the public—so it seems. In the way you present yourself to fellow public safety officers and to the world, you are quite assertive to the point that others may have told you in very different circumstances that you are aggressive.

When that aggression feels out of control at some level of discomfort in your way of relating to others, you may feel like you would like to receive some assistance from a cop counselor. If you are pushed to see a therapist because you have gotten into trouble due to anger control issues, then you are likely to feel a lack of ease. Do not let this deter you from seeking out help. It is more common that you do not seek help first, but help may seek you after some event. Perhaps you have been quite expressive, more than physically effective, or even have landed in some trouble. For example, you may have been very quick to draw your firearm or get into it when you are on a fire rescue. Maybe you were assisting with an aided case and some third party or the aided becomes too bossy for your comfort as an officer. If this is the case, and although you understandably do not want to be labeled, I would like to help you from the outset as a cop who happens to be a doc. Meaning if you are a firefighter, EMT, or police officer, it is key to realize, you may in fact be a natural scrapper, a tough guy or gal for that matter, and I for one am not going to try to brainwash you to seek help to make drastic changes. No, not at all. I want to talk real and get you to see some consequences that could land you in some really bad places. Placed under a controlling system you hate and kill you inside, and maybe even in the final analysis you killing you! So please stop and hear me. I do not believe in tough love, but compassion for even the toughest of blue, red, and white uniformed colleagues. So I am with you first and foremost: your quest for remaining who you are and in prizing your unique strengths can help you be the best you can be. The best you can be without too much compromise but being more effective than ever.

You and your therapist need to achieve what is called a higher than average tolerance of accepting frustration. For your goals in therapy to work, they need to be moderate while hopeful.

Framing Your Moods and Emotions in Your
Unique Public Safety Personality Style

You are likely to get quite angry, rant, and sometimes explode when your space is threatened. That space may include physical violations of your own personal space. Personal space can include a threat to your feeling you are dealing with a rivalry when anyone invades your personal space. When you are temporarily upset and agitated, you lose your own sense of inhibition, and may strike out with a calculated vengeance. Your activity level is a restless drive, but not for seeking approval from significant others, like, for example, the addictive hyperexcited officer. You're driven with an exacting emotional self-control. Sarcasm matched by subtle or even explicit attacks on the culture of your own public safety agency is common. In an agitated mood you are likely to express you "have control at all times" coupled with "not feeling a thing."

Existentially Relating to Me, You, Others:
Ecologically and Ethologically Speaking

Ethologically speaking, a fear of vulnerability and a defensive armor against being hurt make superb sense. This makes sense from a territorial imperative for an alpha officer. It is not only physical; your defense is existentially layered in the ethological and cultural aspect of what space means to you. *Your mood can become inflamed, so to speak, when you feel invaded.* The twist here is that when someone insults your sense of what you feel entitled to receive, your immediate response is fight. Hence, hostility escalates as a way of relating and even finding meaning in being so argumentative and entrenched in your view of how and why an officer must be a certain way. Namely, that officer revolves around yourself and your own needs. Your physical sense of adrenalin rising may be enhanced when you also feel a boss challenges your sense of who you are. I have noticed with officers with your style it is hard to allow others to have the respect they too have earned. This imbalance can lead to volatile situations boiling from lukewarm mixtures, often innocently or naively delivered, being misinterpreted. Interestingly perhaps, you can recount violent retaliation toward someone because they "dared to disrespect you." No guilt is felt, but if you can characterize a feeling, it is simply righteous indignation. You have a keen emotional excitement in recounting morbid aspects of critical incidents. However, you react with rage when you feel wronged, or pushed into doing something you evaluate as being wronged, or pushed into doing something you perceive as a trivial slight. That slight is interpreted as a major slight and disavowal of another person's right to relate dissent from your own view.

In relating to others you may have observed in yourself, or heard others tell you about, an intensity to consume what you can from others in terms of respect and control. It is critical that in honestly confronting your style, a more socialized and practical purpose can be learned. Learning that serving others brings a higher level of pleasure than a tendency to buck the tide and do things your way or the highway as an exclusive motto. Anything overused, as you well know, gets boring, stale, and rusty, even slogans and an exclusive path. This initial goal is a very difficult one and one that is well worth the effort. An exploration of why excessive aggression may be intense and relentless as your first response to stress may help you achieve significant gains for insight. Insight that will work on duty as much as off duty.

An exercise in identity mode reversal. This appeals to your professional pride as a highly motivated officer with a cutting edge—without losing the prime cut, you can ease the slice into what works for you and the other person who may be perceived as a dull, slow, and even somewhat incompetent person: Officer W has a problem with her boss, who she considers to be a loser; she calls her boss KO Z.

Dr. Dan: I really would like to understand and feel what it's like to be in your place. Perhaps you could play the boss, incompetent KO, while I get to play you.

Firefighter Officer W: Why should I want to be anyone but me, Doc? That's psychobabble crap. You aren't female—how could you be me? Why should I want to be anyone but me? Especially a loser boss who cannot get it right and I hate and would like to smash in. Of course I can't and won't. I'll fight tooth and nail until she is out.

Dr. Dan: Well, maybe that's how you see it. But, I really would like to know how it feels to be you. By you being her you can help me find out how much of a loser she is, on one hand, as you put it so often. But maybe some other way of thinking of her will emerge if you let your anger out as you see it. That is, if you look at the consequences by kind of imagining how it feels to be her, as she may see it. Let's see if we can get her to roast a bit in the hot seat. Does that make sense or should we toss away our experiment? What do you think, Officer W?

Firefighter Officer W: [Looks with the most amused look, as if to say to me, are you kidding, Doc? W has learned to experiment as it may benefit her to open up a bit and humor my suggestions.] Okay Doc Dan, let's play it up, but I would rather you be her and me be me.

Dr. Dan: I think that is a good idea, but right now I would like you to suspend your need to change our agreed on plan. Does that still work for you, Officer W? [I await her response and do not repeat a pattern

Officer W had noticed with me in our former sessions. That pattern was her need to make our work go as she would insist. Without any ownership of her need to control the sessions, which made our work almost impossible to be effective.] Yes or no?

Firefighter Officer W: Okay, Doc, I am with you. I did agree. Okay go for it! [Officer W then lets loose with some contradictions in her boss's directives, but nothing that is really too harsh or vindictive from a realistic perspective.] Well, Officer W, what are you going to do with my directive?

Dr. Dan: [Being Officer W] I see the truth in your directive at least in part Firefighter Captain M. I would like to bring to your attention I am doing my job as best as I can. I am wondering if you could illustrate by example how I could fill out that form again as you would like me to?

Firefighter Officer W: [Playing the captain] Well listen, I do not want to be here to hold your hand. Got it, Officer W? I am really getting tired of it. Are you as smart as all that [Officer W received an award in the firefighter training academy]? I am unaware of why you are not getting it and you are so smart. Is it your training as a Catholic school girl maybe? We can get Father ABC in and he can hold your hand. Is that better for you?

Stopping the experiment here: In letting loose in her role-play we explore the dynamics of sexism, sent emails, and religious as well as other biases directed against Officer W. The follow-up we worked on was the question of Officer W bringing this to her boss's attention in writing as well as verbally. Some dysfunctional myths explored included the fact Officer W was truly dealing with some violations of Equal Employment Opportunity. She had a number of options to exercise, if she so desired, making this fact known immediately to her supervisor. Desist calling her boss. She, after all, was not a boss but a supervisor. In working through her anger and rage over her situation, much was uncovered to her benefit. One gain was her validation that she was in fact taking way too much abuse from her employer, although going to the authorities was not her option. She was respected and validated as she need not be silent, or on the other hand get aggressive automatically, thereby losing her advantage of being on the right in this situation. She learned her value as a worker and her biased supervisor who was a bully. She informed her she was aware of discrimination and to desist in writing, to which her supervisor retaliated. She tried to make Officer W's life a miserable hell. In our work she stood by her chosen stance to tolerate the frustration without acting out in turn, even if she felt it was deserved.

She redirected her natural tendency, which was to get aggressive to her advantage. She let her supervisor's bias and unfair treatment, including email track records, be a record her attorney could take on and settle as her advocate in dealing with what truly emerged as a hostile workplace. Discovery with her attorney churned out a lot of painful rehashing settled with a stipend for her endurance and ultimately a better position.

Officer W learned the invaluable lesson of letting go of her need for control and aggressive behavior as a sword to substitute for trust in the trustworthy. Trust could be earned and was indeed extended to her attorney, as trustworthy. She no longer thinks it is weak to assert herself. The results are not stunning, but have helped impact on her style with other relationships, including her boyfriend, her parents, and other folks in her life.

Your Personality Patterns: Ecological and Ethological Sensibility: Why You Act So

In understanding the complexity of your own personality it is crucial to embrace the fact your tendency for aggression is by itself not good or bad per se. It is a tendency you were born with. Think about it: someone who decides to use their aggressive nature to work as an engineer brings much happiness to many people, ensuring a personal and socially good outcome. The desire to manipulate things, be competent in making changes, and a driven passion to shake, rattle, and roll are used as a public safety officer within your eco-ethological niche with precise effect. In a way, truth be told, you make the best of soldiers when called on in the field of duty for a certain tough-mindedness: your public safety-mindedness may be as an EMT in emergency medical response, or as a medic doing rescue and recovery work. Under fire many an EMT has experienced hardly appropriate recognition when dealing with the worst of terrorism and natural catastrophes.

As a firefighter, doing rescue work that calls for tough-mindedness in dealing with ongoing raging fires and riot situations of domestic unrest, and recovery situations that would challenge the greatest archeologist alive. As a police officer, dealing with the myriad challenges you are called on, such as disorder control situations, terrorism, or chaotic events emerging suddenly.

As a corrections officer, having to deal with a takeover, hostage situation, or natural catastrophe or terrorist attack can be as distressing and calling on your innate aggression to emerge in the moment of chaos.

However, your very tendency to be called on for your tough-minded thirst for power, control, and even aggression that is ethologically motivated in part and rewarded could become the thorny consequences. Thorny when you allow yourself full indulgence. Meaning when you believe you are the wronged and offended party, a tendency for being a consuming and defending soldier emerges. It is clear that the ethological motivation is there for your thoughts, behaviors, and meaning you have learned and naturally react to and why.

It is realizing your strength in part makes superb sense as an alpha male/female. Winning a battle does not mean you have won the war. I like to offer Frank Sinatra's song: "I did it my way ... and now the end is near and I close the final curtain ... regrets I've had a few, but more, much more than this I did it my way ..." Fine, like Frank, please wear your hat the way you like. Autonomy is important. But, even Frank Sinatra knew the importance of being soft at times, in order to be truly hard. Meaning it is likely when one says might must be forceful, in many cases it works well when dealing with strong-arm bad guys. But as a steady staple it can bring crushing losses. The balance you need to make existentially is what is most important to you. If it is truly getting ahead, and being number one is your goal, then power is best served in a way in which you need not blow out your partner's candles to light your own. Being the tough officer you are with an even more independent tough-minded way of thinking is good. Winning over your partner on the job—needs to feel valued—in turn she will value you. The harder you push, the harder the pull back. So letting go is not only valued but also indeed wins the day for you rather than ruining it.

It is better to win than to lose, but in winning one wins the day when enlisting another trustworthy person's help. Let's look at another example with Officer W. Illustrating Officer W's gain may assist with your own rehearsal of social skills, assertiveness, and prioritizing goals of connecting to others, the world, and ultimately back to yourself.

A snippet of our early work follows, in which Officer W reassesses why and how to better be able to tolerate her situation with a sense of humor infused in a dark place in her life. Her gains, I suspect, will last a lifetime.

Firefighter Officer W: Doc, she is a real xxyy. I feel like slapping her in the face at times when she looks like a hag and goes on like a horned toad she witch devil b-tch. I cannot really keep my cool. I am just going to blast her when she goes off again. She is jealous and very mean-hearted. She is always trying to comment on what is wrong with me. I do not think I can tolerate the frustration anymore, even though I am using the disputes as to the consequences of my letting losoe.

Dr. Dan: What makes you tolerate her almost intolerableness? I repeat, almost intolerable barrage of what you have thus discovered is intolerable nasty and mean-hearted comments. I believe she has done this trash talk. It is not a private relationship. A work relationship is one that is not tolerable from an EEO perspective, as you know.

Firefighter Officer W: Okay Doc, the reason I do not do the complaint is I do not want to lose my job by getting physical, and the consequences would be all hell broke loose. It is hard enough being a firefighter and woman you know.

Dr. Dan: Yes, we have discussed this at length, and it is extremely challenging, which you have done remarkably well. Okay, on a scale of 1 to 10, as a range of desire to really slap your boss, how high is it right now as you are telling yourself she is a hag witch b-tch?

Firefighter Officer W: I get so aggravated: "it" almost hurts. [W motions at her stomach area and gesticulates painful inchoate bursts of woeful expression.] So to answer your question, it is 11 of 10. Are you happy now?

Dr. Dan: [I do not ignore Firefighter Officer W's painful reference to me being happy at her pain. As we also learned, her traumatic past colluded with her current state in exacerbating a style that has locked her into covering herself from injury. Her letting me know she is at the fringe of tolerance and ready to blow off the steam allows an intervention designed to help her tolerate the exquisite annoying supervisor she needs to temporarily tolerate for the upcoming months.] I am not happy, and in fact with you feel grieved you are having to deal with this painful situation. So let's go on and work on it together. Okay, again you be her.

Firefighter Officer W: [Goes on in the ugly diatribe she is listening to by her supervisor, including comments about her religion, her weight, her age, her lack of ability, which is objectively untrue, as confirmed by her long track record. We also establish her response is to document and assert an EEOC due to the relentless arrogance of her supervisor, who would not diminish her stance. Failing to acknowledge she too was an employee who must follow constitutional respect and regard of others' civil and religious rights. Her goal is twofold: doing her work well and documenting the track record her supervisor left behind.] I will not hold your hand, Firefighter Officer W, anymore, and you are just not cutting it except in your own mind. Now you could leave me alone and not waste my time and better straighten up your mess soon, got it!

I review how I want to imagine Officer W wants to react with a tirade. A verbal response right back at her supervisor in rhyme and verse. I explain this to let her know I do get how upsetting it could be to deal with a tirade if I were in her shoes. Instead, I answer with self-empowerment and refusing to let her disempower me. I start by saying I can visualize my boss as a witch hag or I can also visualize her as a toothless bulldog who has no bite but a ridiculous bark in a purple dress barking all day long. I then go on to illustrate by asking Firefighter Officer W to do the same, and at the same time modeling my response to her supervisor in a brief statement, such as "Thank you for bringing to my attention what you consider a generalization of my work product. I would like it if you could let me know in writing what you would like me to improve on specifically so I can get on it right away, Captain." This difficult situation, as we reviewed and reassessed the dilemma that Firefighter Officer W was in as a potential catch-22, was redirected with her good work and imagination into a success and survivorship in which she was handsomely taught her own sense of humor and her ability to tolerate the so-called intolerable with a gain in outcome, personal and professional.

Keep in mind I was as corrected as a fallible cop doc. Officer W was able to appreciate our alliance, which is creating and confirming or disconfirming our working hypotheses and goals in therapy. Upon our exploration we discovered Officer W's courage and choice to not react with forthright anger, rage, ranting, and raging in a regrettable moment as a poor solution adversely impacting on all the facets of her life. Therapy is truly healing, even in the sometimes unheard losses undergirding anger, aggression, and even at times sadistic escapes an officer can act on—unstopped in his or her mind indeed.

I have afforded Officer W a skill to feel or understand another perspective, and in this regard our therapeutic objective was met as a team. And it is only a beginning.

Our Personality Style Peer's Most Traumatic Event in Officer W's Own Quoted Viewpoint

The one event that I will tell you about occurred on xx/xy/yy. Upon arriving on the scene we encountered other officers entering a parking garage. We observed a radio car full of bullet holes. As we entered the garage we observed a male lying dead on the garage floor, a so-called victim, a drug deal gone bad. As we went deeper in the garage to conduct a search we were fired upon by a perp ducking behind a parked car. We found cover behind cement pillars and other autos and returned fire. It was exciting. I could feel my adrenaline surge. It was gratifying to see the perp dying from our return fire. I placed a flashlight in his eyes and said, "Guess where you're going? It ain't heaven." The other cops looked away. I didn't. I couldn't care less. He was a perp. I wish those guys weren't wusses. I did not lose any sleep anytime after this incident. It was a good shooting and that's that. I felt proud: one less shit stain in the world. I felt this was necessary force and felt no anxiety, anger, or sadness. I was just doing my job. I hope he enjoyed every knot in his last shampoo. [This is not an isolated renarration, but consistent in this officer's style.]

Impact of Traumatic Loss in My Own Unique Personality Style: On Duty and Off Duty

It is also not so apparent how loss impacts on you in hidden ways. Loss is not only surrounded by sad feelings. Loss is also an experience of missing some aspect of yourself you may be trying to recapture again. When your power is so entangled with force you may feel stripped and even naked when your duty status is changed. This is set in a personality you have learned in surviving on the streets and in protecting yourself from being exposed to harm. Protecting yourself from harm, as you have seen, is quite significant for street survival and status in your unit. But the force is the aspect that acts like a lever for conflict when compromise, modification, and openness to change are called for; when you try to force your will on others—consequences can and are disaster.

How Your Public Safety Personality Style Is Different from Other Public Safety Styles

Like all personality styles, yours has a range that encompasses direct acting out, which can be mild in consequences to severe. Unlike the hyperexcited personality style, you are not on a quest for approval; you desire, if not demand, being in control of any situation you are given in the public safety domain. Your style of policing, firefighting, or EMT work is dyed in the cast of holding a long-term grudge, never-ending lists of injustices: if you are called to the front you will let go with bloodlust with equal and intense passion as any bad guy. Like the officer with the hyperexcited style, an intense, almost addictive craving for high excitation, intensity, and challenge exists. Hyperfocused personality officers are fearful of their own compulsions, and try to deny and repress almost any aggressive tendency, while you are much more likely to resonate in your own aggressive tendencies and even behaviors at times.

Initial Inroads to Lay Out Your Own Map for Trauma and Grief Therapy

A lasting impact in your own lifestyle, if accepted in the vein of reality and tragic optimism, is achieving harm reduction. Harm reduction is a worthwhile goal of therapy.

What Does Harm Reduction Mean in Real Terms?

Harm reduction means reducing hostility, the raging, the ranting, and consequent troubles you have flirted with throughout your career, short or long as it is: reducing the aggression without giving up your learned sensibility within your own eco-ethological niche and natural tendency to be an alpha officer in the group.

Why Invest in Doing Harm Reduction?

First, acknowledging how sensible it is to at times be protective and guarded as an officer when you are dealing with volatile situations leaves you with an understanding. Your understanding that working on harm reduction is no less valuable than working on sugar intake as a diabetic, or dust inhalation as an asthmatic. It may hold no more labels or negative connotation when you realize you are superbly equipped for dealing with very difficult tactics your style affords at times with brilliant results.

Second, not all others are trustworthy and responsive. You are the most likely to be able to form boundaries made in concrete. Being selective in how and why you allow others into your life circle is critical for your own health and as a public safety officer. This selectivity works well as a defense to protect your own safety. Your selectivity acts as your own inner perimeter, protecting you from uncertainty and chaos in street situations. On the other hand, it also blocks your connection to others who want to relate compassion with you. Pain hidden in bricks of loss is the foundation of those very walls you erected to shield you.

Third, in changing your approach in certain situations it is important to realize you may gain even more by being effective in street situations you encounter. For example, you may get the real bad guy in an investigation if you ally yourself to folks on the scene, rather than just launch an approach that reduces all participants as if they are the same. By being selective when calm is established, escalation can always be employed, that is, after facts are gathered. By that time you will likely not have to employ an all-encompassing aggressive posture.

Fourth, in entering therapy you may find a challenging situation with a perp, an aided case, an arsonist, an unruly civilian, or even another public safety officer may lead back to an encounter with yourself. Some losses captivated you from not only not moving forward, but also believing you have advanced in having a very tough armor that is as impervious to pain as an American bulldog. Some of the walls of resistance against being too empathic as weakness actually do what you want to accomplish quite well. But remember, walls of resistance not only keep others out but keep you trapped within yourself. Without space to breathe your fears out and inhale the wishes to let your guard down when it is okay to do so. .

Is Harm Reduction the Beginning or the End of Therapy for Your Personality Style?

You may start with harm reduction and keep with your style, which is geared to practical cost-benefits ratio. That cost-benefit ratio leaves soft and touchy-feely expressions to officers you tolerate but would never emulate. You may target harm reduction, and that is a fine goal to achieve. But also in the final analysis and no pun intended, or fun being poked, you may realize very different results than you began with, or imagined about others, and even yourself. You may in the process grieve and mourn losses you felt disdain toward initially. Compassion may emerge for those you thought you would never choose to embrace, including a hidden dimension of your own personality style.

Be aware when something you do not like goes down, you are least likely to feel remorse. In having a lack of guilt at least expressed, self-reflection is neither sought nor accepted except when begrudgingly and with resistance. You are likely to view someone who presents with credentials of experience or education with the first thought of "Who does this jerk think he or she is, better than me, I need no education?" It is time here to stop and pause and realize this person as a professional may offer assistance in ways you are not trained in. You will most likely benefit from. Overcoming your own resistance is what will serve you best in the long and short run, as you witnessed with Firefighter Officer W.

You can be the exquisite officer for tracking down and taking out the bad guys, such as terrorists, bank robbers, and kidnappers. I am not saying you have to be doing any of these activities, but it is not alien to your personality style. In a sense, your own rational, reasoning, and analytic skills as an officer with your personality style, at times in your driven style, can drive you off the cliff of reason. This is markedly so when the ecological niche of your ethological motivation calls for eliciting pain for those who have stalked, attacked, or terrorized innocent citizens.

It is possible that in being called to carry out such incredibly difficult jobs that call for the very ability to be aggressive and not bend in compassion when dealing with terrorists, for example, you can begin to identify with the aggressors. This coupled with the fact you may have a natural tendency for this exacting demand to protect innocent people from being victims of a jihad on humanity. It is sensible you were chosen or even more so competed for positions that call on establishing a level of relatedness through pain as a medium of communication. It is critical to keep up, with much extra effort to civilian outlets, and not lose your own self-image as a decent person. Decent even above being an officer and even in the most stressful of eco-ethological niches. Repeated attempts at connection with others who are compassionate, even if it is your peer support officer and a cop or military doc, are well worth the effort. Loyalty, commitment to values, and ideals, even in this most trying of situations, can be forged if you work hard at not losing faith in your overall goal. It is a challenge to use your own resilience as humanity that affords a shield to enable you to do your job well here and not lose the compass of your own moral coordinates. It is here that a cop doc can affect the most assistance in you being helped to strengthen your own resolve.

Disputing the self-destructive belief, as comforting as it feels at times, that as an officer you are always right and entitled to have your demands met, period—as simple as that! Even if you are 97% right as the physicist Heisenberg asserted aggressively with honest truth, "3% need always be accorded error in the world of the physical universe."

Heisenberg's idea is a sensible copping-in statement for you. Whether you're fighting fires, rescuing civilians from accidents, tornadoes, and tsunamis, or taking down terrorist cells, Heisenberg's practical and sensible truth is one to keep in your Sam Browne belt attached to your core attitude: remembering a humbling reality helps even the toughest soldier. That truth reality is that even gravity, quantum forces, and elusive strings may connect in complex ways we can predict, except at least 3% of the time that is never predictable. Well certainly as a great soldier who is tough-minded as you are, the reality for you is strength includes being aware of your own weakness. Weaknesses even without remedies like the universe we live in. You can keep revolving even if at times evolution does not occur as much as you demand it. You are subject to what you wish, and by the grace of an ultimate power greater than yourself revolves the fact as to whether success is confirmed or not. That is a leap of faith, but so are our core beliefs of physics, psychology, and assumptions you and I have about the world we live in.

Let's Get Real: Your Public Safety Personality Style: Officer and Cop Doc's Corner

Officer B is a middle-aged emergency medical technician supervisor. Although Officer B is not a fully practicing Catholic, he remains faithful to his religious convictions. That conviction as a Catholic includes bearing his sufferings with humility and forbearance. Humility is defined by Officer B as having faith in a higher being and bearing suffering with human dignity. Officer B intimates his faith has been lost in a whirlwind of the tempest of rescue and recovery work in an elite citywide unit. Officer B has worked through the pits of endless and brutal suffering he has encountered over the years. This spark of faith is shaded in loss and needs to be ignited as a light of existential motivation in his losses. His losses have turned a bright cloud of optimism and ideals into the dark furrows of an ugly twister. Tornadic spirals envelop his optimism. His experience of close to 20 years in emergency response is coupled with promotions to different areas of the city. All his commands are described as extremely busy to very busy commands. Officer B has a penchant for underestimating danger, but he is now suffering from sciatic nerve damage, bulging lumbar discs, and asthma, which is causing him to be evaluated to leave the streets. Leaving the streets is nothing less than pulling an active combat veteran medic back into the bleachers at a medical auditorium introducing gross anatomy. What we did identify were 54 specific traumatic events out of hundreds estimated. He told me upfront: "I'm fine, Doc, nothing is really wrong. I need excitement. The detail I am being placed in really sucks and left me feeling empty. My wife asked me to see you. I'll give you a try."

Officer B: As you can see, it is simple. I am used to working in a hot house and that is apparent. So in any case, Doc, there is nothing wrong with me and I am just doing my job. There you go—kid's dead, perp's gone, and I am now the one with the problem. Is that because I am not stressed and want to stay in my house? Can you imagine that, Doc?

Dr. Dan: [Pausing and reflecting on the need for Officer B to have me listen to him. I do really understand he is a combat veteran and will not be displaced and taken away from his unit if he could help it. In hearing his work is valuable I assure him, I hear him, and I am listening first.] I am with you, B, and appreciate how it might seem as if I too will agree with your wife. I may say, hey it's time to move on, get with the program, and leave behind your losses on the curb.

Officer B: I got it all out okay. So what is there to talk about now the traumatic event most serious to me is what I just laid on you. Simple as all that, okay, Doc?

Dr. Dan: You're right. It is a simple as all that. What it is that you let me know felt like a repeat loader filled with some powerful moments you recalled in your generous gift to me. That gift of events layered with a tragic DWI accident and a kid dying in front of you, a reckless murder of a kid by another kid, you being assaulted, a drug dealer being shot and killed in front of his family, a partner is killed in the line of duty, and a perp being taken down. Sounds like one layer of loss on top of another without stop and with chaos to follow.

Officer B: It is as simple as that, Doc, and nothing more. No psychoanalyzing here, okay?

Dr. Dan: No psychoanalyzing here: agreed! Does it strike you in needing to capture the incredible rush of adrenalin and emotion it is hard to imagine how damn hard it is to just take the huge mess you did not make? The mess you are accepting as your responsibility as being simple as all that. Without giving yourself a break to stop and reflect on what is really going on here, it seems you keep rushing through your losses.

Officer B: Okay what is going on here, Doc?

Dr. Dan: I am unsure I could give you any answer, except to say let's try to make sense of "it." "It" means the incredible trauma you have expressed. That is the sensibility of how and why it is so difficult to capture the disappointments, shock, and losses as you experienced "it." "It" as it happens in your own ecological niche, and with your own survival in mind. Does that make sense as a goal we can work on together, Officer B?

Officer B: Yeah, it does, Doc. What should I start with and how?

Dr. Dan: How about whatever you shared first, if that makes sense to you?

Officer B: Yeah that kid who died. It was pretty bad. I did what I had to do, but it was hearing the screams of the kid's parents that was so bad, you know what I mean?

Dr. Dan: Can you tell me, as only you know and I want to know? I am listening, B. [I lean forward and listen with deep intention. Attention with intention to hear what B is expressing beyond only his words. I glean the undercurrent of his emotions and soulfulness so dimly expressed, but whispered between his pauses and stoicism.]

Officer B: It was a nightmare listening to the shrill holler of the mother and father chocked up with horror on their faces. The perp being taken away in cuffs in a stupor was eerie. I could not do anything. It was surreal as everyone tipped the car over, and the guy in the car himself was in la la land, toasted and bruised all over. The kid looked terrible, like a lifeless clay doll. It was too much to see. You know what I mean, but it just is what I had to do. Nothing much I could have done, you know? Really, Doc. [Expression is genuine and relating to me the intensity and shock of being there] Is it really necessary to pull this out of me now? I mean, worse was the kid who shot his brother accidentally and those animals trying to get the kid to take the wrap and get them out of it. Is that incredible? Framing a kid who is totally innocent, unlike the number's runner I told you about. I confess clearly, Doc, I couldn't care a rat's ass about the numbers runner. Hey Doc, please do not push the issue okay. It really means nothing. I am not a bleeding heart liberal. I do not care, so do not ask me again! I mean the only thing was too bad his wife and kid were in the vehicle [the numbers runner]. I mean anyhow I am not to blame. I could not do a thing anyhow. You know what I mean? Hey, you were a cop I am an EMT supervisor. I prioritize and do not believe in all the diagnoses so much, but just get the job done. It is as simple as that. Who cares, he is a low life, not like that innocent angel, you know? Anyhow go ahead, what now? Do you think I am feeling guilty over the numbers runner being wasted in front of his family? You are dead wrong! No way, Doc! His responsibility, his outcomes—not mine! Tough luck, I am not paid to care. You are.

Dr. Dan: I would go ahead now to an interesting puzzle. That puzzle, B, is I think you are struggling with, and at the same time gifting me with. I think in some way you realize you apparently do care more than a rat's ass to confess in part to me that in all that denial you bombard me with you do care about the numbers runner who ran out of luck! Bad luck as your rescue effort squeezed down in the brutality of his murder. What do you think, Officer B?

Officer B: Doc, are you going liberal on me? Shame on you from blue to pink, that is something, wouldn't you say? I'm only ribbing you. [Grinning with "ha ha" murmured in a guttural way, with strong aversion in his looking away from me and then looking at me with a grin, but with some pain in his eyes as his power of silence sets in]

Dr. Dan: [While not ignoring the hostility and the absurd need to devalue me, I realize Officer B is needing to do to me what he feels he needs to do with his feelings. I represent his emotional side and his desire to connect, but under armor so hard he will not let me in. Letting me in to explore his feelings with ease is not happening. No problem. It is not about me but about Officer B's losses, which are overwhelming him—at least I have accepted as a hunch to explore. I firmly go back and pursue B's lead. I am not leaving him in denial of what is so unacceptable that he can let go and feel it is okay to actually feel sad about the brutal murder of a gambling man in front of his kids.] Let me ask you, Officer B, you insist on me accepting you do not give a rat's ass about the murder of the numbers runner in front of his wife and kids, and then as you put it to me in your own words, "you confess to me" and then warn me not to push the issue, and his responsibility is not yours: What do you make of that and why you are so bent on not letting go with me?

Officer B: That is right, Doc Dan, I couldn't give a rat's ass and I am willing to confess that to you. Does that strike you that I couldn't care less—do you get it? Can we move on now and already pass this trauma? Perhaps you are so into it and onto it. What do you think of that, Doc, for an interpretation? I know how you think, I read your clinician's guide [referring to my original book, 2007]. There is no redemption here. That is it and it is all that simple.

Dr. Dan: You wish you could convince me that I should believe you. On one level, as you consciously read my book and as you may have realized on an eco-ethological niche, your motivation for survival in the tough and unemotional public safety profession of EMT officer you have learned well. On another dimension of your existential unconscious you are confronting me to witness with you what is so important to you. Do you know what that is, my dear Officer B?

Officer B: [With change in emotion and in a less defensive and genuine willingness to open up to understanding his motivation, which was now becoming an issue of a joint puzzle, in part what Officer B was aware of and in part was genuinely somewhere in the lighter part of his unconscious] Doc, are you saying I really care about that skell of a guy? You mean that he is someone to really feel sorry for, like a dad of some kid who gambles away his life and couldn't care less for his kids with emotions? [Pausing and with a change of anger and eyes looking down with a sad, if not almost teary look] Oh yeah, moan about him and say how sad. You know what, Doc? F-ck him! I am not responsible for the world—that is your job, Doc—with your psychobabble stuff, not mine. I do not know why I even bother with this.

Dr. Dan: You bother with our therapy work because like the work you do on the street, it is worth the pain. Yes, even the pain of you struggling and suffering, or you wouldn't do it, as we have understood over many sessions. The need to let me know how hard and how much of a struggle it is is our ritual we have agreed on without stating—every session, till we hit loss.

Officer B: Okay so I need to collect my issues and pile it on you so you could know how it feels—right, Doc? But okay, even I do that I can't help it, okay—so what? I still do not need to confess to you. You are my doc, not a priest and not even Catholic; you are a Jewish cop doc. So what can you know about confession? Anyhow, as I said, I am confessing simply because I do not know how to make it clearer. Doc, I do not care for that emotional mushy touchy-feely stuff. What do you think I am, some kid? Listen, I am a man with my own free will as you keep insisting, and I can get up and walk out of here if I want! If I walk out you will have nobody to analyze. That is it, are you happy now, Doc? Look at what you made me do!

Dr. Dan: Tough and hard what you have been through. It is, I imagine, your fear you may be abandoned by me. Resolve of that guy who you mourn when you confess your worse fear of mourning the young boy and wife's loss of witnessing their own dad and husband being murdered for a toss of the dice. It feels cheap and even cheaper to lower yourself to allow a feeling of compassion for a rat. What is a rat?

Someone who is a two-face liar who shows one face and has another face undercover. How hard for the angel of a boy you noted when we first spoke of your trauma. Those were your words, and I imagine you may wonder why it is so hard to allow your loss to be expressed.

Officer B: I am a half of a man, a Mensa, gosh. [I look in puzzlement.] You know, Doc, you are looking at least a half European guy. A guy who lost his manhood. Am I not?

Dr. Dan: Why would you be so harsh on yourself? Suppose you can just for a moment humor me and for my sake let go. Could you let me know what you would like to have me hear? I am listening and truly want to know, B? Feeling as if you have been taken down as a man is a horrid fear and experience to encounter in your value of yourself. I would truly like to listen. [Quiet]

Officer B: Dad, you know [breaking in sobbing and looking down as if he shamed himself in the worst imaginable way]. Dad was a heavy drinker. I mean, you know, a gambling man with the horses, OTB, and rum and coke way too often. But dad was a good man, you know. I mean, I know he got beat a number of times. I was just a kid. I mean a little boy who witnessed this in the streets of Irish, Italian, and some black folk and Hebs like you, Doc, no offense. You know, my best friend is a Jew. [I nod with no offense, as it is B's way of expression and hope to distract and test me once again. I will address it soon]. Anyhow, Doc, he was a good guy. A real good guy and a hard worker, but the alcohol got to him and he died eventually of pseurosis, organic dementia, and liver damage. [Long silence and looking up as if he awoke] Well it is all okay anyhow. What does that have to do with all this? It is like I want to confess to you that I miss my dad or something like that.

Dr. Dan: It is so hard to witness. But you are courageous enough to confess to me how much you do miss Dad. How hard it is to gain absolution for yourself by making me as the "Heb" priest. Well, if you undermine me you can let your loss rest well with someone hardly worth the effort. Yet you just allowed yourself to confess and witness for yourself contrition and forgiveness for what you could not prevent. As much as you wished in your heart of hearts to rescue your dad. As an EMT supervisor with the tragic death of the father and husband of the numbers runner who was murdered in cold blood, you were brought right back to that moment of powerlessness and guilt. A shrink cop doc is a good enough father you needed to test now— even as imperfect as I truly am—to again see if you could get me to abandon or be harsh with you.

Officer B: I am a good EMT supervisor, aren't I, Doc? I mean, so what if I can't save the world, or even my dad, or that poor kid's dad, or woman's husband?

Dr. Dan: I think you know the answer to that question as well. You realize you too are a good enough EMT supervisor and like me can't save the world. Confessing your own doubt about letting go with loss as you witness is not of shame to me—quite the opposite. Perhaps we have opened the front door so your loss may be let free from hiding in the back door. What do you think?

Officer B: Well for a Heb cop doc you are one of a kind. I think I am not so weird, I guess, but I will not wear pink and don't try to get me to do that. [With a smile and some humor directed with me and in our direction, I nod assent. A lot of work awaits us, and some wrestling over issues that is fine for this officer with a hyperaggressive personality style. We will survive. Officer B and I are resilient and have agreed on the many worthy struggles a cop doc and professional public safety officer need to tackle 1 week at a time.]

The Idiosyncratic Hyperintuitive Public Safety Personality Style

What Motivated You toward Swearing Your Own Oath as a Public Safety Officer

"I asked my dad (a retired detective) for advice about what I should do with my life. He told me, 'Become a cop to stop crime, and provide a stable income for a family.'" My officer-patient paused, reflected, and said, "I did just that, and here I am with the Superman blues."

"I am a civic-minded gal and I could apply my creativity to tackling the bad guys, kind of like a genius sleuth without a portfolio."

"I could be a great EMT on the streets while I become an RN in the ER room, and then a physician or maybe a clinical psychologist like you. I can do interventions and write about it in essays."

Psychological Survival Defenses within Your Own Public Safety Personality Style

How does a creative and highly perceptive officer as yourself respond to trauma when your natural tendency is avoiding emotional expression of loss coupled with being overly dependent on others' approval? Complicated loss of original and cumulative trauma is not often expressed directly. Avoidance of emotional hurt is sunk in beliefs of personal inadequacy, shame, and guilt that is expressed indirectly. How? Indirect expression of loss and emotional withdrawal may be presented through an abstract use of language. I call this use of language "idiosyncratic metaphors," meaning your own unique metaphors hold losses you experience in place of the harsh reality most other officers directly express. This is not negative or psychologically unhealthy. Many officers with your style use idiosyncratic metaphors as artistic and creative conduits—holding losses and to a degree allowing expression—indirectly.

When abstraction becomes the replacement for reality the effect is an unhealthy toxicity. For instance, an officer with your style, rather than saying, "I feel overwhelmed," will say, "I am stuck in the ninth cylinder." In place of saying, "The knife soaked in blood of an innocent victim stabbed to death," he will say, "The miasma of the grim reaper came back." Amusing oneself and one's clinical psychologist or psychiatrist at some level of departure from reality is an escape. It is more than amusing that in part you are more likely than not to be highly intelligent. Your use of idiosyncratic metaphors can serve as motifs for the grist of work you and your cop doc are challenged with in therapy: on the other hand, both you and your cop doc may fall into amusing yourselves over the idiosyncratic metaphors in place of the underlying riptide of your traumatic losses. Staying in a dance that is fascinating is not as effective in unraveling the core of your trauma, loss, and terror of working through to the depth of your existential dilemmas. However, your idiosyncratic metaphors are not a lack of you having "reality testing," although some therapists may mistake your style for just that. Rather, indirect ways of expressing your painful losses may help shield you quite effectively from the effects of fear and guilt, being terrorized by the inner unresolved interpretations you weave with the full brush of your own artistic and creative tendencies. Undeserved shame that is equally protected with all your creativity is a distortion of what you can truly express. Even more so, how you can live if you are able to overcome the defenses that imprison you. Think of your avoidance as a seesaw of distortions that pleads for expression: fear, loss, guilt, anxiety, and anger by direct emotional expression is only let out impulsively. Impulsively with a tendency to undermine your ability and sabotage yourself. Cryptically expressing what you desire to express to other officers is preferable to forfeiting being misperceived. Symbols are the paint itself that beg interpretation and are offered as clues, rather than taking the risk to disclose your trauma and loss history. It is not an inability, or even unwillingness on your part—it is an unconscious process frozen in a defense you have learned well to protect. Protection against being rejected and experiencing dejection.

Numbness with a need to express creativity and solutions to problems is striking to other officers. It serves a defense you employ with peers that makes you acceptable and even likeable as nonthreatening. It may help you bury your own disheartened anguish, but it blocks your full creative expression and productivity. It includes being able to tolerate making a stand directly without fearing the possibility of rejection. The hyperintuition hides your full and genuine potential contributions, aids your own disavowal of healthy competition, asserting your own needs, and appreciation of your own creative potential.

The fact stands that you are more likely than not to make highly effective and insightful public service officers: firefighter investigators and arson specialists, patrol, detectives, rescue, or EMT/medics in elite and specialized units. Adaptively, at best your creativity is owned up to spontaneously, where your trauma and grief experiences are artistically expressed through specialized outlets. Here you can genuinely and directly in an applied way express yourself. Many officers with your style learn how to uniquely fit within your own adaptive niche without therapy. Allowances for your creative contributions often afford many allowances by supervisors. Supervisors who are similar to you or different usually can learn to appreciate your unique gifts, which allow you to be the exception to the rules. This allowance further reinforces your gifts, but in a way traps you in your idiosyncratic defenses against expressing losses and claiming the unique value of your own life as an individual.

Framing Your Moods and Emotions in Your Unique Public Safety Personality Style

Often you may find when you are challenged with an intriguing puzzle to solve your mood becomes anchored in restlessness, irritability, and anxiety. It is important to attempt to work on establishing boundaries in your relationships as your tendency for dependency may slip into codependency instead of interdependency with those most significant in your life. Developing these boundaries includes valuing your own abilities, not disabilities in avoidance and withdrawal patterns. Your hypervigilance by overly identifying with being an officer all the time is likely to be enacted with peers. It is at the roots a desire for your peers' approval and acknowledgment hidden in symbols, or again idiosyncratic metaphor rather than directly asking for attention. Irritable moods are triggered when you feel rejected or neglected with intense energy. The text by Dr. Gilmartin (2002) is very helpful in gaining an understanding by a doc who also was a police lieutenant for many years. Keep in mind that your ability to draw from your losses and weave creative fantasies from the harshest realities is not always a negative outlet if, all other things being equal, it is not extreme or dissociative.

Existentially Relating to Me, You, Others:
Ecologically and Ethologically Speaking

Your relating to others likely includes avoidance when off duty to major and large social events. You are more likely to have a self-reflective introverted style. This is not unusual for a highly intelligent officer who avoids being free with his or her exquisite gifts. You in turn are more likely to present as less competent in self-descriptions than is usually the case, unless dealing with a bully type of supervisor. Safety and trust are always a core underlying issue for you. When you are faced with fear of losing your safety net and trust, you are likely to set up a hyperintuitive shield. Hypervigilance is another way of looking and thinking about the world of public safety in a defense that is well established (see Conroy and Hess, 1992; Gilmartin, 2002). Their work clearly laid down the socialization forces inside tracks of public service agencies where power is expressed through the step-and-ladder structure.

Your perception of insecurity is also offset by your own strength to be highly intuitive in perceiving the struggles you go through. It is your gift in which overdrive, or what I call hyperintuition, filters into your thoughts and emotions as ethological responses, feelings, and your own behavioral patterns. The trauma experiences you have in the form of dreams, mental representations, and creative ideas as well as oppressive fears and fantasies are kept secret.

Secret until they may emerge in artistic form. It is key to understand artistic does not mean only painting, sketching, or even musical or poetic pieces. Artistic can mean the way you conduct an investigation or close it. It can also mean the style in which you articulate an interview with a victim/complainant, or even interpret a crime scene, or set some bold hypotheses about a crime pattern. It can mean your initiating a bold medical procedure, or ambulatory intervention with an aided case with unique results. Artistic can be how you chose to create a more effective fire escape route, or response on the scene of a hazardous material situation unfolding.

It is equally confusing at times to see the ingenuity of your thought patterns yield to coercion: it is as if a stop sign halts your path in a deadlock. Yielding to your fear to step up and onto the plate when your own initiative is called for is tragic as much as it is comic in results. This is a significant ethologic block where you give power to the force of anyone but yourself. For example, it is easy to say, "Well you know, Doc, it's the job" (public service agency), where you surrender your own choice and responsibility to others. For instance, changing assignments (horizontal mobility) or promotion through (vertical mobility) is often rejected outright. It is only with guarantees absolving you of changes—that you are likely to accept changes as things that are done and happen to you in a passive way.

The underpinnings of this behavior are matched by survival ethologically in your own ecological niche. What is as snug as a carpet mite in a dusty carpet? It may be dusty, but dust is comforting. A mite may say it is my bed at night and I am used to it, so why change what works? It is better to be a carpet mite than being out there exposed to the elements as a lady bug: beautiful, free to eat aphids, and waiting to be caught in a spider's web. This logic was delivered more than once in hidden brilliance. Brilliance as a diamond trapped in a graphite coal mine. Let's look at a snippet of an officer with your hyperintuitive style:

Detective C: Hey Doc, why should I exchange my great position for one where I am put at risk for demotion? Getting in trouble with the bosses, and putting my neck in the guillotine does not work. Chop shop undercover may be what I want to get into investigations. But do I really? No, Doc, I don't. The unit I am in is much safer, and at least I know what to do and how to keep from getting in trouble. I am like the fly on the wall. I don't need to show off and make waves to get into Organized Crime Control Bureau (OCCB).

Dr. Dan: By not making waves but being the ace in the hole where you are the gadfly on the wall, is it not true that you can hear it all, are involved with it all, but can afford being snug as a bug in the rug?

Detective C: Doc, I thought you showed me how I am really being artistic in my detail. I am not really snug, am I?

Dr. Dan: I do not really know that answer. Why not tell me what you mean to express when you say you are as fixed as a fly on the wall—as you put it?

Detective C: It is being an artist that I embrace in my role as an investigator. Yeah, I mean, as I said, it would be great to move into OCCB and do some heavy investigations and get my second grade [a higher status as detective]. Why take the risk? I am anonymous. Where I am everyone knows me and my role in the team. I could do my 20 years on my head here. Why make it harder for myself?

Dr. Dan: Great question for a detective who is happy with being a third grade, if that is the case. But, are you truly happy? More important, is your current assignment meaningful to you now?

Detective C: No [expressed with passionate emotion]! You knew that answer: Are you laughing at me, Doc? [Detective C stops and immediately corrects himself.] I know you like me, Doc, and I feel we are friends at times, you know? [I stay silent, which iterates I am a cop doc and that is my identity here: taking away nothing from my collegial and friendly caring attitude as his therapist. He tried to evade the question and his own answer. Detective C continues to speak to me.] It is my dream to go to OCCB, but then I have to do wire taps. Maybe I'll get identified and capped! What if they make me on a job? The hard core of my current unit may not offer promotion, but it is like southern comfort—sweet and good for any afternoon. It's a way to get through my 20, which is in countdown mode, Doc. What can you say after that?

Dr. Dan: Not much to say except you remain a true artist. Like me, you know well how to paint illusions: illusions to comfort you. An illusion, not too different than many artists draw.

Detective C: How so? Tell me what you mean, Doc.

Dr. Dan: I would like you to use your psychological imagination and think of an artist such as being a director of a film. A director remains unscathed by the discontent of whatever is presented by having a distance from the actual real danger on set, and on cue with the producer. Danger escaped at least in the active and rolling umbrella of the lenses on the camera. But unacknowledged and unconsciously veiled in his recording events are sequences frozen in tabloid frames. Projections for the director are projections for you, Detective C. Know why? I'll tell you why—because what you have projected are your idiosyncratic frames of metaphor frozen in the reality of their passive content. Passive means you are not active but just subject too. Meaning not active in your wishes, desires, and losses all hidden from your view. In other words, although you recorded all your trauma and losses in your brain within your own eyes. Like the director you're blind to the producer of your own creative life behind the scene. Guess why? Because, they are recorded as is your initiative in your blind spot. I am here to reflect that fact back to you and let you make your own choice when your vision is clearer? Make sense, Detective C?

Detective C: Holy smoke, Doc! I see what you mean. I am blind to my own need for being passive, with my choice to stay or try to get into the detail I want. That is the miasma. isn't it?

Dr. Dan: That is an interesting metaphor. Let's tear it down no more as we have reached the core meaning. You with me, C?

Detective C: I am, my dear Dr. Watson Rudofossi. I know it is my choice and I do not want to always be behind the director's lenses, but my own. [I nod and our work continues.]

Dr. Dan: [We explore the metaphors, including C's, which is the forgotten language of dreams, illusions, and reality we all have to deal with in a world set up with trauma and losses.] Detective C, as you recognized, the producer directing his experience is truly an illusion. It is also a reality in the moment—as a creative public safety officer, it holds the same tactical arrangement. Like the film you watched as a self-help assignment. It is important, Detective C, to put the director, writer, and producer [Mr. Emmanuel Di Feliciantonio Martin, MFA work, *A Summer in the Life of Earnest Rosenberg* (2002)] in the frame of the exquisite humanity he presents it in. Let me ask you, why would I suggest this film to you as an ace detective? After all, I use this film to illustrate examples of the indefatigable human spirit in my undergraduate and graduate students at NYU in a number of psychology classes.

Detective C: [Without hesitation, with renewed vigor] Doc, I am no producer like Mr. Di Feliciantonio Martin, who clearly is a genius and got me to see some amazing things, like Earnest being in the most squalid of places, and his spirit to raise his faith in a higher being. I mean, how he struggles and returns to a deep level of humanity and compassion you keep bringing in to the mix. But, look at me. [With a grin, a smirk that gave a moment of snide recourse as a last-ditch defense] Doc, me, I mean what should I say? C, take a look world, there he is, the NYPD detective in the raw?

Dr. Dan: Let's stop and pause for a moment and look at the whole picture, Detective C. We have looked at the hero in the film who is truly a remarkable person of character in the director's spotlight. Was it not inspiring to you, C, to see an artist hidden under the veil of struggle with the mean streets of New York? Dealing with some violent folk, and keeping his moral compass in challenges that would bowl most folks over like pins aligned for a fall. Earnest's redemption included his desire to discover himself and transcend his circumstances by living through them, witnessing what he lived through and placing artwork for all to see from Italy to New York Soho galleries. Is that an amazing accomplishment, where Earnest represents the ability for redemption as the finest of city dwellers and workers from the heart and soul of the concrete jungles in his calling as an artist?

Detective C: Doc, absolutely he is a cool and stand-up artist who made it by his faith and love of his calling to do what he felt could bring some light to the world. I mean, his world was pretty dark. But what did you mean by asking me about the whole picture? Isn't Earnest's victory from the concrete streets apparent without stealing or hurting another person, even when under intense pressure?

Dr. Dan: That is a beautiful question, C. No, it is not the full picture. What about the ingenious director, Mr. Di Feliciantonio Martin, who

like you, me, and all-behind-the-scene public safety officers, struggles with his vicarious trauma of being a participant observer. By
participant observer I mean being there in reality. I have the privilege of being able to get Mr. Di Feliciantonio Martin to see my students at NYU at times he is available. What strikes me about the
film, and as you may have hinted, is who is behind the lenses. Well
in his case Emmanuel gets involved by knocking at the doors of
perdition and unapologetically capturing what is in his heart and
soul when confronting the poverty, the abuse, the ugly and painful human condition until the light of redemption he encounters
in the person under the veil is unveiled. In that way his courage
and spirit are hidden behind the screen. Is that not much different
than your soulfulness hidden in losses untold? While I am shining
some light on the qualities that make you the artistic sleuth you
truly are, what do you think about your responsibility to yourself,
Detective C?

Detective C: Yeah, I guess so. I realize you may have meant me to see that even
like the real man behind the genius of Emmanuel as a producer is
a real person. A man who understands the real deal and doing the
right thing. I guess I may also be doing some important work. An
interesting way of thinking, Doc. Hum. [Detective C thinks a bit
about my point and example and why!]

Dr. Dan: [I pause for a few moments, letting the fracture of his hyperintuitive
style shift.] Exactly as you put it C, a producer and director on the
mean streets searching for redemption in others, Mr. Di Feliciantonio
Martin does his share in the work that called him to do what he does
so well. More so, Emmanuel leaves a print that is an artistic record of
his work, in part unseen, but in earnest emotionally felt by all. Felt by
all who realize his ingenious humility, which casts plastic transpar-
ency to the winds of the East River and takes liberty of expression as
his muse. In Emmanuel's case, as in yours now and perhaps mine,
your creativity helps you look within. Looking within to produce
what you have inside you for others without to peak at. If you look
at your defenses and relationship strategy without labeling or judg-
ing, let me ask you, C, have you not in some way achieved a truly
brilliant eco-ethological existential analytic attitude in your ongoing
adaptation of artful sleuthing with compassion? [Detective C continues and nods with enthusiasm.] Your work on expressing yourself
in your poems remains your own legacy, which you can work toward
publishing. But even if not published, writing it for your own record
is worth the effort. In a way, in a different path but similar destina-
tion, you are no different than a genius producer as Emmanuel Di

Feliciantonio Martin, who helped place artist Mr. Rosenberg's art in Soho galleries in New York and Italy. Earnest, once homeless in New York, where you pounded a beat, now in dignified measure displays his artworks without apology and as eloquent expression of the soulfulness within, placed without for all to gain insight as they wish. Just as you redeemed so many lost souls day in and day out, so did our producer. While he made a record in his films for prosperity and all to see, you may leave a poem for all to read. Your own unique testament, if you so choose. Even if you choose not to put your work out there, or it does not make it to publication, I have witnessed your work and that means one more person knows you and your work— some accomplishment. Am I right, Detective C? [Detective C smiles and works in earnest to achieve his calling slowly and gradually in the work ahead of us, in his good time and pace.]

Like Detective C in an existential analysis, it is torturous for you and your therapist to cull out a beautiful black pearl in a calcified oyster bed. A bed laid out in a coral reef with the tiger shark fending off all losses as his gain. That shark is denial of your strength, creativity, and will to faith in your calling, and the source beyond our concrete world. That calling is ever present, right here and right now. Perhaps like me you have big ears to lean over and listen to that call within you.

On an existential dimension your passive approach to life, no matter how significant your contributions, protection, and niche afforded during an active career, may fall apart when you retire. The impact of your duty status changes: restricted, modified, retired may leave you feeling otherwise thrown off your horse, so to speak, and left in the dirt and dust. The dusty heals of your own rodeo show of traumas, and ever-hidden elusive efforts where losses abound, can leave you in the doghouse and pony pen circle. Your rejection of mobility is typical of giving your power to the forces of external control, rather than self-initiative. Typical rationalizations I have encountered are the following:

"There is very little danger for me here in this detail, so why bother to put myself on the front line?"
"I know the streets, and who would do my job if I didn't stick with it as I do?"
"The job made me a patrol cop, and that's where I'll remain. It sucks though."
"It's all hooks and kissing up when you become a boss. Why bother being a brown nose?"

Knowledge is power when the metaphors become springboards for action and resolution.

Your Personality Patterns: Ecological and Ethological Sensibility: Why You Act So

Underlying your avoidant strategy and hypervigilance toward danger are some real fears. The fear, however, is against being scrutinized from within your ranks. Internal prosecution, that is, internal affairs probes, the DA, chief medic officer, or battalion chief going after you (this is not impossible and not without a basis, but nonetheless is an unusually heightened fear). Roots of this fear and similar fears of being sought out and found out usually unveil family dynamics that have led to a fear of personal initiative. Another fear you experience is taking your own initiative, and if you step wrongly, being prosecuted by external agencies in the limelight.

Avoidance and withdrawal is a style in which you may relate to other officers. For example, not being disturbed, and getting one's paycheck safely and retiring without incident. That may be an outward goal, but one that is conflicted inside in your heart of hearts. Specifically, many conflicts may emerge when you vacillate between trusting and mistrusting your spouse, family, friends, and department. Your mistrust may be more a perceived anticipation of your trust being violated and a fear, if you are genuinely vulnerable, that you will be hurt, and that is not paranoia: it is a fear of being abused and misused. It is not unusual that trust and confidence, that genuine empathy could be enlisted on your behalf by family, friends, and fellow officers is tested by you.

For example, when you present vigilantly with a passive-aggressive approach. Your angle of passive withdrawal when you sense aggression in a tone, a word, or a directive is truly aggressive, but without letting it out directly. That indirect passive-aggressive tactic is not much different than your use of idiosyncratic metaphors, at least initially, when a good deed, kind word, or support is proffered. Eventually you and your cop counselor can whittle away at these fears you defend yourself against so strongly. Your avoiding being outgoing is another way you keep being hurt away from you. The best defense is a strong offense, but no offense is better than one cached in passive aggression. Think about your personality pattern for a moment as ethologically sensible. How and why? In a public safety ecology where many violations of the need for safety and trust in others occur on a subtle and explicit dimension, the smartest officers are likely to use an escape from the inevitable pain and suffering endured. Being introverted (rather than being a social butterfly—you prefer residence in your own cocoon) and introspective (looking into your own self, rather than looking at others) is your personality style. Your powers of introspection develop well beyond the realm of other officers'. Your use of fantasy may help compensate for fear of death, your perceived loss of power and control over your own feelings of loss. You are a master of adaptive functional dissociation: your dissociation exists in a unique style in your strategy of having two sides, one exposed to others as passive and the other hidden from yourself as aggressive.

Discussion of Development of Personality Style

Avoiding too much risk in public safety career development is the norm. Yet, you are likely to have mastered an adequate toleration of discomfort, doing your job adequately and without notice. You are the master of creating an epiphany characterized by a lulling hush. Why and how this persists as functional dissociation, numbness, and avoidance is a difficult question. I suggest it is selected because it offers you a high survival value in your eco-ethological niche and your unique imprint in how you make that happen. That lulling hush is your way of self-soothing that is afforded and conditioned in your eco-ethological niche. It helps you remain at a level that you can avoid the experience of being overwhelmed. It takes exquisite adaptation and creativity to achieve the ambiance you craft in the first place in your niche.

But we are back again to the question of why do you tend to use abstract patterns of speech and idiosyncratic styles of presentation? Why does such an intelligent and creative person, as you are at times, litter conversation with cryptic and elusive ways of expression rather than a more direct and balanced presentation?

Expressing your discontent through passive indignation may be a safe way of distancing yourself from active aggression. It may even feel self-righteous, as a way to be elusive to others.

Elusive is powerful, and after all you are not acting out in anger, but holding anger in. The world-leading authority on anger disorders, Professor and Dr. DiGuiseppe, who himself was a police officer for a short time, discovered there are many different styles of expressing anger. One such style relevant here is called anger-in, and is associated with many cardiovascular and neurological disorders. Holding in expressions of anger is not the same as not having it. To the contrary, it becomes as irritable as bowels when waste is held in and needs to be transformed into appropriate emotional expression. Holding it in is not healthy, nor is it effective.

In a way it is important to realize your anger-in is also a rebellion against the feeling of being forced to conform when your style is creative and you are thinking of expressing yourself uniquely. Ambiguity presented leaves the internal standards of status quo intact, and is likely tolerated by peers and supervisors alike, and can be defended as nonresistance if you are accused of being a nonteam member. The idiosyncratic metaphors you use blunt the edge of owning up to dissatisfaction while expressing your pangs of discontent by being ambiguous. While at times your discontent is strong in your anger held within, your strategy makes sense on an ethological dimension. Why? If you use a protesting voice you are likely to experience a strong removal of rewards for even excellent behavior. Rebellion is not tolerated in a public safety ecology. Your response is a passive-aggressive stand that is not clearly rebellious and therefore will likely be tolerated. It may help to realize the sense of power you gain is subtle, but rewarding to you personally. It effectively keeps your distance with others shrouded in mystery, by being aloof, intriguing, and hence attractive within your own eco-ethological unit. From the eco-ethological focus your selection of resistance and image making, while not fully conscious, is quite adaptive. For example, from your academy training through your EMT, firefighting, or police street patrol assignments, keeping a low profile is overlearned and reinforced. Think about it: your avoidant strategy helps you avoid the risk of negatively being singled out, for you remain active below the radar screen and protected from being ostracized. Minimal risk means minimal danger of getting involved in any dangerous situation where you can be singled out.

What is evident is you are not in fear of objective danger; in fact, the paradox here is you are more than likely to be quite courageous in public safety actions. But you are also likely to get physical aches and pains after an event of trauma, with all kinds of imagined fears of prosecution far from the reality of the event. Your own idiosyncratic expression of vigilance and avoidance is beautifully described as a broken heart or soul. Fear and avoidance of existential anxiety thwart your development as a full-filled officer and individual. Until you confront the pain directly and emotionally let out your grief and pain with one significant other you are stuck in your own world of escape. That significant other may be, and in fact often is, your therapist, which is initiated through your peer support officer. Tolerating and embracing your own existential anxiety may precede any real growth, which must result from painful confrontations with your own fears of loss. Loss hidden from your own awareness and creative expression. A purging of your mind of toxic accumulation of unspoken, undefined, and symbolic abstraction of traumatic loss is corequisite to growth. Your grief cycles into idiosyncratic symbolism that remains unshared and undiscovered—unless you get to express the emotional weight you've stocked behind it.

Our Personality Style Peer's Most Traumatic Event in Detective C's Own Quoted Viewpoint

I've been involved in many events through the years. Some I remember, but all I want to forget.

I've responded to many 10-XX (calls for assistance by other officers) and made many arrests and seen plenty of hurt and dying people. I'm tired, okay, tired of seeing it. I don't understand how people can hurt other people for no apparent reason. I've lost friends on the job because of violence, and I'm tired of it. I can do what I have to. Don't get me wrong, I'm a good soldier and I've always been. I can't take seeing it again and again like pictures that pop up. I've felt confused and weak. I just want to be able to let it roll off again. I want you and my other doctors to help me get back to feeling strong, like I was. I remember working on a midnight shift, 15 years ago August, with my old partner.

We were assigned to sector A-D in Red Hook houses. We got a job for a female stabbed. I remember the address. It was in the projects. We had trouble with our car, which I remember was stalling on us.

We got there, the ambulance guys, EMT were already there working on her. I looked at her. From my point of view she was upside down on the floor. I asked her, "Who stabbed you?" She said, "Ms. L." I made the arrest.

She was dying right then and there. So I solved my first homicide. Fuck! I would rather have been able to have stopped my first homicide! I wished so much I could have saved the poor kid from the f-cking reaper! I was in all night at the station house filling out paperwork and safeguarding the perp. In the morning I went with Detective X to the Kings County Morgue to ID the body. There she was—nude on the table—with that 95 tag on her toe. She hadn't been chopped up yet.

Impact of Traumatic Loss in My Own Unique Personality Style: On Duty and Off Duty

Detective C goes on to describe his losses and express his shock and effort to undo the very traumatic loss of the victim he witnesses.

Detective X asked the doctor to stick a probe into the girl's stab wound. It went in all right, all the way in. I remember [at that moment] telling her in my mind: "Hey, please, your only a kid, D, come on get up! I was just talking to you. Come on now, what happened?" The probe freaked me out. I remember Detective X laughed and pointed out that if in the event I got murdered I'll be on the same table. Talk about freaky, like a miasma leaking out. I felt this wet electricity early in my police career, maybe 3 years in the bag. Still to this day I see myself on the project landing, talking to

D upside down. She still looks frantic to me. It makes me feel frantic too. I got department recognition for this arrest. So what? People will kill at the drop of a hat. I must be watchful and wary for that possibility. Especially in the work I do. After this any job coming over in the projects would make me super alert, as I saw what happened that night. Between two females no less! I must be on guard at all times against horror and disappointment because I know either will trip me up if I get caught otherwise. That's why I just do my job and watch my back. And my priority is to collect a check every 2 weeks.

Detective C: Do you see, Doc, why it is naïve to care about the work you do and let go in a real way? After all, what will happen when you allow others to know how you really feel? I do not want any recognition; the less they know about me, the better. The only mirror they can look into is their own, not mine, and that is how I like it. I can be a super sleuth with you as my dear Dr. Rudofossi Watson: I do appreciate your help but refuse opening up anymore. As I said, collecting the check every 2 weeks and then monthly once I finish with the job is where my head is at. Do you see what I mean?

Dr. Dan: [I pause and think of what Detective C is truly offering me to unravel.] I do not see what you want me to see. I see what lies behind the mirror of your own illusion. You know you use but prefer to reflect on mine to envision, so you can disown it. You desire being the super sleuth to the worlds within. You invite me to the triangle to unravel clues as Dr. Watson and Rudofossi in the two worlds you live in. One is fantasy and one is the hard cold reality of murder.

Detective C: Maybe that is true, as you are allowing me to see and figure out with you. Although maybe it is not so. I mean, I really think maybe somewhere subconsciously I do really care at how this can happen without someone stopping their inner anger and not acting on it. I mean, it is very difficult to deal with being dissed and left out in the cold to die on a cold gray blood-soaked stairwell.

Dr. Dan: Yes, C, please go on with your description. I am listening [pause for a number of lone silent minutes and reflections].

Detective C: Yes, I fantasize a lot about being able to help, but I know the reality versus fantasy. I am educated and not dumb. [Reflecting in gesture by putting up his hand to cover his face and in deeper and genuine expression] It is so weird, I mean, seeing a young African American girl dying on the stairwell and the smell of her piss. It is weird, as if I smelled it before somewhere. The feeling I could do nothing at all and I did not really know how I could bare her death like someone or something was going to save the day. But no one ever did save the day, Doc. It is not supposed to end that way. Why did it? What do you have to say for yourself what could you or any doc do? It is all for nothing? As I said to you earlier, why bother?

Dr. Dan: Yes, a good question and a real one you need to answer for yourself day by day alone. It sounds like the best escape from your angst and painful losses where you are rendered a mere mortal, as I am too. It is sometimes too harsh to bear without fantasy to escape the tragedy of life's sorrow.

Detective C: Yeah, Doc, I do care a lot. I guess. But put the wicked witch's mirror up on the wall for her evil hag's face, where even Batman could not conquer the miasma of both worlds where no real answer lies for anyone except the ninth cylinder. Not even you could figure it with me. Even if we were partners, right? [Silence for 5 minutes. I listen in respect for C's next thoughts in his good time.] Why are you so quiet? It is the truth, right? I mean, there is no real answer to figure out, Dr. Dan.

Dr. Dan: The desire to create a world in which you desire to not only solve the crimes, but to figure out the painful loss as to "Why?" is like the wicked witch hag. Is the wicked hag in a way a metaphor to passively accept the harsh reality that is very painful and without rhyme and reason? You do your job well, but not the aftermath of having opened up your pain in that mirror you see into at night. At night, so to speak, all alone. It is good to escape to the retention of your pension and the future of a monthly dole, as you associated to earlier. Well, it makes sense to hold in and control what you can. Doubly not be targeted by others who may notice. In our space it is easier to join both worlds together, including the sadness without guilt, perhaps for what you could not prevent in deed.

Like with Detective C, what was originally your own genuine creative impulse and empathetic connection to others as a rookie officer in overly optimistic goals is experienced as a severe loss. A loss of innocence battered through repeated expectations shattered into the split of so many fragmented losses. Maladaptation ensues. The economic solution in a hierarchical structure of power is your creation of a sacred and private world of shadows. A world of shadows where retreat, avoidance, and hyperintuition tragically replace the balanced substance of healthier assertion, competition, and creativity. In part, this is the weight of trauma, bureau-pathology, and stigmatization, not weakness on your part. Nonetheless, it is only in uniting the real world of losses in the unique way you envision creative expression that you are freed. It is not the only path, but a very effective and worthy path to work through with a therapist, as Detective C and I have begun to, and you may with your own therapist.

How Your Public Safety Personality Style Is Different from Other Public Safety Styles

Unlike other personality styles thus far explored, many officers with your style, although keeping a low profile, so to speak, paradoxically pride themselves on being an "odd" man or woman in the unit, agency, or department. You are not similar to hyperaggressive officers in how you process anger, as you have a passive style where anger is held within. The addictive hyperexcited style thrives on excitement and gets into frays; you are likely, by comparison, to avoid conflict.

Avoidant strategies may emerge in your unique style of adaptation to an environment where your exquisite sensitivity toward human anguish and suffering is personalized and internalized. In such an internal world, as you have seen in my work with Detective C as an example, it makes superb sense to withdraw from others and not to expose yourself to being labeled vulnerable. Grief and trauma are not worked through, but split into the world of illusion, fantasy, and wishes to undo the reality of the shock of losses webbing your public safety identity and functional world.

Your tendency is similar to the hyperexcited, where a genuine caring for sacred victims is ever present. Guilt almost always unearned in reality is sadly owned in secret. Your tendency for self-blame and guilt unwarranted is accepted as if you are defective and responsible for the multiple losses in trauma experienced. This maladaptation engenders your tendencies to become hyperintuitive, avoid making a stand openly that you genuinely believe in, and being directly assertive. The maladaptive consequence of an unusually highly intelligent officer as you likely are is apathy and boredom. Your retreat from living eventually stills your passion with unquiet silent thunder. It may stunt your own development and ability to grow through productive competition and genuine cooperation. Parsimony, such as avoidance and withdrawal, makes sense to preserve energy on one hand. While keen for a tortoise and ergonomics, it hardly suffices for human living. Avoidant and hyperintuitive schemas are revealed through the following statements:

"A good officer understands the least you do, the better."
"Avoid any trouble; the goal is pick up your paycheck every other Thursday period."
"When off duty, avoid crowded areas to avoid being involved with perps."

Further, having your hyperidiosyncratic intuitive approach creates a diminished likelihood that you will enjoy being a team player (avoidant tactic), yet still you are likely to be highly dependent on the group for survival. Compensation is a unique strategy you are likely to use with more adept results than any other officer style, save the hyperfocused style. You usually find a valued skill and offer your best within the group you belong to within your eco-ethological niche. Your distinct skill affords you a large payoff in terms of ethological satisfaction. In an advanced hierarchical society like public safety a specialized skill in healthy intuitive approaches affords you a selective advantage in comparison to other officer-patients. In fact, one of the wonderful assets you have as a proffered specialized skill is that you are unusually learned and sophisticated in your repertoire. The reciprocity you give is rewarded by being left alone and by gaining benefits in full view of your own hyperintuitive and idiosyncratic style. When balanced and integrated with your tendency for creativity, your style epitomizes balanced adaptive ethological evolution in action.

Initial Inroads to Lay Out Your Own Map
for Trauma and Grief Therapy

The challenge for yourself and your therapist, if you choose to embark on such a course of working through, is a redirecting of hyperintuition into a healthier expression of intuition, resilience, and productivity. I suggest such a strategy includes quite a bit of renarration of trauma, in part accomplished by your own exploration of what idiosyncratic metaphors personally mean to you: stop and think about what are the ideas that repeatedly emerge in your own metaphors, analogies, and descriptions of sensory material, especially losses you may not want to address at first.

How to Move Your Own Hyperintuition into
Expansion and Inclusive Intuition

Expand self-vigilance to include wider circles of relatedness you may attempt to do gradually and with your therapist's assistance. Behavioral experiments are excellent ways of doing so as the two of you assess experiments gradually.

Your experiments may include gradual movement toward risk taking that targets healthy ambition and competition, for example, taking promotional exams, and specialized assignments with increasing complexity. While doing so, note your thoughts about maladaptive myths you may discover you are living by and with.

Do rehearsals, role-plays, and tangible experiments where you get to directly express your own creative ideas and involvement in work settings and social events.

These experiments are ideally rehearsed initially with the therapist, or if you are comfortable with a peer support officer, and worked through by doing it. Note your fears and successes when you go beyond the fear of being disapproved of or feeling inadequate or guilty. Write down your thoughts as you conquer some fears and those holding you back. This is great material to work through with a therapist cop counselor/cop doc.

As you achieve growth and self-mastery is gained, peer support officers may be enlisted in building social circles.

Use your own artwork, diary, and verbal metaphor to express your world of fantasy, illusion, and metaphor. The goal is not to eliminate it but to integrate your creativity into the world of trauma and loss you have experienced. That is the real public safety world, which can in fact handle the harsher reality of direct expression that you anchor your growth in. Gradual growth in which you have set some goals, including competiveness and achievement, as a real and lasting contribution within your own life. Your life as an officer and individual.

Since you are the most likely of personality styles to have an above-average intelligence, take the challenge of complex and involved existential and artistic-oriented approaches to express your own PPS-CPTSD.

The essence of your growth is best achieved by working through the religious and metaphorical motifs without fighting them as irrational, archaic, or primitive, and expressing them with a mental health professional who will help you work through to a deeper understanding and redirection to spiritual growth. You can also do this of course yourself, but it is much more meaningful to share with another.

I remind myself, as you need to, when working through, many conflicts will emerge and what is hidden for and so yearned for as well is your desire for relatedness and understanding. You can help yourself by seeking actively and directly toward reintegrating your own broken soul toward spontaneous healing.

Your repair work is a healing process that includes your own ability to express loss without shame, and that takes time, but begins with your first step. Optimism and reinvestment in life are allowed expression after your emotional release of pain and loss is expressed. An example of how toxic loss remains built up and not expressed is presented in the inimitable style of Dr. Fritz Perls, as an army psychotherapist:

A soldier was referred after suffering from big welts all over his body and with a deep despair in his eyes.... I put him under Pentothal and learned that he had been in a concentration camp. I spoke German to him and led him back to his moments of despair and removed the crying block. He really cried his heart out, or shall we say he cried his skin out. He woke in a state of confusion and then he really worked at the typical experience of being completely and freely in the world. At last he had left the concentration camp behind and was with us. The welts disappeared. (Perls, 1979, p. 90)

Dr. Perls may have used a modified eco-ethological existential analytic approach. It is likely in part the unique aspects of Perls' empathy helped the soldier's loss to be expressed. In the eco-ethological approach Dr. Perls worked with the original traumatic loss the officer-patient experienced. That loss may be described as a quantum psychic moment of the death camp. The trauma may be conceived as a point in the patient's life where human time becomes defined by the narrowing of human space beat into him from the ashen welts experienced through repetitive trauma. The cumulative lumps of unreleased toxins bore witness to unspoken loss. It was perhaps Dr. Perl's attitude that did not repeat what this victim officer-patient had experienced with others. That is, in the joint work and empathy that was bidirectional in his work with the patient respectfully, trust was gained in allowing him to express his considerable and cumulative loss. Because the therapist cared enough to help facilitate the loss being expressed, Dr. Perl's passionate, non-judgmental, and existential approach worked. His patient exchanged the map of hyperintuition as victim for the vitality that hard work through direct expression of traumatic loss freed in him as a survivor.

Let's Get Real: Your Public Safety Personality Style: Officer and Cop Doc's Corner

Placing the Wet Electricity of the Sixth Sense in Focus

In the eco-ethological existential analysis your narration of trauma and loss may be viewed as a map. Your map may guide you into a more clear understanding of how you actually process loss in your own unique interpretation of trauma.

It may also clarify what defenses you have developed in protecting yourself from being vulnerable to the losses so difficult to process in the complexity of accumulated traumas. In the example to follow I will again visit Detective C's hypersensitivity and vigilance against loss. Here you will witness a fine peer officer of superb intellect and gifted as an investigator indirectly express his losses. This snippet of our working through, like other examples, will suffice in giving you an opening to seek your own help and to put the work in this section on your own personality style in perspective. Please pay attention to the way Detective C describes very painful losses. For example, as feeling vibrations; having a sixth sense about people no longer present, but felt; sensing an aura is present somewhere nearby. This final example suffices to illustrate to you an attempt to reach out to me as therapist and to engage me in facilitating Detective C's expression of losses left unexpressed. I suggest you understand Detective C's symbolic representations as his own meaning of indirectly expressed loss. Using an eco-ethological existential analytic approach, we work together to define, normalize, and more directly express the losses Detective C experienced in trauma. The payoff in Detective C's case is the direct expression and freedom of creative expression as the realities of repetitive trauma and loss are fleshed out together. At this point keep in mind Detective C and I have an alliance together, and have clarified working on trauma and loss as an important aspect of our agreed on goals in therapy. Our task is to gain direct expression of loss in the trauma while helping Detective C to value his inestimable worth as a survivor beginning on a path of even more stunning growth, which followed.

Detective C: Doc, just tell me what to do. I'm tired, okay? I just can't figure out how an innocent girl can die like that. The pictures pop up again and again. The miasma of the grim reaper hovers around her face. I cannot feel anything. [Detective C presents this trauma with minimal emotional expression, but in a deep and strong-pitched voice.] Well, how do I get rid of this grim reaper?

Dr. Dan: C, once again, I have no magical technique or pill. In fact, it seems like you'd like me to give you the answers. I would like to understand what comes to mind with the image of the 'grim reaper' coming up when you think of death? [I pause to hear a response, none follows.] It is no wonder, but understandable. If I am getting it right, and I may be far off, you are sick and tired of the physical arousal each time you see the face of the girl as the grim reaper hovers around her face. The reaper's sword you've described maybe the long knife that stabbed T, and the grim reaper's face replaces the girl's grim expression while dying and pleading as your eyes picked up and held her there for a long time (silence). [I let my understanding of Detective C's genuine experiences underlying his metaphors lead me. They are quite rich, although seemingly awkward at first. I feel and think Detective C may be too scared to identify vulnerability, fear, and cry openly. I chose not to remain silent. I grab for the metaphors to clarify what I believe is blocking expression of loss.] Detective C: [Eyes becoming slightly teary with gaze aversion] You know I've done all I could [alluding to guilt, I make note to return at a later time]. Why did she have to die on the landing on the 13th stair of the 7th stairwell, upside down? She told me Ms. L and she had disagreed about a boy. T gave me a dying declaration. T said,

"Mrs. L told me that will teach me to be disrespectful. She pointed at her stomach. She said she was scared." [I saw a slice cut deep inside and the thick red blood.]

Dr. Dan: [I visually observed fear, as if written on Detective C's face.] What are you experiencing right now as you are seeing her at this moment?

Detective C: [Without missing a heartbeat and with genuine expression let loose] Wet electricity jumping up and down my body. You know, that sixth sense we discussed when she was dying. The EMT thought she may make it, and told me so. The miasma was all around. I knew she was worse off than she made out. Then the f-cking job and anyhow ... [distracted to unrelated event, in part understandably to avoid once again the pain].

Dr. Dan: [Interrupting and encouraging Detective C to let loose and continue] The wet electricity sounds like a very painful experience; while it is difficult, it is important to stay with it.

Detective C: [Trusting the process and me as his therapist] It's the striding through circumstances, a jolt, a miasma is there [directly looking at me intensely studying my responses]. It's a real miasma when her face pops up. I feel the grim reaper is right there with us. [Detective C scans the room with his eyes, as if he is tracking something he cannot see but senses as fear associated with the horror imprint of T's death.] It feels like wet electricity right now. [I don't attempt to get to the roots of these metaphors no matter how interesting; we will explore these metaphors later.]

Dr. Dan: It appears if we look at what's happening now, your experience of the grim reaper is not a ghost, or evil spirit, but the painful loss of seeing a grim face on T, a dying girl—flashing some real fears back into your mind's eye. The experience of striding through circumstances makes sense as a homicide seen again and again. The shock of the death and seeing such a young woman murdered by another older woman is jolting, shocking to your depth. I imagine for you, Detective C, it felt like wet electricity. Mrs. L stabbing T was your first homicide as a detective 15 years ago; if that's not a miasma, I don't know what is.

Detective C: [Silence and sadness in tone of voice, teary-eyed, no expression for a few minutes, a deep sigh] I remember the time I started to feel the miasma, and see the grim reaper in the shadows of her face like a dream or vision. I feel weird talking about it. It's chaos, you know. It is like the feeling I told you about. You and I are Greek soldiers in ancient times, and you are my centurion, Doc, healing me from the bad stuff we saw.

Dr. Dan: [Silence. I need to process where Detective C is going. I get frustrated and think I may need a new hypothesis. I have not disconfirmed the original one yet. I know Detective C is not psychotic or paranoid. I chose to continue and keep to my stance. I go for putting the riddle presented to me as a gift, which it truly is for a therapist who is attuned.] Detective C, it seems like the journey you are taking us on is one of finding clarity in a miasma, a miasma that makes a lot of sense in the context of ancient Greek times. [Detective C had shared with me readings about the oracle at Delphi, where Socrates went in his quest to find order in chaos—reason and purpose behind the tragic comedy of murder.] The grim reaper moves in and out of the miasma of sorrow unexpressed. This miasma is where you courageously endured wet electricity as jolts to your soul, seeing her stab wound, red blood, and the urine smells you described before as senseless offering to a false god of rage. It may be in part you wish to invite me as your therapist to find order with you in the senseless murder through your beautiful metaphors. As long as we remember, they are metaphors—why not in the sacred relationship we are building? [This is a paradoxical intervention to help Detective C realize in our existential analysis I can witness and value the pain and loss underlying the metaphors, and tolerate the more direct expression of loss with my full support for the healthy expression now released. My intervention tends to be helpful to Detective C.]

Detective C: [Tears in eyes, crying, and followed by a smile that is genuine] I mean, it hurts to see this young gir's beautiful life wiped out by this self-righteous, mean-hearted bitch! Imagine, how evil is murder? Over what, Doc? Being dissed? Come on, that's madness, isn't it? It's not me that's mad, it's this chaotic situation and many more like it.

Dr. Dan: No, it not you! It's hard and difficult to express. As you're doing right now, Detective C.

Our work continues: clarity and directness followed. By not relinquishing the joint quest with Detective C to find sensibility and a rational creative approach to what begun with an overvalued use of metaphors, we have begun to establish a new and healthier way of expression, identification, validation, and exploration of losses in our therapeutic alliance. Much work follows and progress has already shined in some light in this dark miasma ready to spring forth hope—no pun intended—as we now move on to the next profile, which will focus our attention a bit heavily.

Controlled Hyperfocused Public Safety Personality Style

What Motivated You toward Swearing Your Own Oath as a Public Safety Officer

The essence of what motivated officers with your own style to join a public safety career was:

> "Job security, a reliable and decent profession with good promotional opportunities."
> "Being an officer felt natural to me. I wanted to maintain peace and order in people's lives!"
> "As an EMT I knew I could accomplish saving lives."

Psychological Survival Defenses within Your Own Public Safety Personality Style

How does an officer capable of intense concentration, being fully attentive and pragmatic, deal with the quantum psychic moment of trauma?

What happens to the rituals that served as predictable security against what is now shattered by the impact of original trauma?

It is natural for an officer with your style of approach, and a need for answers to search for structure and order in chaos that strikes suddenly. Your search for order is nested in your mapping of tactics, rules, and a sense of order in your strategy to survive in an unpredictable eco-ethological niche. Your strength is in the nest of aftershocks: when crumbling facades of safety block your path, you become solution-oriented. Practices that should have or must have kept you safe invariably will fail. When failure occurs, your respite is to hyperfocus attempts at learned and often complex rituals. Notably after a trauma, your tendency is to feverishly attempt to undo loss. Your attempts to solve rather than confront or experience loss are of course an ever-heightened intensified defense against that very loss. The original symbolic value of the wish for rituals to ward off harm is not forgotten, but is almost always sunk under the waves of conscious awareness. This is so, for in your assessment of things not working out, even a tactic your focus highlights failures that in moderation is healthy, but as in all your defense is to retreat into a perfectionistic pitch. The epitome is the captain going down with his ship. Please pause and genuinely think about that. If one said the captain will go down to the gates of hell with his troops, human empathy and heroism emerge. Heroism doubtless is heard, but the ship, even the *Titanic*, will not care less if the captain sinks with her or not: it is a hull of metal and steel, and it is tragic when any officer loses track of his or her inestimable worth, even when millions of dollars are at stake. Life is priceless, as all officers are; no material ever is. This submerging under your existential unconscious makes superb sense in your hiding your losses, which on the one hand to help you view yourself as perfect. On the other hand if you are lacking in perfection, then, to compensate for your loss of meaning all you have to do is heighten your own perfectionism to a fevered pitch and, again, you are on the road again. It is when you slow down that the crushing effect of self-imposed perfectionism cascades into a collapsed ideal. But again, let's move in for a more intimate view at an example of Officer TQ. Officer TQ is in her mid-fifties. She has made an active decision to retire after two and a half decades of public safety work. While she begins emptying out her locker she finds an older radio holder and begins to cry profusely. Initially many psychiatric labels are fixed to Officer TQ with sudden effect. I will spare the details save one fact: the peer support officer, the battalion chief, and the captain all may think they are clinical psychiatrists/psychologists without portfolios—they are not.

In my dismissing the labels affixed erroneously on Officer TQ, she and I learned using an eco-ethological existential analysis: that the radio holder discovered over years of loss had unique and meaningful significance to not only Officer TQ, but also as she shared it in life with Officer KO.

Firefighter Officer TQ: [As if staring out in vacant space with no rental signs in sight, she began to get morass in her expression of deep painful loss, easily mistaken for despair and severe depression. Her attempt was to keep me distracted.] The radio case has a lot of memories for me; they are no use to Officer KO anymore. I remember some moments when he acted in a cute way. You see this double stitch? He pulled on it once and joked about me being a silly lady who had no idea how attractive I am. I would tell him I was fat and ugly. I mean, we had our moments but never really mixed business with pleasure, but all in all I loved KO. [TQ goes on to express the leather case and some of the sewn fix-ups; each lining was woven with experiences that held meaning.]

Dr. Dan: It seems like every frayed line of leather that folded in on itself represented many positive, timeless moments shared with your partner KO over a decade of firefighting before he died in the line of duty.

Firefighter TQ: Hey, I did not do anything to save him, even though I knew he was sick and had hit the bottle too much. I knew he wanted to express a lot, well me too. I mean, we had a rough time when we lost a firefighter. You know what I mean? Anyhow, Doc, enough of me. I am just freaked out. Why bother? I am the old fat, ugly, and unwanted horse. I mean, I did all I could to be a stand-up and critical firefighter over the years and gave up a lot, and now what do I have to show for it all? I have a boyfriend but no real marriage, and a whole lot of injuries from the years. Where do you begin with what has happened to me and where I am now with death a few years ahead of me? Well maybe if I am luckier than my partner, a few years more. I cannot believe I cried over a radio holster—what a shame and what a loser. So what can you say about me, Dr. Dan? Are you going to try to get me to see I am not so ugly, not so fat. or old? Go ahead. Try, because it will not work. [TQ is so upset and needs me to tolerate and care to confront her real pain and not judge, minimize, or distract her away from "it."]

Dr. Dan: [I sense and listen as my eardrums hear her silent tears; my eyes focus in on her painful breathing, and the beauty of a fellow officer who in her years of serving others has never stopped and paused. Never paused to hear her own genuine grief she is entitled to expressing and allowing full ventilation. I think as I often do, if God gave free will, who is any person to take it away? Soulful tears are the most sacred gifts one can share with his or her therapist. I accept even the silent tears, but what I hear, smell, and sense in the constricted tightness of stale air allowed escape. Tears and annoyance at me emerge as she just nods.] I sense the pain like stale air needing escape and expression; like the transmissions on the radio they are unheard but still echoing inside, with all the feelings you hide so well and so long. Because you and I cannot switch that radio on, we can sense the importance of the radio runs together. That is, if you trust me. I will await the transmission as you remember it. That is, if you care to share it with me. That is why I have the big ears to listen so well.

Firefighter Officer TQ: It is horrid. The smoke is black and gray and it is hot as hell. The officer is in shock, going into cardiac arrest. No words are exchanged when he is dying and no one to say, "I love you brother! Do not die. Fight please. Breathe again!" It is surreal and nothing can help him. I wish God would come down and take him back to us. Where is his voice, is that it? Where is his breath? Can a man die like this, in his uniform? Is it all a lie? I mean, how come no one heard the pain when I screamed out? It sucks, it really sucks! Crying and heaving inside out for me to witness. What did I labor for all my life—to be single and a loner? Now without much to show, including all these words for all my work and life. Is this what it is about in the end?

Dr. Dan: A very good question to think about—the labor of your life, and the loss of no returns. Is it truly losses without any returns for you, TQ?

Firefighter TQ: Doc, had I done everything by the book. I followed what I had to do! Even in the CPR I should have really made a difference. It is too late and in reality, it is pure absurdity, as much as me, myself, and I—I'm simply helpless and it is all hopeless!

Dr. Dan: [Pausing and acknowledging in a low and deep voice the immense pain of existential angst and near despair] My sister officer, it is incredible to stop and think of the time and energy you have given in your brave firefighting spirit and will to saving lives. It appears in this moment, among others to come, that the well of all your efforts is dried up. But not the tears in the well of your red-shot eyes, where all the losses you hold in your heart's cache are swollen. The tears you are letting out can take the worst fire out. TQ: the fire burning inside of guilt and pain of your partner dying and feeling powerless with all the by-the-book tactics you used. The fire of passion to be the eternal firefighter lost in giving back the holster to call direct assistance as needed by your peers. It is scary and painful, is it not? [TQ is sobbing while holding it back as best as possible.] It is incredible how many lives you have saved side by side with the angels of your creator. Do you believe it is really possible you are alone ever? Is it possible to reach out to gain ground and use the sand of relief in all the good you have done to extinguish the fire burning within your soul and heart? In your losses you forgot your hidden strengths and gains. One gain not insignificant is the connection with me here and now. Are you alone right here and now? [Staring directly so eye contact is established]

Firefighter TQ: [Looking at me with tears and sniffling and a grin breaks out] I guess my peers have not really abandoned me. I am retiring and can still see you as well, even if you are a cop and not a firefighter. I mean a cop doc. You are here, aren't you?

Dr. Dan: I hope you trust I truly am here for you. I hope you do not have to reach across and poke me to check out if I am real, but you may do so if needed. [Firefighter TQ grins again with a raised eyebrow.] Believe me, you would not be the first to see if I am real and poke me. I am very real and very much here. I am as here as you are. It is in sharing the beginning of your emotional bondage you have wrapped yourself in and trusting me to help you unwrap "it" that may feel so strange. Have I lost my sensibility, or does that make sense to you?

Firefighter TQ: It is very surreal, Doc, but yes, it feels good to let it go and get it out. You are here with me. I am not alone.

Dr. Dan: I am here, and I am not Swiss cheese. But neither was the peer support officer or the captain that did care about you to help you get some assistance to work on this very real pain you are experiencing, TQ, as you have privileged me to understand with you.

As we continue to explore her losses and her assumptions about her identity as a firefighter, TQ is not absurd, not hysterical, or suffering from any personality defect. TQ's hyperfocus in part predisposed her belief that she was to blame for all that went wrong. She never stopped and considered the reality of her partner as a young firefighter dying and the many associations of guilt she carried. TQ's complex grief had many layers needing unfolding within the hours of work we had left to explore in the space of her exit signs, all left closed as options she was to discover with me.

Discovery in the space of time now wide open with all the possible choices she had to make. We had begun work that was needed. In essence, that radio holder was a symbol that afforded FD Officer TQ a grasp on her life, which in her narrowed vision closed in on her with retirement and changes in her aging. The radio holder was a rich transitional link to her past that, on one hand, held space in frozen time. On the other, the tyranny is it held her blocked in her losses with no insight for future choices and the freedom of new opportunities awaiting her. We held the moments that were meaningful and shared with her partner in a log written down to capture their value and meaning when she cared to go back in time and revisit. Genuine expression led to an insight that a dynamic exploration revealed. The death of her friend and partner provoked shared vulnerability, survival guilt, anger, anxiety, and buried loss with me. Those shared memories emerged when the radio holder revealed a tip of her pain and loss that even the best intentions and stringent rituals could not prevent at the heart of the matter, lost and now gradually regained in Firefighter Officer TQ's gain. The telescopes of her genuine losses were long ones that burrowed down to a spiral of death, denied agape love, and a loss that remained buried and unheard. Allowing herself healthier expression of her many losses freed Officer TQ's gain in ways she never knew were possible. Without harsh, self-imposed rules and limits to halt expression of loss under fire, in Officer TQ's case the lightness of fresh air was released.

Framing Your Moods and Emotions in Your Unique Public Safety Personality Style

What stands out in your personality style is a gauge that reads in neon lights: constant overdrive, running in high gear with nonstop energy. A less pronounced but ever present anxiety and agitation lie undertow. Your resistance against pleasure, relaxation, and genuine levity is hand in hand with disavowed traumatic loss. Your hyperfocus may be a way of communicating with yourself, as well as others, shifts in your mood. How? Ethological aggression communicated through your feverish pitch of constant work may signal to others agitation and pain, in a way that is acceptable in public safety culture. For example, mordant gallows humor may not be real humor but avoidance of loss through distancing yourself from traumatic loss. This avoidance and denial for the short term is adaptive and works well on the scene of the trauma.

In many public safety eco-ethological niches gallows humor is all too common, idealism is high, and conflicts over the contradictions are not unusual. Let's take a look at a process that impacts on mood and emotions with officers who have a hyperfocused personality style. Peer pressure may initially press you to exchange shock and grief for giggles. The pressure to not allow expression of grief is keen. This is particularly so when the victim is considered a worthy victim or a perp, or someone who in some way deserves what he or she did in fact get. In many cases, in socially acceptable ways you can, as all folks to some degree or another do. That is, compromise your spiritual, religious, cultural, or philosophical existential angst silently. Upset can occur emotionally when you lose a lot of energy that you invest in temporary coping tactics to help you get past chronic attempts at adapting to humor you find humorless and you truly disdain.

Existentially Relating to Me, You, Others: Ecologically and Ethologically Speaking

Existentially your response to trauma provokes what I call intense hyperfocus leading to a search. That search holds a promise to recover what was lost and what remains lost. With a tendency toward hyperfocusing an implosion, where aggression, excitement, and loss ever present are masked in new and more involved rituals to defend against grieving. That implosion may be an attempt at compensation, when rules and rituals are no longer effective in keeping away the repressed loss. The rituals you have laid out act as buffers to protect you from many losses, but no longer can be bought out and afford you the ability to ward off danger. When a critical mass accumulates, exhaustion sets in, and an emotional implosion may occur.

Your hyperfocus style serves a very important existential purpose; your ability to constrict your emotions forces you into a way of relating by doing things and purpose in behaviors that leads to very harsh self-discipline. Along with this tendency you become prone to reducing your achievements, which keeps you distant from your genuine accomplishments and at a fevered pitch. Your commitment to work is a straight-edged razor, no ridge of imperfection allowed. A sure sign is how you absorb or learn the procedural guide of the public service department you are attached to as a member of the service. Sometimes hundreds of pages of minutiae are committed to memory, along with a rigid adherence to that rule-based guide. Asking for a procedure and witnessing you dictate encyclopedic knowledge is confirming. Your walled defenses are as impenetrable as armor. Your style is as functional and important as an existential eco-ethological defense can be. This defense works to reinforce your public safety identity. However, no matter what you accomplish in concrete goals on the job, the tragic moment is almost everyone appreciates your Herculean effort and achievement: the irony is the one who never lays down his chisel for a wreath, not even for a blinking moment of genuine pleasure, is no one less than you! While most officers would feel a deep sense of accomplishment, efficacy, and pleasure when promoted to the rank of captain (executive level) and achieving an MA degree, you consider it "just another goal/phase accomplished." "What's next?" is not only a question you ask, but one you have answered before it even comes up in your anticipatory mind.

Your Personality Patterns: Ecological and Ethological Sensibility: Why You Act So

Your restless search for perfection is never satiated in the waters that waft through straits of self-imposed exactitude. Perfectionism is mastered. The wish underlying your uniform of armor of perfectionism in part is a desire for invulnerability and immortality. Reaching the accumulated mental and professional knowledge of your own profession means achieving a walking armor that renders you impervious to pain, loss, and ultimately death. The more you experience traumatic loss, the more goals are established. Goals that detour you from what will be your own inevitable confrontation with PPS-PTSD. While your driven tendency is a key ethological emotion, your own idealism and selflessness are both strengths and weakness. An idealism that is unusually attractive to the sparkle that radiates in you as a young recruit. This sparkle illumines your way up the fire ladder, gun smoke, and ambulatory calls to the full plumes of being a senior and tenured commander. Your matter of fact attitude lays cement troves that act as flood gates where cumulative traumatic losses become stale tears in an ever-increasing constricted dry well. Truth be told, emotional repression may lead to your distraction with so many different tasks that genuine living may be stalled for an entire career.

Our Personality Style Peer's Most Traumatic Event in Detective W's Own Quoted Viewpoint

Approximately 15 years ago, while working for emergency medical services in Brooklyn, I responded to a call for a woman in labor. This would normally be a routine transport to the hospital, but it was not. We arrived on the scene and proceeded up to the apartment. The door was slightly opened. We knocked, but no one answered. We looked in and we could see an elderly lady mopping the floor.

We called out to her that EMS was here, but she did not respond. We then saw a male walking in the apartment and called out to him, but he also did not respond. We then entered the apartment and asked the lady who was mopping up water if she called for an ambulance. She did not say anything, as if we were talking a different language. We proceeded as protocol, went further into the apartment: to our left, in another room, we saw a female on the couch with blood dripping down from between her legs. We ran over to her and quickly thought she was the female in labor. However, we soon realized she had already given birth. We shouted, "Where is the baby?" Still nobody answered. After a short time, I pieced it all together and ran into the bathroom. It was there that I found the baby in the toilet, with its head actually looking like it was stuck in the hole in the bottom of the bowl. I pulled the newborn infant out of the toilet. I had a job to do.

My partner called for the police as I was attempting mouth to mouth on the infant. The baby had a pulse of about 50, but for a newborn this is not enough to sustain life. The baby was also in respiratory arrest. I continued resuscitation efforts until the police arrived, and I immediately told the officer to take me to the hospital in the radio motor police vehicle (RMP). My partner stayed to care for the mother. The baby died a couple of days later. The mother was charged with murder. Sometime after the incident I ran into a police sergeant who became involved in that investigation that night. He told me that it was in the paper that the mother was acquitted in a jury trial. I did not understand how this could be. She had tears in her eyes and the jury was shaking their heads.

Her defense was that she did not know she was pregnant and the baby just fell into the bowl, a ridiculous story. Her past history involved prostitution arrests and she had two other kids somewhere. This incident has stayed with me over the years. Thinking about it, talking about it, I am angry how someone can betray a beautiful little baby. Every once in a while I relive this incident in a bad dream. I guess I have gone over this event for many years when I was remembering it. I have gone over my steps in responding and I did everything proper. I studied hard and long as an EMT and was the third top graduate in my class.

Impact of Traumatic Loss in My Own Unique Personality Style: On Duty and Off Duty

The wish many officers with your style embrace as an emblem close to their suit of armor is being a perfect soldier. What is excruciatingly painful is when your own perception may be very biased against yourself for violating a standard you have written in your heart as a standard to follow. A violation of a rule you have imposed on yourself no matter how supported within the eco-ethological niche is experienced as a loss. You are capable of exacting through intense guilt, anxiety, and even more hyperfocus ruminations about how badly you acted and the need for confession and punishment. In that way of coping with loss, you actually perpetually suffer the consequences of your self-corrective mechanism, which to this point may have been vaguely within your knowledge but more likely unconscious. Again, this mechanism remains under your own control. Also, it is a means to undo what you consider to be a wrong or bad behavior, or screwing up, that you believe you have committed.

Your personality of hyperfocus more often than not transfers into your personal relationships. When you are confronted with the most painful traumatic losses, you wear the armor of being unaffected, and strongly act as if it is simply routine

For example, you may hear yourself saying often, "Aha, I let it roll right off me, just like a duck" or "I snap out of 'it'—no problem." Your veneer is sensible when put in a developmental perspective. What is meant is your childhood likely had role model(s) reinforcing a tough presentation and being able to endure traumatic experiences without flinching. You have learned the tactical maneuvers to protect your loved ones from vulnerability against a perceived dangerous world. Your learned strategy is not without evolutionary value and perceptual sensibility. This phenomenon in Holocaust survivors' children includes guardedness, hording, and rituals to defend against vulnerability shaped by trauma: in fact, like Holocaust survivors, your assumptions of suspicion, agitation, and anxiety may be selectively transmitted to family members across generations and into careers. It is far from accidental that your style seemed to be represented by veterans from the Armed Services, and extended police and public safety families. In this case the rituals you may have learned really are shared defenses keeping danger away from your own family. This can turn into situations that may provoke extreme over-protection. The term *control freak* is a stupid label taken out of developmental context and may contribute to simplistic notions of little value. Control may be understood in the eco-ethological perspective, as a learned defense strategy against perceived vulnerability to loss. Again, by understanding the sensibility of your strategy in public safety eco-ethological niches, you may work on changing your style without condemning your learned tactics to ward off losses.

An extension of this perspective is observed in adaptive functional dissociation where behavioral consequences of warding off expression of losses become apparent. For example, an officer may achieve everyday duties without missing a day of work while being severely depressed. For instance, fighting to stay on duty rather than be relieved of full-duty status, even when warranted medically, without penalty. At the core of denial and being a martyr for the cause, as we shall see soon in another case example.

The therapeutic value of this so-called defense of humor is as effective as all paper tigers. This defense of using dark humor has been praised as a way of coping. I have seen it used as a mechanism of denial and undergirding pain that emerges as a corked bottle filled with bubbling rage that blows later than sooner. The real Bengal tiger of grief emerges in the living chamber of one's memories; with all its ferocity loss is heard as a yelp when it hides a biting roar trapped in silent echoes. Adaptively, as an officer with this style, you epitomize the backbone of public service. You are the good soldier that goes on and on in spite of all adversities faced. The problem is eventually you will collapse into an implosion of loss in trauma that erupts into the present. That eruption of loss into the present is when you may have to face a retirement, an injury on duty or line of duty. Your identity is surrounded by granite with "officer" on and off duty. When you feel your own identity as an officer is lost or made obsolete, it is a traumatic loss you are hardly prepared for. An example may be taken from the Noble prize winner for peace in 1986: Eli Wiesel in his novel based on some very real experiences expressed this phenomenon so well. Professor Wiesel explains how thousands of young partisans survived the fascists' wave over Poland: "They fought hunger, conquered fear, and outmaneuvered the myriad perils that had plagued them during the reign of Night. But once the world had more or less returned to 'normal', they gave up. They were abruptly forced to realize to what extent they were depleted. And vanquished. And stigmatized. And alone" (Wiesel, 1962, p. 10).

In their identity as hyperfocused officers this tragedy would have a sadly comic relief without any humor when the train of thoughts, focus on work, and its products are brought to an abrupt halt. With that halting the rush of losses come to take their tolls and demand expression. If one is not aware of what is happening existentially, how can they know they are not losing their minds, and neither did they have to deal with it all alone? They did not have the benefit of this wisdom at that time—fortunately you do. You have the option to seek to work through losses right here and now. Let's see how a brief window of therapy illustrates how quiet desperation can turn into the fiery inferno of loss as it gets quenched in tears begging to be released in a trusted connection.

Dr. Dan: Can you stop and pause for a moment, EMT Officer E?

EMT Officer E: Yes, Doc, I can—what's up? Did I say anything wrong? I did all I had too, right? I mean you don't think I could have messed up? She drowned her own infant in shit and piss. Can you imagine that even Clorox was found in the water? I followed protocol to the dot.

Dr. Dan: [Gently interrupting the onslaught of an inquisition self-imposed] No, Officer E. I am going to ask you to listen to what you just shared with me and tell me if you can kindly share with me your losses as you see them.

EMT Officer E: Okay, Doc, I mean I am a good EMT and I do what I have to and do it so well and almost perfectly, but it is incredible still. This witch kills her infant and she walks away because of some liberal judge who just does not get it. How can I deal with that it is just impossible to fix this system? It is really standard operating procedure. I know the reality but I studied and did squat. You get the picture, Doc?

Dr. Dan: I get how incredibly frustrating it is to deal with a revolving door system of justice at times for EMTs, cops, and firefighters. I see the picture of the reality of a sick and ill woman drowning her helpless infant in a toilet. A precious infant where you put shit and piss contrasts with you doing the very best human effort possible to save her life. How can that happen, E? When you gave the very best and worked so hard at rescuing even the most impossible case as this infant? You give not only all your technique, but all your heart and soul. How heartbreaking when your incredible investment in being the best EMT fails so hard even though you did all any human or angel could have done!

EMT Officer E: I could have done better [the tears start to well up and his lips start shaking with true emotions of passion]. I did do what I felt I should do. I did my job. It is as simple as that, Doc, you know, simple as that and I failed. I wish I could have brought that little angel back. She could have been a mommy one day. She could have been the daughter my wife and I tried to get and can't. A little princess in a toilet. How could I bear this pain? It is sick man, so sick. I feel like I could rip that bitch apart. How could she do that and yet she is sick, so sick herself, isn't she? I cannot bear this work. It is too hard, Doc. [Breathing heavily and in glassy eyes with tears and resolute strength drawn in his Spartan armor, he looks at me.] It is a breeze, Doc. Maybe you think it is hard as hell, but I can handle it and that is as simple as that, as I say. I just will get better as a medic in training, and this will never happen again. Do you get it now? Can we go on please to a more important topic?

Dr. Dan: Do you really want to close the door on your own internal witnessing? Is your own pain and loss and broken heart for the very real human infant who died unmourned, except by you and your peers going to remain unmourned in silence? With every ounce of decency in your heart, you are protesting against the inhumane human evil deeds, are you not, even though they are born in the tragic moments of insanity? Insanity you witnessed when a princess you would have adopted is now dead—in spite of your most courageous and professional attempts.

Sobbing continues with Officer E realizing he is all too human and has every right to mourn her loss. Save not owning guilt he has not earned, and here needs not own. Tissues are consumed in the pads to buffer pain needing release. We work on a prayer and a poem to honor Princess Mary's loss and the very humane courage as Officer E agrees he will write her a letter and pray for her soul.

How Your Public Safety Personality Style Is Different from Other Public Safety Styles

The hyperintuitive officer uses the defense of withdrawal from vulnerability against loss in the shade of fantasy and abstraction; the hyperexcited become addicted to higher and higher thresholds of excitement and risk taking to ward off loss in trauma. Your personality style places a hyperfocus as a concrete, automated armor of defense to seal off discharging intense aggression, hostility, anxiety, shock, and guilt. Under intense pressure of PPS-CPTSD, your armor of hyperfocus becomes dissociated and your clarity becomes confused.

Let's take another look at how patterns in your relationships differ across each personality style. How are these differences manifested? In part, the hyperaggressive officer displaces and projects rage at feeling any hurt or losses. This officer's tendency is to inflict stinging revenge directly, and he or she finds it hard to let go of control—he or she hurts others. The hyperexcited jumps into situations risking great damage and pain to self, undoing his or her vulnerability and sense of loss of an ideal image he or she creates of self. The hyperintuitive personality officer shuns the traumatic loss through metaphors that fantasy veils in his or her shadow as intellectual and unreachable echoes of loss. As a hyperfocused officer you may develop a tolerance for more and more pain through a hidden masochism that is self-directed, and hardly conscious. Masochism sets your bar so high in perfectionism that when you experience pain, you take that as a salve for success. In fact, your tendency for masochism continues with a higher and more intense tolerance for frustration that would make most other officers cringe.

Initial Inroads to Lay Out Your Own Map for Trauma and Grief Therapy

You are likely to present as Dapper Danielle: flawless, meticulous, fastidious, down to the pressed, button-down, starched, Oxford blouse. The shine on your Dapper Danielle's shoe is spit polish. Another clue is your service record is notable in hardly any absences, sicknesses, or rarely line-of-duty injuries.

Although in fact, if we look under the cover of your own need for perfection, more often than not, you are likely to have received injuries on duty, or line-of-duty injuries. It is more than of interest that you have a reluctance to report your injuries or even admit them to yourself in some extreme cases. At times you do report your injury on duty; your immediate tendency for minimizing your own injury becomes less than apparent. I ask you to patiently attend to the sensibility of why this seemingly odd behavior may be entrenched in your personality style: in part learned and in part your unique tendencies for hyperfocusing.

Adaptively, it makes superb sense ethologically, where prowess and a resistance to complaining about any injury are rewarded as being tough and resilient. Your tendency to be perfectionistic has extended to work and, in your own self image, a line of duty or off duty injury is viewed as external to you. This makes sense from an ethological survival mode in which being vulnerable means being weak. In your eco-ethological perspective your focus is to turn attention to the job, as distinct from yourself. Injury, as is true of psychological injury, including the label of trauma, is taken as a weakness and vulnerability to be guarded against. Your ability to think and act in critical moments is highly valued. An injury leaves you feeling almost inept and unable. This is existentially a pit with severe consequences over time and experiences you are apt to have as a public safety officer. In the annals of police and public safety there are officers of the most outstanding character save their one deadly flaw of perfectionism that felled their lives at the apex. I do not need to review this history; it is for the purpose of understanding yourself I bring this up. You know the fact you are not perfect as an officer, perhaps although acknowledged on an intellectual dimension, is not yet absorbed at the deepest core of your existential self-awareness and experience.

Being equally adept at climbing the rank order of strategic responsibility is an adaptation shaped within your personality style's strength. It is your tendency to excel that cultivates your own outstanding acts of courage, and role consistency necessary as a leader in some way, shape, or form within the public safety eco-ethological niche you have laid out as your own domain. Your strength is likely seen by peers and your own supervisors through your acts of courage, the fact you are a good team player, and your consistency in optimal task completion. In turn, your motivation for survival appears to be expressed in rituals that act as repeated behaviors that reinforce your need to be satiated with the thirst of unconscious wishes for immortality, perfectionism, and behavioral repetition, which guard against a fear of death, a fear of self-destructive impulses that emerge when things go awry from the map you have laid out in your head. It is a natural pattern for you to take responsibility for whatever goes wrong, without much thought. You drum to repeated patterns of familiarity that are struck like a dormant match that blind you from seeing you are lighting your own fire of impossible standards. What could be the reward in all this feverish control of your impulses? It is the control over error, imperfections, ambiguity, and the insight of your fallibility as not weakness but the humane condition. It is the control of being a victim or at a loss of being able to be the exquisite rescuer, recovery expert professional who saves the day with equanimity. The equanimity of being focused even when faced with the worse losses imaginable is an incredible strength. The rote behavioral pattern motivated by deeply layered conflict with loss is defended against in a manner that perpetuates that very loss from being expressed. When you encounter the accidental firearm discharge, the aided case going south in spite of your exquisite command presence and decision-making skills that unusually save the day, the child that dies in the fire in spite of the most valiant rescue efforts, and the recovery of body parts instead of fully living folks saved from the fire, you are struck hard. All of your fiber is invested so deeply in your focus on the job. Natural sequences of life events may provoke your belief that you have failed. Insight, whether by a department doc or peer support officer, may at first be perceived as a hostile indifference to your very real shock and loss if he or she does not know your sensitivity. Sensitivity buried under the armor of presenting yourself with Spartan strength. This imperfection pointed out to you is interpreted as a hostile attack. It ripens your heightened resistance to vulnerability as an experience of weakness and shame of failure. Rumination and obsessing over failure and the idea you have let yourself down, and your troops, exact a toll on your keeping things under control. Your existential reservoir is depleted. You crash in a number of ways that are truly crisis for you and those you work with, as well as loved ones. When the spillage of upset at failure occurs, the result can run the range of extremes acting out at one end of the spectrum. You may act in a way that is typically self-destructive and permanently damaging. You may also act out in ways you would normally consider strike out against your very core being. Those behaviors can be toward you or others you would never imagine doing. These actions go against your adept skills, where your ability is known, and invaluable to others in your unit. Without doubt you are an officer who does not embarrass the agency/department by stepping out of your assigned identity mode, which is forged in disciplined cadence. When you experience traumatic losses that reach the tolerance level breaking point, your rebellion is likely to not be dramatic, but subtle in resistance.

Doubt and uncertainty are heightened as the feeling you have lost control, which is terrorizing to your own personal sense of life and your expectations of living. Traumatic loss may be dealt with in an entirely different and equally disturbing way. The content of your style of processing losses when trauma has reached the level of implosion is expressed existentially as moral anxiety. Meaning through your own internal self-evaluation, guilt worthiness, and responsibility you weigh yourself by the scale of impossibly high personal standards. On the other side of the scale is adequacy or inadequacy comparisons, and achieved or failed spiritual goals. It is usually the failure of a situation where even superman may fail that you judge yourself with quiet rumination. You sulk and sink in fear of retaliation by others in the unit, the internal affairs, and the outside community and judicial system. In turn, you live a horror out alone and frightened, which strikes against your image of who you are and what you have relied on for yourself.

Two ways of coping occur: One is you redirecting your "moral anxiety" to an even heightened level of defending against being vulnerable. A fevered pitch to self-conditioning may include an exhaustive immersion into the rituals of extreme discipline. That rigid discipline acts as a buffer to your overwhelming feelings of vulnerability and expression of fear, shock, anger, anxiety, and guilt over traumatic loss. The assumptions of doing things to protect you and others from harm have failed, as they will ultimately. This is not a personal shortcoming but the nature of the world of public safety. In your style more so than in the others, the world colored by danger and unpredictability hyperfocuses survival. Outside fortresses failed to protect you by following all the rules and regulations. Vulnerability, risk of interdependency, and change in status or domestic situations provoke your greatest opportunity to seek peer support. Physical injury, marriage, divorce, promotion, or change of status may also be cause for your initiating therapy. In initiating therapy please consider your amazing strengths as resources to value.

Your likely strengths are a rare quality in public safety, including your ability to reject addictive outlets that are destructive. Another is an unusually high level of being able to tolerate difficult demands made on your body, mind, and spiritual resources. At the core of your being you have an ability to fit into the demanding rank structure of public service agencies. Your hyperfocus is extraordinary in staying with complex problems until you come up with a solution.

Further, a stoicism dating from Marcus Aurelius as a living philosophy, not in place of religion or faith but in what he called a philosophical attitude toward life, may be exquisitely helpful for an officer with your personality style. This philosophy is also one that has bred a modified version of psychotherapy formulated by Dr. Albert Ellis in his seminal contribution called *Rational Emotive Behavioral Therapy* (Ellis, 1962, 1973). Stoicism is mistaken for being unfeeling and emotionally unaware—this is not the case. Stoicism supports responsibility, the ability of choice and tolerance of frustration, which may help you as it accords with your nature more than any other personality style. Rational Emotive Behavior Therapy (REBT) as a therapy is an excellent choice, helping you enjoy and appreciate a rational and emotionally sensible expressiveness that promotes self-acceptance and pleasure. Self-direction and rational experiments to tolerate and express emotions and pleasure may gradually facilitate the ability to tolerate vulnerability and growth.

In public service to vaunt a challenge is responded to with your style as an officer offering himself as an oblation in the service of duty that can become all too real.

Accommodating for your personality style are certain readily available niches. For instance, administration, analysis, desk duties, operational duties, training, and inspections, as well as elite rescue units where your desire for heroic sobriety is called on. Details needing organization and implementation are excellent venues to use your tendency for hyperfocus, where it pays off in large surpluses for all involved.

The strategy of my suggested approach is for you to begin to work on your tendency, which is on the right pole through the left pole, illustrated below in exercises you can think of and do for yourself. My hope is you will do this with your peer support officer and family and open the envelope to include your cop doc. The following model I developed may serve you as a helpful guide for expressing emotional empathy and wisdom supported and structured from A to Z:

Idealism <_____> Practical allowance for compromise

Perfectionism <_____> Realistic allowance of being error-bound

Selfless <_____> Self-interest and compassion for self and others

Invulnerable armor <_____> Boundaries of duty

Functional numbness <_____> Emotional expression

No pleasure allowed <_____> Responsible pleasure

Silent martyrdom for others <_____> Team player with your own voice

Silent agreement: Peer pressure <_____> Experiment: Your example as a model for others

Self-image: I must be perfect <_____> Accept and value yourself as imperfect

Worthy of insults: Self and others <_____> Unconditional self-appreciation

Rationalization, intellectualism <_____> Experiencing life in all
   its hues

Impervious to pain <_____> Learning to say I'm
   hurting, and can use a hug

Identifying loneliness and expanding your circles of friends and community involvement with non-public service professionals helps expand pleasure, involvement, and growth.

Let's Get Real: Your Public Safety Personality Style: Officer and Cop Doc's Corner

D is a lieutenant of Hispanic American origin, a patrol veteran, married with two children. He presented with feeling worn out and anxious, but could not understand why. Lieutenant D let me know right off the bat, "Therapy is not really what I need, but I am here to get to know what a cop doc is all about. I don't mind as much now because, after all, you are a retired sergeant." I accepted his roundabout excuse for coming in. I began in earnest to develop a working relationship with him on his terms. Our alliance soon became a success by keeping my attitude consistent with working beyond the wall of resistance he set up for us. In our work, a context emerged where his style was transmitted with the armor and courage and brilliance of three generations of military, police, and public safety officers. My first hypothesis was Lieutenant D did not learn to identify his feelings, and did not know how to express his emotions as he experienced them. Lieutenant D's polished surface and at times gruff attitude barked out resistance.

The second hypothesis I had was the major trauma in Lieutenant D's life was the catastrophe of 9/11. He was as an active member in recovery efforts and his loss remained unspoken. The first hypothesis of his lack of learning how to identify and express his feelings was on the money; the second hypothesis regarding 9/11 was on my sleeve; in part, I was wrong. I had to revise my second hypothesis after disconfirmation. I had structured my approach on the trauma of 9/11. In part it was 9/11. In larger part his trauma telescoped back to a decade earlier. The original trauma as well as the 9/11 trauma linked anger with loss needing our attention and understanding—without which Lieutenant D would still be carrying his losses like a cancer needing immediate removal.

Lieutenant D offers us a path to possible loss. While seeking to find out what loss is pressing in his heart of hearts, his narrative graciously helps us understand the natural unfolding leading to his original trauma. Lieutenant D discloses being a former seminary student who became an all but ordained Roman Catholic priest. He aspired to be the only male to carry the torch as a priest in his traditional Roman Catholic family. Instead, he exchanged his priest's frock and vows of celibacy for marriage to a lovely nurse practitioner. An LNP with whom he fell in love, and as he put it, "She is my first love, the uniform and shield of the NYPD my second."

He never grieved the loss of his aspiration to be a priest. Compounding this loss was ambivalence he experienced in his abrupt change from all but a priest to a life of marriage. Upon earning his shield and firearm, he was assigned to an urban war zone as a rookie street cop. A tendency in many hyperfocused officers in Lieutenant D's case no different is disavowing feelings toward a loss and to move on in the cadence of whatever beat the chief drummer is playing. That is, on the surface of the chief drummer while holding his own; even if he or she is a chief, there is always a commissioner, and beyond that there is always a mayor, and so on. So returning to Lieutenant D, marching in cadence to department rules and regulations he maintained being happy. Happy for Lieutenant D meant being content in his current position. Lieutenant D adopted a strategy that kept him sharp as a soldier drummer in achieving the job goals. Sharp and yet stuck voiceless in a closed soundproof drum vacuumed in a vault of hidden losses. That vacuum telescoped to traumatic loss, the earliest of original trauma, where two events merged. The first homicide and first dead person he experienced telescoped back from 9/11 to a decade ago. As a rookie beat officer Lieutenant D was shocked to experience "indifference among his fellow officers" with dealing with the sacredness of death and the dead victims encountered. Lieutenant D's cultural and religious training and his personal beliefs and assumptions colored his trauma and grief. A point not to be lost is, if I viewed his loss as being a crybaby or whining, my stance would have helped silence his own voice and values. I could have also interpreted his traumatic loss as exaggerated hysteria. Why? By saying to myself that accepting gallows humor in its lighter shade, rather than the dark side from which he viewed it, is normal and his traumatic losses are just exaggerations that are irrational and dismiss them any further work. Understanding his perspective is key. It is key to you with this personality style, as I educate clinicians in my guides to never lump any individual into a group and to interpret trauma as a group, as that hinders your own unique loss from being expressed. The key here is understanding your own loss and the way you experience it is critical in unraveling the treatment, so it is important to disclose how you perceive your losses to a therapist that understands he or she is learning anew with you. The process works in dialogue as the "talking cure." Helping Lieutenant D recover his lost voice was part of his self-healing. His making an active self-directive stance of redemption in an impoverished setting was his own value, long lost in his deepest personal religious conviction as a Roman Catholic officer and as he experienced his loss. You can do the same in your grief work. 9/11 was a historic turning point in masculinity where public expression of emotions, including grief, was made more acceptable.

In Lieutenant D's experience 9/11 was a painful reminder of how different he experienced his response to death and loss over a decade ago. At 9/11 Lieutenant D observed officers and dogs hurting badly. As a lieutenant he was a far cry away from his life as a rookie where he experienced overwhelming loss and its suppression when he dealt with his first homicide and DOA recovery safeguarding scene. The initiation of Lieutenant D as a patrol officer to gallows humor was not experienced as something normal. Instead, it was a rather painful event. This painful experience emerged when what he held sacred was first disenfranchised and experienced as shame, guilt, and cowardice in his conformity to gallows humor. This guilt would have been buried with his memories hidden in a cache. Caches unopened with losses do not go away and build in toxicity. They are holding losses that will burst open at some later time, perhaps with the fury of a waterspout landlocked for 20 years. 9/11 did hold that expression for Lieutenant D when his armor started to show the wear and tear of hidden losses. His vivid image of police dogs in the craters of dirt and clay digging for any vestige of life was a sacred experience where their calloused paws could not hold the fiery heat anymore. In this setting something different did emerge for Lieutenant D. Rituals and public service respect of the dead were equilateral across the board. This respect worked in a paradoxical way for Lieutenant D, as the new respect for the dead flew in the face of his earlier experiences as a cop. His earlier losses, where his own expectations of how his ideal image of himself and other officers were long discarded.

Lieutenant D, as all officers, came on the job with his own ideals, usually supplemented by the fine pure ideals of the academy. Ideals shattered like a snowball thrown in a furnace: the mean streets of the city's criminal underworld and less than noble scenes of death and mayhem. Quite a contrast for the idealistic officer.

For Lieutenant D as a rookie patrol officer it became a litany of questions that would haunt him in silence and avowed duty as a newbie: how it should have been and how he must have acted was a harsh internalized task master. Officer D's mental acrobatics in part led to self-loathing, where accusations against himself "for being a moral and spiritual lame duck" may be likened to a cold front over a hot region as the streets of NYC. Officer D did not lose self-denigrating ideas and beliefs about himself. He converted his religious beliefs into a feverish pursuit of rituals and other activities without rest to turn his conscience away from his own self-reflections. He did not seek an enlightened priest for the same reason he did not seek me as a therapist. Why? Because Officer Lieutenant D felt shame and that he was a sham: regardless of the truth he would not confront, he sank deeper in denial and loss. Why?

It turned out he could no longer bear the motif of what he perceived as the cross on his back in the face of a catastrophe. His harsh self-deprecation and castigation without respite may well have served a need to punish himself. That masochism in part may have satiated his guilt and need for self-punishment. Under the surface of his anxiety was a desire to express his loss so long and perpetually reexperienced through the rituals surrounding his life. Those very rituals kept his unexpressed losses from being identified and worked through. Panic attacks signaled a desire to flee both his sorrow and the process of exposing his loss. It opened an avenue to explore his real fear and moral anxiety.

This led to a specific avenue of intervention where Lieutenant D's perceived failure to live up to ideals he wished to fulfill was disenfranchised with abrupt coercion to conform to the group norm. It led to an existential, dynamic reassessment in response to his individual loss as he experienced his own unique PPS-CPTSD. With this brief context in mind, let us attend to a segment of my exploratory work with Lieutenant D and how the shift from 9/11 moved as a telescope backwards to original traumatic loss a decade earlier. Once we addressed the backdraft, we were able to move forward. No pun for firefighters and EMTs, but please read through and see, with changing the demands, how these losses can easily apply to you. That said, just as the existential journey apply to your losses, so can it to your healing.

Lieutenant D's initial denial of feeling loss, pain, trauma, or stress yielded a riptide undercurrent that exposed the abyss he felt in the gap between ideals and the reality of the warfront on domestic terrorism on the streets of NYC during 9/11. That is as Lieutenant D shifts into Officer D. His experience in his unique way as an outstanding officer with the hyperfocused personality style will certainly enlighten your understanding as it did mine. Losses as they emerge are tackled together and offered as an outline, in fact, a fragment of the real work accomplished. But a sample is all that is needed to understand a pebble fractures from a rock. Let's listen together:

Lieutenant D: Going through the rubble, the dogs looking like they were battered. Seeing them, you look and say, "What did I do?" Looking at the heavy and real job you kind of just see we're on the outskirts of the morgue. They looked like zombies, that is, the other cops and EMTs. FDNY no better—the walking dead on this job: after you see bodies the first few times you take your mind off of it. Then it doesn't bother you no more, matter of fact. [He giggles with a fearful expression, not genuine, but not false—just anxious.]

Dr. Dan: You say they looked like zombies, the cops and EMTs, the walking dead on this job; after you see bodies the first few times you take

your mind off of it. What does that "it" mean to you, Lieutenant D?
What comes to your mind?

Lieutenant D: We were going through the rubble … the dogs looked like
they were battered; seeing them, you look and say [in comparison],
what did I do? The K-9 units did the heavy and real job. What did
I do? [Pause and silence for a moment or two] What did I really
do? [Looking straight at me with a glaze in his eyes as if he is miles
away from me] Just to see them, you know. We were in outskirts
of the morgue. They all looked like zombies. They looked like the
walking dead. On this job, after you see bodies the first few times
you know and then you take your mind off of "it." [Repeating himself as if to convince himself he is re-visioning the reality of the
carnage and death he actually did see. Perhaps, as we realized later,
it is a defense to hope somehow reality remains untrue, at the core
of the words as we have seen earlier used by survivors of terrorism: *surrealistic, twilight zone*, or as with Lieutenant D, *zombies*
or the *walking dead*.] The first few times you see dead bodies you
turn away, you know? [looking up, as if asking himself, "Why this
ordeal?" Staring into space and a tracking movement from his eyes,
which close with a giggle as nervous laughter].

Dr. Dan: I would like to know where that giggle signals us to go, where you
are first seeing dead bodies?

Lieutenant D: The first few times you know you're horrified. I mean, with my
background, I see dead bodies as holy. No matter what. You know,
guys are there taking pictures with Polaroids; they love it and get
into it. Photo albums, you know [nervous giggle spells anxiety and
fear about even discussing it].

Dr. Dan: You said you learned to live with it, meaning you may have felt very
different at first. Seeing the dead bodies and the pictures taken and
placed in albums, what was that experience like for you?

Lieutenant D: You don't like it, you know. Sometimes you get there, someone
died, and you think it could be someone's father, husband, wife,
or sister. Show some respect, you know! I realize the academy and
puzzle palace is one thing—reality another. A lot of times I kept
silent. I was trying to figure out what was so funny. Someone died;
you would sit on the body and wait until the medical examiner
[ME] came, after the emergency medical technician [EMT] confirmed it. A dead on arrival [DOA] is now a body tag on the toe.

Dr. Dan: Tell me what body tag comes to mind right now. Tell me about
the victim and where you are. My big ears are open. [I lean forward attentively and look in his eyes, undaunted in my message of
accepting, not avoiding what he will say.]

Lieutenant D: A lot of times in the back of my mind there was nothing I could do. It's part of life, but I thought, "What if the guy's got no relatives?" What's left when you're all alone without anyone to even ID him? I feel bad I keep everyone together; it's part of life. It adds pressure. Sometimes when you think about it, you almost feel like a robot. You go through the motions. You feel awkward—you really don't know what to say. You got to keep everyone together in these situations.

Dr. Dan: It's very hard, I imagine, for you to be able to express that feeling of going through the motions and that experience of feeling like a robot in your mind's eye. What comes to mind right now?

Lieutenant D: [A long pause, perhaps a few minutes. I almost never interrupt these meaningful pauses. The reason I do not interrupt these pauses is it takes time for all folks to remember and speak about traumas and the losses associated with the past.] I remember my first homicide, December 30, 1988. It's snowing on xx Street and yy Avenue. I am eating with my partner. Windows cracked. Midnight tour about 0430 hours and it's starting to snow flurries outside. We go over to this job of "man down" with sirens blaring. It seemed like forever, after we arrived for night watch to come. Big xxx case, 2 years the wife set up her husband. I never forget his face, the guy lying there. I had a few months of nightmares afterwards. I first did the paperwork, then feeling bad for the guy. He was set up and murdered to collect on an insurance policy. She never got to it. The guys were giggling on the crime scene. I never forget how I kept it in. I was a rookie. One guy takes pictures and says this is a good killing, like as if it is an animal being displayed. I kept it in.

Dr. Dan: What did you keep in? [The nightmares will be addressed later. His major association in the therapeutic moment was the repetition of his expression "keeping it in." I choose to follow what meaning this phrase "keeping it in" held in Lieutenant D's thoughts. I followed his lead in our exploration by attending to his own associations: his associations were not free, and loaded with symbolic and psychological meaning. The reason it is so important to follow the lead is Lieutenant D, here Officer D, is talking from a different mindset and state of reference, and I want to understand that mindset with him. In other words, I am being educated as to how Officer D understands and processes his own losses and the reason it is so difficult to let them out in free expression.]

Lieutenant D: I kept it in.

Dr. Dan: I would like to hear what you kept in [silence].

Lieutenant D: I can't. [Silence, then expression moves to real anger—a smirk, then followed with a defensive grin, and then a vanishing giggle.]

They were acting like they just couldn't care less. One detective just lit up a smoke. Even my partner said, "Well, be happy, don't worry. It's all over, dude." This guy was barely dead, murdered without hope, and he was so young it was sick, depraved.

Dr. Dan: It appears you felt sick over the murder, and seeing the victim in a street gutter. No one realized how nauseated and hurt you felt when you witnessed the murder. What you felt was bad enough—a cold-blooded murder was magnified with what then appeared to be a callous response by your fellow officers. A callous response right in front of the body of the dead husband murdered for a few thousand dollars. That image would not go away. It has not gone away if we think about it together.

Lieutenant D: It was sick and depraved. All I did was stay silent instead of saying what I felt. What did I do? I just giggled!

Dr. Dan: What did you want to express at the crime scene, if you felt you could express it then?

Lieutenant D: The murder of an innocent man by his wife for a golden bull. This innocent man was sacrificed for nothing but a few cheap dollars. The sanctity of his marriage tossed out for some cheap green paper. Is that worth a life? How insane, Doc. It is insanity to see how cheap life is taken. We are the better, the finest, the righteous, and we just go along with the madness like we are dealing with zombies as DOAs. It is crazy. I mean, like the way we all looked at the site [meaning the Twin Tower pits] is how I wished we would have been at that DOA. Weird!

Dr. Dan: It sounds like you were very angry over the betrayal of your values and being placed in the middle of a cesspool left in the wake of the attack on our city, but that it is so confusing to imagine you felt loss at seeing the way that guy was treated on the streets, slain in cold blood by his wife for a few grand. Does that make sense, Lieutenant D?

Lieutenant D: Believe it or not, Doc, it makes a lot of sense. Truth be told, the guy even a brother in blue was cruising for a bruising. I felt like laying him out. One of the guys I would die for, but he just didn't realize how upsetting it was to see him snap shots at the DOA guy. My brother [an officer] said, "Take it easy, lighten up. I was a cop too and it is just the job. Let it roll off." I tried to let it roll off. It hurt bad, it stung. You know, I just went on as if it did not bother me. You know, like the guy who died in the toilet taking a load and he had a heart attack and was a loner. The endless jokes I laughed at was a farce. I feel like a fraud right now when I think of it. I laughed at each joke, like I thought it was really funny. Do you know what I mean?

Dr. Dan: I think I know what you mean. That giggle, I would call it, we have learned is a way to express feeling weird, as you put it, or a bit concerned about being put on the spot, or hot seat. Is that what you mean by laugh, D?

Lieutenant D: Yeah, that's what I mean. How can you really tell I am not really laughing? [D stops in a long moment and then smiles genuinely. At that pivotal moment his smile turns into a release of tears that flow out like streams released with some strong sighs and breaths of relief, thankfully.]

Dr. Dan: It is painful to hold back all that grief over losing an aspect of yourself, or what you had to give up in becoming the lieutenant you are today D.

Lieutenant D: I betrayed my faith and my belief in the dignity of death, and I knew better, but I was no better than any kid from East Cup Cake Long Island, laughing at what we all knew was wrong. I just went along with everyone else. No heroic guy, just a dude. You know what I mean, Doc?

Dr. Dan: It was and is a hard cross to bear witness to and for yourself, Lieutenant D.

Lieutenant D: That guy was only in his sixties, and dying on the toilet of a heart attack. Is that terrible or what? He was defecating. The taking of pictures was hard to bear. I mean, when I think of it, it is holy terror and hell. What is in us to do that? Why do we do that stuff? Am I sick or are those officers sick, and don't they get it. What is really weird is I really can't get it and I can't get myself. Why do I go along with them and do nothing at all?

Dr. Dan: Let's stop, Lieutenant D. Why do you imagine those guys take pictures, knowing what you do from our work on losses and trauma?

Lieutenant D: Doc, I don't know. You get the big bucks, Doc. I can't imagine why except they think it is a big joke and I just went along with it too.

Dr. Dan: Okay, let's think about it then. Did you really think it is funny, or did you go along with the officers taking the pictures as a way of coping with the stress of death and somehow feeling as if the horror of it all was too hard to swallow in the moment?

Lieutenant D: I did not do what I knew was wrong and bad. I could have got them to see the truth that a dead body is sacred to God and that a person who dies needs to be respected as such. I was and am as equal in my blame for being, to be honest, cowardly by not doing my best to stop it.

Dr. Dan: Did the pictures keep a record of the death, and do you think it in some way may have immortalized the officers' eternity by showing

them a record they did not die, but cheated death at the heart of
their motivation, and their laughing was like your giggling? In
other words, not a real laughter at the tragic, but a way to distance
you from the pain of death in your heart of hearts, as little as you or
I may like to admit that fear of death most of us mere mortals have.

Lieutenant D: Perhaps, that is really strange and weird. [Pause and long silence:
Then as if that inextricable light bulb lit up, his expression changed
with drastic emotion.] You may be right, and in that case they were
scared as much as I was to deal with death, except in reverence, but
then why didn't they act somber when they took pictures?

Dr. Dan: I do not really know that answer. But perhaps we can think about
it together. A reasonable interpretation we may have is that they
felt they were capturing the moment of trauma and holding it captive. Rather than that moment holding them captive in fear, the
picture was not so much the dead, but the reality of their own survival. Surviving death, and sharing their ritual of capturing it with
laughter, as in making light of it. As real as your giggle at times
with abandon of fear, and anxiety relief, while deep inside you are
not laughing at all.

Lieutenant D: I never felt that way, but perhaps that really makes sense. I
am trying to wrap my head around that. It does make sense, and
maybe it does make sense. I'm not really sure, Doc.

Dr. Dan: Look, it is hard to wrap our head around some traumatic losses, but
our heart can grasp at times what the mind cannot fathom completely. Think about this and tell me if I am wrong, if I am D, and if
I am right, tell me what you make of what I am about to say. Is that
okay with you? [Lieutenant D nods in a head shake, a universal yes
back to me.] Well, when you described the pit at the tower site, did
you call that site and the officers zombies?

Lieutenant D: Yeah, well they were—I mean, not real zombies, but they looked
like the walking dead. I mean, the dogs and them and me, I guess
it is weird now that you mention it. Did I sink that far from my
original belief and values as a Catholic and imagine a priest, me?

Dr. Dan: Let's think of what just happened. You do remember feeling like
a zombie and the walking dead. Yet, you cannot fathom how
sacredly the dead were treated, and still it was overwhelming in
loss and grief for you. Loss strikes in a telescope returning often
to the original losses you experienced, including your values and
views as a genuine man of faith. Faith in your religious belief, not
your creed, but in your heart of hearts. You were not laughing at
the sacred dead at 9/11, but mourning them in your unique way,

as were other officers. Can it be they too felt weird and disturbed doing the same thing back over 10 years ago in the borough?

Lieutenant D: Yeah, oh my God. That is probably what they were doing and I was accusing them and worse. Do you know how guilty I have been and for how long I have held this in?

Dr. Dan: Well, right here and now let's look at your insight as renewed faith and discovery of your genuine feelings and what you can do as Lieutenant D now. Not as a rookie officer in how you deal with your own losses and help others.

Lieutenant D and I went on to discovering different dimensions of unexpressed losses. We uncovered each loss while redeeming the beauty of his faith and indefatigable compassion, laid fatigued by years of hidden, unexpressed grief. Losses needing mourning in prayers and renewed rituals that were meaningful in the faith of his ancestry and with a newfound confidence of the changes he could forge. Lieutenant D realized his potential as a leader among his peers.

Lieutenant D now flexibly models his reverence for the dead as a gift, unapologetically. His model is one that other officers may embrace, absent the hostility as a true leader: no hell and brimstone in the cornice laid out in his real self. The best example to reflect his own thoughts and actions expressed freely is his own example. Freely without the cost of guilt and unexpressed trauma anymore. The losses so hidden and so shameful at first become a point that pivoted into critical and sorely needed grief and trauma work. Lieutenant D gradually is helped to make sense of how he has replaced his genuine warm and empathic self with a hyperfocus in becoming a perfect soldier. By blocking loss he remained stuck in disillusionment, shock, hatred, and disgust. This became his own issue with death as his personal cross to bear. What was guilt around his imagined violations and self-punishment was exchanged through insight. That insight rediscovered changed his approach into self-assertion and less harsh judgment of himself, others, and the world.

As with all five personality profiles, evolution in one's existential analysis, seeds sown may bear fruit you never imagined. Psychological imagination demands officers who serve others to refocus and enlighten their own resilience and adaptation to what comes natural to some, and most officers, including the author of this work, strive to achieve. So let's now go on to the last profile, which will likely transform your style into a more adaptive and resilient personality.

Adaptive Intuitive Public Safety Personality Style

What Motivated You Toward Swearing Your Own Oath as a Public Safety Officer

"To help people!"

"To learn, and try to do the best job I can."

"Doing the right thing, while making a secure living for myself and my family."

"To have a respectable profession, while making an honest living."

Psychological Survival Defenses within Your Own Public Safety Personality Style

What makes your personality style resilient and socially intuitive where practical, emotional, and creative intelligence come together in a way that maximizes healthier adaptation?

In some officers with your style a natural tendency for adaptation is active. It is clear that being intuitive and emotionally intelligent can lead to clues that support survival. Survival in your eco-ethological niche demands flexibility, and the intuitive intelligence to cull options. What specific tendencies help you punctuate the landscape of repetitive trauma with an ability to thrive? A tendency of flexibility, hardiness, and curiosity toward seeking novel solutions to problem situations is one side of the key to understanding your style. This key is present regardless of other tendencies, traits, and features.

The other side of your personality style is learned ethological tendencies shaped in an ecological niche are modified by your will to learn how to transcend force with attitude. Your attitude to transcend the eco-ethological niche that can reduce survival to despair is transformed by your will to embrace meaning. Officers with your style take responsibility for actions in the agency worked for. Your ability to remain somewhat aloof to maintain integrity, and independence in decision-making skills, is a wisdom you develop. You are not a paragon of justice, strength, or courage. You're with it by being able to forge your will to communicate without giving in to apathy, or overt hostility. This is not without work. I suggest your style emerges within the crucible of loss in trauma. It is the upheaval that comes with trauma that provokes your emotional thirst to experience life. This is especially piqued in the face of repeated experiences of loss, trauma, death, and terrorism. The selective value of your adaptation requires an exquisite emotional intelligence and the ability to use it and learn from it. The ability to confront the meaningfulness of life is not without a price. Here the lessons are not fleeting but are learned and in part stable. Rather than become bitter from the hard luck handed to you, your tendency is to establish alternatives and optional paths. The levels of options in the most extreme cases you turn into opportunities. When given grime and dung, you heap it together into fertile hills, and till the seeds of your own insight until fruit grows. It is a strong sense of commitment to actualization that is not endlessly thought about, dreamed of, but lived. Your style has a wide range, from moderate adaptation to being highly actualized.

Framing Your Moods and Emotions in Your Unique Public Safety Personality Style

A striking aspect of your mood appears to be a self-regulation that is expressive and on an even keel. Absent from your emotional and mental makeup is an exaggerated masochism or sadism, but ever present is assertiveness. Your mood and emotional regulation observed are generally on an even keel. This is not to say that you have no issues with anger, anxiety, relationships, or PPS-CPTSD: I am suggesting your keen radar for adaptation has helped you in likely learning to balance the extremes dealt with in your unit. Moderation of mood and affect is not automatic but something you strive for. You have most likely worked hard to get to a better balance than all of the other personality styles of public safety—this achievement entails motivation and resilience.

Spontaneity to take opportunities as they avail themselves to you, rather than impulsiveness, avoidance, or procrastination, is a component of your eco-ethological approach within your unit.

Existentially Relating to Me, You, Others: Ecologically and Ethologically Speaking

Activities like being involved in the community and being culturally aware and service-oriented are more likely than not. Many of you bring spiritual/ existential beliefs and meaningful activities and hobbies outside of public service culture in your own sphere, privately or openly. In part your active seeking of unique skills for establishing yourself in your area of interest and responsibility is motivated by an ownership of a calling, not just duty. Pursuits you tend in your sown field of desire likely range from artwork to sports to martial arts. Many of your peers with your personality style held varied interests and even dual professional or vocational certifications, including attorney, teacher, architect, funeral director, nurse, engineer, auto mechanic, or chef. Many personality profiles of officers with your style obtained rank at one level, or appointment, as represented in greater numbers than most other styles.

Expressively and interpersonally your willingness holds a high toleration of discomfort, pain, and dealing with objective fear. The strength to work through traumatic loss-filled experiences makes you quite resilient, unique, and with an inner ability to thrive. An example was Correction Officer V, who had a serious trauma where she was injured in the line of duty: doing her rounds of safety checks, she suffered an assault.

Correction Officer V: Yeah, Doc, it is hard to be in prison with the inmates. I mean, I feel as locked up sometimes with them. I know some folks in there are not guilty. I mean some are skells to the end, violent and cruel sadists. Some inmates are not and just are in wrong places at wrong times. I was in a wrong place at the wrong time that day and got struck hard by a bad guy.

Dr. Dan: Can you tell me what comes to mind when you think back to that moment of being in the wrong place at the wrong time, getting hit hard by a bad guy?

Correction Officer V: It sucks. I mean, excuse the French: he was a vicious dude with little mind for anyone. He was making himself the alpha guy in the lot. I got in between and received a hit not intended for me but I was jumped, however you put it. He had no reason to care to be respectful, or a decent human being. He was brutal.

Dr. Dan: It seems like you kind of get, as we reviewed last session, he had motivation to prove himself in the pen, but you clearly did not do anything to provoke his assault and your injury was not your lack of anything save his lack of any sense. Especially a sense of decency, as you put it.

Correction Officer V: I think he got his just desserts in getting restrained and is in the can for a good reason. You know, it is not pleasant, it hurt. I feel at times I can get jumped and the skells inside can get over to a degree. But I am no easy ticket, I fight back as needed. When I am challenged, I know how to defend myself. Okay, I know it can happen, but it hurts how I could get jumped. Hey, even being a fair and decent officer. It is a difficult place, not that you ever were a correction officer or deputy sheriff, but you know it is really hard being inside with some inmates—to tell you the truth, who could only be called animals. You know, as I told you, some are like bull terriers. I cannot express that feeling, as it is not politically correct you know [raising her eyebrows and furrowing her lips in a twisted pucker—as if to say, "The irony of hypocrisy is the begin and end all"].

Dr. Dan: [Gently and leaning forward to listen closely] I know you are upset. I also imagine you would like to unload what you are feeling without being corrected politically, or with rules and regulations correction-wise, here and now. Here and now where you can let down your guard, no pun intended. Do you know what I mean? [I have gained a trusting relationship with Officer V, who enjoys sharing her anxiety and frustration with the system we both know will not change anytime soon.]

Correction Officer V: Yeah, the raw deal, Doc Dan, is the way things are in the bull pen. It is just that. I know the nice ones. I know the soft ones, the exploiters, the survivors, the predators, the instigators, and the ones who are decent in the system. I just can't believe it happened to me, you know? I am innocent. I did not deserve being attacked. I know it happens. But it is very upsetting and I am at a loss. But I have begun to see friends and family while off of work rather than sitting with the tube—I am connecting.

Correction Officer V and Dr. Dan continue in their dialogue. Officer V in reassessing her initial response to try and see where she may have made a tactical error. Objectively no error was committed, and she did not dwell on trying to find where she could have, would have, and should have acted differently. It was not apparent at first, but with consensus by her own supervisors and peers she no longer blamed herself based on the evidence. She also learned to quickly appreciate the good work she did as we worked on the assault that she suffered. At the time she was pursuing a BA in engineering. She did not demand straight A's, although preferring A's, she was content with doing well enough. The same moderation and ambition balanced out in her ambition to become the next highest rank of captain. She carefully weighed her choices. She realized it would be worth it, set out a realistic strategy, and pursued it. She succeeded. Correction Captain V certainly realized she could maintain her moral compass even in the "pits of bull pens." Ensuring decent folk with very tragic situations and ecological niches of prison could also benefit from her exquisite humanity. Her humanity asserted her voice of conscience even after suffering unfairly and wrongly for acts she never caused.

Your Personality Patterns: Ecological and Ethological Sensibility: Why You Act So

Flexibility is the core in your personality style, along with stability and consistency. Moral anxiety, objective fear (fear based on real dangers), and existential angst commingle in you as an officer. The ability to sublimate your energy in a willingness to speak your voice of humanity, sensitivity, and empathy for others with action emerges in trials you endure. It is not easy to maintain an even keel in a profession replete with multiple detours to dissociation, complicated grief, delayed/chronic trauma, and addictive disorders—and complex PTSD. You are not likely to hold on to dreams of being invulnerable. Whether you learned this fact of life in the heat of fighting fires, or bruises and fractures wrestling perps, or aided cases going down, or in riots in cells, you learned this lesson. Not only are the heels of your feet vulnerable, but so is everything along the path leading to your brain's orbs: that is your strength—humility is one of the most powerful tools in the war on terror, beginning with the internal struggle with trauma and loss that threatens to terrorize you from within. At times your inability to change outcomes is a reality filled with losses—losses that are not allowed transformations into anchors of despair become buoys to mark recovery in gradual healing. Buoys of hope to hold you afloat even in the most turbulent and terror-filled seas.

The key you are able to grasp in therapy or remarkably in your own introspection is your openness to change, risking vulnerability, and listening to other perspectives without relinquishing your own moral compass. As I have shared with you, self-disclosure and expressing your own vulnerabilities are windows to let fresh perspective in. For example, an officer who came in for a few sessions told me directly she was feeling troubled about retirement and "wanted to explore options for insight" with me. Money issues and choices related to practical aspects of retirement were expressed, along with her feelings, including loss of a meaningful profession and career. Since she was young, being in her mid-forties, enjoying the prospect of a new challenge and second career "seemed logical to me, and why not," she asserted. She was fully aware it would be difficult, a novel experience, and one at which some peers jibed. After working on an existential calculus where she weighed the pros and cons as a balance of experience and emotion with the practical benefits, she chose to retire. She set time for relaxation and set about doing it. She was stimulated and interested. She pursued her new career. In her early fifties she is now making the move to a new and promising career.

Our Personality Style Peer's Most Traumatic Event in Lieutenant D's Own Quoted Viewpoint

The police experience most traumatic for me was being part of a volunteer search and recovery team with the U.S. Coast Guard for the TWA Flight 800 recovery effort. As a ranking member of the department I spent many days and nights recovering, searching, and photographing bodies and body parts.

The tension physically grew at first once we were notified a boat was coming in with bodies. As we suited up I knew each group would be in worst shape than the one before. I didn't know what to expect.

Those sights and smells will never leave my memory. I was truly saddened and upset for a while after the loss of so many lives and imagined how they felt at impact. Their family members' tragic loss, and anger at the senselessness of it all, with the possibility it could have been prevented.

Impact of Traumatic Loss in My Own Unique Personality Style: On Duty and Off Duty

Your personality style affords a special advantage not so apparent when dealing with losses. Your edge is not in your outward approach to life as much as your inner defenses against losses and how your defenses help you process your experience of losses.

A very mature defense that comes more natural to officers who either are oriented toward sublimation or learn to embrace it is a topic worthy of discussion but not in the space available here. What is of most importance is you can successfully channel your losses in trauma to resolution in spite of the odds against you doing so. The ability to channel what are unavoidable conflicts into productive and rewarding substitutions has a wide range. What becomes evident is your ingenious adaptation within your working eco-ethological niche: in some cases creative work where your trauma experiences are reframed into programs of change. Change in small ways to momentous reform seeks expression and connection with others.

The other defense against traumatic loss is your will to believe in the fundamental goodness within yourself and others without indiscriminant naivety. Some examples are achievement of a professional standard combining equity and empathy toward peers, subordinates, and supervisors, which is realistic, not idealistic. You have earned the respect of peers and you are liked by most of your fellows. Establishing a place for yourself in your ecological niche, even where there was none, out of ingenuity and tenacity, willing to take the risk, means accepting and embracing your own vulnerability.

How Your Public Safety Personality Style Is Different from Other Public Safety Styles

Your personality style epitomizes the ability Sigmund Freud spoke about in sublimation of tendencies that might otherwise be acted out, or inwardly torturous for you. Meaning you are able to take your tendencies for aggression, vigilance, excitement, and hyperfocus, and channel them in pleasurable and healthy expressiveness. For instance, while excitement, aggression, vigilance, creativity, and ideals are present in your style, none dominate your outlook and overpower you—none are neglected. You channel your drives, tendencies, and emotions productively in a mature, socially acceptable way. That path you choose may include self-interest and the interest of others, not the overidealism of the hyperfocus, or a need for overexcitement to feel good, or a hyperintuitive abstraction as a main conduit of maladaptation. Sadism, masochism, and overt aggression as a dominant motivation are not present. Compassion and emotional empathy were more freely expressed at the start of therapy or ambulatory interventions. This edge of emotional presence gives your personality style an edge in resilience and adaptation among your peers.

Initial Inroads to Lay Out Your Own Map for Trauma and Grief Therapy

The inroad to help you get motivated for trauma and grief therapy may be captured in two words: *maturity* and *equanimity*. Your self-image here is one of a professional and private person who is confident and relaxed about life and its challenges. You are not blind to the real dangers in public safety, including personal vulnerability and psychological burnout. Believing, rather than knowing, your personal sacrosanct peace of mind is not a preference, but an intentional direction.

What emerges again in different descriptions of officers is a mindset of an internal sense of direction and belief you can embrace in the here and now of living. That is, even when at some time in your career you find you are in the depth of trauma and loss. Tolerance of ambiguity infused with cautious optimism is a strong balance for equanimity. This is neither without hard work nor inborn, but your tendency to learn and use what you learned. This is adaptation. Flexibility of mind and openness in many ways is not so apparent in what is noticeably thought by other officers as being aloof. What is interesting is much faith and belief in the ultimate meaning in life and the source of life when you are challenged as illustrated in the case example that closes this chapter. What is characteristic in your personality style is the absence of religiosity, or the outward expression of piety, as well as the drive for short-term hedonism. This deserves some more attention from you. Existential meaning and choice did not come natural here. As with any of the other officers, exploration and work needed in a genuine therapy approach are embraced. The will to believe in a dimension of your existence beyond material walls is what your existential motivation transcends.

What you cannot move in excited passion, physically through force, in fantasy and creative endeavor, or even in hyperfocus, to a place you so wish for is pursued until the potential meaning you seek is revealed. Your personality style may be the rare fortune of your natural tendency to evolve or learn. Regardless, your potential is actualized within the suffering and learning curve of experiencing equanimity of your belief and faith in the source of genuine self-transcendence. Healthy competition is not a dirty phrase rejected. Single-mindedness when it comes to important values is not let go of, whether it's difficult, and is answered with integrity. Maintaining friendships with public service peers and civilians outside of the job is your strength. Refusal to buy into the tendency of being a stiff shirt, where the hub of your identity is usually pinned on officer's collars, is left on the hook of your own locker, when you leave work. With all that said, it is quite relevant that in working with the therapist, an attitude for you to embrace therapy needs to be met with your own desire for self-growth and creative expression. While being active in taking responsibility for your own direction is important, letting go and accepting insight the other professional cop doc offers is crucial. The ability to trust or learn to trust even after experiencing severe loss is not easy. While it may be easier to respect therapy and embrace optimism, it is crucial to allow the therapist entry into the depth of your losses. Loss and trauma need to be confronted, not avoided, repressed, or diverted. Sublimation and equanimity can allude the forceful losses hidden in shame and presentation. A high level of motivation toward genuine well-being and self-insight is an ongoing project. This makes your work in collaboration with your therapist no less stimulating or challenging. You are likely to be a participant in therapy with the ability to engage in the full encounter of a therapeutic relationship through learned trust. Bibliotherapy, learning new ideas and techniques as in this guide, is one avenue; films are also excellent tools of entry into insight and renarration, depending on the dynamic exploration you are willing to embrace. Please see Appendix B for a list of recommended films and books.

Stop, pause, and reflect; while you may not have achieved your gains easily, or as of yet, they may be right under the surface of your emerging style. What you have in your corner is emotional intelligence and resilience, which in the therapeutic encounter is priceless. Centering your goal in therapy on your existential and philosophical attitude toward life and living is essential.

Staying positive in the fulfillment of your calling is key in your own work with your therapist collaboratively: it is more difficult than I can possibly render justice to. What helps is the results you will see. I choose to illustrate this with one case example of some essentials with one special officer with your personality style, eloquent in heart and soul. The end of our work, truth be told, was a loss for me as for him, as he disclosed.

Let's Get Real: Your Public Safety Personality Style: Officer and Cop Doc's Corner

Shards of Glass and Steel: A Quantum Psychic Moment Transcended for Captain E

Captain E and Dr. Dan are working seriously and in alliance on his experience of complex trauma involving a serious plane wreck with no survivors. Reassessment of his moral anxiety, survivor's guilt, inadequacy, shame, self-blame, objective fear as psycho-physiological inevitability, and renarration of his experience of the trauma are reexamined together. Captain E in this fragment of our working through captures his existential angst and anxiety about the ultimate meaning of life, and his experience of the death and wreckage is gnawing at his core. The following example illustrates a fragment of our existential analysis of complex trauma. Please attend to the underlying challenges faced and confronted together as a captain with a resilient and adaptive public safety personality style as your own.

Captain E: I have been working hard at not avoiding the death and bodies at Flight 800. I've come to realize the recovery effort is in part successful from my corner of the universe. I can own up to that fact now. I still feel an ache when I see the victims: the brains are all over, the carnage in the sea. I try to see the meaning of it all? Don't get me wrong, Doc. [Captain E delivers a stare that means no punches pulled. I accept with a reciprocal look back. I hear you loud and clear in my silent nod.] I mean, I stopped second guessing myself. I accept I did what I had to. I dispute this as irrational. I do believe I did what I had to do. It is good enough. But then what about my faith. Why is it so damn hard to accept? [Silence, looking up and down, teary-eyed] How can...? [Sobbing]

Dr. Dan: [Silence, as grief needs expression] It's very hard to express how it's so damn hard to accept. As you were going to say, How can...? [I let him fill in the blank.]

Captain E: How can a higher being allow this to happen? How can innocent people be killed like this? How can their families be shattered? What is there afterwards? I know I have faith, but I feel my faith in God is pretty weak right now. I feel like I have let go of the strength of faith in a higher being. I feel I am weak in what has been my strength through faith. To tell you the truth, at times now I have my moments where I have little confidence after Flight 800. [Pause] But, I still believe I think it's my own weakness. [In many public service families a refreshing belief in a higher being shines through. I will address what he considers to be weakness, which in his case means he feels inadequate to his real faith. To slip this under the table is to ignore a genuine experience of his life.]

Dr. Dan: Is it weakness, or are you and me, and every thinking human being, trying to seek definitive answers we just can't fathom? Asking the questions means you feel it deeper, and care deeply. Is it enough to ponder the questions, rather than pound yourself for having healthy moments of skepticism?

Captain E: I do ponder, and I guess pound myself at times more than I like. I find it hard to think life goes on when it ended for them. Whole lives ended that day on a flight that ended in the sea. Maybe life is purgatory, a truth that lies under all the coincidences, or destiny of our lives.

Dr. Dan: Maybe it is purgatory. But it seems maybe that truth, as you put it under coincidence, may help us witness the dark moments. That is to remember our life right here and now is precious. Maybe not heaven, nor hell, nor purgatory, nor paradise, but precious is the mystery and hard truth of death and tragedy.

The tragedy of Flight 800 is very difficult to process. Putting it together in Captain E's way of looking at life through faith is a strength he has shared with me. It is fair material to work on and to balance in coping with the trauma and guilt. Again, the vast majority of officers believe in God, whatever religion or creed.

Captain E: You know, I jump to magical thoughts at times. I even think I was meant to experience this event and the trauma. I feel like Frankl, that doc who was in the death camp and came out with faith in God more intact. I mean, that is silly and my ego gets high fluting, comparing myself to his ordeal, right, Doc?

Dr. Dan: Why ask me? You know yourself. I trust your truth. Do you? Let's look at it together. What do you experience when you go back to Flight 800 as part of your history?

Captain E: It sucks in part. I hate the death, the bodies, the blood, the violence. Maybe shot down or accidental, it hurt the innocent. Being a police captain, African American family man in a second marriage, with an estranged son from a first marriage, I know how it feels to hurt. Suffering is history seared into my blood. But I have not let it make me bitter and hate others. Like Frankl, I know it's not easy; you just keep going. But I let out the tears and I don't blame myself like I did years ago.

Dr. Dan: You bet. Like you're doing now, and the hard work you do each day of your life. No retreat from reality. How have you convinced yourself not to let your history, police experience, and beautiful cultural tradition make you bitter and biased? Even though you've dealt with racism from all angles and hatred?

Captain E: I realize. [Pause] Rather, I trust our work. I am not responsible for what I learned is tragic. I did the best I could and my prayers count. The silence of God does not mean he is not listening. My blue color does not run; our police culture has a tradition and pride too. I have a why, a how. I have faith in a creator who has no race and loves us all. I have confidence in myself and others like you, Doc. I choose to believe in good and evil, I need not apologize for my race, my faith of Judaism, or my shield by hiding any of it.

Dr. Dan: Bravo, well said, Captain E. Doesn't sound like you are weak in faith, but expressing some doubts firms up what you know. In fact, it firms up what you believe in your heart of hearts. That's what counts.

Our work continues traversing trauma. An existential need seeks to quench a dried, parched inner thirst. A thirst calling for sensibility and kindness in a world shattered by trauma and grief. Without a deep sense of calling, a courage to embrace a vocation where life is imperiled, you and other officers would not join up as public service professionals, uniform and civilian alike. A dry style that denies your unheard need for meaning is bound for an excursion that docks and leaves the port vacant, no matter how otherwise functional your attempt to deny losses: Louis Armstrong called it soul. The difference is compassion, empathy, and persistence goes a long way when cop doc and public safety officer embrace genuine loss and internal witnessing together. Pure objectivity is a tombstone. I for one cannot deny the expression of humanity of self as well as the officer I am privileged to work with.

Suffice to say the rewards are worth every bit of effort and resilience you will need to cherish qualities in yourself that truly existential analysis will bring out with your cop doc.

Conclusion: Five Public Safety Personality Styles and Complex Trauma Syndromes

This chapter in its entirety may be viewed as an entire guide, a path, a bridge into the styles that you as a public safety officer are likely to present with. My hope is that you read each chapter as its own guide. I equally hope it is not used as some modern-day guide to styles of police personality in only a prescriptive way. That use may erroneously achieve placing you as a humane being into a diagnostic category. I also hope it is not used as an overly optimistic formula, implying your work, your peer support officer, and cop doc's work is easy. It is not. Pure objectivity is found in ivory granite tombstones and porcelain dolls. The real, warm human being you are may be lost through taking labels too seriously, including the potential abuse of my police personality styles. The caveat is that the language of science is qualitatively and historically limited. It is relative to a degree, and on another level it is a dynamic language to describe and tentatively understand your personality style. It is all about semantics, is it not? Including ones we can be tempted to guide us—as our own ideals. What we do best in our resilience as officers is complemented by the resilience in each of the public safety styles I presented you with. In writing this book I have come to the realization, public or private, that if you and I dare to go out of the shadows of our private sense, we all have a common sense waiting to be discovered! As long as I live, I suggest you may follow your adaptive, intuitive senses as well as your scientific senses. To legislate what is right and wrong can only be a disaster. The key is to remind ourselves almost always that we are mere mortals. That being so, our active listening includes self-confrontation and growth, not miraculous hiding and ignoring of trauma and loss with strict and impervious boundaries.

The one minority that generality has not achieved real understanding and empathy is the police and public safety officer. To serve is a profile in courage! In humility, while no one can pinpoint the actual physical embodiment of the essence of our own resilience and courage to face the most challenging moments in our lives, new fads or idols for entertainment in quick fixes try to supplant the essence of your own choice and responsibility. It is the source within you that reflects a nonphysical source without. It is best reflected in the wisdom of Churchill, another favorite public safety officer, "There go I, but for the grace of God." "There is no atheist in the fox hole" is equivalent to saying regardless of one's religious belief or lack of it, there is meaning in the world and in your own life, and the source of that meaning is ultimate: while you and I may not be immortal, eternal, or awesome, the source of your strength and ingenuity is. Further, it is only in your priceless and unique style that your own shine can be redirected for the map your moral and existential compass directs you too. That is a balance in intuition, and it is the diploma without portfolio you graduate with upon completing this book. Simper Fidelis!

Professor Viktor Frankl's equation is: despair equals suffering without meaning. The moment one has a reason to endure suffering, pain, and even death is the moment suffering has meaning and despair has ended. Carpe diem—live well and now—choose life!

Professor Nachmun closes this guide with a gem—Advice as complex as trauma and simple as the timelessness of truth: "Don't give up. Despair does not exist at all! If you believe that it is possible to ruin, then believe as an individual that it's possible to rectify ... there's no despair in the world at all" (Besancon, 2004).

References

Besancon, I.I. 2004. *Courage*, Monreal, CA: Chadash Publishers.

Conroy, D. 2008. Personal conversation about coping with severe loss and trauma and methods of relief.

Conroy, D., and Hess, K. 1992. *Cops at risk: How to identify and cope with stress.* Placerville, CA: Custom Publishing Company.

Creelman, T. 2007. Personal conversation on Professor Creelman's approach with police suffering severe deception and betrayal by spouses. An existential spiritual approach complementing the eco-ethological existential analytic theory and treatment.

Einstein, A. 1954. *Ideas and opinions.* New York: The Crown Publishing Group.

Ellis, A. 1962. *Reason and emotion in psychotherapy.* New York: Lyle Stuart Publishers.

Ellis, A. 1973. *Humanistic psychotherapy.* New York: McGraw-Hill Paperbacks.

Frankl, V. 1978. *The unheard cry for meaning.* New York: Simon & Schuster.

Frankl, V. 2000. *Man's search for ultimate meaning.* Cambridge, MA: Perseus Publishing.

Gaines, J. 1979. *Fritz Perls: Here and now.* New York: Celestial Arts Press.

Gilmartin, K.M. 2002. *Emotional survival for law enforcement.* Tucson, AZ: E-S Press.

Grossman, D. 2004. *On combat: The psychology and physiology of deadly conflict in war and peace.* New York: PPCT Research Publications.

Heisenberg, W. 1971. *Physics and beyond: Encounters and conversations.* New York: Harper & Row.

Kitaeff, J. 2011. *Forensic psychology.* Boston: Prentice Hall Publishers.

Leenaars, A. A. 2004. *Psychotherapy with suicidal people: A person centered approach.* West Sussex, England: John Wiley & Sons.

Leenaars, A. 2010. *Suicide and homicide-suicide among police.* Amityville, NY: Baywood Press.

Moeller, H. G. 2006. *The philosophy of the Daodejing.* New York: Columbia University Press.

Morris, D. (1994). *The naked ape trilogy: Naked ape; human zoo; intimate behavior.* London: Jonathan Cape Publishers.

Nachmun B. 2008. *The gentle weapon. timeless wisdom from the teachings of the Hasidic master.* Woodstock, VT: Breslov Research Institute.

Orwell, G. 2005. *George Orwell, why I write.* New York: Penguin Books.

Pavlov, I. 1941. *Conditioned reflexes and psychiatry.* New York: International Publishers.

Rudofossi, D. 1997. *The impact of trauma and loss on affective differential profiles of police officers.* Ann Arbor, MI: University of Michigan.

Rudofossi, D.M. 2007. *Working with traumatized police officer patients: A clinician's guide to complex PTSD.* Amityville, NY: Baywood Publishing Company.

Rudofossi, D.M. 2009. *A cop docs guide to public safety complex trauma syndrome: Using five police personality styles.* Amityville, NY: Baywood Publishing Company.

Shneidman, E. 1996. *The suicidal mind.* Oxford: Oxford University Press.

Shneidman, E. 1993. *Suicide as psychache. A clinical approach to self-destructive behavior.* Northvale, NJ: Jason Aronson.

Wambaugh, J. 1987. *The choir practice.* New York: Dell Books.

Wiesel, E. 1962. *The accident.* New York: HarperCollins.

Wilber, D. 2010. Interview and report with author.

Zinnser, W. 2004. *Writing about your life: A journey to the past.* New York: Marlowe and Company.

Appendix A: The Real Memo Book Insert for Antidote for Terrorism, Burnout, and Deployment

Any memo book insert needs to be filled with powerful and meaningful information. In deciding what to put in, I had to choose what to not put in. I had to make some key choices for your use in the field. I resonated with being a street cop and my peers at the after-shift breakfast clubs after the midnight-to-eights. Having been shot at, arriving on scene to a volley of shells spraying the streets on a midnight-to-eight, and dealing with my own trials throughout my own life, including many tragic losses, betrayals as one of the worst of traumas and challenges, a flight making an emergency landing, being on a four-alarm fire, and dealing with more than my share of the bad guys and gals, I always reflected how I wish I had a spiritual insert that could connect me to the source of strength and courage, the creator.

As with many other peers as a cop and a cop doc later, I prayed in silence and even sometimes in the noisy loud streets in the hood. A quiet spot where you can have some down time to let loose and pray to God is so important. I yearned for a spiritual piece that was not written for Joe Q and Mary X civilian, but for cops, firefighters, and EMTs. The brief few pages for an ER RN and medic, to pick up and find some solace in.

When I was in Brooklyn North central booking or Manhattan South and no prison van duty was asked for to pick up some overtime (OT) after a collar and wrestling on the streets where my shield was almost ripped off my chest, I wanted a few moments for me. If you could relate to that same yearning as I had then, like me you could take a cardboard box as a makeshift bed and pick up a coffee and read a good book or tabloid for a while. Before long, you, like me, could be schmoozing with cops from other commands or departments. It was interesting and a great bond to hear similar war stories from smaller departments that had some incredible officers: for example, Port Authority PD, New York Seagate PD, or NYHRA PD, or NY DEP PD. But even after socializing and reading and grabbing a bite to eat, I was hungry for what was soulful and fulfilling. That soulful need aches for fulfillment in almost every office I have worked in was inside my knapsack and under my abnormal psychology text. What was it that I wanted so bad and provoked me to find a haven with? Who or what can speak to the emotions and mind of a firefighter after doing a rescue operation and finding he has a charred body of a kid to deal with? Who can the EMT/medic go to after she has just dealt with an elderly man run over because the bus driver could not stop for a moment to let him pass safely? What about the emergency service unit (ESU) officer who had to calm the suicidal teen down who blew his brains out after trying to talk him down and she did her very best?

No it is not *Family Guy* or the *Simpsons*, it is not reality TV and not *American Idol*. It was a small, unique, timeless composition of heartfelt passion poured out by the public safety hero for all officers and good for all times. The young shepherd who sung poems and fought wars against the terrorists of his time. The man who wore his humility in fearing God as a shield in conquering the lion and bear by placing his own life on the line while protecting his flocks. Look at the courage and soul of a shepherd who flung a stone at a giant who boasted of his might makes right with fear and threats of violence. Such courage by a young shepherd is a timeless guide for the darkest of times. Who is this soldier? Well, this best of soldier artists was none other than the king warrior poet of all times: King David, the son of Jesse.

A hero of his times, and perhaps of all time. He lives in our minds and souls as well as actions in making a stand. A stand not in the sand of fame and glory but for his faith in the will to believe in ultimate meaning and the source of all creation—against the transient threats of terror and destruction.

David struck terror in the terrorists! Goliath, huge as a tree and as arrogant in his own pride as a god with a small *g*, fell like the mighty rigid oak struck with the thunderous crack of a bolt of faith. Faith in the choice of David to walk with equanimity and not bow to force but stand his ground. All monuments, pyramids, and giant oaks are held by their roots. Heaven can uproot and splinter the arrogance of believing any human force is eternal. Humility is the sustenance that showers dew on the trembling and washes away fear. Said another way, the very creator who gives life can take it—lifting the scrapper in the field to the heights of power. The shepherd boy who fought wolves and bears deep in the wells of narrow straits where others feared and bowed to the idols of their times in fear, want, and servile conformity refused to do so boldly. David in a sense was a public safety officer shielded by his attitude and direction with attention to his mission of freedom. David, pumped with courage and determination, took out his slingshot held in his creator hands as the source of his power against force. David was armed with real-deal humility and with utmost courage refused bowing to an arrogant terrorist.

David's armor was a rock chosen from the very field Goliath threatened to bury him as yet another scheme he counted on, after all he was a giant. Goliath relied on his body armor and shock tactics of deception and fear. Goliath played out the thousand amusements of gladiators and their idyllic circuses of might makes right. The Philistines cheered at the mendacity as they bowed to their own illusions.

David stopped and paused not to a better sword and armor but to the source of all warrior officers and spoke the very words that have become immortalized and etched in many officers' hearts and souls, Psalm 27, while taking arms against a sea of forceful coercion and tyranny. Goliath ramrod straight leaned on his horse of metal and iron, showing his thighs of muscles while resting his sword, as if to pose. David turned his intention and redirection in one superbly placed shot. David slung his faith, and in a moment that lays the idols and the terrorists in the dust, so he slays his enemy, Goliath.

His enemy, yours, and mine are as old as dirt pillars and as modern as fifth columns, such as Osama bin Laden and his serial killers: David made the stand for light in darkness and the horizon of sunshine ushering into the dawn of despair, hope, faith, and promise. So did David compose his psalms. In the pits of doom despair lies on one side of the warrior's choice to sink into addiction, amusement, and withdraw in self and other loathing or to make a choice and fertilize the seeds of redemption. Faith is the dew that resurrects and redirects each officer, and his or her unique manna found in the ecology of suffering endured in each loss hidden in that specific trauma. The development of new life emerges in the very ecology and ethological demands of each trauma—redirected in internal witnessing and motivation to live well.

The poets, as all artists, are inspired with the sword of creativity. Swords that cannot be sheathed in a fascism that muffles the enemy within, and without with silence and illusions. Being bold is sometimes called for when civilizations of decent people are threatened. The indecent terrorists are trying to steal away our freedom of choice, initiative, and the will to believe in meaning within, without, and in the world.

Resistance and defiance are called for in your own mission in this context and time: that time is now! What psalm is the right choice? Psalm 27 is often quoted by many rabbis, priests, and ministers, and other clergy members: contrary to the stubborn man I am, I will ask you to enjoin me with the Fifth Psalm. Why the Fifth Psalm?

The Fifth Psalm is in my opinion a shield for dealing with the onslaughts against flesh, psyche, and most important, your own soul. As soldiers in public safety you are heir to cement being hurled in heaps of politically correct pyramids where the apex is held by the nadir of society, who mimic the elite. King David was chosen also because he was the shepherd-soldier-warrior-poet who was as humane as you and me. David was chosen as king perhaps because as he made some major mistakes, he overcame his own temptations and mistakes the flesh is heir to. In the face of all his fears, as we all face, he earned his shield as the real shepherd of his flock. No easy mission.

Those of you who fight the good fight can never lose the source of all strength of justice and compassion over evil. That source is there go I but for the grace of God! You are truly a courageous warrior, and the work of your hands becomes your own poetry in the most quantum power when you believe and act in earnest in the only domain you truly own. That domain, as the American Indian said, is the space you occupy, right here and right now. Your conscience, responsibility, and voice to assert freedom to will your own belief in the source and soulfulness that dwells within your own journey of life! If an army stood against you and you had your creator on your side, who could withstand the power of truth enveloped in such compassion and justice? You as an officer are one of the worthiest of those who make a stand for protecting and caring for all of humanity God so beautifully created—you!

Psalm 5 was inspired by one of the bravest of all kings with heart, rhythm, and soul. In reading the psalm, in brackets under each bold line in his words are my reflections, which may help you as a brother or sister officer in red, blue, or white.

Song of David: To my sayings give ear, God. Perceive my thoughts: Heed the sound of my outcry, my King and my God!
[Ears listen to vibrations as felt in the senses. Your mind perceives thoughts and what is truly being hidden as well as directly expressed. Heeding outcries may be understood as musical outbursts, each with its own unique rhythm—unlike noise. Such musical sounds passionately sung are shaped in concert with reason appealing to God as the king of all kings. God, who created each of his humane beings, certainly can hear the silent vibrations stirring in the deepest depth in your heart. He understands the words you cry out with before you even speak them as articulate sounds of faith. God listens to the unique orchestration of each soldier in the field of a battle that must be fought in unison. The sounds and orchestration of a composer who orchestrates resistance against a force that attempts to squelch the very choices all human beings are given as inalienable. God gives free will and no human can take it from you.]
To you alone I pray! God at dawn, hear my voice as I prepare myself for you, anticipating You!
[David prays as the most worthy of weapons shield the warrior king—his shield of faith. He gets ready for battle and to

war against his enemies, those who epitomize sudden stalking ambushes. David, the poet-warrior, ends this line with believing God is with him when he says, "I anticipate You!" You is capitalized. Why? The confidence in knowing you are he/she, as you are on the side of the angels in the unique style you have. Whether you're the hyperfocused or intuitive or aggressive or excited personality style. That fact is, the battles against those trying to destroy the freedoms we hold sacred are worthy opponents to be stopped. Right in the midst of dawn is David's certain vision beyond his physical that a new sunrise will be forthcoming. Isn't faith awesome—as it connects you to your source?]

For you are not a god who desires wickedness, no evil sojourns with You.

[Being discouraged by the small gods, as written in the original psalms in its original form of expression, is telling. As if a human can ever be a god. David reminds himself, as you might have, of one indubitable fact: that times weathering will not fade in the fads of his day, as not in ours. That fact is that although many tyrants have made pyramids and monuments while alive in their own image, the twilight of the little gods will eclipse. But the opposite holds as true. That is, the triumphs of those who fight terrorists, mental slavery, and oppression are met by poets, writers, and leaders who God places to stand strong against the storms of inhumanity. Evil's darkness is shadowed in the light of truth.]

The twisted distortion of slanderers and illusionists may not stand firm before your eyes.

[Those who focus on targeting heroes and heroines by attacking their honesty, integrity, and the very difficult duties of their mission and calling are cunning in their retaliation. Slander is bound to fail and in unsteady, consistent fashion, fall. For example, a military doc who is overseas at great risk of his life is interrogating terrorists and those who are caught in a den of terrorism. He must use unconventional means to crack his case. He is judged by a jury of one peer in an organization sympathetic to terrorists in the guise of human rights.

A peer in education and training as a shrink, but who has no experience in combat or trauma terrorism on the battlefield experienced by our soldiers. In being so self-righteous he or she is biased and slanders the one he or she should protect and give allegiance too. An allegiance to the very country the military doc serves as a profile in courage. That profile in courage, as President

Kennedy said, is in service, as our fine and major military doc
exemplified. The peer doc who judged him so harshly may have
had intentions to show compassion to the enemy, but in his or
her zeal he or she acted in concert, and in illusionist distortion
mocked the very fight for civil rights in an uncivil manner at
a hero. Sleeping with the enemy is having compassion for terrorist suspects, not the officers fighting them. Compassion is not
ensuring sleeper cells are allowed rest in the Trojan horses in the
heart of our democracy.

Victims of these Trojan horses placed in the midst of the fog of
extreme perfidy held up by a fifth column selling out to protecting groups that hate Americans, Catholics, Jews and Christians,
Buddhists, Taoists, Hindus, and Sufis and moderate Muslims.
Methods of counterterrorism are tough and harsh. But, not doing
what must be done to obtain information in time of war will lead
to death, not of one, but thousands. But I will say if saving one
life is saving the whole world, then the contrary fits. What is that
contrary? If one spills the blood of an innocent man who is a
shepherd by throwing him to the rabid wolves, that bloodlust
leads to the tragic suffering of the entire world.]

You despise all evildoers, and doom speakers of deception!

[Politically correct pseudo-intellectuals threaten democracy and
ultimately are the greatest axis ensuring the rise of fascism. When
scientists try to show selective targeting of groups and selectively
label their opponents using economic coercion by not giving
voice to conservative viewpoints in medicine, psychology, and
psychiatry, this is domestically strong-arm tactics. It is economic
tactics of terror. The Nazis started by boycotting the underlings
or undesirables as losing voice in their new order. Those who
report lies about people or label in extremes are as false-hearted
as those accused under their rubric of doublespeak and hot air.
Calling officers pigs and fascists, they need to look in their own
mirror and see the image they despise.]

The bloodthirsty and deceitful man God abhors.

[Do not despair with suffering through your battles with evil
without knowing God knows all the evil terrorists do. Ultimately
prayers that are laced with evil are not answered. How can one
be sure as an officer in the field of battle? The dividing line is
one of heart and soul. Please go back and remember God knows
even the stirrings of your heart—he most assuredly knows your
enemies as well. The reason they are your enemies is that in their
own free will they chose to appoint little gods as their object of

worship. Evil chants as noisy chimes orbiting around their illusions. The prayers of the bloodthirsty and slanderous testify against them.]

As for me, through your abundant kindnesses, I will enter your House. [Where can you find the Almighty? The question back, my brother and sister officer, is: Where can you go and not find him? Observe as you do as a public safety officer and see his creations. How can you not see the awesome power of the creator in the very miracle of life and the gifts of your many interventions and rescues. Look in the mirror and think of the amazing work you do in cocreation with the creator! Stop, pause, and reflect as a public safety officer keeping the cities safe: look deep in the mirror and ask yourself the question: If you did not patrol, investigate, and solve crime and prevent it by your presence, how would society stand?

Firefighters, if you did not put yourself in the teeth of the fiery inferno by rescuing so many when you douse out raging fires where you meet them, who would dare fight such a destructive force? Terrorists on a domestic scale as well as a global scale lust to burn people alive. How many people have you saved from being burned alive by doing the job? Stop, pause, and reflect as you douse out the doubt and uncertainty of your calling and station in the ultimate firehouse.

As an EMT you receive the very unfair shake-off: yet, stop, pause, and reflect with me please. Ask yourself: If it were not for your own courage and integrity when faced with such harsh challenges as a police officer, firefighter, EMT officer when others are in need of rescue—who would do the work you have done and continue to do? You ensure the patient gets to the ER RN and MD. Street rescues revive the almost dead to life. Just as you enter the EMT house, the firehouse, or police service area, precinct, or district as a cocreator and rescuer with the ultimate healer. Rest assured you have a seat in his house. Well where is his house, which David eludes to? For an officer, his house is your house. For where you truly do the amazing work you do, be sure the life-saving rescue and recovery operations are tickets for your own awesome reservations to reside in the creator's house.]

I will prostrate myself toward Your Holy Sanctuary in Awe of YOU! [Humility asks one not to bow to fads, fashion, bribes, and temptations, but to surrender and bow to your creator, who expects you to do kindness and compassion with justice in your corner of the universe where you stand. Leaders who bow to others to win points often fear man. Why fear man? It is reasonable and sensible to fear the creator of man. If you can be so deceived in fear of man, then you have little humility, but cunning and poverty. In this one line the safe haven of sanctuary is not fearing what others think as long as you know in your heart of hearts and your mind that you are doing the right thing!]

God guide me in Your Righteousness, because of my watchful enemies. Make your way straight before me. For in their mouth there is no sincerity. Their inner thought is treacherous. Their throat an open grave. Their tongue they equivocate.

[For officers we are beset with temptations, and not only external. The internal temptation is to give up to despair as suffering, which is inevitable, and life itself is a series of accidents with no meaning. Resist, and embrace your will to believe in meaning within your day-to-day life. Embrace the guide of the right way, that is, doing the right thing! No one does anything perfectly that is humane. Stop, pause, and patiently hold back your anger and rage when provoked. Please resonate on David's wisdom here. The glib of words in your enemies litter glitter in the strings of provocations and accusations in their slander: it seems the public at times never get you, and often politicians and media folks are reactionary—as if one officer making an error means you and all officers are all bad and guilty. Do not miss the reality that other politicians and media reporters are open to your suffering. Patience wins the day and the instigators will rue their day, even though you never wish this on them. How the very schemes they have designed to remove you from the world and your job as an officer will capture them in the very schemes made to harm you. That is the power of faith. Study the history of tyrants, fascists, and murderers and you will see for yourself the evidence of this truth. The enemy seeks your sense of despair—you cannot prevent suffering. But, you can preserve the assurance that you are doing the right thing! You will not be alone when you cry out. The best 10-13 is when you know your own creator is right there with you.]

Declare them guilty, O God may they fall short in their own schemes—they will topple. For their many sins cast them away, For they have rebelled against You!

[If you look at Nero, Sadam Hussein, Adolph Hitler, Mussolini, and other tyrants who build empires on bloodlust, each died as the very idols in their own image, as gods with a small g, toppled. Mussolini was thrown on a pile of his own bowels! Adolph Hitler was buried in the bunker he cowed in as a mass murderer of all times. Sadam Hussein was hung on the very cedar he made for his victims; the noose he made for innocents became a fitting collar for this mass murdering perp. Agendas for killing and destruction sought to destroy others became the very devices in which each fell prey to his own deceptive scheme. God does have a sense of humor, when man has his design, as King David's son warns, and God has his plan, or as sometimes interpreted, he laughs. As a public safety officer, thank God in your heart that you temper mercy with justice in your calling, you serve God when you care for people.]

And all who take refuge in You—will rejoice! Forever they will sing joyously. You will shelter them. Those who love Your name will exult in You; When You, God will bless the righteous.

[Unlike the tyrants and fascists throughout the most turbulent times you face as an officer when you are attacked in body, soul, reputation, and trial with an evil opponent. Like a tsunami after the quantum moment of trauma splits your psyche like a quake that rips apart the very ground you walk on—refuge exists for you! The narrow strait exists with a welcome sign that you can take refuge in. That sacred of places is within the chambers of your heart and in the sacred space of your own soul. No one can take away your will to live in the belief of life's sacred meaning. Your calling is unique, and so is your refuge in the shelter of calling God's name. His name is the music of your song as only you can sing it in the style you were given and developed in his service. God's favor is his love for you.]

Enveloping "me" with favor like a Shield! [His love and yours for him is your shield!]

Appendix B: Bibliotherapy and Film Therapy for Officers and Families

Many more films and books of worth are out there. These are at the top of my list.

Flight 93: A Review of the Movie: Film Therapy

Flight 93 is a classic film. It will truly last stand the test of time, and in time I believe tragically as well as comically turn out to be prophetic in three dimensions. It is our tragedy to bear as civilized humane beings: it is ultimately comic in the end for those advocating terrorism.

One dimension is it presages more tragedy in the wings of our experiences with radical Islamic totalitarian fascists. It is unlikely that in time we will not be hit by another wave of these fascists: that is, the more destruction they hurl at the civilized world, the stronger we as civilized people will unite and strike back.

The second dimension is it illustrates the fact of a higher source of inspiration to guide our emancipation from radical fascists who would totally believe Americans to lay back and be conquered as weak and inept because we are kind and compassionate as a people. It is our kindness and compassion as a people with a united culture of tolerance and compromise that make us a great nation and identity as a people.

It is hatred of mercy and justice that brings out the worst in all people. Unlike those who sit idly by as terrorisms ply their terror, and others who may hide in ever-illusive peace with those who stand for terror, we as Americans and our allies, like Israel, do not. The poignant genius of Hillel beckons a cry for meaning in this age of terrorism. If we are not for ourselves, who will be for us? If we do not wage war on the terrorists, who will? If we do not lead the world in our battle, what are we? If not now, when?

The third dimension of common folk is finally coming to the head of our attention rather than the tail. How is this so in an age where *American*

Idol has prime-time TV. Well, being brave and having the courage to stand up and to act has the potential force to inspire many Americans to appreciate the real heroes of everyday life. Alas, the consumer market is ripe for learning that heroes are not made on the marble stages where thespians dance. For those arenas are where silhouettes may entertain our imagination, but the genuine heroes sweat, grunt, and are raw and drawn from the kiln. That kiln is fired up in the crucible of rare existential moments from ground zero to eternity—not in a tune or beat to drum up dazzle, but rather those who pound the beat of life whether on a street district as a police officer, emergency technician, a firefighter, or a brave civilian in tune with the humanity that emerges in responsible choices of using force when needed to preserve peace.

It is with this context in mind that the film *Flight 93* pays marginal attention to other tragedies that occurred that day and other days. The tragedy of Flight 93 aspires to the message it sends out: the victory for the terrorists is enflamed in a pyrrhic pyre!

Flight 93 achieved life in death that was not in vain. It took what was an attack on the soul of America and in a descent into the earth it opened up hope for all of us to memorialize not in a reified testament, but in a war that was just and is just! It has become embedded in the caverns of every American's mind, with a roll call for resistance and victory with the elegant words "Let's roll." As a NYC cop doc I can never forget the witnessing of scores of officers and public safety as well as ordinary citizens who all became a band of extraordinary folk that day and in the weeks to follow. The ushering in of one flight into the Trade Center followed by another with precision only cowards could muster in razing down what symbolized the world coming together in peace and harmony. Well, that is what terrorists cast—fascisms might make right, violence to minorities who are not of their faith, and lust for blood. The terrorists stand for all we are against as Americans, in opposition to life, liberty, and peace. The president at the time of his leadership called this column an arch of evil. That arch of terrorism is the world's Achilles' heel, and in order to survive, terrorists and their evil must be destroyed. It is exactly what our heroes of the day did in unison—united we stand, divided we fall. They fell, but in that fall they brought human dignity to a new level in their death. It was not in vain; it is tragic and to be mourned in depth by all of us. The blood of their offering is sown in a renewal of this memorable past into the future of revolt against an evil internal and external. Evil is evil and no excuse or attempt to humanize what is inhumane can suffice. This film illustrates the blood thirst and terror that terrorists fulfill without apology—it also shows how so-called plain folk are the salt of the earth. Their flight is our plight, their fight against fright—their courage is inspiration for all of us willing to learn. They are our heroes—they are us—they are the finest of America; let us witness their plight with them. Please see it for heaven's and for earth's sake. It is worth the investment indeed!

The Lake House

A cached deployment film for all time and with timelessness in the space of conscience awareness. It is one of not relinquishing what time can do in the rip of time's tide to stave off despair, which is a state of mind and soul. It is the ability to transcend the gust of pain and anguish when a man and woman are separate in time while the spaces they occupy are in synch with one another. Assignments in the federal government, including the long sojourn of soldiers and agents as well as police who are also soldiers in reserve services, are on call at times for long periods of time. This film is romantic and an antiterrorism buster for in the depth of a journey with a seemingly inexplicable ending, the power and miracle of love between a man and woman—as natural as nature itself—where the power of faith is regenerative. Regenerative as creativity and creation itself: sexy and meaningful in its splendor of overcoming the fads of passivity and dwelling in shadows as love rebirths destiny in the faith in the breaking light of day into night.

Inglorious Bastards

This is the 2009 film in which film producer Tarantino outdoes himself. This film reverses the identity of victims and places the hyperexcited, hyperfocused, hyperintuitive officers as heroic, and they are. It is somewhat overdone in the bloody scenes, but in spirit it is done well, as in the dirty dozen updated. It is a way-out-there film, but is really as American as one can imagine being. Jewish American soldiers hell bent and giving some of the hell back to the cowardly Nazis who can prey on unarmed citizens and pillage them and control them as slaves until they have manipulated and murdered them in cold blood. The greatest payback is the troops sent behind enemy lines like special agents on assignment are able to engulf the worst tyrants in the world in the fire they set on the world. It is interesting as much as it is politically incorrect, but then again who cares to be PC in a world that is real and not Peter Pan. We are talking about the U.S. Armed Services. Service is delivered in five stars to the enemy, where their heads roll instead of ours. The bad guy loses as the loser he or she is without apology in a grand way.

Black Hawk Down

This movie is the epitome of American courage and the modern Leonitis reborn in Colonel McKnight, who stays his ground on the front line in Mogadishu with a rain of fire on his head. He stands his ground with his troops and does not relinquish his moral compass of leadership in the face of death by overwhelming odds. He has the audacity of humility, not pride, and trusts in God unapologetically. As in his leadership and his groundbreaking work, his credo is his life experience and his life's work on the field of battle and leadership to the soldiers and law enforcement and public safety officers he teaches night in and day out. Leave no one behind is his mantra in war, and his leadership is as ancient as King David's. He leads by example not by rhetoric. He is a true solider, and poet in action. His troops and their courage are indomitable, as is their leader in fighting terrorism in Afghanistan in the early 1990s around the time of the first World Trade Center attack. His shield of faith is his glory to the end: a legend in our times and a leader to be heard.

The Cult of the Suicide Bomber and *21 Hours at Munich*

These are narrated by the heroic and incredible Special Agent and former CIA Agent Robert Baer. Both works hold back no punches and look at the chilling effect of the terrorists and their motivations. Special Agent Baer as a tenured and expert field agent operates a smooth understanding that captures a wide net into and around the mind of the terrorist. If you take your time in watching and rewatching this non-PC film that is done so well, you will see the evidence of the death drive of the terrorist and the leadership as gods with small *g*'s that have historically led a berth of innocent blood spilled around the world hemispheres folded in on one another.

Uprising

This one of the best resistance films to Nazism as terrorism and extreme totalitarianism in force. It is a true story based on eyewitness accounts, including documents pulled from terror headquarters in Berlin and the SS before they could be burned as the millions of innocent victims that emerged from Hitler's quest for total death and destruction to the German people. A little man with a dream of hatred and death conquered half of the world, but was put in their place by a few of the so-called inferior races as the Jews, mainly with Polish resistance support, held back the German army for over a month in a battle that symbolically is a trademark of the universal heroism of the officers who choose to not give up and take pride in their faith that God did not make men and women to be slaves. The heroes are men and women who resisted to the final battle, some even surviving the war on terror. An example of the humane spirit with faith! Freedom fighters have been so maligned in this last decade, but this is the meaning and the spirit.

Hotel Rwanda

This movie, produced and directed in 2004, was and remains a testament to one man's incredible resistance to terrorism in the real-life hell of Rwanda genocide in the hero Paul Rusesabagina of Hotel Des Mille Coolines. The murder in cold blood of Africans, especially Christians, is not forgotten or forgiven. One million innocent souls were murdered. By standing and doing what he knew intuitively in his voice of conscience, Paul was able to rescue over a thousand men, women, and children who were bound to the chains of death. It is an inspiring film of the determination of a man with heart and soul and courage of a lion.

God Grew Tired of Us: The Lost Boys of Sudan

This film is heartbreaking as much as it is uplifting when children are made into adults and tears are like sulfur when you view the decency of the innocent made into soldiers who have to fight against a Jihad of ethnic cleansing by radical Islamists. It is sometimes washed in PC as being a civil war, but what is civil in tearing out the heart and souls of Christian kids and burning them alive and ambushing unarmed civilians without care for the damage inflicted in a terrorist dream of destruction and death—which must never be proud? The other side of hell is the paradise these young fellows make when they are faced with the dream of a real refrigerator and bus and the other gifts we take for granted. They are shocked by the pictures of nude people, as they truly are living the dream they hoped in their spiritual and complex lifestyles in Sudan, as they are displaced with the vagaries and blessings of U.S. life. Freedom is hard won, and they in their courage and security do not forget the scores of thousands left behind. It is a great film, for it shows clearly the decency of many Africans who are under siege by fascist terrorists who would like to homicide them, as all of us who are not of the same ilk.

300

This film is a docudrama, but one that cannot be missed in the war on terror. No doubt the struggle of Leonitis is made exquisite and as real as a F5 tornado laying down in the metropolis of Athens as Sparta's king, who was born a soldier and officer, took charge of the fight to war on an enemy that expected bowing down and homage rather than a fight. As long as Leonitis bowed in homage he was promised security and payment. He could not be bought or laid to rest in a peaceful bondage to lose all he cherished and loved. Love and creativity took him to a level of sacrifice and helped him overcome the fear most men live with and die with. He did not glory in death and revel in conquering his enemy. His hoorah as the soldiers on the domestic front took arms against a deluge of force and with power of faith and meaning stood their ground in battle till death without relinquishing their love of freedom and justice. It is a timeless film, and its message so scared the Iranian minister of propaganda, who along with Goebbels denies the Holocaust. But why fear of a film, as said in the guide, it was a book that led to the hell of fascism and communism worldwide as totalitarian regimes of the left and right. This film threatens the idea that the war of terrorist sponsored states are inenvitably the victor rather than the doomed. The Spartans victor not in battle but in the Victory they led by their own meaningful and timeless sacrifice that is worthwhile remembering now as then.

The Hero's Journey by Joseph Campbell

This is the story of the existential anthropologist whose wisdom and reach of insight traverse deep into the cultural motif or myths we live by. His own courage and genius is laid out in a lifetime of work and historical context. The motivations underlying his creative work and commitment to not falling prey to terrorism and fascism are beautifully laid out in this film, in which the unsung hero is the narrator himself.

Catch 22: Directed by Mike Nichols and Written by Joseph Heller

One of the best war films ever insofar as it speaks to the absurdity of the condition of war. *Catch 22* is best seen and then read. It is not an antiwar film or I would have trashed it a long time ago. It is a film that speaks to the reality of the absurdity of a politically correct version that has turned on itself in a spiral of doublespeak and double bind. It is the fact that we know we all are at risk at war, and it is dangerous and we have human fear that makes it so real. Being stuck in the madness of a war on terrorists in which one must go by the conventional formula of combat really is another way of looking at *Catch 22* from a different angle, from the right to center rather than from the left of nowhere.

Fahrenheit 451: Directed by Francois Truffaut and Written by Ray Bradbury

One of the most chilling and realistic nightmares of what public safety fire-fighters can become if they lose their moral compass, and in fact, the beauty is if it is gained back. It is one film and book that needs special attention in a world of mind and freedom becoming eclipsed in a censorship that excludes God, family values, and religion as owned by the very founders of our amazing country, and the grace bestowed on you and I who have served and fought for the very freedoms not ever taken for granted if we are not to lose them in the most sacred places in our own heart and soul.

Books to be Read

Man's Search for Meaning by Viktor Frankl

This book is one of the top hundred ever published. It has been recommended by the pope and the grand rabbi and folks of all religions. It is the his-story of one man's battle with terrorism and fascist murderers. A public service officer, Dr. Viktor Frankl stood his ground of being humane in the worst struggle in hell, Auschwitz. He survived without losing his soul or courage and faith in God. His style of therapy, which is in part modified in my own treatment of trauma and grief, is brought to light by the founder himself.

Maximilian Kolbe: The Saint of Auschwitz by Elaine Murray Stone

This Catholic priest epitomizes the sacrifice of a man who has transcended his own desire to live with the meaning of the ultimate sacrifice for another man's life. In his trail of resistance he is led to hell, beaten, and brutalized by the viral terrorists who celebrate and revel in death and destruction. Instead of throwing anyone to the wolves to save his life, Father Kolbe places the Jewish star of David next to his heart while remaining Catholic to the end—he insists his life be offered in place of the younger man's, although he himself is a young man. His death is not celebrated, but his life and courage, of which he is the finest of the finest public safety officers. He nobly resists the brutality of terrorists as he uses his shield of conscience in a timeless and eternal cover to his own indomitable spirit of humane being. He is honored as a saint by Catholics, Christians, and Jews in Israel for all time.

Cops at Risk by Denny Conroy

This book is written by one of the wisest and tenured cop docs around, who has over three decades of being a cop and a cop doc. He writes so well you can feel his breathing and wise sage words come from his mouth when you are on the road, in a public vehicle and parked for a moment, or at home and reeling from a day's work on the job. He elaborates on what counts and what is key in being a real-deal cop and corrections officer with the reality of experience of being in the saddle. If I was a rookie or senior officer considering retiring, I would take hold of the wisdom offered for a small price for peace of mind and buy his guide, which covers a lot not covered in other books. Cop's cop. His work speaks volumes as does his experience, which in itself tells of his wisdome and effectiveness. Cop Doc Denny distills his wisdom as a cop doc to anyone who chooses to listen whether on the beat or a commander making a major decisive move in a strategic war against terror or service to his/ her community.

Suicide and Suicide Homicide among Police by Anton Leenaars

This book is a short but powerful guide that explains in a novel way by the leading expert in this field how not to fall into the trap of constricting your options and losing balance in the true imprint of terror you and I fight in law enforcement and military operations, analysis, and administration. It is filled with fact and delivered with literary brilliance and flow. You may pick up the book and get so much out of it for not only yourself, but also a peer or family member in the other enemy within, which is the giving up, or despair faced in the most trying of times as a police and public safety officer. Doc Antoon is the leader in the world, perhaps, in suicide, and his many other books are helpful to the public safety peer leader or support officer seeking to gain information that is gained from the saddle of experience as a cop doc in Canada and here in the United States when we are blessed to have him visit.

Streets of Mogadishu: Leadership at Its Best by Colonel Danny McKnight

Political correctness at its worst. This book is written by the national hero of a leader under fire whose tenacity only equals his genius in offering lessons that need to be taken to the living room of every sensible American police and public safety officer and his or her family members—whether you or your loved one is in the military, federal, state, city, or local level of service, the command presence of this man, who is a rare and ingenious leader, needs to be heard as his wisdom is not from the pulpit of political and academic intrigue. His wisdom of heroism cannot be gained in training alone, but from the deepest reservoir of what character is defined as. In the crucible of what would make most soldiers pause for a long time when he was faced with dealing with terrorists who were overwhelming in force, he stood his power of faith and creativity to the next level. The power of his integrity and lessons learned are delivered with ingenuity and grace of making a stand for the country and values we all cherish in police, public safety, and military communities. He puts political correctness where it belongs, in the worst handicap we have sunk to, and helps guide the leader in you and me out and in the day of light that is genuine as he is incredible as a modern Leonitis proven!

On Killing and *On Combat* by Dave Grossman

Dave Grossman is a professor of psychology at West Point and at the DEA, FBI, and scores of other agencies and departments. A Pulitzer Prize writer who has a heart of a lion and the strategy of a Churchill in his craft as a teacher and writer. The fact is Lt. Col. Dave Grossman developed the field of killology and combat psychology that will have far-reaching implications and insight for decades, if not centuries. His cop and military genius strategy I can testify has helped officers I have worked with. In working through complex trauma syndromes, Lt. Col. David Grossman's two classic works, *On Killing* and *On Combat*, create a dynamic duo for street, public safety, and military use in the field. The strategic importance of these works is a framework that exposes the reality of violence and the mendacity of ignorance about the differences between the bad guys and good guys. The critical importance to a field officer is that he or she did not kill a terrorist, domestic or foreign, but has done his or her job in a heroic manner that moves him or her in a way that aids and fosters healing. Death and killing is not minimized but is given context and real existential meaning without apology for being a soldier. Anyone who is in policing and public safety at the leadership to soldier level will gain by reading and understanding the psychology of combat and killing. I would venture to say this is the most astute and ingenious thinker in the field that has broken through the barrier of trainer and strategist to educate all of us in the very field of science that owes its direction to the creative genius behind its development. Like Colonel McKnight, Lt. Col. Dave Grossman is one of the bravest heroes in countless missions in the field of public safety combat in the U.S. Rangers overseas!

Handbook for Police Psychology by Jack Kitaeff

Former U.S. major military, cop doc, and attorney, Jack Kitaeff has written some bestselling works in the field of forensic psychology, science, and law. His encyclopedic work is the *Handbook*, which is a guide to every aspect of police psychology you could ever want to know about. I would say of all guides in existence, it is the most comprehensive and readable book by the leaders in the field of police psychology and psychiatry. Doc Kitaeff knows what he is talking about and writes with a deep message that underscores all his work, which is caring for the troops and officers in a way that is uniquely gifted and profound! Please buy this book if you want to assess the entire field of police and public safety psychology in way that is non-PC but is real as the beat you pound. Indispensible for anyone who wants to know the scope of the profession and its many branches, it is brought to you in plain English that is understandable and key to your foundation of policing and public safety.

Emotional Survival of Law Enforcement by Kevin Gilmartin

Lieutenant and doctor, Kevin Gilmartin has brought the word *hypervigilance* into national prominence, and the whole idea of emotional intelligence and survival in the world of police and public safety. He is the leader; although others have followed and also integrated his original work, he is the pivotal mind and cop doc behind understanding the mindsets and ways of sabotaging that the job creates. He does more by also offering a way through and out of the mire officers are drawn into.

Don't Sweat the Small Stuff and *Walk Like a Chameleon* by Gary Aumuller

These books may sound like easy, simple guides, but they are anything but simplistic. In fact, Cop Doc Gary Aumuller uses a perspective in part that takes the different types of styles all people use in relationships and ensures the reader understands his or her core defenses and strengths. In addition, he puts it well and in understandable storytelling based on real cases of how emotional extinction can happen to you if the wrong mate is chosen. In doing so, he also offers advice that is priceless for officers and their families in dealing with their own foibles and dilemmas. He is one of the foremost leaders in the area of family and personal care in the world of police psychology.

Mettle—Developing Mental Toughness Training for LE by Dr. Laurence Miller

Dr. Miller has written many books and even more articles. This book is an exquisite work in which the reader can gain an education in the sources and branches of stress in the most updated form by integrating theory and practice in a way that brings together his wealth of experience in Palm Beach, Florida, as a police psychologist. It is a book that can appeal to you as a police, public safety, or military instructor, with examples that get to the issue of developing the toughness mentally to cope with issues from society as well as clinical problems that are uniquely personal.

Death Work Police, Trauma, and the Psychology of Survival by Vincent E. Henry

Dr. Henry is another NYPD sergeant, as myself, who presents some aspects in common with my work but uniquely offers a different and brilliant exposure of policing and being on the job. He highlights resilience in different developmental epic roles forged in gaining one's police identity, such as the rookie experience of death, the patrol sergeants, the crime scene investigators, and homicide detectives, among others. A real gem and with deep pearls of wisdom. Proud to be a fellow sergeant and cop doc in the same department that shaped Cop Doc Henry. This book is truly bound to be a classic, if not already.

Index